George Willis Cooke

George Eliot

A critical study of her life, writings and philosophy

George Willis Cooke

George Eliot
A critical study of her life, writings and philosophy

ISBN/EAN: 9783337236762

Printed in Europe, USA, Canada, Australia, Japan

Cover: Foto ©Thomas Meinert / pixelio.de

More available books at **www.hansebooks.com**

GEORGE ELIOT

A CRITICAL STUDY

OF HER

LIFE, WRITINGS AND PHILOSOPHY.

BY

GEORGE WILLIS COOKE,

AUTHOR OF "RALPH WALDO EMERSON: HIS LIFE, WRITINGS AND PHILOSOPHY."

BOSTON AND NEW YORK:
HOUGHTON, MIFFLIN AND COMPANY.
The Riverside Press, Cambridge.

PREFACE TO SECOND EDITION.

The publication of a new edition of this work permits me to say that the essay on "The Lady Novelists," quoted in the seventh chapter, was written by George Henry Lewes. Its opinions, however, are substantially those of George Eliot, and they will be found in harmony with her own words. Confessing to the error, I yet venture to let the quotations, and the comments on them, stand as at first made. The three poems mentioned on page 75, were among the latest of the productions of George Eliot's pen.

It has been suggested to me that I have not done perfect justice to George Henry Lewes, especially in what I say of his books on the Spanish drama and the life of Goethe. I have carefully reconsidered what I wrote of him, and find no occasion for any change of judgment, though two or three words might properly give place to others of a more appreciative meaning.

My book has met with much greater praise than I could have expected. Its errors, I have no doubt, are quite numerous enough; and yet I venture to think the main thought of the book is correct.

MARCH, 1884.

CONTENTS.

GEORGE ELIOT.

I.

EARLY LIFE.

THE poet and the novelist write largely out of personal experience, and must give expression to the effects of their own history. What they have seen and felt, gives shape and tone to what they write; that which is nearest their own hearts is poured forth in their books. To ignore these influences is to overlook a better part of what they write, and is often to lose the explanation of many features of their work. Shakspere is one of those who are of no time or place, whose words gain no added meaning in view of what he was and how he lived; but it is not so with a great number of the best and most inspiring writers. The era in which they lived, the intellectual surroundings afforded them by their country and generation, the subtle phases of sentiment and aspiration of their immediate time and place, are all essential to a true appreciation of their books. It is so of Goethe, Byron, Shelley, Hugo, Wordsworth, Emerson, and how many more!

As we must know the eighteenth century in its social spirit, literary tendencies, revolutionary aims, romantic aspirations, philosophy and science, to know Goethe, so must we know the nineteenth century in its scientific attainments, agnostic philosophy, realistic spirit and humanitarian aims, in order to know George Eliot.

She is a product of her time, as Lessing, Goethe, Wordsworth and Byron were of theirs; a voice to utter its purpose and meaning, as well as a trumpet-call to lead it on. As Goethe came after Lessing, Herder and Kant, so George Eliot came after Comte, Mill and Spencer. Her books are to be read in the light of their speculations, and she embodied in literary forms what they uttered as science or philosophy.

Not only is a poet's mind affected by the tone of thought about him, but his personal experiences and surroundings are likely to have a large influence on what he writes. Scott was deeply affected by the romantic atmosphere of his native land. Her birthplace and youthful surroundings had a like effect on George Eliot. The Midland home, the plain village life, the humble, toiling country folk, shaped for her the scenes and characters about which she was to write. Some knowledge of her early home and the influences amidst which her mind was formed, help largely to an appreciation of her books and the views of life which she presents in them.

The Midland region of England she has pictured with something of that accuracy with which Scott described the Border. It is a country of historic memories. Near by her childhood home was the forest of Arden and Astly Castle, the home of Sir John Grey, whose widow, Elizabeth Woodville, became the queen of Edward IV. This was also one of the homes of Henry Grey, Duke of Suffolk, who was found in a hollow tree near by after his rebellion; and the home, likewise, of his daughter, Lady Jane Grey. In another direction was Bosworth Field; and within twenty miles was Stratford-upon-Avon. The ancient city of Coventry was not far distant. It was not these historic regions which attracted her, however, so much as the pleasant country, the common people, the quiet villages. With observant eyes she saw the world about her as it was, and she entered into the heart of its life, and has painted it for us in a most sympathetic, appreciative spirit. The simple, homely, unromantic life of middle England she has made immortal with her wit, her satire, her fine description, and her keen love of all that is human. She herself recognized the importance of her early surroundings. In one of her letters she used these words:

> It is interesting, I think, to know whether a writer was born in a central or border district — a condition which always has a strongly determining influence. I was born in Warwickshire, but certain family traditions connected with more northerly districts made these districts a region of poetry to me in my early childhood. I was brought up in the Church of England, and have never joined any other religious society, but I have had close acquaintance with many Dissenters of various sects, from Calvinistic Anabaptists to Unitarians.

The influence of the surroundings of childhood upon character she has more than once touched upon in her books. In the second chapter of *Theophrastus Such*, she says, —

> I cherish my childish loves — the memory of that warm little nest where my affections were fledged.

In the same essay she says, —

> Our Midland plains have never lost their familiar expression and conservative spirit for me.

In *Daniel Deronda* she most tenderly expresses the same deep conviction concerning the soul's need of anchorage in some familiar and inspiring scene, with which the memories of childhood may be delightfully associated. Her own fond recollections lent force to whatever philosophical significance such a theory may have had for her.

> A human life should be well rooted in some spot of a native land, where it may get the love of tender kinship for the face of the earth, for the labors men go forth to, for the sounds and accents that haunt it, for whatever will give that home a familiar, unmistakable difference amidst the future widening of knowledge; a spot where the definiteness of early knowledge may be inwrought with affection, and kindly acquaintance with all neighbors, even to

the dogs and monkeys, may spread, not by sentimental effort and reflection, but as a sweet habit of the blood.

Mary Ann Evans was born at South Farm, a mile from Griff, in the parish of Colton, Warwickshire, England, November 22, 1819. In after years she adopted the abbreviated form of her name, and was known by her friends as Marian. When she was six months old the family moved to Griff House, which was situated half-way between Bedworth, a mining village, and the manufacturing town of Nuneaton. In approaching Griff from Nuneaton, a little valley, known as Griff Hollows, is passed, much resembling the "Red Deeps" of *The Mill on the Floss*. On the right, a little beyond, is Griff House, a comfortable and substantial dwelling surrounded by pleasant gardens and lawns.

Robert Evans, her father, was born at Ellaston, Staffordshire, of a substantial family of mechanics and craftsmen. He was of massive build, tall, wide-shouldered and strong, and his features were of a marked, emphatic cast. He began life as a master carpenter, then became a forester, and finally a land agent. He was induced to settle in Warwickshire by Sir Roger Newdigate, his principal employer, and for the remainder of his life he had charge of five large estates in the neighborhood. In this employment he was successful, being respected and trusted to the fullest extent by his employers, his name becoming a synonym for trustworthiness. Marian many times sketched the main traits of her father's character, as in the love of perfect work in "Stradivarius." He had Adam Bede's stalwart figure and robust manhood. Caleb Garth, in *Middlemarch*, is in many ways a fine portrait of him as to the nature of his employment, his delight in the soil, and his honest, rugged character.

Caleb was wont to say that "it's a fine thing to have the chance of getting a bit of the country into good fettle, and putting men into the right way with their farming, and getting a bit of good contriving and solid building done — that those who are living and those who come after will be the better for. I'd sooner have it than a fortune. I hold it the most honorable work that is." Robert Evans, like Caleb Garth, "while faithfully serving his employers enjoyed great popularity among their tenants. He was gentle but of indomitable firmness; and while stern to the idle and unthrifty, he did not press heavily on those who might be behindhand with their rent, owing to ill luck or misfortune, on quarter days."

While still living in Staffordshire, Robert Evans lost his first wife, by whom he had a son and a daughter. His second wife, the mother of Marian, was a Miss Pearson, a gentle, loving woman, and a notable housewife. She is described in the Mrs. Hackit of "Amos Barton," whose industry, sharp tongue, epigrammatic speech and marked character were taken from life. Something of Mrs. Poyser also entered into her nature. She had three children, Christiana, Isaac and Mary Ann. The house at Griff was situated in a rich landscape, and was a large, commodious farm-house of red brick, ivy-covered, and of two stories' height. At the back was a large garden, and a farm-yard with barns and sheds.

In the series of sonnets entitled "Brother and Sister," Marian has given some account of her early life. She had the attachment there described for her brother Isaac, and followed him about with the same persistence and affection. The whole of that poem is autobiographical. The account of the mother gives a delightful glimpse into Marian's child-life:

Our mother bade us keep the trodden ways,
  Stroked down my tippet, set my brother's frill,
Then with the benediction of her gaze
  Clung to us lessening, and pursued us still
Across the homestead to the rookery elms,
  Whose tall old trunks had each a grassy mound,
So rich for us, we counted them as realms
  With varied products.

The early life of Marian Evans has, in many features of it, been very fully described in the story of

Maggie Tulliver. How far her own life is that of Maggie may be seen by comparing the earlier chapters in *The Mill on the Floss* with the "Brother and Sister." The incident described in the poem, of her brother leaving her in charge of the fishing-rod, is repeated in all its main features in the experiences of Maggie. In the poem she describes an encounter with a gipsy, which again recalls Maggie's encounter with some persons of that race. The whole account of her childhood life with her brother, her trust in him, their delight in the common pleasures of childhood, and the impression made on her by the beauties of nature, reappears in striking similarity in the description of the child-life of Maggie and Tom. These elements of her early experience and observation of life have been well described by one who knew her personally. This person says that "Maggie Tulliver's childhood is clearly full of the most accurate personal recollections."

Marian Evans very early became an enthusiastic reader of the best books. In an almanac she found a portion of one of the essays of Charles Lamb, and remembered reading it with great delight. In her seventh year a copy of *Waverley* was loaned to her older sister. She became herself intensely fascinated by it, and when it was returned before she had completed it she was thrown into much distress. The story so possessed her that she began to complete it in writing, according to her own conception. When this was discovered, the book was again secured for her perusal. This incident she has described in a sonnet, which appears as the motto to the fifty-seventh chapter of *Middlemarch*.

They numbered scarce eight summers when a name
  Rose on their souls and stirred such motions there
As thrill the buds and shape their hidden frame
  At penetration of the quickening air:
His name who told of loyal Evan Dhu,
  Of quaint Bradwardine, and Vich Ian Vor,
Making the little world their childhood knew
  Large with a land of mountain, lake and scaur,

And larger yet with wonder, love, belief,
  Toward Walter Scott, who living far away
Sent them this wealth of joy and noble grief.
  The book and they must part, but day by day,
    In lines that thwart like portly spiders ran,
    They wrote the tale, from Tully Veolan.

Not only was she a great reader, but she was also a diligent and even a precocious student, learning easily and rapidly whatever she undertook to acquire in the way of knowledge.

She was first sent, with her brother Isaac, to a free school in the village of Griff. Among her mates was William Jacques, the original of Bob Jakins in *The Mill on the Floss.* When seven years old she went to a girls' school at Nuneaton. Her schoolmates describe her as being then a "quiet, reserved girl, with strongly lined, almost masculine features, and a profusion of light hair worn in curls round her head." The abundance of her curling hair caused her much trouble, and she once cut it off, as Maggie Tulliver did, because it would not "lie straight." "One of her school-fellows," we are told, "recalls that the first time she sat down to the piano she astonished her companions by the knowledge of music she had already acquired. She mastered her lessons with an ease which excited wonder. She read with avidity. She joined very rarely in the sports of her companions, and her diffidence and shrinking sensibility prevented her from forming any close friendship among her school-fellows. When she stood up in the class, her features, heavy in repose, were lighted by eager excitement, which found further vent in nervous movements of her hands. At this school Marian was well taught in English, with drawing, music, and some little French."

Leaving this school at the age of twelve, she went to that of the Misses Franklin in Coventry, a large town a few miles distant. To the careful training received there she was much indebted, and in after years often spoke of it with the heartiest appreciation. One of her friends, Edith Simcox, has given an account of this school and of Marian's studies there. "Almost on the outskirts of the old town of Coventry, towards the railway station, the house may still be seen, itself an old-fashioned five-windowed, Queen Anne sort of dwelling, with a shell-shaped cornice over the door, with an old timbered cottage facing it, and near adjoining a quaint brick and timber building, with an oriel window thrown out upon oak pillars. Between forty and fifty years ago, Methodist ladies kept the school, and the name of 'little mamma,' given by her school-fellows, is a proof that already something was to be seen of the maternal air which characterized her in later years, and perhaps more especially in intercourse with her own sex. Prayer meetings were in vogue among the girls, following the example of their elders; and while taking, no doubt, a leading part in them, she used to suffer much self-reproach about her coldness and inability to be carried away with the same enthusiasm as others. At the same time, nothing was farther from her nature than any sceptical inclination, and she used to pounce with avidity upon any approach to argumentative theology within her reach, carrying Paley's *Evidences* up to her bedroom, and devouring it as she lay upon the floor alone."

During the three years Marian attended this school she held aloof from the other pupils, was grave and womanly in her deportment. She acquired Miss Rebecca Franklin's slow and precise method of speaking, and to her diligent training owed her life-long habit of giving a finished completeness to all her sentences. It seems that her imagination was alive at this time, and being slowly cultivated. She was in the habit of scribbling verses in her books and elsewhere.

A fellow-pupil during the time she was a member of this boarding-school has given these reminiscences of Marian's life there: "She learned everything with ease," says this person, "but was passionately devoted to music, and became thoroughly accomplished as a pianist. Her masters always brought the most difficult solos for her to play in public, and everywhere said she might make a performer equal to any then upon the concert stage. She was keenly susceptible to what she thought her lack of personal beauty, frequently saying that she was not pleased with a single feature of her face or figure. She was not especially noted as a writer, but so uncommon was her intellectual power that we all thought her capable of any effort; and so great was the charm of her conversation, that there was continual strife among the girls as to which of them should walk with her. The teachers had to settle it by making it depend upon alphabetical succession."

Leaving the school in Coventry at the age of fifteen, Marian continued her studies at home. The year following, her mother died; and this event, as she afterwards said, first made her acquainted with "the unspeakable grief of a last parting." Soon after, her older sister and her brother were married and left home. She alone remained with her father, and was for several years his housekeeper. "He offered to get a housekeeper," says Miss Blind, "as not the house only, but farm matters had to be looked after, and he was always tenderly considerate of 'the little wench,' as he called her. But his daughter preferred taking the whole management of the place into her own hands, and she was as conscientious and diligent in the discharge of her domestic duties as in the prosecution of the studies she carried on at the same time." Her experiences at this period have been made use of in more than one of her characters. The dairy scenes in *Adam Bede* are so perfectly realistic because she was familiar with all the processes of butter and cheese making.

In 1841 her father gave up his business to his son and moved to Foleshill, one mile from Coventry. A pleasant house and surroundings made the new home attractive, and her habits of thought and life became more exact and fastidious. The frequent absence of her father gave her much time for reading, which she eagerly improved. Books were more accessible, though her own library was a good one.

She zealously began and carried on a systematic course of studies, such as gave her the most thorough results of culture. She took up Latin and Greek with the head master of the Coventry grammar-school, and became familiar with the classic literatures. French, German and Italian were read in all the master-pieces of those languages. The Old Testament was also studied in the original; at the same time she became a proficient player on the piano, and obtained a thorough knowledge of music. During several years of quiet and continuous study she laid the foundations of that accurate and wide-reaching knowledge which was so notable a feature of her life and work. It was a careful, systematic knowledge she acquired, such as entitled her to rank as an educated person in the fullest sense. Her painstaking thoroughness, and her energetic application, were as remarkable at this time as in later years. Her knowledge was mainly self-acquired, but it was in no sense superficial. It is difficult to see in what way it could have been improved, even if the universities had been open to her.

Her life and her studies at Coventry have been well described by one who knew her. We are told that "in this somewhat more populous neighborhood she soon became known as a person of more than common interest, and, moreover, as a most devoted daughter and the excellent manager of her father's household. There was perhaps little at first sight which betokened genius in that quiet gentle-mannered girl, with pale grave face, naturally pensive in expression: and ordinary aquaintances regarded her chiefly for the kindness and sympathy that were never wanting to any. But to those with whom, by some unspoken affinity, her soul could expand, her expressive gray eyes would light up with intense meaning and humor, and the low, sweet voice, with its peculiar mannerism of speaking — which by the way wore off in after years — would give utterance to thoughts so rich and singular that converse with Miss Evans, even in those days, made speech with other people seem flat and common. Miss Evans was an exemplification of the fact that a great genius is not an exceptional, capricious product cf nature, but a thing of slow, laborious growth, the fruit of industry and the general culture of the faculties. At Foleshill, with ample means and leisure, her real education began. She acquired French, German and Italian from Signor Brezzi. An acquaintance with Hebrew was the result of her own unaided efforts. From Mr. Simms, the veteran organist of St. Michaels, Coventry, she received lessons in music, although it was her own fine musical sense which made her in after years an admirable pianoforte player. Nothing once learned escaped her marvellous memory; and her keen sympathy with all human feelings, in which lay the secret of her power of discriminating character, caused a constant fund of knowledge to flow into her treasure-house from the social world about her."

Marian Evans early showed an unusual interest in religious subjects. Her parents belonged to the Established Church, while other members of the family were zealous Methodists. Religion was a subject which occupied much of their attention, and several of them were engaged in one way and another in its inculcation. Marian was an attentive listener to the sermons preached in the parish church, and at the age of twelve was teaching in a Sunday school held in a cottage near her father's house. Up to the age of eighteen she was a most devoted believer in Christianity, and her zeal was so great that Evangelicalism came to represent her mode of thought and feeling. She was a somewhat rigid Calvinist and full of pious enthusiasm. After her removal to Coventry, where her reading was of a wider range and her circle of friends increased, doubts gradually sprang up in her mind. In a letter written to Miss Sara Hennell she gave a brief account of her religious experiences at this period. In it she described an aunt, Mrs. Elizabeth Evans, who was a Methodist preacher, and the original of Dinah Morris in *Adam Bede.*

There was hardly any intercourse between my father's family, resident in Derbyshire and Staffordshire, and our family—few and far-between visits of (to my childish feeling) strange uncles and aunts and cousins from my father's far-off native country, and once a journey of my own, as a little child, with my father and mother, to see my uncle William (a rich builder) in Staffordshire—but *not* my uncle and aunt Samuel, so far as I can recall the dim outline of things—are what I remember of northerly relatives in my childhood.

But when I was seventeen or more—after my sister was married and I was mistress of the house—my father took a journey into Derbyshire, in which, visiting my uncle and aunt Samuel, who were very poor, and lived in a humble cottage at Wirksworth, he found my aunt in a very delicate state of health after a serious illness, and, to do her bodily good, he persuaded her to return with him, telling her that *I* should be very, very happy to have her with me for a few weeks. I was then strongly under the influence of Evangelical belief, and earnestly endeavoring to shape this anomalous English-Christian life of ours into some consistency with the spirit and simple verbal tenor of the New Testament. I *was* delighted to see my aunt. Although I had only heard her spoken of as a strange person, given to a fanatical vehemence of exhortation in private as well as public, I believed that I should find sympathy between us. She was then an old woman—about sixty—and, I believe, had for a good many years given up preaching. A tiny little woman, with bright, small, dark eyes, and hair that had been black, I imagine, but was now gray—a pretty woman in her youth, but of a totally different physical type from Dinah. The difference—as you will believe—was not *simply* physical; no difference is. She was a woman of strong natural excitability, which I know, from the description I have heard my father and half-sister give, prevented her from the exercise of discretion under the promptings of her zeal. But this vehemence was now subdued by age and sickness; she was very gentle and quiet in her manners—very loving—and (what she must have been from the very first) a truly religious soul, in whom the love of God and the love of man were fused together. There was nothing highly distinctive in her religious conversation. I had had much intercourse with pious Dissenters before; the only freshness I found, in our talk, came from the fact that she had been the greater part of her life a Wesleyan, and though *she left the society when women were no longer allowed to preach*, and joined the New Wesleyans, she retained the character of thought that belongs to the genuine old Wesleyan. I had never talked with a Wesleyan before, and we used to have little debates about predestination, for I was then a strong Calvinist. Here her superiority came out, and I remember now, with loving admiration, one thing which at the time I disapproved; it was not strictly a consequence of her Arminian belief, and at first sight might seem opposed to it, yet it came from the spirit of love which clings to the bad logic of Arminianism. When my uncle came to fetch her, after she had been with us a fortnight or three weeks, he was speaking of a deceased minister, once greatly respected, who from the action of trouble upon him had taken to small tippling, though otherwise not culpable. "But I hope the good man's in heaven, for all that," said my uncle. "Oh, yes," said my aunt, with a deep inward groan of joyful conviction, "Mr. A's in heaven—that's sure." This was at the time an offence to my stern, ascetic, hard views—how beautiful it is to me now!

One who has been permitted to read the letters of Marian Evans written to this aunt, has given the following account of them, which throws much light on her religious attitude at this period: "Most of the epistles are addressed to my 'dear uncle and aunt,' and all reveal George Eliot's great talents. The style is elegant and graceful, and the letters abound in beautiful metaphor; but their most striking characteristic is the religious tinge that pervades them all. Nearly every line denotes that George Eliot was an earnest biblical student, and that she was, especially in the years 1839 and 1840, very anxious about her spiritual condition. In one of these letters, written from Griff to Elizabeth Evans, in 1839, she says she is living in a dry and thirsty land, and that she is looking forward with pleasure to a visit to Wirksworth, and likens her aunt's companionship and counsel to a spring of pure water, acceptable to her as is the well dug for the traveller in the desert. That the most affectionate and loving relationship existed between the eminent author and Mrs. Elizabeth Evans, is apparent from this correspondence. The inmost secrets of George Eliot's heart are laid bare in these letters to the famous Methodist preacher, who was at that time her dearest friend. She is ever asking for advice and spiritual guidance, and confesses her faults with a candor that is rendered additionally attractive by reason of the polished language in which it is clothed. When quite a girl, George Eliot was known as pious and clever; and in the letters she wrote in 1839, when she was twenty years old, the cleverness has grown and expanded, although she is not so sure about her piety. She says that 'unstable as water thou shalt not excel,' seems to be a description of her character, instead of the progress from strength to strength that should be experienced by those who wish to stand in the presence of God. In another letter she admits that she cannot give a good account of her spiritual state, says that she has been surrounded by worldly persons, and that love of human praise is one of her great stumbling-blocks. But in a letter written in 1840 the uncertainty has gone from her mind, and she writes that she has resolved in the strength of the Lord to serve him evermore. In a later communication, however, she does not appear so confident, and admits that she is obliged to strive against the ambition that fills her heart, and that her fondness of worldly praise is a great bar and hindrance to spiritual advancement. Still she thinks it is no use sitting inactive with folded hands; and believing that the love of God is the only thing to give real satisfaction to human beings, she hopes, with his help, to obtain it. One of the letters is chiefly devoted to the concern felt by Marian Evans at Elizabeth Evans' illness; and another, written at Foleshill, betrays some humor amid the trouble that afflicts her about her own future. Their outward circumstances, she writes, are all she can desire; but she is not so certain about her spiritual state, although she feels that it is the grace of God alone that can give the greatest satisfaction. Then she goes on to speak of the preacher at Foleshill, with whom she is not greatly pleased: 'We get the truth, but it is not recommended by the mode of its delivery,' s how she writes of this divine; yet she is charitable withal, and removes the sting by adding that more good may sometimes be obtained from humble instruments than from the highest privileges, and that she must examine her own heart rather than speak unkindly of the preacher. Up to this period it is evident that Marian Evans' views upon religion were orthodox, and that her life was passed in ceaseless striving for the 'peace that passeth understanding;' but in 1843 a letter was written to Elizabeth Evans by a relative in Griff, in which Marian Evans is spoken of, and the change in her religious opinions indicated. She writes that they are in great pain about Mary Ann; but the last portion of the letter, dealing more fully with the subject, has unfortunately got lost or destroyed. The close association of George Eliot with Derbyshire, as well as her love for the quaint village of Wirksworth, and its upright, honest, God-fearing people, breaks forth in more than one of these communications."

Partly as the result of her studies and partly as the result of contact with other minds, Marian began to grow sceptical about the religious beliefs she had entertained. This took place probably during her twenty-third year, but the growth of the new ideas was slow at first. As one of her friends has suggested, it was her eagerness for positive knowledge which made her an unbeliever. She had no love of mere doubt, no desire to disagree with accepted doctrines, but she was not content unless she could get at the facts and reach what was just and reasonable. "It is seldom," says this person, "that a mind of so much power is so free from the impulse to dissent, and that not from too ready credulousness, but rather because the consideration of doubtful points was habitually crowded out, one may say, by the more ready and delighted acceptance of whatever accredited facts and doctrines might be received unquestioningly. We can imagine George Eliot in youth, burning to master all the wisdom and learning of the world; we cannot imagine her failing to acquire any kind of knowledge on the pretext that her teacher was in error about something else than the matter in hand; and it is undoubtedly to this natural preference for the positive side of things that we are indebted for the singular breadth and completeness of her knowledge and culture. A mind like hers must have preyed disastrously upon itself during the years of comparative solitude in which she lived at Foleshill, had it not been for that inexhaustible source of delight in every kind of intellectual acquisition. Languages, music, literature, science and philosophy interested her alike; it was early in this period that in the course of a walk with a friend she paused and clasped her hands with a wild aspiration that she might live 'to reconcile the philosophy of Locke and Kant!' Years afterward she remembered the very turn of the road where she had spoken it."

The spiritual struggles of Maggie Tulliver give a good picture of Marian Evans' mental and spiritual experiences at this time. Her friends and relatives were scandalized by her scepticism. Her father could not at all sympathize with her changed religious attitude, and treated her harshly. She refused to attend church, and this made the separation so wide that it was proposed to break up the home. By the advice of friends she at last consented to outwardly conform to her father's wishes, and a partial reconciliation was effected. This alienation, however, had a profound effect upon her mind. She slowly grew away from the intellectual basis of her old beliefs, but, with Maggie, she found peace and strength in self-renunciation, and in the cultivation of that inward trust which makes the chief anchorage of strong natures. She bore this experience patiently, and without any diminution of her affection; but she also found various friends among the more cultivated people of Coventry, who could sympathize with her in her studies and with her radical views in religion. These persons gave her the encouragement she needed, the contact with other and more matured minds which was so necessary to her mental development, and that social contact with life which was so conducive to her health of mind. In one family especially, that of Mr. Charles Bray, did she find the true, and cordial, and appreciative friendship she desired. These friends softened the growing discord with her own family, and gave her that devoted regard and aid that would be of most service to her. "In Mr. Bray's family," we are told by one who has written of this trying period of her career, "she found sympathy with her ardent love of knowledge and with the more enlightened views that had begun to supplant those under which (as she described it) her spirit had been grievously burdened. Emerson, Froude, George Combe, Robert Mackay, and many other men of mark, were at various times guests at Mr. Bray's house at Rosehill while Miss Evans was there either as inmate or occasional visitor; and many a time might have been seen, pacing up and down the lawn or grouped under an old acacia, men of thought and research, discussing all things in heaven and earth, and listening with marked attention when one gentle woman's voice was heard to utter what they were quite sure had been well matured before the lips opened. Few, if any, could feel themselves her superior in general intelligence; and it was amusing one day to see the amazement of a certain doctor, who, venturing on a quotation from Epictetus to an unassuming young lady, was, with modest politeness, corrected in his Greek by his feminine auditor. One rare characteristic belonged to her which gave a peculiar charm to her conversation. She had no petty egotism, no spirit of contradiction; she never talked for effect. A happy thought well expressed filled her with delight; in a moment she would seize the thought and improve upon it — so that common people began to feel themselves wise in her presence; and perhaps years after she would remind them, to their pride and surprise, of the good things they had said."

She was an ardent reader of Emerson and other thinkers of his cast of thought, and some traces of this early sympathy are to be seen in her books. On his second visit to England Emerson spent a day or two at the house of Charles Bray, with whose writings he had previously become acquainted. Emerson was much impressed with the personality of Marian Evans, and more than once said to Bray, "That young lady has a calm, serious soul." When Emerson asked her somewhat suddenly, "What one book do you like best?" she at once replied, "Rousseau's *Confessions*." She cherished this acquaintance with Emerson, and held him ir grateful remembrance through life.

The painful experiences of this period are undoubtedly reflected in another of her autobiographic poems, that entitled "Self and Life." She speaks of the profound influence the past had over her mind, and that her hands and feet were still tiny when she began to know the historic thrill of contact with other ages. She also makes Life say to Self, in regard to her pain and sorrow:

> But all thy anguish and thy discontent
> Was growth of mine, the elemental strife
> Towards feeling manifold with vision blent
> To wider thought: I was no vulgar life
> That, like the water-mirrored ape,
> Not discerns the thing it sees,
> Nor knows its own in others' shape,
> Railing, scorning, at its ease.
> Half man's truth must hidden lie
> If unlit by sorrow's eye.
> I by sorrow wrought in thee
> Willing pain of ministry.

The intellectual surroundings of Marian Evans at this time gave shape to her whole after-life. There were now laid the foundations of her mode of thinking, and her philosophic theories began to be formed. It was in the home of one of her friends she learned to think for herself, and it was there her positivist doctrines first appeared. Charles Bray was affected by the transcendental movement, and was an ardent admirer of Newman, Emerson and others among its leaders. This interest prepared him, as it has so many other minds, for the acceptance of those speculative views which were built up on the foundation of science when the transcendental movement began to wane. The transcendental doctrines of unity, the oneness of mind and matter, the evolution of all forms of life and being from the lowest, the universal dominion of law and necessity, and the profound significance of nature in its influence on man, as they were developed by Goethe, Schelling, Carlyle and Emerson, gave direction to a new order of speculation, which had its foundations in modern science.

Bray was an ardent phrenologist, and in 1832 published a work on *The Education of the Feelings*, based on phrenological principles. In 1841 appeared his main work, *The Philosophy of Necessity;* this was followed several years later by a somewhat similar work, *On Force, its Mental and Moral Correlates.* His philosophy was summarized in a volume published in 1871, which was entitled *A Manual of Anthropology*. He also wrote pamphlets on "Illusion and Delusion," "The Reign of Law," "Toleration," and "Christianity." In his work on necessity he promulgated very many of those ideas which have formed so prominent a part of the philosophy of George Eliot. The dominion of law, the reign of necessity, experience as the foundation of knowledge, humanity as an organism that develops a larger life for man by the aid of experience and tradition, — these are among the doctrines of the book. There is every reason for believing that in the teachings of Charles Bray, Marian Evans found many of the main elements of her philosophy, and with his aid her opinions were largely shaped.

Mrs. Bray was also a woman of large intelligence, and of a mind freely open to new theories. She wrote a *Physiology for Schools* and a school-book on *Duties to Animals*, which have been well received by the public and used as text books in the schools of the Midland counties. In 1882 she published a little book on the *Elements of Morality*, consisting of a series of easy lessons for Unitarian Sunday schools and for home teaching. To the Brays, Marian Evans owed much in the way of sympathy, culture and direct influence. Perhaps more than any other persons they gave tone and direction to her mind. One who knew them has said, "Besides being a practical as well as theoretical philanthropist, Mr. Bray was also a courageous impugner of the dogmas which form the basis of the popular theology. Mrs. Bray shared in this general largeness of thought, while perhaps more in sympathy with the fairer aspects of Christianity."

A brother and a sister of Mrs. Bray's, Charles C. Hennell and Sara S. Hennell, also had a large influence on Marian Evans during this period. It was Charles Hennell who induced her to translate Strauss, and it was Sara Hennell to whom she wrote about her aunt after the publication of *Adam Bede*. Hennell's *Inquiry concerning the origin of Christianity* was published in 1838, and appeared in a second edition in 1841. In the latter year the book was read by Marian Evans, after a faithful perusal of the Bible as a preparation for it, and quickly re-read, and with great interest and delight. She then pronounced it "the most interesting book she had ever read," dating from it a new birth to her mind. The book was translated into German, Strauss writing a preface for it, and that interpreter of Christianity praised it highly. Hennell rejected all supernaturalism and the miraculous, regarding Christianity as a slow and natural development out of Judaism, aided by Platonism and other outside influences. He finds the sources of Jesus' teachings in the Jewish tendencies of the time, while the cause of the supremacy of the man Jesus was laid in a long course of events which had swelled to a crisis at the time of his appearance, and bore him aloft to a height whence his personal qualities told with a power derived from the accumulated force of many generations. Jesus was an enthusiast who believed himself the predicted king of the Jews, and he was a revolutionist expecting to establish an earthly kingdom for the supremacy of Judaism. Jesus was largely influenced by the Essenes, but he rejected their austerity. Hennell found a mixture of truth and error in the Gospels, and believed that many mythical elements entered into the accounts given of Jesus. A thorough rationalist, he claimed to accept the spiritual essence of Christianity, and to value highly the moral teachings of Jesus. In a later work on *Christian Theism* he finds an argument for belief in God mainly in nature. In his conclusions he is not far from F. W. Newman and Theodore Parker; but he does not give the credit to intuition and the religious faculty they do, though he is an earnest believer in God, and inclined to accept Christianity as the highest expression of religion.

Sara S. Hennell early published *An Essay on the Skeptical Tendency of Butler's Analogy*, and a Baillie prize essay on *Christianity and Infidelity: An Exposition of the Arguments on Both Sides*. A work of much merit and thought appeared from her pen in 1860, under the title of *Thoughts in Aid of Faith*. In this work she follows her brother, Strauss, Feuerbach and Spencer in an interpretation of religion, which constantly recalls the theories of George Eliot. In a series of more recent books she has continued the same line of thought. The early and intimate friendship of Marian Evans and Miss Hennell may explain this similarity of opinion, and the beliefs they held in common were doubtless developed to a greater or less extent even when the former lived in Coventry.

Another friend of this period was a German scholar by the name of Brabant, resident in England, a friend of Strauss, Paulus, Coleridge and Grote. Grote described him as "a vigorous self-thinking intellect." A daughter of Dr. Brabant first undertook the translation of Strauss, and she it was who married Charles Hennell. After this marriage Miss Evans offered to take to Dr. Brabant the place of his daughter, and did act as his housekeeper for some months.

Marian Evans was surrounded at the most impressible period of her life by this group of intellectual, free-thinking people, who seem to have fully indoctrinated her with their own opinions. None of them had rejected Christianity or theism, but they were rationalists in spirit, and eager students of philosophy and science. Here were laid the foundations of the doctrines she afterwards held so strongly, and even during this period very many of the theories presented in her books were fully developed. Here her mind was thoroughly prepared for the teachings of Comte, Spencer and Lewes; and her early instructors had gone so far in their lessons that the later teachers had little to do more than to give system to her thoughts.

It was essential to George Eliot's novel-writing that she was educated amidst religious influences, and that she earnestly accepted the religious teaching of her childhood. Not less important was her humble home and her association with the common life of the people. Through all her work these influences appear, coloring her thought, shaping her views of life, and increasing her sympathies and affections. Her tender, enthusiastic love of humble life never lost any of its quickening power. The faith of childhood was lost, but its memory was left in a warm appreciation of all phases of religious life and a heartfelt sympathy with all the sorrows and aspirations of men.

Her father's health becoming very poor, Marian spent the next two or three years in the care of him. She read to him most of Scott's novels, devoting several hours each day to this task. During this period she made a visit to the Isle of Wight, and there read the novels of Richardson. Her father died in 1849, and she was very much affected by this event. She grieved for him overmuch, and could find no consolation. Her friends, the Brays, to divert and relieve her mind, invited her to take a continental tour with them. They travelled extensively in Belgium, Germany, Switzerland and Italy. Her grief, however, was so excessive as to receive little relief, and her friends began to fear the results. On their return to England they left her at Geneva, where she remained for nearly a year. After some months in a boarding-house near Geneva she became an inmate of the family of M. D'Albert Durade, a Swiss water-color painter of some reputation, who afterwards became the translator of her works into French. She devoted the winter of 1849–50 to the study of French and its literature, to mathematics and to reading. Her teacher in mathematics soon told her that she was able to proceed without his aid. She read Rousseau and studied the French socialists. M. Durade painted her portrait, making a remarkable picture. The softness of the clear blue eyes, in which is expressed a profound depth of thought, is one of its characteristics.

M. Durade accompanied her to England in the spring of 1850, and she went to live with her brother, where she remained for a few months. The old family differences about religion had alienated the brother and sister so far intellectually that she accepted an invitation from the Brays to find a home with them. Her sadness and grief continued, and her health was not good. Her fits of nervousness and of tears were frequent, but her studies continued to occupy her mind. She delighted to converse with Mr. Bray, and other persons of earnest thought had their influence on her mind. Among these was George Dawson, the famous preacher who cut himself loose from all denominations.

II.

TRANSLATOR AND EDITOR.

IT was while living at Foleshill, and amidst the intellectual influences of awakening radicalism, that Marian Evans undertook her first literary labor. This was the translation of the *Leben Jesu* of David Strauss. A book so daring in its interpretations of the origin of Christianity excited much attention, and especially among those who had broken away from the old religious beliefs. The work of translation was at first undertaken by Miss Brabant, who soon married Charles Hennell. Then the task was taken up by Marian Evans, who gave three years to it, renewing her Hebrew studies for the purpose, and the book was published in 1846. The work was thoroughly done, so much so that Strauss complimented the translator on its accuracy and correctness of spirit. Concerning the translation the *Westminster Review* had this word of praise to offer: "We can testify that the translator has achieved a very tough work with remarkable spirit and fidelity. The author, though indeed a good writer, could hardly have spoken better had his country and language been English. The work has evidently fallen into the hands of one who has not only effective command of both languages, but a familiarity with the subject-matter of theological criticism, and an initiation into its technical phraseology." Another critic said that "whoever reads these volumes without any reference to the German, must be pleased with the easy, perspicuous, idiomatic force of the English style. But he will be still more satisfied when, on turning to the original, he finds that the rendering is word for word, thought for thought and sentence for sentence. In preparing so beautiful a rendering as the present, the difficulties can have been neither few nor small in the way of preserving, in various parts of the work, the exactness of the translation, combined with that uniform harmony and clearness of style which impart to the volumes before us the air and the spirit of an original. A modest and kindly care for his reader's convenience has induced the translator often to supply the rendering into English of a Greek quotation when there was no corresponding rendering into German in the original. Indeed, Strauss may well say, as he does in the notice which he writes for this English edition, that, as far as he has examined it, the translation is *et accurata et perspicua.*"

The book had a successful sale, but Marian Evans received only twenty pounds, and twenty-five copies of the book, for her share of the translation. A little later she translated Feuerbach's *Essence of Christianity*, receiving fifty pounds for this labor. It was published in 1854, but the sale was small, and it proved a heavy loss to the publisher. While translating Strauss she aided a friend interested in philosophical studies (probably Charles Bray) by the translation, for his reading, of the *De Deo* of Spinoza. Some years later she completed a translation of the more famous *Ethica* of the same thinker. It was not published, probably because there was at that time so little interest in Spinoza.

The execution of such work as this, and all of it done in the most creditable and accurate manner, indicates the thoroughness of Marian Evans' scholarship. Though she doubtless was somewhat inclined to accept the opinions she thus helped to diffuse, yet Miss Simcox tells us that "the translation of Strauss and the translation of Spinoza were undertaken, not by her own choice but at the call of friendship; in the first place to complete what some one else was unable to continue, and in the second to make the philosopher she admired accessible to a friendly phrenologist who did not read Latin. At all times she regarded translation as a work that should be undertaken as a duty, to make accessible any book that required to be read; and though undoubtedly she was satisfied that the *Leben Jesu* required to be read in England, it would be difficult to imagine a temper more naturally antipathetic to her than that of its author; and critics who talk about the 'Strauss and Feuerbach period' should be careful to explain that the phrase covers no implication that she was at any time an admirer or a disciple of Strauss. There are extremes not only too remote but too disparate to be included in the same life."

Marian Evans did not become an admirer or disciple of Strauss, probably because she preferred Charles Hennell's interpretation of Christianity. It is certain, however, that she was greatly affected by Feuerbach, and that his influence was ever after strongly marked in her thinking. The teachings of Charles Bray and Charles Hennell had prepared her for the reception of those of Feuerbach, and he in turn made her mind responsive to the more systematic philosophy of Comte. Bray had taught her, along with Kant, to regard all knowledge as subjective, while Hennell and her other friends had shown her the objective falsity of Christianity. Thus her mind was made ready for Feuerbach's leading principle, that all religion is a product of the mind and has no outward reality corresponding to its doctrines. According to Feuerbach, the mind creates for itself objective images corresponding to its subjective states, reproduces its feelings in the outward world. In reality there is no objective fact corresponding to these subjective ideas, but what the mind conceives to exist is a necessary product of its own activity. The mind necessarily believes in God, which is man's way of conceiving his species and realizing to himself the perfect type of his own nature. God does not exist, and yet he is a true picture of man's soul, a necessary product of his feeling and consciousness. All religious ideas are true subjectively, and Christianity especially corresponds to the inward wants and aspirations of the soul. To Feuerbach it is true as a poetic interpretation of feeling and sentiment, and to him it gives the noblest and truest conception of what the soul needs for its inward satisfaction.

The influence of Feuerbach is to be seen in the profound interest which Marian Evans ever took in the subject of religion. That influence alone explains how it was possible for one who did not accept any religious doctrines as true, who did not believe in God or immortality, and who rejected Christianity as a historic or dogmatic faith, to accept so much as she did of the better spirit of religion and to be so keenly in sympathy with it. It was from the general scepticism and rationalism of the times she learned to reject all religion as false to truth and as not giving a just interpretation of life and its facts. It was from Feuerbach she learned how great is the influence of religion, how necessary it is to man's welfare, and how profoundly it answers to the wants of the soul. Like so many keen minds of the century, she rejected, with a sweeping scepticism, all on which a spiritual religion rests, all its facts, arguments and reasons. She knew only nature and man; inspiration, revelation, a spiritual world, had no existence for her. Yet she believed most thoroughly in religion, accepted its phenomena, was deeply moved by its spiritual aims, yearned after its perfect self-renunciation. Religion was to her, however, a purely subjective experience; it gave her a larger realization of the wants of humanity, it revealed to her the true nature of feeling. To Feuerbach she owed this capacity to appreciate Christianity, to rejoice in its spiritual aims, and even to accept it as a true interpretation of the soul's wants, at the same time that she totally rejected it as fact and dogma.

In the spring of 1851 she was invited to London by John Chapman, to assist him in the editorship of the *Westminster Review*. Chapman had been the publisher of her translations, and she had met him in London when on the way to the continent the year before. He was the publisher of a large number of idealistic and positivist works, representing the outspoken and radical sentiment of the time. The names of Fichte, Emerson, Parker, Francis Newman, Cousin, Ewald, H. Martineau, and others of equal note, appeared on his list. The *Westminster Review* was devoted to scientific and positivist views, and was the organ of such writers as Mill, Spencer, Lewes and Miss Martineau. It was carefully edited, had an able list of contributors, but its advanced philosophical position did not give it a wide circle of readers. It gave careful reviews of books, and had able departments devoted to the literature of each of the leading countries. Marian Evans did much of the labor in preparing these departments and in writing special book reviews. Her work was thoroughly done, and shows wide reading and patient effort. Her position brought her the acquaintance of a distinguished and brilliant company of men and women. Under this influence her powers widened, and she quickly showed herself the peer of the ablest among them. Herbert Spencer has said that at this time she was "distinguished by that breadth of culture and universality of power which have since made her known to all the world." We are told by another that "her strength of intellect, her scholarship and varied accomplishments, and the personal charm of her manner and conversation, made a deep impression on all who were thrown into her society."

Dr. Chapman then lived in the Strand, and Marian Evans became a member of his family, sharing in its interests as well as in its labors. She was extremely simple in her habits, went but very little into society, and gave herself almost exclusively to her duties and to metaphysical studies. A fortnightly gathering of the contributors to the *Review* was held in Mr. Chapman's house, and on these occasions she came to know most of the scientific and positivist thinkers of England at that time. Harriet Martineau invited her to Ambleside, and she was a frequent guest at the London residence of Sir James and Lady Clarke. She visited George Combe and his wife at Edinburgh in October, 1852, going to Ambleside on her return.

While assisting Mr. Chapman, Marian Evans contributed only one article, beyond her editorial work, to the pages of the *Westminster Review*. The work she did, almost wholly that of digesting and reviewing new books, could have been little to her taste. It must have been a drudgery, except in so far as it aided her in the pursuit of her studies. Occasionally, however, she must have found a task to her mind, as when, in the summary of current English literature for January, 1852, she had Carlyle's *Life of Sterling* in hand. Her notice of the book is highly appreciative of Carlyle's genius, and full of cordial praise. This passage gives her idea of a true biography:

We have often wished that genius would incline itself more frequently to the task of the biographer, — that when some great or good personage dies, instead of the dreary three or five volumed compilations of letter, and diary, and detail, little to the purpose, which two-thirds of the reading public have not the chance, nor the other third the inclination, to read, we could have a real "Life," setting forth briefly and vividly the man's inward and outward struggles, aims and achievements, so as to make clear the meaning which his experience has for his fellows. A few such lives (chiefly, indeed, autobiographies) the world possesses, and they have, perhaps, been more influential on the formation of character than any other kind of reading. But the conditions required for the perfection of life writing, — personal intimacy, a loving and poetic nature which sees the beauty and the depth of familiar things, and the artistic power which seizes characteristic points and renders them with life-like effect, — are seldom found in combination. *The Life of Sterling* is an instance of this rare conjunction. Its comparatively tame scenes and incidents gather picturesqueness and interest under the rich lights of Carlyle's mind. We are told neither too little nor too much; the facts noted, the letters selected, are all such as serve to give the liveliest conception of what Sterling was and what he did; and though the book speaks much of other persons, this collateral matter is all a kind of scene-painting, and is accessory to the main purpose.

The earliest of the regular articles, and the only one printed while she was the associate editor of the *Review*, is on "The Lady Novelists." It appeared in the number for July, 1852, and contained a striking discussion of woman's place in literature, a defence of woman's right to occupy that field she can best cultivate, with a clear and just criticism of several of the most prominent among lady novelists. She was quite full in her treatment of Jane Austen and George Sand, praising as well as criticising with insight and fine discrimination. At the outset she defines literature as an expression of the emotions, and gives a remarkably clear and original description of its functions.

Her editorial connection with the *Westminster Review* continued for about two years, until the end of 1853. For the next three years she was a contributor to its pages, where there appeared "Woman in France: Madame de Sablé," in October, 1854; "Evangelical Teaching: Dr. Cumming," October, 1855; "German Wit: Heinrich Heine," January, 1856; "The Natural History of German Life," July, 1856; "Silly Novels by Lady Novelists," October, 1856; and "Worldliness and other-Worldliness: the Poet Young," January, 1857. Two other articles have been attributed to her pen, but they are of little value. These are "George Forster," October, 1856, and "Weimar and its Celebrities," April, 1859. The interest and value of nearly all these articles are still as great as when they were first published. This will justify the publication here of numerous extracts from their most salient and important paragraphs. As indicating her literary judgment, and her capacity for incisive characterization and clear, trenchant criticism, reference may be made to the essay on Heine, which is one of the finest pieces of critical writing the century has produced.

Heine is one of the most remarkable men of this age; no echo, but a real voice, and therefore, like all genuine things in this world, worth studying; a surpassing lyric poet, who has uttered our feelings for us in delicious song; a humorist, who touches leaden folly with the magic wand of his fancy, and transmutes it into the fine gold of art — who sheds his sunny smile on human tears, and makes them a beauteous rainbow on the cloudy background of life; a wit, who holds in his mighty hand the most scorching lightnings of satire; an artist in prose literature, who has shown even more completely than Goethe the possibilities of German prose; and — in spite of all charges against him, true as well as false — a lover of freedom, who has spoken wise and brave words on behalf of his fellow-men. He is, moreover, a suffering man, who, with all the highly wrought sensibility of genius, has to endure terrible physical ills; and as such he calls forth more than an intellectual interest. It is true, alas! that there is a heavy weight in the other scale — that Heine's magnificent powers have often served only to give electric force to the expression of debased feeling, so that his works are no Phidian statue of gold, and ivory, and gems, but have not a little brass, and iron, and miry clay mingled with the precious metal. The audacity of his occasional coarseness and personality is unparalleled in contemporary literature, and has hardly been exceeded by the license of former days. Yet, when all coarseness, all scurrility, all Mephistophelean contempt for the reverent feelings of other men, is removed, there will be a plenteous remainder of exquisite poetry, of wit, humor and just thought. It is apparently too often a congenial task to write severe words about the transgressions committed by men of genius, especially when the censor has the advantage of being himself a man of *no* genius, so that those transgressions seem to him quite gratuitous; *he*, forsooth, never lacerated any one by his wit, or gave irresistible piquancy to a coarse allusion, and his indignation is not mitigated by any knowledge of the temptation that lies in transcendent power. . . .

In Heine's hands German prose, usually so heavy, so clumsy, so dull, becomes, like clay in the hands of the chemist, compact, metallic, brilliant; it is German in an *allotropic* condition. No dreary, labyrinthine sentences in which you find "no end in wandering mazes lost;" no chains of adjectives in linked harshness long drawn out; no digressions thrown in as parentheses; but crystalline definiteness and clearness, fine and varied rhythm, and all that delicate precision, all those felicities of word and cadence, which belong to the highest order of prose. And Heine has proved that it is possible to be witty in German; indeed, in reading him, you might imagine that German was pre-eminently the language of wit, so flexible, so subtle, so piquant does it become under his management. He is far more an artist in prose than Goethe. He has not the breadth and repose, and the calm development which belongs to Goethe's style, for they are foreign to his mental character; but he excels Goethe in susceptibility to the manifold qualities of prose, and in mastery over its effects. Heine is full of variety, of light and shadow: he alternates between epigrammatic pith, imaginative grace, sly allusion, and daring piquancy; and athwart all these there runs a vein of sadness, tenderness and grandeur which reveals the poet.

The introduction to this article contains a wise comparison of wit and humor, and makes a subtle discrimination between them. German wit she finds is heavy and lacking in nicety of perception; and the German is the only nation that "had contributed nothing classic to the common stock of European wit and humor" previous to the present century. In Heine she found both in a marked degree, so that he is unlike the other writers of Germany, having a flavor and a spirit quite his own.

Her essays on Dr. Cumming and the poet Young were largely of a theological character. They are keen in their thrusts at dogmatic religion, sparkling with witty hits at a make-believe piety, and full of biting sarcasm. Her entire want of sympathy with the men she dissects, makes her sometimes unjust to them, and she makes them worse than they really were. The terrible vigor of her criticism may be seen in her description of Dr. Cumming and his teaching. She brings three charges against him, and defends each with ample quotation, wit, sarcasm, argument and eloquence. She finds in his books unscrupulosity of statement, absence of genuine charity, and a perverted moral judgment. These essays much resemble Thackeray's dissection of Swift for their terrible sarcasm, their unmerciful criticism, and their minute unveiling of human weakness and hypocrisy. It is possible that Thackeray was her model, as his lecture was first delivered in 1851 or 1852; but, at least, she is not at all his inferior in power to lay bare the character and tendencies of the men she selected for analysis. Her keen psychological insight was shown here in a manner as brilliant and as accurate as in any of her novels. She may have done injustice to the circumstances under which these men were placed, their religious education, the social conditions which aided them in the pursuit of the lives they lived; and she may not have been quite ready enough to deal charitably with those who were blinded, as these men were, by all their surroundings and by whatever of culture they received; but she did see into the secret places of their lives, and laid bare the inner motives of their conduct. It was because these men came before the world as its teachers, holding up before it a special ideal and motive for its guidance, that she criticised them. In reality they were selfish, narrow, worldly; their teaching came from no deep convictions, nor from a high moral purpose; and hence her criticism. She laid bare the shallowness of their thoughts, the selfishness of their purposes, and the spiritual unfruitfulness of their teachings. Criticism so unsparing and so just, because based on the most searching insight into character and conduct, it would be difficult to find elsewhere.

Dr. Cumming's mind is evidently not of the pietistic order. There is not the slightest leaning towards mysticism in his Christianity — no indication of religious raptures, of delight in God, of spiritual communion with the Father. He is most at home in the forensic view of justification, and dwells on salvation as a scheme rather than as an experience. He insists on good works as the sign of justifying faith, as labors to be achieved to the glory of God, but he rarely represents them as the spontaneous, necessary outflow of a soul filled with divine love. He is at home in the external, the polemical, the historical, the circumstantial, and is only episodically devout and practical. The great majority of his published sermons are occupied with argument or philippic against Romanists and unbelievers, with vindications of the Bible, with the political interpretation of prophecy, or the criticism of public events; and the devout aspiration, or the spiritual and practical exhortation, is tacked to them as a sort of fringe in a hurried sentence or two at the end. He revels in the demonstration that the Pope is the Man of Sin; he is copious on the downfall of the Ottoman empire; he appears to glow with satisfaction in turning a story which tends to show how he abashed an "infidel;" it is a favorite exercise with him to form conjectures of the process by which the earth is to be burned up, and to picture Dr. Chalmers and Mr. Wilberforce being caught up to meet Christ in the air, while Romanists, Puseyites and infidels are given over to gnashing of teeth. But of really spiritual joys and sorrows, of the life and death of Christ as a manifestation of love that constrains the soul, of sympathy with that yearning over the lost and erring which made

Jesus weep over Jerusalem, and prompted the sublime prayer, "Father, forgive them," of the gentler fruits of the Spirit, and the peace of God which passeth understanding — of all this, we find little trace in Dr. Cumming's discourses.

Even more severe is her account of the poet Young. She speaks of him as "a remarkable individual of the species *divine*." This is her account of his life:

He is on the verge of fifty, and has recently undergone his metamorphosis into the clerical form. Rather a paradoxical specimen, if you observe him narrowly: a sort of cross between a sycophant and a psalmist, a poet whose imagination is alternately fired by the "Last Day" and by a creation of peers, who fluctuate between rhapsodic applause of King George and rhapsodic applause of Jehovah. After spending "a foolish youth, the sport of peers and poets," after being a hanger-on of the profligate Duke of Wharton, after aiming in vain at a parliamentary career, and angling for pensions and preferment with fulsome dedications and fustian odes, he is a little disgusted with his imperfect success, and has determined to retire from the general mendicancy business to a particular branch; in other words, he has determined on that renunciation of the world implied in "taking orders," with the prospect of a good living and an advantageous matrimonial connection. And no man can be better fitted for an Established Church. He personifies completely her nice balance of temporalities and spiritualities. He is equally impressed with the momentousness of death and of burial fees; he languishes at once for immortal life and for "livings;" he has a vivid attachment to patrons in general, but on the whole prefers the Almighty. He will teach, with something more than official conviction, the nothingness of earthly things; and he will feel something more than private disgust if his meritorious efforts in directing man's attention to another world are not rewarded by substantial preferment in this. His secular man believes in cambric bands and silk stockings as characteristic attire for "an ornament of religion and virtue;" hopes courtiers will never forget to copy Sir Robert Walpole; and writes begging letters to the King's mistress. His spiritual man recognizes no motives more familiar than Golgotha and the skies; it walks in graveyards, or it soars among the stars. His religion exhausts itself in ejaculations and rebukes, and knows no medium between the ecstatic and the sententious. If it were not for the prospect of immortality, he considers it would be wise and agreeable to be indecent or to murder one's father; and, heaven apart, it would be extremely irrational in any man not to be a knave. Man, he thinks, is a compound of the angel and the brute; the brute is to be humbled by being reminded of its "relation to the stalls," and frightened into moderation by the contemplation of death-beds and skulls; the angel is to be developed by vituperating this world and exalting the next; and by this double process you get the Christian — "the highest style of man." With all this, our new-made divine is an unmistakable poet. To a clay compounded chiefly of the worldling and the rhetorician, there is added a real spark of Promethean fire. He will one day clothe his apostrophes and objurgations, his astronomical religion and his charnel-house morality, in lasting verse, which will stand, like a Juggernaut made of gold and jewels, at once magnificent and repulsive; for this divine is Edward Young, the future author of *Night Thoughts*.

She says, "One of the most striking characteristics of Young is his *radical insincerity as a poetic artist*."

Indeed, we remember no mind in poetic literature that seems to have absorbed less of the beauty and the healthy breath of the common landscape than Young's. His images, often grand and finely presented, lie almost entirely within that circle of observation which would be familiar to a man who lived in town, hung about the theatres, read the newspaper, and went home often by moon and star light. There is no natural object nearer than the moon that seems to have any strong attraction for him, and even to the moon he chiefly appeals for patronage, and "pays his court" to her. . . . He describes nothing so well as a comet, and is tempted to linger with fond detail over nothing more familiar than the day of judgment and an imaginary journey among the stars. . . . The adherence to abstractions, or to the personification of abstractions, is closely allied in Young to the *want of genuine emotion*. He sees Virtue sitting on a mount serene, far above the mists and storms of earth: he sees Religion coming down from the skies, with this world in her left hand and the other world in her right; but we never find him dwelling on virtue or religion as it really exists — in the emotions of a man dressed in an ordinary coat, and seated by his fireside of an evening, with his hand resting on the head of his little daughter, in courageous effort for unselfish ends, in the internal triumph of justice and pity over personal resentment, in all the sublime self-renunciation and sweet charities which are found in the details of ordinary life.

In these essays there are various indications of her religious opinions, and those of a decided character. In that on Dr. Cumming, she has this word to say of the rationalistic conception of the Bible:

He seems to be ignorant, or he chooses to ignore the fact, that there is a large body of eminently instructed and earnest men who regard the Hebrew and Christian scriptures as a series of historical documents, to be dealt with according to the rules of historical criticism, and that an equally large number of men, who are not historical critics, find the dogmatic scheme built on the letter of the scriptures, opposed to their profoundest moral convictions.

This statement is suggestive of her position on religious subjects:

The best minds that accept Christianity as a divinely inspired system, believe that the great end of the Gospel is not merely the saving but the educating of men's souls, the creating within them of holy dispositions, the subduing of egoistical pretensions, and the perpetual enhancing of the desire that the will of God — a will synonymous with goodness and truth — may be done on earth. But what relation to all this has a system of interpretation which keeps the mind of the Christian in the position of a spectator at a gladiatorial show, of which Satan is the wild beast in the shape of a great red dragon, and two thirds of mankind the victims — the whole provided and got up by God for the edification of the saints?

She calls Dr. Cumming's teachings "the natural crop of a human mind where the soil is chiefly made up of egoistic passions and dogmatic beliefs." Then she deals with that belief in this trenchant fashion:

Happily, the constitution of human nature forbids the complete prevalence of such a theory. Fatally powerful as religious systems have been, human nature is stronger and wider than religious systems, and though dogmas may hamper, they cannot absolutely repress its growth: build walls around the living tree as you will, the bricks and mortar have by and by to give way before the slow and sure operation of the sap. But next to the hatred of the enemies of God which is the principle of persecution, there perhaps has been no perversion more obstructive of true moral development than this substitution of a reference to the glory of God for the direct promptings of the sympathetic feelings. Benevolence and justice are strong only in proportion as they are directly and inevitably called into activity by their proper objects; pity is strong only because we are strongly impressed by suffering; and only in proportion as it is compassion that speaks through the eyes when we soothe, and moves the arm when we succor, is a deed strictly benevolent. If the soothing or the succor be given because another being wishes or approves it, the deed ceases to be one of benevolence, and becomes one of deference, of obedience, of self-interest, or vanity. Accessory motives may aid in producing an action, but they presuppose the weakness of the direct motive; and conversely, when the direct motive is strong, the actions of accessory motives will be excluded.

In writing of Young she says, —

The God of the *Night Thoughts* is simply Young himself "writ large" — a didactic poet, who "lectures" mankind in the antithetic hyperbole of mortal and immortal joys, earth and the stars, hell and heaven, and expects the tribute of inexhaustible applause. Young has no conception of religion as anything else than egoism turned heavenward; and he does not merely imply this, he insists on it.

She contrasts Young with Cowper, preferring the

latter because he dwells more on the things of a common and simple life.

In Young we have the type of that deficient human sympathy, that impiety toward the present and the visible, which flies for its motives, its sanctities, and its religion, to the remote, the vague and unknown: in Cowper we have the type of that genuine love which cherishes things in proportion to their nearness, and feels its reverence grow in proportion to the intimacy of its knowledge.

This warm human sympathy is all she cares for in religion.

See how a lovely, sympathetic nature manifests itself in spite of creed and circumstance! Where is the poem that surpasses the *Task* in the genuine love it breathes, at once toward inanimate and animate existence — in truthfulness of perception and sincerity of presentation — in the calm gladness that springs from a delight in objects for their own sake, without self-reference — in divine sympathy with the lowliest pleasures, with the most short-lived capacity for pain? Here is no railing at the earth's "melancholy map," but the happiest lingering over her simplest scenes with all the fond minuteness that belongs to love; no pompous rhetoric about the inferiority of the brutes, but a warm plea on their behalf against man's inconsiderateness and cruelty, and a sense of enlarged happiness from their companionship in enjoyment; no vague rant about human misery and human virtue, but that close and vivid presentation of particular deeds and misdeeds, which is the direct road to the emotions. How Cowper's exquisite mind falls with the mild warmth of morning sunlight on the commonest objects, at once disclosing every detail and investing every detail with beauty! No object is too small to prompt his song — not the sooty film on the bars, or the spoutless teapot holding a bit of mignonette that serves to cheer the dingy town lodging with a "hint that nature lives;" and yet his song is never trivial, for he is alive to small objects, not because his mind is narrow, but because his glance is clear and his heart is large.

Her contributions to the *Westminster Review* indicate that Marian Evans had read much and well, and that she was possessed of a thoroughly cultivated mind and much learning. To their preparation she gave herself diligently, writing slowly, after a careful study of her subject and much thought devoted to a faithful thinking out of all its parts. It has been many times suggested that these articles gave indication only of learning and studious effort. They certainly give strong hint of these, but also of much more. That on human life shows how much she had thought, and how thoroughly and philosophically, on one of the largest problems; while the one on Heine indicates her penetrating literary judgment and her capacity for analysis and interpretation. These essays are not mere compilations, mere digests of learned information; they are studies of large subjects done in a large and inspiring manner. Her essays on the poet Young and Dr. Cumming, and the two on lady novelists, as well as that on Heine, show many indications of that subtle power and that true genius which were displayed in her later work. There was genius displayed in these articles, without doubt, and genius of a high order. It was genius not as yet aware of itself, and not yet at the height of its power and capable of its truest expression, but genius nevertheless. Many of the most striking characteristics of her novel-writing were shown in these essays. Here was the same love of common human life; the same interest in its humbler forms and expressions; the like penetrating analysis and subtle portrayal of character; a psychological method of the same probing and comprehensive nature. Her main philosophical ideas were indicated here, though not given that clear and incisive expression they afterwards received. When she wrote of the *natural history* of German life she indicated in the very title of her essay one of her main theories, and her conception of man as a social being was brought out in it. These essays fully indicate that her opinions were already formed, that the leading ideas she was to give expression to in her novels had been arrived at by diligent study and thought, and that she had equipped herself with ample reasons for the acceptance of the opinions she held. Their chief defect is in their occasional arrogance of expression, as if the writer had not yet wholly escaped the superior airs of the young woman elated with the greatness of her knowledge, and a certain rudeness and vehemence of statement not seen later. It is a defect that is not very prominent, but one that is apparent enough to mar some of the best of these pages. It was one she never wholly outgrew, though in her novels her large information was usually so managed and subordinated as to give little annoyance to the intelligent reader.

It must be quite evident to any reader of her *Westminster Review* contributions, that Marian Evans would never have attained to any such high literary eminence as an essayist as that which she has secured as a novelist. Readable as are her essays, — and the five just named are certainly worthy of a place in her complete works, — yet they are not of the highest order. She could attain the highest range of her power only when something far more subtile and intrinsic was concerned. That this is true may be seen in these essays; for even here she writes the best only when she has human motives, feelings and aspirations to weigh and explain. That she could dissect and explain the inner man they made apparent enough; but her genius demanded also the opportunity to create, to build up a life of high beauty and purpose from materials of its own construction. Her *Review* articles gave her a high place in the eyes of her friends, and their chief value seems to have been, that they caused these friends to see that she could do other and better work, and led them to induce her to apply her genius in a direction more congenial to its capacity.

III.

MARRIAGE.

IN 1853 Marian Evans became the wife of George Henry Lewes. He had married at an early age a woman possessed of many charms of person. They went to live in a large house at Kensington with five other young couples, keeping house on a co-operative arrangement, with many attractions of social entertainment therewith. One result was the desertion of her home by Mrs. Lewes in connection with one of the men into whose company she was constantly thrown by this manner of life. She soon repented, and Lewes forgave her, receiving her back to his home. A second time, however, she left him. His having condoned her fault made it impossible for him to secure a divorce according to the laws of England at that time. He seems to have done what he could to retain her faithful devotion to her marriage relations, so long as that seemed possible.

When Lewes and Marian Evans met, on her going to live in London, and after his wife had deserted him, there sprang up a strong attachment between them. As they could not be legally married, she agreed to live with him without that formality.

It is to be said of this affair that George Eliot was very far from looking at such a problem as Goethe or George Sand would have looked at it, from the position of personal inclination. Yet we are told by Miss Blind that she early entertained liberal views in regard to divorce, believing that greater freedom in this respect is desirable. There could have been no passionate individualistic defiance of law in her case, however. No one has insisted more strongly than she on the importance and the sanctity of the social regulations in regard to the union of the sexes. That her marriage was a true one in all but the legal form, that she was faithful to its every social obligation, has been abundantly shown. She was a most faithful wife to Lewes, and the devoted mother of his three children by the previous marriage, while she found in him that strong, self-reliant helpmate she needed.

Her marriage under these circumstances required no little individualism of purpose, and some defiance of social obligations. Her intimate friends were unable to comprehend her conduct, and she was alienated from most of them. Especially her friends in Coventry were annoyed at such a marriage, and were not reconciled with her for a long time, and not until they saw that she had acted with a conscientious purpose. She was excluded from society by this act, and her marriage was interpreted as a gross violation of social morality. To a sensitive nature, as hers assuredly was, and to one who so much valued the confidence of her friends as she did, such exclusion must have been a serious cross. She freely elected her own course in life, however, and she never seems to have complained at the results it brought her. That it saddened her mind seems probable, but there is no outward evidence that she accepted her lot in a bitter or complaining spirit. No one could have written of love and marriage in so high and pure a spirit as everywhere appears in her books with whom passion was in any degree a controlling influence. In *Adam Bede* her own conception of wedded love is expressed out of the innermost convictions and impulses of her own heart, when she exclaims, —

> What greater thing is there for two human souls, than to feel that they are joined for life — to strengthen each other in all labor, to rest on each other in all sorrow, to minister to each other in all pain, to be one with each other in silent unspeakable memories at the moment of the last parting.

In *Felix Holt* there is a passage on this subject which must have come directly from her own experience, and it gives us a true insight into the spirit in which she accepted the distrust of friends and the coldness of the world which her marriage brought her.

A supreme love, a motive that gives a sublime rhythm to a woman's life, and exalts habit into partnership with the soul's highest needs, is not to be had when and how she will: to know that high initiation, she must often tread where it is hard to tread, and feel the chill air, and watch through darkness. It is not true that love makes all things easy; it makes us choose what is difficult.

Throughout her novels she exalts marriage, never casts any slur upon it, treats it as one of the most sacred of all human relations. She makes it appear as a sacrament, not of the Church, but of the sublime fellowship of humanity. It is pure, holy, a binding tie, a sacred obligation, as it appears in her books. When Romola is leaving Florence and her husband, her love dead and all that made her life seem worthy gone with it, she meets Savonarola, who bids her return to her home and its duties. What the great prophet-priest says on this occasion we have every reason to believe expressed the true sentiments of George Eliot herself. He proclaims, what she doubtless thoroughly believed, that marriage is something far more than mere affection, more than love; that its obligation holds when all love is gone; that its obligation is so sacred and binding as to call for the fullest measure of renunciation and personal humiliation. As throwing light on George Eliot's manner of looking at this subject, the whole chapter which describes the meeting of Romola and Savonarola deserves to be read. That portion of it in which Savonarola gives his views of marriage may here be reproduced, not as giving the doctrine of the Church, but as presenting the positivist conception of marriage as interpreted by George Eliot.

His arresting voice had brought a new condition into her life, which made it seem impossible to her that she could go on her way as if she had not heard it; yet she shrank as one who sees the path she must take, but sees, too, that the hot lava lies there. And the instinctive shrinking from a return to her husband brought doubts. She turned away her eyes from Fra Girolamo, and stood for a minute or two with her hands hanging clasped before her, like a statue. At last she spoke, as if the words were being wrung from her, still looking on the ground.

"My husband — he is not — my love is gone!"

"My daughter, there is the bond of a higher love. Marriage is not carnal only, made for selfish delight. See what that thought leads you to! It leads you to wander away in a false garb from all the obligations of your place and name. That would not have been if you had learned that it is a sacramental vow, from which none but God can release you. My daughter, your life is not as a grain of sand, to be blown by the winds; it is as flesh and blood, that dies if it be sundered. Your husband is not a malefactor?"

Romola flushed and started. "Heaven forbid! No; I accuse him of nothing."

"I did not suppose he was a malefactor. I meant that if he were a malefactor your place would be in the prison beside him. My daughter, if the cross comes to you as a wife, you must carry it as a wife. You may say, 'I will forsake my husband,' but you cannot cease to be a wife."

"Yet if — oh, how could I bear —" Romola had involuntarily begun to say something which she sought to banish from her mind again.

"Make your marriage sorrows an offering, too, my daughter: an offering to the great work by which sin and sorrow are being made to cease. The end is sure, and is already beginning. Here in Florence it is beginning, and the eyes of faith behold it. And it may be our blessedness to die for it: to die daily by the crucifixion of our selfish will — to die at last by laying our bodies on the altar. My daughter, you are a child of Florence; fulfil the duties of that great inheritance. Live for Florence — for your own people, whom God is preparing to bless the earth. Bear the anguish and the smart. The iron is sharp — I know, I know — it rends the tender flesh. The draught is bitterness on the lips. But there is rapture in the cup — there is the vision which makes all life below it dross forever. Come, my daughter, come back to your place!"[1]

Again, when Dorothea goes to see Rosamond to intercede in Dr. Lydgate's behalf with his wife, we have an expression of the sacredness of marriage, and the renunciation it demands of all that is opposed to its trust and helpfulness. Dorothea says, -

"Marriage is so unlike everything else. There is something even awful in the nearness it brings. Even if we loved some one else better than — than those we were married to, it would be of no use" — poor Dorothea, in her palpitating anxiety, could only seize her

[1] Chapter XL.

language brokenly — "I mean, marriage drinks up all our power of giving or getting any blessedness in that sort of love. I know it may be very dear — but it murders our marriage — and then the marriage stays with us like a murder — and everything else is gone. And then our husband — if he loved and trusted us, and we have not helped him, but made a curse in his life — "

If Marian Evans rejected the sanctions which society has imposed on the love of man and woman in the legal forms of marriage, it was not in a wilful and passionate spirit. There are reasons for believing that she was somewhat touched in her youth with the individualistic theories of the time, which made so many men and women of genius reject the restraints imposed by society, as in the case of Goethe, Heine, George Sand, Shelley and many another; yet she does not appear to have been to more than a very limited extent influenced by such considerations in regard to her own marriage. The matter for surprise is, that one who regarded all human traditions, ceremonies and social obligations as sacred, should have consented to act in so individualistic a manner. She makes Rufus Lyon say — and it is her own opinion — that "the right to rebellion is the right to seek a higher rule, and not to wander in mere lawlessness." Her marriage, after the initial act, had in it nothing whatever of lawlessness. She believed there exists a higher rule than that of Parliament, and to this higher law she submitted. To her this was not a law of self-will and personal inclination, but the law of nature and social obligation. That she was not overcome by the German individualistic and social tendencies may be seen in the article on "Weimar and its Celebrities," in the *Westminster Review*, where, in writing of Wieland as an educator, she says that the tone of his books was not "immaculate," and that it was "strangely at variance with that sound and lofty morality which ought to form the basis of every education." She also speaks of the philosophy of that day as "the delusive though plausible theory that no license of tone, or warmth of coloring, could injure any really healthy and high-toned mind."

In the article on "Woman in France," she touches on similar theories. As this article was written just at the time of her marriage, one passage in it may have a personal interest, and shows her conception of a marriage such as her own, based on intellectual interest rather than on passionate love. She is speaking of

> the laxity of opinion and practice with regard to the marriage tie. Heaven forbid [she adds] that we should enter on a defence of French morals, most of all in relation to marriage! But it is undeniable that unions formed in the maturity of thought and feeling, grounded only on inherent fitness and mutual attraction, tended to bring women into more intelligent sympathy with men, and to heighten and complicate their share in the political drama. The quiescence and security of the conjugal relation are, doubtless, favorable to the manifestation of the highest qualities by persons who have already attained a high standard of culture, but rarely foster a passion sufficient to rouse all the faculties to aid in winning or retaining its beloved object—to convert indolence into activity, indifference into ardent partisanship, dulness into perspicuity.

Her conception of marriage may have been affected by that presented by Feuerbach in his *Essence of Christianity*. In words translated into English by herself, Feuerbach says, "that alone is a religious marriage which is a true marriage, which corresponds to the essence of marriage—love." Again, he says that marriage is only sacred when it is an inward attraction confirmed by social and personal obligations; "for a marriage the bond of which is merely an external restriction, not the voluntary, contented self-restriction of love—in short, a marriage which is not spontaneously concluded, spontaneously willed, self-sufficing—is not a true marriage, and therefore not a truly moral marriage." As a moral and social obligation, marriage is to be held sacred; its sacredness grows out of its profound human elements of helpfulness, nurture and emotional satisfaction, while its obligation rises from its primary social functions. It does not consist in any legal form, but in compliance with deep moral and social responsibilities. Some such conception of marriage as this she seems to have accepted, which found its obligation in the satisfaction it gives to the inner nature, and in the fulfilment of social responsibilities. The influence of Comte may also have been felt in the case of both Lewes and Marian Evans; they saw in the marriage form a fulfilment of human, not of legal, requirements.

While there is no doubt they would both gladly have accepted the legal form had that been possible, yet they were sufficiently out of sympathy with the conventionalities of society to cause them to disregard that form when it could not be complied with. They regarded themselves, however, as married, and bound by all the ties and requirements which marriage imposes. They proclaimed themselves to their friends as husband and wife, and they were so accepted by those who knew them. In her letters to literary correspondents she always mentioned Lewes as "my husband." The laws of most civilized nations recognize these very conditions, and regard the acceptance of the marriage relation before the world as a sufficient form.

Those who have written of this marriage, bear testimony to its devotion and beauty. The author of the account of her life and writings in the *Westminster Review*, an early and intimate friend, says the "union was from the first regarded by themselves as a true marriage, as an alliance of a sacred kind, having a binding and permanent character. When the fact of the union was first made known to a few intimate friends, it was accompanied with the assurance that its permanence was already irrevocably decreed. The marriage of true hearts for a quarter of a century has demonstrated the sincerity of the intention. 'The social sanction,' said Mr. Lewes once in our hearing, 'is always desirable.' There are cases in which it is not always to be had. Such a ratification of the sacrament of affection was regarded as a sufficient warrant, under the circumstances of the case, for entrance on the most sacred engagement of life. There was with her no misgiving, no hesitation, no looking back, no regret; but always the unostentatious assertion of quiet, matronly dignity, the most queenly expression and unconscious affirmation of the 'divine right' of the wedded wife. We have heard her own oral testimony to the enduring happiness of this union, and can, as privileged witnesses, corroborate it. As a necessary element in this happiness she practically included the enjoyment inseparable from the spontaneous reciprocation of home affection, meeting with an almost maternal love the filial devotion of Mr. Lewes's sons, proffering all tender service in illness, giving and receiving all friendly confidence in her own hour of sorrowful bereavement, and crowning with a final act of generous love and forethought the acceptance of parental responsibilities in the affectionate distribution of property, the visible result of years of the intellectual toil whose invisible issues are endless."

Their marriage helped both to a more perfect work and to a truer life. She gave poise and purpose to the "versatile, high-strung, somewhat wayward nature" of her husband, and she "restrained, raised, ennobled, and purified" his life and thought. He stimulated and directed her genius into its true channel, cared for her business interests with untiring faithfulness, made it possible for her to pursue her work without burdens and distractions, and gave her the inspiration of a noble affection and a cheerful home. Miss Edith Simcox speaks of "the perfect union between these two," which, she says, "lent half its charm to all the worship paid at the shrine of George Eliot." She herself, Miss Simcox proceeds to say, "has spoken somewhere of the element of almost maternal tenderness in a man's protecting love: this patient, unwearying care for which no trifles are too small, watched over her own life; he stood between her and the world, he relieved her from all those minor cares which chafe and fret the artist's soul; he wrote her letters; in a word, he so smoothed the course of her outer life as to leave all her powers free to do what she alone could do for the world and for the many who looked to her for help and guidance. No doubt this devotion brought its own reward; but we are exacting for our idols and do not care to have even a generous error to condone, and therefore we are glad to know that, great as his reward was, it was no greater than was merited by the most perfect love that ever crowned a woman's life." Mr. Kegan Paul also writes of the mutual helpfulness and harmony of purpose which grew out of this marriage. "Mr. Lewes's character attained a stability and pose in which it had been somewhat lacking, and the quiet of an orderly and beautiful home enabled him to concentrate himself more and more on works demanding sustained intellectual effort, while Mrs. Lewes's intensely feminine nature found the strong man on whom to lean in the daily business of life, for which she was physically and intellectually unfitted. Her own somewhat sombre cast of thought was cheered, enlivened and diversified by the vivacity and versatility which characterized Mr. Lewes, and made him seem less like an Englishman than a very agreeable foreigner."

This marriage presents one of the curious ethical problems of literature. In this case approval and condemnation are alike difficult. Her own teaching condemns it; her own life approves it. We could wish it had not been, for the sake of what is purest and best; and yet it is not difficult to see that its effects were in many ways beneficial to her. That it was ethically wrong there is no doubt. That it was condemned by her own teaching is so plain as to cause doubt about how she could herself approve it.

Lewes had a brilliant and versatile mind. He was not a profound thinker, but he had keen literary tastes, a vigorous interest in science, and a remarkable alertness of intellect. His gifts were varied rather than deep; literary rather than philosophical. As a companion, he had a wonderful charm and magnetism; he was a graceful talker, a marvellous story-teller, and a wit seldom rivalled. His intimate friend, Anthony Trollope, says, "There was never a man so pleasant as he with whom to sit and talk vague literary gossip over a cup of coffee and a cigar." By the same friend we are told that no man related a story as he did. "No one could say that he was handsome. The long bushy hair, and the thin cheeks, and the heavy mustache, joined as they were, alas! almost always to a look of sickness, were not attributes of beauty. But there was a brilliance in his eye which was not to be tamed by any sickness, by any suffering, which overcame all other feeling on looking at him."

George Henry Lewes was born in London, April 18, 1817. His grandfather was a well-known comedian. His education was received in a very desultory manner. He was at school for a time in Jersey, and also in Brittany, where he acquired a thorough command of French. Later he attended a famous school in Greenwich, kept by a Dr. Burney. After leaving school he went into a notary's office, and then he became a clerk to a Russia merchant. His mind was, however, attracted to scientific and philosophic studies, and he betrayed little interest either in the law or in commercial pursuits. Then he took up the study of medicine, giving thorough attention to anatomy and physiology. It is said that his horror of the dissecting-room was so great as to cause him to abandon the purpose to become a physician. All this time his mind was steadily drawn to philosophy, and he gave as much time to it as he could. The bent of his mind was early developed, and in 1836, when only nineteen, he had projected a treatise on the philosophy of mind, in which he proposed to give a physiological interpretation to the doctrines of Reid, Stewart and Brown. At the age of twenty he gave a course of lectures on this subject; and to this line of thought he held ever after. One of the influences which led to his departure from a strict interpretation of the Scotch metaphysicians was the influence of Spinoza. As indicating the eagerness with which he pursued his studies in all directions, and the earnestness of his purpose at so early an age, his own account of a club he attended at this time[1] may be mentioned. In this account he describes a Jew by the name of Cohen, who first introduced him to the study of Spinoza, and who has mistakenly been supposed to be the original of Mordecai in *Daniel Deronda*.

The sixth member of this club, who "studied anatomy and many other things, with vast aspirations, and no very definite career before him," was Lewes himself, in all probability. His eager desire for knowledge took him to Germany in 1838, where he remained for two years in the same desultory study of many subjects. He became thoroughly acquainted with the German language and life, and gave much attention to German literature and philosophy. On his return to England, Lewes entered upon his literary career, which was remarkable for its versatility and productiveness. In 1841 he wrote "The Noble Heart," a three-act tragedy, published in 1852. His studies of Spinoza found expression in one of the first essays on the subject published in England. In 1843, he published in the *Westminster Review* his conclusions on that thinker. His essay was reprinted in a separate form, attracting much attention, and in 1846 was incorporated into a larger work, the result of his studies in Germany and of his interest in philosophy. In 1845, at the age of twenty-nine, he published a history of philosophy, in which he undertook to criticise all metaphysical systems from the inductive and scientific point of view. This work was his *Biographical History of Philosophy*. It appeared in four small volumes in Knight's weekly series of popular books devoted to the diffusion of knowledge among the people. Lewes touched a popular demand in this book, reaching the wants of many readers. He continued through many years to elaborate his studies on

[1]Fortnightly Review, April 1, 1866, introductory to the article on Spinoza.

these subjects and to re-work his materials. New and enlarged editions, each time making the book substantially a new one, were published in 1857, in 1867 and in 1871. No solid book of the century has sold better; and it has been translated into several continental languages.

Lewes did not confine himself to philosophy. Other and very different subjects also attracted his attention. His mind ranged in many directions, and his flexible genius found subjects of interest on all sides. In 1846 he published a little book on *The Spanish Drama: Lope de Vega and Calderon*, a slight affair, full of his peculiar prejudices, and devoted mainly to an unsympathetic criticism. The following year he gave to the world an ambitious novel, *Ranthorpe*. It seems to have been well read in its day, was translated into German and reprinted on the continent by Tauchnitz. The plot is well conceived, but the story is rapidly told, full of incident and tragedy, and there is a subtle air of unreality about it. The experiences of a poet are unfolded in a romantic form, and the attempt is made to show what is the true purpose and spirit in which literature can be successfully pursued. To this end there is a discussion running through the book on the various phases of the literary life, much in the manner of Fielding. *Ranthorpe* would now be regarded as a very dull novel, and it is crude, full of the sensational, with little analysis of character and much action.

It was read, however, by Charlotte Brontë with great interest, and she wrote of it to the author in these words: "In reading *Ranthorpe* I have read a new book — not a reprint — not a reflection of any other book, but *a new book*. I did not know such books were written now. It is very different to any of the popular works of fiction; it fills the mind with fresh knowledge. Your experience and your convictions are made the reader's; and to an author, at least, they have a value and an interest quite unusual." In

1848, Lewes published another novel of a very different kind — *Rose, Blanche and Violet.* This was a society novel, intended to reach the minds of the ordinary novel-readers, but was not so successful as the first. It has little plot or incident, but has much freshness of thought and originality of style.

The same year appeared his *Life of Robespierre*, the result of original investigations, and based largely on unpublished correspondence. Without any sympathy of opinion with Robespierre, and without any purpose of vindicating his character, Lewes told the true story of his life, and showed wherein he had been grossly misrepresented. The book was one of much interest, though it lacked in true historic insight and was clumsily written. While these works were appearing, Lewes was a voluminous contributor to the periodical literature of the day. He wrote, at this time and later, for the *Edinburgh Review*, the *Foreign Quarterly*, *British Quarterly*, *Westminster Review*, *Fraser's Magazine*, *Blackwood's Magazine*, *Cornhill Monthly*, *Saturday Review*, in the *Classical Museum*, the *Morning Chronicle*, the *Atlas* and various other periodicals, and on a great variety of subjects. His work of this kind was increased when in 1849 he became the literary editor of *The Leader* newspaper, a weekly journal of radical thought and politics. His versatility, freshness of thought and vigor of expression made this department of *The Leader* of great interest. His reviews of books were always good, and his literary articles piquant and forcible. In the first volume he published a story called *The Apprenticeship of Life.* In April, 1852, he began in its columns a series of eighteen articles on Comte's Positive Philosophy. In connection with the second article of this series he asked for subscriptions in aid of Comte, and in the third reported that three workingmen had sent in money. These subscriptions were continued while the articles were in progress, and amounted to a considerable sum. In 1854 these essays were republished in Bohn's *Scientific Library* under the title of *Comte's Philosophy of the Sciences.* The *Leader* was ably conducted, but it was radical and outspoken, and did not receive the support it deserved. In 1854 his connection with it came to an end.

While connected with *The Leader*, Lewes had turned his attention to Goethe, and made a thorough study of his life and opinions. After spending many months in Weimar, and as a result of his studies in Germany, he published in 1855 his *Life and Works of Goethe.* It was carefully re-written in 1873, and the substance of it was given in an abbreviated and more popular form a few years later. This has usually been accepted as the best book about Goethe written in English. Mr. Anthony Trollope expresses the usual opinion when he says, "As a critical biography of one of the great heroes of literature it is almost perfect. It is short, easily understood by common readers, singularly graphic, exhaustive, and altogether devoted to the subject." On the other hand, Bayard Taylor said that "Lewes's entertaining apology hardly deserves the name of a biography." It is an opinionated book, controversial, egotistic, and unnecessarily critical. It was written less with the purpose of interpreting Goethe to the English reader than of giving expression to Lewes's own views on many subjects. His chapters on Goethe's science and on his realism are marked by an extreme dogmatism. The poetic and religious side of Goethe's nature he was incapable of understanding, and always misrepresents, as he did that side of his nature which allied Goethe with Schiller and the other idealists. Lewes was always polemical, had some theory to champion, some battle to fight. He did not write for the sake of the subject, but because the subject afforded an arena of battle for the theories to the advocacy of which he gave his life.

With the completion of his *Life of Goethe*, Lewes

turned his attention more than ever to physiological studies, though he had continued to give them much attention in the midst of his other pursuits. In 1858 appeared his *Seaside Studies*, in which he recorded the results of his original investigations at Ilfracombe, Tenby, Scilly Isles and Jersey. This volume is written in a plain descriptive style, containing many interesting accounts of scenery and adventure, explanations of the methods of study of animal life at the seashore, how experiments are carried on, the results of these special studies, and much of controversy with other observers. It combines science and description in a happy manner. Another result of his physiological studies was a paper "On the Spinal Cord as a Centre of Sensation and Volition," read before the British Association for the Advancement of Science, in 1858. This was followed the next year by three published addresses on "The Nervous System," in which he presented those theories which were more carefully developed in his latest work, where he gave a systematic account of his philosophy. From this time on to his death the greater part of his energies were given to these studies, and to the building up of a philosophy based on physiology. A popular work, in which many of his theories are unfolded, and marked throughout by his peculiar ideas in regard to the relations of body and mind, was published in 1858. This was his *Physiology of Common Life*, a work of great value, and written in a simple, comprehensive style, suited to the wants of the general reader. In the first volume he wrote of hunger and thirst, food and drink, digestion, structure and uses of the blood, circulation of the blood, respiration and suffocation, and why we are warm and how we keep so. The second treats of feeling and thinking, the mind and the brain, our senses and sensations, sleep and dreams, the qualities we inherit from our parents, and life and death. In 1860 he printed in *The Cornhill Magazine* a series of six papers on animal life. They were reprinted in book form in 1861, under the title of *Studies in Animal Life*. More strictly scientific than his *Seaside Studies*, they were even more popular in style, and intended for the general reader. While these books were being published he was at work on a more strictly scientific task, and one intended for the thoughtful and philosophic reader. This was his *Aristotle: a Chapter from the History of Science, including Analyses of Aristotle's Scientific Writings*, which was completed early in 1862, but not published until 1864. As in his previous works, Lewes is here mainly concerned with an exposition of his theories of the inductive method, and he judges Aristotle from this somewhat narrow position. He refuses Aristotle a place among scientific observers, but says he gave a great impulse towards scientific study, while in intellectual force he was a giant. The book contains no recognition of Aristotle's value as a philosopher; indeed his metaphysics are treated with entire distrust or indifference. His fame is pronounced to be justifiably colossal, but it is said he did not lay the basis of any physical science. It is a work of controversy rather than of unbiassed exposition, and its method is dry and difficult.

Early in the year 1865, a few literary men in London conceived the project of a new review, which should avoid what they conceived to be the errors of the old ones. It was to be eclectic in its doctrinal position, contain only the best literature, all articles were to be signed by the author's name, and it was to be published by a joint-stock company. Lewes was invited to become the editor of this new periodical, and after much urging he consented. The first number of *The Fortnightly Review* was published May 15, 1865. It proved a financial failure, and was soon sold to a publishing firm. The eclectic theory was abandoned, and the *Review* became an agnostic and radical organ under the management of its second editor, John Morley. Lewes edited six volumes, when, in 1867, he was obliged, on account of his health, to resign his position. He made the *Review* an independent and able exponent of current thought, and he kept it up to a very high standard of literary excellence. His own contributions were among the best things it contained, and give a good indication of the wide range of his talent. In the first volume he published papers on "The Heart and the Brain," and on the poetry of Robert Buchanan, as well as a series of four very able and valuable papers on "The Principles of Success in Literature." In the second volume he wrote about "Mr. Grote's Plato." In the third he dealt with "Victor Hugo's Latest Poems," "Criticism in relation to Novels," and "Auguste Comte." In this volume he began a series of essays entitled "Causeries," in which he treated, in a light vein, of the passing topics of the day. He wrote of Spinoza in the fourth volume, and of "Comte and Mill" in the sixth, contributing nothing to the fifth. After Morley became the editor, in the ninth and tenth volumes, he published three papers on Darwin's hypothesis, and in 1878 there was a paper of his on the "Dread and Dislike of Science." He also had a criticism of Dickens in the July number of 1872, full of his subtle power of analysis and literary insight.

Lewes in early life had a strong inclination to become an actor, and he did go on the stage for a short time. He wrote and translated several plays, one of his adaptations becoming very popular. He wrote dramatic criticisms for the *Pall Mall Gazette* and other journals, during many years. In 1875, a volume of these papers was published with the title, *On Actors and the Art of Acting*. It treated in a pleasant way, and with keen insight, of Edmund Kean, Charles Kean, Rachel, Macready, Farren, Charles Matthews, Frédéric Lemaitre, the two Keeleys, Shakspere as actor and critic, natural acting, foreign actors on our stage, the drama of Paris in 1865, Germany in 1867, and Spain in 1867, and of his first impressions of Salvini. Another piece of work done by him was the furnishing, in 1867, of an explanatory text to accompany Kaulbach's *Female Characters of Goethe.*

The last years of Lewes's life were devoted to the preparation of a systematic exposition of his physiological philosophy. As early as the year 1858, he was at work on the nervous system, and, soon after, his studies took a systematic shape. In his series of volumes on the *Problems of Life and Mind* he gave to the world a new theory of the mind and of knowledge. In the first two volumes, published in 1874, and entitled *The Foundations of a Creed*, he developed his views on the methods of philosophic research. These were followed in 1877 by a third volume, on *The Physical Basis of Life.* After his death his wife edited two small volumes on Psychology, which included all the writing he left in a form ready for publication. His work was left incomplete, but its publication had gone far enough to show the methods to be followed and the main conclusions to be reached.

Concerning the work done by Lewes in philosophy, there will be much difference of opinion. He did much through his various expositions to make the public familiar with the inductive methods of inquiry and with the conclusions of positive thought. He made his books readable, and even popular, giving philosophy an exposition suited to the wants of the general reader. At the same time, he was polemical and dogmatic, and more concerned to be clever than to be exact in his interpretation. Into the meanings of some of the greatest thinkers he had little clear insight, and he is seldom to be implicitly trusted as an expositor of those whose systems were in any way opposed to his own. His limitations have been well defined by Ribot, in his *Contemporary English Psychology.*

"Mr. Lewes lacks the vocation of the scholar, which, indeed, is generally wanting in original minds. His history resembles rather that of Hegel than that of

Ritter. His review of the labors of philosophers is rather occupied with that which they have thought, than with their comparative importance. He judges rather than expounds; his history is fastidious and critical. It is the work of a clear, precise and elegant mind, always that of a writer, often witty, measured, possessing no taste for declamation, avoiding exclusive solutions, and making its interest profitable to the reader whom he forces to think." Ribot speaks of the work again as being original but dogmatic and critical. He says it belongs to that class of books which make history a pretext for conflict. "The author is less occupied with the exposition of facts than he is with his method of warfare; he thinks less of being exact than of being clever. . . . He has evidently no taste, or, if we prefer so to put it, he has not the virtue necessary to face these formidable folios, these undigested texts of scholastic learning, which the historian of philosophy ought to penetrate, however repulsive to his positive and lucid mind."

On the other hand, Mr. Frederic Harrison has described the great success of the *Biographical History of Philosophy*, and made it apparent what are its chief merits. "This astonishing work was designed to be popular, to be readable, to be intelligible. It was all of these in a singular degree. It has proved to be the most popular account of philosophy of our time; it has been republished, enlarged, and almost re-written, and each re-issue has found new readers. It did what hardly any previous book on philosophy ever did — it made philosophy readable, reasonable, lively, almost as exciting as a good novel. Learners who had been tortured over dismal homilies on the pantheism of Spinoza, and yet more dismal expositions of the pan-nihilism of Hegel, seized with eagerness upon a little book which gave an intense reality to Spinoza and his thoughts, which threw Hegel's contradictories into epigrams, and made the course of philosophic thought unfold itself natu rally with all the life and coherence of a well-considered plot. . . . There can be no possible doubt as to the success of this method. Men to whom philosophy has been a wearisome swaying backward and forward of meaningless phrases, found something which they could remember and understand. . . . For a generation this 'entirely popular' book saturated the minds of the younger readers. It has done as much as any book, perhaps more than any, to give the key to the prevalent thought of our time about the metaphysical problems. . . . That such a book should have had such a triumph was a singular literary fact. The opinions frankly expressed as to theology, metaphysics, and many established orthodoxies; its conclusion, glowing in every page, that metaphysics, as Danton said of the Revolution, was devouring its own children, and led to self-annihilation; its proclamation of Comte as the legitimate issue of all previous philosophy and positive philosophy as its ultimate *irenicon* — all this, one might think, would have condemned such a book from its birth. The orthodoxies frowned; the professors sneered; the owls of metaphysic hooted from the gloom of their various jungles; but the public read, the younger students adopted it, the world learned from it the positive method; it held its ground because it made clear what no one else had made clear — what philosophy meant, and why philosophers differed so violently."

This extravagant praise becomes even absurd when the writer gravely says that this book "had simply killed metaphysic." A popular style and method gave the book success, along with the fact that the temper of the time made such a statement acceptable. It cleverly indicated the weak places in the metaphysical methods, and it presented the advantages of the inductive method with great eloquence and ingenuity. Its satire, and its contempt for the more spiritualistic systems, also helped to make it readable.

His later work, in which he develops his own positive conclusions, has the merit of being one of the best expositions yet made of the philosophy of evolution. In view, however, of his unqualified condemnation of the theories of metaphysicians, his system is one of singular audacity of speculation. Not even Schelling or Hegel has gone beyond him in theorizing, or exceeded him in the ground traversed beyond the limits of demonstration. He who had held up all speculative systems to scorn, distanced those he had condemned, and showed how easy it is to take theory for fact. Metaphysic has not had in its whole history a greater illustration of the daring of speculation than in the case of Lewes's theory of the relations of the subjective and objective. He interprets matter and mind, motion and feeling, objective and subjective, as simply the outer and inner, the concave and convex, sides of one and the same reality. Mind is the same as matter, except that it is viewed from a different aspect. In this opinion he resembles Schelling more than any other thinker, as he does in some other of his speculations. As a monist, his conclusions are similar to those of the leading German transcendentalists. Indeed, the evolution philosophy he expounds is, in some of its aspects, but a development of the identity philosophy of Schelling. In its monism, its theory of the development of mind out of matter, and its conception of law, they are one and the same. The evolution differs from the identity philosophy mainly in its more scientific interpretation of the influence of heredity and the social environment. The one is undoubtedly an outgrowth from the other, while the audacious flights of speculation indulged in by Lewes rival anything attempted even by Schelling.

Lewes was one of the earliest English disciples of Auguste Comte, and he probably did more than any other person to introduce the opinions of that thinker to English students. He was a zealous and yet not a blind disciple, rejecting for the most part the later speculations of Comte. Comte's theories of social and religious construction were repugnant to Lewes's mind, but his positive methods and his entire rejection of theology were acceptable. Comte's positivism was the foundation of his own philosophy, and he did little more than to expand and more carefully work out the system of his predecessor. In psychology he went beyond Comte, through his physiological studies, and by the adoption of the methods and results of evolution. His discovery of the sociological factors of mind was a real advance on his master.

George Eliot's connection with Lewes had much to do with the after-development of her mind. An affinity of intellectual purpose and conviction drew them together. She found her philosophical theories confirmed by his, and both together labored for the propagation of that positivism in which they so heartily believed. Their lives and influence are inseparably united. There was an almost entire unanimity of intellectual conviction between them, and his books are in many ways the best interpreters of the ethical and philosophical meanings of her novels. Her thorough interest in his studies, and her comprehension of them, is manifest on many of her pages. Her enthusiastic acceptance of positivism in that spirit in which it is presented by Lewes, is apparent throughout all her work. Their marriage was a companionship and a friendship. They lived in each other, were mutual helpers, and each depended much on the advice and counsel of the other. Miss Mathilde Blind has pointed out how thoroughly identical are their views of realism in art, and on many other subjects they were as harmonious. They did not echo each other, but there was an intimate affinity of intellectual apprehension and purpose.

Immediately after their marriage, Lewes and his wife went to Germany, and they spent a quiet year of study in Berlin, Munich and Weimar. Here he re-wrote and completed his *Life of Goethe.* On their return to England they took a house in Blandford Square, and began then to make that home which was soon destined to have so much interest and attraction. A good part of the year 1858 was also spent on the continent in study and travel. Three months were passed in Munich, six weeks in Dresden, while Salzburg, Vienna and Prague were also visited. The continent was again visited in the summer of 1865, and a trip was taken through Normandy, Brittany and Touraine. Other visits preceded and followed, including a study of Florence in preparation for the writing of *Romola*, and a tour in Spain in 1867 to secure local coloring for *The Spanish Gypsy*. In 1865, the house in Blandford Square was abandoned for "The Priory," a commodious and pleasant house on the North Bank, St. John's Wood. It was here Mr. and Mrs. Lewes lived until his death.

IV.

CAREER AS AN AUTHOR.

UNTIL she was thirty-six years old Mrs. Lewes had given no hint that she was likely to become a great novelist. She had shown evidence of large learning and critical ability, but not of decided capacity for imaginative or poetic creation. The critic and the creator are seldom combined in one person; and while she might have been expected to become a philosophical writer of large reputation, there was little promise that she would become a great novelist. Before she began the *Scenes of Clerical Life*, she had written but very little of an original character. She was not drawn irresistibly to the career for which she was best fitted, and others had to discover her gift and urge her to its use. Mr. Lewes saw that the person who could write so admirably of what a novel ought to be, and who could so skilfully point out the defects in the lady novelists of the day, was herself capable of writing much better ones than those she criticised. It was at his suggestion, and through his encouragement, she made her first attempt at novel-writing. Her love of learning, her relish for literary and philosophical studies, led her to believe that she could accomplish the largest results in the line of the work she had already begun. Yet Lewes had learned from her conversational powers, from her keen appreciation of the dramatic elements of daily life, and from her fine humor and sarcasm, that other work was within the range of her powers. Reluctantly she consented to turn aside from the results of scholarship she had hoped to accomplish, and with many doubts concerning her ability to become a writer of fiction. The history of the publication of her first work, *Scenes of Clerical Life*, has been fully told, and is helpful towards an understanding of her career as an author.

In the autumn of 1856, William Blackwood received from Lewes a short story bearing the title of "The Sad Fortunes of the Rev. Amos Barton," which he sent as the work of an anonymous friend. His nephew has described the results that followed on the reception of this novel by Blackwood, and its publication in *Blackwood's Magazine*. "The story was offered as the first instalment of a series; and though the editor pronounced that 'Amos' would 'do,' he wished to satisfy himself that it was no chance hit, and requested a sight of the other tales before coming to a decision. Criticisms on the plot and studies of character in 'Amos Barton' were frankly put forward, and the editor wound up his letter by saying, 'If the author is a new writer, I beg to congratulate him on being worthy of the honors of print and pay. I shall be very glad to hear from him or you soon.' At this time the remaining *Scenes of Clerical Life* were unwritten, and the criticisms upon 'Amos' had rather a disheartening effect upon the author, which the editor hastened to remove as soon as he became sensible of them, by offering to accept the tale. He wrote to Mr. Lewes, 'If you think it would stimulate the author to go on with the other tales, I shall publish "Amos" at once;' expressing also his 'sanguineness' that he would be able to approve of the contributions to follow, as 'Amos' gave indications of great freshness of style. Some natural curiosity had been expressed as to the unknown writer, and a hint had been thrown out that he was 'a clergyman,'—a device which, since it has the great sanction of Sir Walter Scott, we must regard as perfectly consistent with the ethics of anonymous literature.

"'Amos Barton' occupied the first place in the magazine for January, 1857, and was completed in the following number. By that time 'Mr. Gilfil's Love Story' was ready, and the *Scenes of Clerical Life* appeared month by month, until they ended with 'Janet's Repentance' in November of that year. As fresh instalments of the manuscript were received, the editor's conviction of the power, and even genius, of his new contributor steadily increased. In his first letter to the author after the appearance of 'Amos Barton,' he wrote, 'It is a long time since I have read anything so fresh, so humorous and so touching. The style is capital, conveying so much in so few words.' In another letter, addressed 'My dear Amos,' for lack of any more distinct appellation, the editor remarks, 'I forgot whether I told you or Lewes that I had shown part of the MS. to Thackeray. He was staying with me, and having been out at dinner, came in about eleven o'clock, when I had just finished reading it. I said to him, "Do you know that I think I have lighted upon a new author who is uncommonly like a first-class passenger?" I showed him a page or two—I think the passage where the curate returns home and Milly is first introduced. He would not pronounce whether it came up to my ideas, but remarked afterwards that he would have liked to have read more, which I thought a good sign.'

"From the first the *Scenes of Clerical Life* arrested public attention. Critics were, however, by no means unanimous as to their merits. They had so much individuality—stood so far apart from the standards of contemporary fiction—that there was considerable difficulty in applying the usual tests in their case. The terse, condensed style, the exactitude of expression, and the constant use of illustration, naturally suggested to some the notion that the new writer must be a man of science relaxing himself in the walks of fiction. The editor's own suspicions had once been directed towards Professor Owen by a similarity of handwriting. Guesses were freely hazarded as to the author's personality, and among other conjectures was one that Lord Lytton, whose 'Caxton' novels were about the same period delighting the readers of this magazine, had again struck a new vein of fiction. Probably Dickens was among the first to divine that the author must be a woman; but the reasons upon which he based this opinion might readily have been met by equally cogent deductions from the *Scenes* that the writer must be of the male sex. Dickens, on the conclusion of the *Scenes*, wrote a letter of most generous appreciation, which, when sent through the editor, afforded the unknown author very hearty gratification.

"While 'Mr. Gilfil's Love Story' was passing through the magazine, the editor was informed that he was to know the author as 'George Eliot.' It was at this time, then, that a name so famous in our literature was invented. We have no reason to suppose that it had been thought of when the series was commenced. It was probably assumed from the impossibility of a nameless shadow maintaining frequent communication with the editor of a magazine; possibly the recollection of George Sand entered into the idea; but the designation was euphonious and impressive.

"Before the conclusion of the *Scenes*, Mr. Blackwood felt satisfied that he had to do with a master mind, and that a great career as a novelist lay open to George Eliot; and his frequent communications urged her warmly to persevere in her efforts. When 'Janet's Repentance' was drawing to a close, and arrangements were being made for re-issuing the sketches as a separate publication, he wrote to Mr. Lewes, 'George Eliot is too diffident of his own powers and prospects of success. Very few men, indeed, have more reason to be satisfied as far as the experiment has gone. The following should be a practical cheerer,'—and then he proceeded to say how the Messrs. Blackwood had seen reason to make a large increase in the forthcoming reprint of the *Scenes*. The volumes did not appear until after the New Year of 1858; and their success was such that the editor was able, before the end of the month, to write as follows to Lewes: 'George Eliot has fairly achieved a literary reputation among judges, and the public must follow, although it may take time. Dickens's letter was very handsome, and truly kind. I sent him an extract from George Eliot's letter to me, and I have a note from him, saying that "he has been much interested by it," and that "it has given him the greatest pleasure." Dickens adheres to his theory that the writer must be a woman.' To George Eliot herself he wrote in February, 1858, 'You will recollect, when we proposed to reprint, my impression was that the series had not lasted long enough in the magazine to give you a hold on the general public, although long enough to make your literary reputation. Unless in exceptional cases, a very long time often elapses between the two stages of reputation, the literary and the public. Your progress will be *sure*, if not so quick as we could wish.'"

The success of the *Clerical Scenes* determined the literary career of Mrs. Lewes. She began at once an elaborate novel, which was largely written in Germany. It was sent to Blackwood for publication, and his nephew has given a full account of the reception of the manuscript and the details of giving the work to the public.

"*Adam Bede* was begun almost as soon as the *Scenes* were finished, and had already made considerable progress before their appearance in the reprint. In February, 1858, the editor, writing to Mr. Lewes, says, 'I am delighted to hear from George Eliot that I might soon hope to see something like a volume of the new tale. I am very sanguine.' In a few weeks after, the manuscript of the opening chapters of *Adam Bede* was put into his hands, and he writes thus to Lewes after the first perusal: 'Tell George Eliot that I think *Adam*

Bede all right — most lifelike and real. I shall read the MS. quietly over again before writing in detail about it. . . . For the first reading it did not signify how many things I had to think of; I would have hurried through it with eager pleasure. I write this note to allay all anxiety on the part of George Eliot as to my appreciation of the merits of this most promising opening of a picture of life. In spite of all injunctions, I began *Adam Bede* in the railway, and felt very savage when the waning light stopped me as we neared the Scottish border.' A few weeks later, when he had received further chapters, and had reperused the manuscript from the beginning, Mr. Blackwood wrote to George Eliot, 'The story is altogether very novel, and I cannot recollect anything at all like it. I find myself constantly thinking of the characters as real personages, which is a capital sign.' After he had read yet a little further he remarks, 'There is an atmosphere of genuine religion and purity that fears no evil, about the whole opening of the story.' George Eliot made an expedition to Germany in the spring of 1858, and the bulk of the second volume was sent home from Munich. Acknowledging the receipt of the manuscript, the editor wrote to Lewes, 'There can be no mistake about the merits, and I am not sure whether I expressed myself sufficiently warmly. But you know that I am not equal to the *abandon* of expression which distinguishes the large-hearted school of critics.' *Adam Bede* was completed in the end of October, 1858, and Mr. Blackwood read the conclusion at once, and sent his opinions. He says, 'I am happy to tell you that I think it is capital. I never saw such wonderful efforts worked out by such a succession of simple and yet delicate and minute touches. Hetty's night in the fields is marvellous. I positively shuddered for her, poor creature; and I do not think the most thoughtless lad could read that terrible picture of her feelings and hopeless misery without being deeply moved. Adam going to support her at the trial is a noble touch. You really make him a gentleman by that act. It is like giving him his spurs. The way poor Hetty leans upon and clings to Dinah is beautiful. Mr. Irwine is always good; so are the Poysers, lifelike as possible. Dinah is a very striking and original character, always perfectly supported, and never obtrusive in her piety. Very early in the book I took it into my head that it would be "borne in upon her" to fall in love with Adam. Arthur is the least satisfactory character, but he is true too. The picture of his happy, complacent feelings before the bombshell bursts upon him is very good.'

"*Adam Bede* was published in the last week of January, 1859. The author was desirous on this occasion to test her strength by appealing directly to the public; and the editor, though quite prepared to accept *Adam Bede* for the magazine, willingly gratified her. Sending George Eliot an early copy, before *Adam Bede* had reached the public, he says, 'Whatever the subscription may be, I am confident of success — great success. The book is so novel and so true, that the whole story remains in my mind like a succession of incidents in the lives of people I know. *Adam Bede* can certainly never come under the class of popular agreeable stories; but those who love power, real humor, and true natural description, will stand by the sturdy carpenter and the living groups you have painted in and about Hayslope.'

"*Adam Bede* did not immediately command that signal success which, looking back to it now, we might have expected for it. As the editor had warned the author, the *Scenes* had secured for her a reputation with the higher order of readers and with men of letters, but had not established her popularity with the public in general. The reviewers, too, were somewhat divided. Many of them recognized the merits of the work, but more committed the blunder of endeavoring to fix the position of the book by contrasting the author with the popular novelists of the time, and by endeavoring to determine from which of them she had drawn her inspiration. In 1859 a review of *Adam Bede* from the pen of one of the oldest and ablest of our contributors was published in this magazine, and on its appearance George Eliot wrote the editor, 'I should like you to convey my gratitude to your reviewer. I see well he is a man whose experience and study enabled him to relish parts of my book which I should despair of seeing recognized by critics in London back drawing-rooms. He has gratified me keenly by laying his fingers on passages which I wrote either from strong feeling or from intimate knowledge, but which I had prepared myself to find passed over by reviewers.' Soon after, *The Times* followed with an appreciative notice of the book which sounded its real merits, and did justice to the author's originality of genius; and by the month of April the book was steadily running through a second edition. Readers were beginning to realize that the *Scenes of Clerical Life* was not a mere chance success, but the work of a writer capable of greater and better things."

It was Mrs. Lewes's desire not to be known to the public in her own personality, hence her adoption of a *nom de plume*. She shrank from the consequences of a literary fame, had none of George Sand's love of notoriety or desire to impress herself upon the world. It was her hope that George Eliot and Mrs. Lewes would lead distinct lives so far as either was known outside her own household; that the two should not be joined together even in the minds of her most intimate friends. When her friend, the editor of the *Westminster Review*, detected the authorship of *Adam Bede*, and wrote to her in its praise, congratulating her on the success she had attained, Lewes wrote to him denying positively that Mrs. Lewes was the author. Charles Dickens also saw through the disguise, and wrote to the publisher declaring his opinion that *Adam Bede* was written by a woman. When this was denied, he still persisted in his conviction, detecting the womanly insight into character, her failure adequately to portray men, while of women "she seemed to know their very hearts."

The vividness with which scenes and persons about her childhood home were depicted, speedily led to the breaking of this disguise. One of her school-fellows, as soon as she had read *Adam Bede*, said, "George Eliot is Marian Evans;" but others were only confident that the author must be some Nuneaton resident, and began to look about them for the author. Some portions of the *Scenes of Clerical Life* had already been discovered to have a very strong local coloring, and now there was much curiosity as to the personality of the writer. A dilapidated gentleman of the neighborhood, who had run through with a fortune at Cambridge, was selected for the honor. While the *Scenes* were being published, an Isle of Man newspaper attributed the authorship to this man, whose name was Liggins, but he at once repudiated it. On the appearance of *Adam Bede* this claim was again put forward, and a local clergyman became the medium of its announcement to the public. The London *Times* printed the following letter in its issue of April 15, 1859: "Sir, — The author of *Scenes of Clerical Life* and *Adam Bede* is Mr. Joseph Liggins, of Nuneaton, Warwickshire. You may easily satisfy yourself of my correctness by inquiring of any one in that neighborhood. Mr. Liggins himself and the characters whom he paints are as familiar there as the twin spires of Coventry. — Yours obediently, H. Anders, Rector of Kirkby."

The next day the following was printed by the same paper: —

Sir, — The Rev. H. Anders has with questionable delicacy and unquestionable inaccuracy assured the world through your columns that the author of *Scenes of Clerical Life* and *Adam Bede* is Mr. Joseph Liggins, of Nuneaton. I beg distinctly to deny that statement. I declare on my honor that that gentleman never saw a line of those works until they were printed, nor had he any knowledge of them whatever. Allow me to ask whether the act of publishing a book deprives a man of all claim to the courtesies usual among gentlemen? If not, the attempt to pry into what is obviously meant to be withheld — my name — and to publish the rumors which such prying may give rise to, seems to me quite indefensible, still more so to state these rumors as ascertained facts. I am, sir, yours, &c., GEORGE ELIOT.

Liggins found his ardent supporters, and he explained the letter repudiating the authorship of the *Scenes of Clerical Life* as being written to further his own interests. He obtained money on the plea that he was being deprived of his rights, by showing portions of a manuscript which he had copied from the printed book. Neighboring clergymen zealously espoused his cause, and a warm controversy raged for a little time concerning his claim. Very curiously, it became a question of high and low church, his own fellow-believers defending Liggins with zeal, while the other party easily detected his imposition. Finally, Blackwood published a letter in *The Times* denying his claims, accompanied by one from George Eliot expressing entire satisfaction with her publisher. A consequence of this discussion was, that the real name of the author was soon known to the public.

The curiosity excited about the authorship of *Adam Bede*, the Liggins controversy, and the fresh, original character of the book itself, soon drew attention to its merits. It was referred to in a Parliamentary debate, and it became the general topic of literary conversation. Its success was soon assured, and it was not long before it was recognized that a new novelist of the first order had appeared.

It is as amusing as interesting now to look back upon the reception given to *Adam Bede* by the critics. It is not every critic who can detect a great writer in his first unheralded book, and some very stupid blunders were made in regard to this one. It was reviewed in *The Spectator* for February 12, 1859, in this unappreciative manner: "George Eliot's three-volume novel of *Adam Bede* is a story of humble life, where religious conscientiousness is the main characteristic of the hero and heroine, as well as of some of the other persons. Its literary feature partakes, we fear, too much of that Northern trait which, by minutely describing things and delineating individuals as matters of substantive importance in themselves, rather than as subordinate to general interest, has a tendency to induce a feeling of sluggishness in the reader."

Not all the critics were so blundering as this one, however, and in the middle of April, *The Times* said there was no mistake about the character of *Adam Bede*, that it was a first-rate novel, and that its author would take rank at once among the masters of the craft. In April, also, *Blackwood's Magazine* gave the book a hearty welcome. The natural, genuine descriptions of village life were commended, and the book was praised for its "hearty, manly sympathy with weakness, not inconsistent with hatred of vice." Throughout this notice the author is spoken of as "Mr. Eliot." The critic of the *Westminster Review*, in an appreciative and favorable notice, expressed a doubt if the author could be a man. He cited Hetty as proof that only a woman could have written the book, and said this character could "only be delineated as it is by an author combining the intense feelings and sympathies of a woman with the conceptive power of artistic genius." The woman theory was pronounced to be beset with serious difficulties, however, and the notice concluded with these words: "But while pronouncing no decisive opinion on this point, we may remark that the union of the best qualities of the masculine and feminine intellect is as rare as it is admirable; that it is a distinguishing characteristic of the most gifted artists and poets, and that to ascribe it to the author of *Adam Bede* is to accord the highest praise we can bestow."

With the writing of *Adam Bede*, George Eliot accepted her career as a novelist, and henceforth her life was devoted to literary creation. Even before *Adam Bede* was completed, her attention was directed to Savonarola as the subject for a novel. Though this subject was in her mind, yet it was not made use of until later. As soon as *Adam Bede* was completed, she at once began another novel of English life, and drawn even more fully than its predecessors from her own experience. Of this new work a greater portion of the manuscript was in the hands of the publishers with the beginning of 1860. She called it *Sister Maggie*, from the name of the leading character. This title did not please the publisher, and on the 6th of January, Blackwood wrote to her suggesting that it be called *The Mill on the Floss*. This title was accepted by George Eliot, and the new work appeared in three volumes at the beginning of April, 1860.

In July, 1859, there appeared in *Blackwood's Magazine* a short story from George Eliot bearing the title of "The Lifted Veil." This was followed by another, in 1864, called "Brother Jacob." Both were printed anonymously and are the only short stories she wrote after the *Clerical Scenes*. They attracted attention, but were not reprinted until 1880, when they appeared in the volume with *Silas Marner*, in Blackwood's "cabinet edition" of her works. In March, 1861, *Silas Marner, the Weaver of Raveloe*, her only one-volume novel, was given to the public by Blackwood.

Having carefully studied the life and surroundings of Savonarola, she now took up this subject, and embodied it in her *Romola*. This novel appeared in the *Cornhill Magazine* from July, 1862, to July, 1863. It has been reported that it was offered to Blackwood for publication, who rejected it because it was not likely to be popular with the public. The probable reason of its publication in the *Cornhill Magazine* was that a large sum was paid for its first appearance in that periodical. In a letter written July 5, 1862, Lewes gave the true explanation. "My main object in persuading her to consent to serial publication was not the unheard-of magnificence of the offer, but the advantage to such a work of being read slowly and deliberately, instead of being galloped through in three volumes. I think it quite unique, and so will the public when it gets over the first feeling of surprise and disappointment at the book not being English and like its predecessor." The success it met with while under way in the pages of the magazine may be seen from a letter written by Lewes on December 18. "Marian lives entirely in the fifteenth century, and is much cheered every now and then by hearing indirectly how her book is appreciated by the higher class of minds, and some of the highest, though it is not, and cannot be, popular. In Florence we hear they are wild with delight and surprise at such a work being executed by a foreigner, as if an Italian had ever done anything of the kind." *Romola* was illustrated in the *Cornhill Magazine*, and on its completion was reprinted by Smith, Elder & Co., the publishers of that periodical.

The success of *Romola* was such as to lead George Eliot to begin on another historical subject, though she was probably induced to do this much more by its fitness to her purposes than by the public reception of the novel. This time she gave her work a poetical and dramatic form. *The Spanish Gypsy* was written in the winter of 1864–5, but was laid aside for more thorough study of the subject and for careful revision. She had previously, in 1863, written a short story in verse, founded on the pages of Bocaccio, entitled "How Lisa Loved the King." Probably other poems had also been written, but poetry had not occupied much of her attention. As a school-girl, and even after she had gone to London, she had written verses. Among these earlier attempts, it may not be unsafe to conjecture, may have been the undated poems which she has published in connection with *The Legend of Jubal*. These are "Self and Life," "Sweet Evenings come and go, Love," and "The Death of Moses."

After laying aside *The Spanish Gypsy* she began on

another novel of English life, and *Felix Holt: the Radical* was printed in three volumes by Blackwood, in June, 1866. Shortly after, she printed in *Blackwood's Magazine* an "Address to workmen, by Felix Holt," in which she gave some wholesome and admirable advice to the operative classes who had been enfranchised by the Reform Bill. In the same magazine, "How Lisa Loved the King" was printed in May, 1869. This was the last of her contributions to its pages. Its publisher gave her many encouragements in her literary career, and was devoted to her interests. After his death she gave expression to her appreciation of his valuable aid in reaching the public, through a letter addressed to his successor.

I feel that his death was an irreparable loss to my mental life, for nowhere else is it possible that I can find the same long-tried genuineness of sympathy and unmixed impartial gladness in anything I might happen to do well. To have had a publisher who was in the fullest sense of the word a gentleman, and at the same time a man of excellent moral judgment, has been an invaluable stimulus and comfort to me. Your uncle had retained that fruit of experience which makes a man of the world, as opposed to the narrow man of literature. He judged well of writing, because he had learned to judge well of men and things, not merely through quickness of observation and insight, but with the illumination of a heart in the right place — a thorough integrity and rare tenderness of feeling.

After a visit to Spain in the summer of 1867, *The Spanish Gypsy* was re-written and published by Blackwood, in June, 1868. During several years, at this period of her life, her pen was busy with poetical subjects. "A Minor Prophet" was written in 1865, "Two Lovers" in 1866, and "Oh may I join the Choir Invisible" in 1867. "Agatha" was written in 1868, and was published in the *Atlantic Monthly* for August, 1869. *The Legend of Jubal* was written in 1869, and was printed in *Macmillan's Magazine* for May, 1870. In 1869 were also written the series of sonnets entitled "Brother and Sister." "Armgart" was written in 1870, and appeared in *Macmillan's Magazine* in July, 1871. "Arion" and "Stradivarius" were written in 1873. "A College Breakfast Party" was written in April, 1874, and was printed in *Macmillan's Magazine* for July, 1878. *The Legend of Jubal and other Poems* was published by Blackwood in 1874, and contained all the poems just named, except the last. A new edition was published in 1879 as *The Legend of Jubal and other Poems, Old and New.* The "new" poems in this edition are "The College Breakfast Party," "Self and Life," "Sweet Evenings come and go, Love," and "The Death of Moses."

To the longer of these poetical studies succeeded another novel of English Life. *Middlemarch: a Study of Provincial Life* was printed in twelve monthly parts by Blackwood, beginning in December, 1871. Five years later, *Daniel Deronda* was printed in eight monthly parts by the same publisher, beginning with February, 1876. This method of publication was probably adopted for the same reason assigned by Lewes for the serial appearance of *Romola.* Both novels attracted much attention, and were eagerly devoured and discussed as the successive numbers appeared, the first because of its remarkable character as a study of English life, the other because of its peculiar ideas, and its defence of the Jewish race. Her last book, *Impressions of Theophrastus Such*, a series of essays on moral and literary subjects, written the year before, was published by Blackwood in June, 1879. Its reception by the public was somewhat unfavorable, and it added nothing of immediate enlargement to her reputation.

Of miscellaneous writing George Eliot did but very little. While Mr. Lewes was the editor of *The Leader* newspaper, from 1849 to 1854, she was an occasional contributor of anonymous articles to its columns. When he founded *The Fortnightly Review* she contributed to its first number, published in May, 1865, an article on "The Influence of Rationalism," in which she reviewed Lecky's *Rationalism in Europe.* These occasional efforts of her pen, together with the two short stories and the poems already mentioned, constituted all her work outside her series of great novels. She concentrated her efforts as few authors have done; and having found, albeit slowly and reluctantly, what she could best accomplish, she seldom strayed aside. When her pen had found its proper place it was not often idle; and though she did not write rapidly, yet she continued steadily at her work and accomplished much. Within twenty years she wrote eight great works of fiction, including *The Spanish Gypsy;* works that are destined to an immortality of fame. From almost entire obscurity her name appeared, with the publication of the *Scenes of Clerical Life*, to attract attention among a few most appreciative readers, and it was destined then to rise suddenly to the highest place of literary reputation with the publication of *Adam Bede*. Her genius blazed clearly out upon the world in the fulness of its powers, and each new work added to her fame, and revealed some new capacity in the delineation of character. Her literary career shows throughout the steady triumph of genius and of persistent labor.

V.

PERSONAL CHARACTERISTICS.

THE home of Mrs. Lewes during the later years of her life was in one of the London suburbs, near Regent's Park, in what is known as St. John's Wood, at number 21, North Bank Street. This locality was not too far from the city for the enjoyment and the use of its advantages, while it was out of the noise and the smoke. The houses stand far apart, are surrounded with trees and lawns, while all is quiet and beautiful. The square, unpretentious house in which the Leweses lived was surrounded by a fine garden and green turf, while flowers were abundant. A high wall shut it out from the street. Within, all was refinement and good taste; there were flowers in the windows, the furniture was plain and substantial, while quiet simplicity reigned supreme. The house had two stories and a basement. On the first floor were two drawing-rooms, a small reception room, a dining-room and Mr. Lewes's study. These rooms were decorated by Owen Jones, their artist friend. The second floor contained the study of George Eliot, which was a plain room, not large. Its two front windows looked into the garden, and there were book-cases around the walls, and a neat writing-desk. All things about the house indicated simple tastes, moderate needs, and a plain method of life.

Mrs. Lewes usually went into her study at eight o'clock in the morning, and remained there at work until one. If the weather was fine, she rode out in the afternoon, or she walked in Regent's Park with Mr. Lewes. In case the weather did not permit her going out, she returned again to her study in the afternoon. The affairs of her household were so arranged that she could give herself uninterruptedly to her work. The kitchen was in the basement, a housekeeper had entire charge of the management of the house, and Mrs. Lewes was carefully guarded from all outside interruptions. She very seldom went into society, and she received but few visitors, except on Sunday afternoons. Her letters were written by Mr. Lewes, with the exception of those to personal friends or an occasional outside correspondent; and all the details of the publication of her books and the management of her business affairs were in his hands. The immediate success of her novels made them profitable to the publisher, and she was paid comparatively large sums for them.

Her evenings were spent by Mrs. Lewes at home, in reading and singing, unless she went to the theatre, as she often did. She walked much, often visiting the zoölogical gardens, and she had a great liking for all kinds of small animals. She greatly enjoyed travelling. Music was her passion, and art her delight. She preferred the realistic painters, and she never tired of the collections she often visited in London.

The health of Mrs. Lewes was never good. She was a constant sufferer, was nervous, excitable and low-spirited. Only by the utmost care and husbanding of her powers was she enabled to accomplish her work. In a note to one of her correspondents she has given some hint of the almost chronic languor and bodily weakness from which she suffered.

> The weather, our ailments, and various other causes, have made us put off our flight from one week to another, but now we are really fluttering our wings and making a dust about us. I wish we had seen you oftener. I was placidly looking forward to your staying in England another year or more, and gave way to my general languor about seeing friends in these last months, which have been too full of small bodily miseries for me to feel that I had much space to give to pleasanter occupation.

Only those who knew her long and well can fitly describe such a woman as Mrs. Lewes. Personal intimacy gives a color to the words used, and a meaning to the delicate shades of expression, that can be had in no other way. One of her friends has described her as being of "the middle height, the head large, the brow ample, the lower face massive; the eyes gray, lighting up from time to time with a sympathetic glow; the countenance sensitive, spiritual, with 'mind and music breathing' from it; the general demeanor composed and gracious; her utterance fluent and finished, but somewhat measured; her voice clear and melodious, moving evenly, as it were in a monotone, though now and then rising, with a sort of quiet eagerness, into a higher note." The same writer speaks of the close-fitting flow of her robe, and the luxuriant mass of light-brown hair hanging low on both sides of her head, as marked characteristics of her costume. Her features were very plain and large, too large for anything like beauty, but strongly impressive by their very massiveness. More than one of her friends has spoken of her resemblance to Savonarola, perhaps suggested by her description of that monk-prophet in *Romola*. Mr. Kegan Paul finds that she also resembled Dante and Cardinal Newman, and that these four were of the same spiritual family, with a curious interdependence of likeness. All these persons have "the same straight wall of brow; the droop of the powerful nose; mobile lips, touched with strong passion kept resolutely under control; a square jaw, which would make the face stern were it not counteracted by the sweet smile of lips and eye." Her friends say that no portrait does her justice, that her massive features could not be portrayed. "The mere shape of the head," says Kegan Paul, "would be the despair of any painter. It was so grand and massive that it would scarcely be possible to represent it without giving the idea of disproportion to the frame, of which no one ever thought for a moment when they saw her, although it was a surprise, when she stood up, to see that, after all, she was but a little fragile woman who bore this weight of brow and brain."

An account of her personal traits has been given by Mrs. Lippincott. "She impressed me," says this writer, "at first as exceedingly plain, with the massive character of her features, her aggressive jaw and evasive blue eyes. But as she grew interested and earnest in conversation, a great light flashed over or out of her face, till it seemed transfigured, while the sweetness of her rare smile was something quite indescribable. But she seemed to me to the last lofty and cold. I felt that her head was among the stars — the stars of a wintry night." Another American, Miss Kate Field, in writing of the English authors to be seen in Florence half a dozen years after George Eliot began her career, was the first to give an account of this new literary star. "She is a woman of large frame and fair Saxon coloring. In heaviness of jaw and height of cheek-bone she greatly resembles a German; nor are her features unlike those of Wordsworth, judging from his pictures. The expression of her face is gentle and amiable, while her manner is particularly timid and retiring. In conversation Mrs. Lewes is most entertaining, and her interest in young writers is a trait which immediately takes captive all persons of this class. We shall not forget with what kindness and earnestness she addressed a young girl who had just begun to handle a pen, how frankly she related her own literary experience, and how gently she *suggested* advice. True genius is always allied to humility; and in seeing Mrs. Lewes do the work of a good Samaritan so unobtrusively, we learned to respect the woman as much as we had ever admired the writer. 'For years,' said she to us, 'I wrote reviews because I knew too little of humanity.'"

These sketches by persons who only met her casually have an interest in the illustration of her character; and they may be added to by still another account, written by Mrs. Annie Downs, also an American, in 1879, and describing a visit to George Eliot two years before her death. "Tall, slender, with a grace most un-English, her face, instead of beauty, possessed a sweet benignity, and at times flashed into absolute brilliancy. She was older than I had imagined, for her hair, once fair, was gray, and unmistakable lines of care and thought were on the low, broad brow. But although a pang pierced my heart as I recognized that most of her life was behind her, so intensely did I feel her personality that in a moment I lost sight of her age; it was like standing soul to soul, and beyond the reach of time. Dressed in black velvet, with point lace on her hair, and repeated at throat and wrists, she made me think at once of Romola and Dorothea Brooke. She talked of Agassiz, of his museum at Cambridge, of the great natural-history collections at Naples, of Sir Edwin Landseer's pictures, and with enthusiasm of Mr. Furnival's Shakspere and Chaucer classes at the Working Men's College. . . She had quaint etchings of some of the monkeys at the zoölogical gardens, and told me she was more interested in them than any of the other animals, they exhibit traits so distinctly human. She declared, while her husband and friends laughingly teased her for the assertion, that she had seen a sick monkey, parched with fever, absolutely refuse the water he longed for, until the keeper had handed it to a friend who was suffering more than he. As an illustration of their quickness, she told me, in a very dramatic manner, of a nurse who shook two of her little charges for some childish misdemeanor while in the monkey house. No one noticed the monkeys looking at her, but pretty soon every old monkey in the house began shaking her children, and kept up the process until the little monkeys had to be removed for fear their heads would be shaken off. I felt no incongruity between her conversation and her books. She talked as she wrote; in descriptive passages, with the same sort of humor, and the same manner of linking events by analogy and inference.

The walls were covered with pictures. I remember Guido's Aurora, Michael Angelo's prophets, Raphael's sibyls, while all about were sketches, landscapes and crayon drawings, gifts from the most famous living painters, many of whom are friends of the house. A grand piano, opened and covered with music, indicated recent and continual use."

One of her intimate friends says that "in every line of her face there was power, and about her jaw and mouth a prodigious massiveness, which might well have inspired awe had it not been tempered by the most gracious smile which ever lighted up human features, and was ever ready to convert what otherwise might have been terror into fascination!" We are told that "an extraordinary delicacy pervaded her whole being. She seemed to live upon air, and the rest of her body was as light and fragile as her countenance and intellect were massive." One of the results of this large brain and fragile body was, that she was never vigorous in health. Only her quiet, simple life, and avoidance of all excitement in regular work, enabled her to accomplish so much as she did. Her conversation was rich and attractive. She talked much as she wrote, was a good listener, never obtruded her opinions, and always had a noble moral purpose in her words.

An American lady has given an interesting account of her home and of her conversation. "No one," says Mrs. Field, "who had ever seen her could mistake the large head (her brain must be heavier than most men's) covered with a mass of rich auburn hair. At first I thought her tall; for one could not think that such a head could rest on an ordinary woman's shoulders. But, as she rose up, her figure appeared of but medium height. She received us very kindly. In seeing, for the first time, one to whom we owed so many happy hours, it was impossible to feel towards her as a stranger. All distance was removed by her courtesy. Her manners are very sweet, because very simple and free from affectation. To me her welcome was the more grateful as that of one woman to another. There is a sort of free-masonry among women, by which they understand at once those with whom they have any intellectual sympathy. A few words, and all reserve was gone. 'Come, sit by me on this sofa,' she said; and instantly, seated side by side, we were deep in conversation. It is in such intimacy one feels the magnetism of a large mind informed by a true woman's heart; then, as the soul shines through the face, one perceives its intellectual beauty. No portrait can give the full expression of the eye any more than of the voice. Looking into that clear, calm eye, one sees a transparent nature, a soul of goodness and truth, an impression which is deepened as you listen to her soft and gentle tones. A low voice is said to be an excellent thing in a woman. It is a special charm of the most finely cultured English ladies. But never did a sweeter voice fascinate a listener, — so soft and low that one must almost bend to hear. You can imagine what it was thus to sit for an hour beside this gifted woman and hear talk of questions interesting to the women of England and America. But I should do her great injustice if I gave the impression that there was in her conversation any attempt at display. There is no wish to shine. She is above that affectation of brilliancy which is often mere flippancy. Nor does she seek to attract homage and admiration. On the contrary, she is very averse to speak of herself, or even to hear the heartfelt praise of others. She does not engross the conversation, but is more eager to listen than to talk. She has that delicate tact — which is one of the fine arts among women — to make others talk, suggesting topics the most rich and fruitful, and by a word drawing the conversation into a channel where it may flow with broad, free current. Thus she makes you forget the celebrated author, and think only of the refined and highly cultivated woman. You do not feel awed by her genius, but only quickened by it, as something that calls out all that is better and truer. While there is no attempt to impress you with her intellectual superiority, you naturally feel elevated into a higher sphere. The conversation of itself floats upward into a region above the commonplace. The small-talk of ordinary society would seem an impertinence. There is a singular earnestness about her, as if those mild eyes looked deep into the great, sad, awful truths of existence. To her, life is a serious reality, and the gift of genius a grave responsibility."

Mrs. Lewes was in the habit for many years of receiving her friends on Sunday afternoons from two to six o'clock. These gatherings came to be among the most memorable features of London literary life. A large number of persons, both men and women, attended her receptions, and among them many who were well known to the scientific or literary world. Especially were young men of aspiring minds drawn hither and given a larger comprehension of life. She had no political or fashionable connections, says Mr. F. W. H. Myers, "but nearly all who were most eminent in art, science, literature, philanthropy, might be met from time to time at her Sunday-afternoon receptions. There were many women, too, drawn often from among very different traditions of thought and belief, by the unfeigned goodness which they recognized in Mrs. Lewes's look and speech, and sometimes illumining with some fair young face a *salon* whose grave talk needed the grace which they could bestow. And there was sure to be a considerable admixture of men not as yet famous,—probably never to be so,—but whom some indication of studies earnestly pursued, of sincere effort for the good of their fellow-men, had recommended to 'that hopeful interest which'—to quote a letter of her own—'the elder mind, dissatisfied with itself, delights to entertain with regard to those younger, whose years and powers hold a larger measure of unspoiled life.' It was Mr. Lewes who on these occasions contributed the cheerful *bonhomie*, the observant readiness, which are necessary for the facing of any social group. Mrs. Lewes's manner had a grave simplicity, which rose in closer converse into an almost pathetic anxiety to give of her best — to establish a genuine human relation between herself and her interlocutor — to utter words which should remain as an active influence for good in the hearts of those who heard them. To some of her literary admirers, this serious tone was distasteful; they were inclined to resent the prominence given to moral ideas in a quarter from which they preferred to look merely for intellectual refreshment. Mrs. Lewes's humor, though fed from a deep perception of the incongruities of human fates, had not, except in intimate moments, any buoyant or contagious quality, and in all her talk — full of matter and wisdom, and exquisitely worded as it was — there was the same pervading air of strenuous seriousness which was more welcome to those whose object was distinctively to *learn* from her, than to those who merely wished to pass an idle and brilliant hour. To her, these mixed receptions were a great effort. Her mind did not move easily from one individuality to another, and when she afterward thought that she had failed to understand some difficulty which had been laid before her, — had spoken the wrong word to some expectant heart, — she would suffer from almost morbid accesses of self-reproach." A further idea of these conversations may be gathered from Mr. Kegan Paul's account. "When London was full," he says, "the little drawing-room in St. John's Wood was now and then crowded to overflowing with those who were glad to give their best of conversation, of information, and sometimes of music, always to listen with eager attention to whatever their hostess might say, when all that she said was worth hearing. Without a trace of pedantry, she led the conversation to some great and lofty strain. Of herself and her works she never spoke; of the works and thoughts of others she spoke with reverence, and sometimes even too great tolerance. But these afternoons had the highest pleasure when London was empty, or the day was wet, and only a few friends were present, so that her conversation assumed a more sustained tone than was possible when the rooms were full of shifting groups. It was then that, without any premeditation, her sentences fell as fully formed, as wise, as weighty, as epigrammatic, as any to be found in her books. Always ready, but never rapid, her talk was not only good in itself, but it encouraged the same in others, since she was an excellent listener, and eager to hear."

At these gatherings the most noted of the English disciples of Comte were to be found, and among them Frederic Harrison, Prof. E. S. Beesley, Dr. Congreve, the director of the London Church of Humanity, and Prof. W. K. Clifford. The English positivists were represented by Herbert Spencer, Prof. T. H. Huxley and Moncure D. Conway. The realistic school of poets and artists came in the persons of its most representative men. Dante Rosetti and Millais, Tourguénief and Burne Jones, DuMaurier and Dr. Hueffner illustrated most of its phases. The great world of general literature sent Sir Arthur Helps, Sir Theodore Martin, Anthony Trollope, C. G. Leland, Justin McCarthy, Frederic Myers, Prof. Mark Pattison and many another. The rarer guests included Alfred Tennyson and Robert Browning. It was no inconsiderable influence which could draw together such a company and hold it together for many years. Of the part played in these gatherings by the hosts, Miss Mathilde Blind has given an account. Lewes acted "as a social cement. His vivacity, his ready tact, the fascination of his manners, diffused that general sense of ease and *abandon* so requisite to foster an harmonious flow of conversation. He was inimitable as a *raconteur*, and Thackeray, Trollope and Arthur Helps were fond of quoting some of the stories which he would dramatize in the telling. One of the images which, on these occasions, recurs oftenest to George Eliot's friends is that of the frail-looking woman who would sit with her chair drawn close to the fire, and whose winning womanliness of bearing and manners struck every one who had the privilege of an introduction to her. Her long, pale face, with its strongly marked features, was less rugged in the mature prime of life than in youth, the inner meanings of her nature having worked themselves more and more to the surface, the mouth, with its benignant suavity of expression, especially softening the too prominent under lip and massive jaw. Her abundant hair, untinged with gray, whose smooth bands made a kind of frame to the face, was covered by a lace or muslin cap, with lappets of rich point or Valenciennes lace fastened under her chin. Her gray-blue eyes, under noticeable eyelashes, expressed the same acute sensitiveness as her long, thin, beautifully shaped hands. She had a pleasant laugh and smile, her voice being low, distinct, and intensely sympathetic in quality; it was contralto in singing, but she seldom sang or played before more than one or two friends. Though her conversation was perfectly easy, each sentence was as finished, as perfectly formed, as the style of her published works."

Among the persons who gathered at The Priory on Sunday afternoons there came to be a considerable number of those who were Mrs. Lewes's devoted disciples. They hung upon her words, they accepted her views of life, her philosophy became theirs. That she would have admitted such discipleship existed there is no reason to believe, and it is certain she did not attempt to bring it about or even desire it. So great, however, was her power of intellect, so noble her personal influence, it was impossible that ardent young natures could refrain from devotion to such genius and speedy acceptance of its teachings. The richness of her moral and intellectual nature aided largely in this heroine worship, but she impressed herself on other minds because she was so much an individual, because her personality was of a kind to command reverence and devotion. It was not merely young and impulsive natures who were thus attracted and inspired, for Edith Simcox says that "men and women, old friends and new, persons of her own age and of another generation, the married and the single, impulsive lovers and hard-headed philosophers, nay, even some who elsewhere might have passed for cynics, all classes alike yielded to the attractive force of this rare character, in which tenderness and strength were blended together, and as it were transfused with something that was all her own — the genius of sweet goodness." Perhaps her influence was so great on those it reached because it demanded high and noble life and thought of her disciples. Her moral ideal was a high one, and she had literary and artistic standards that demanded all the effort of both genius and talent, while her culture was such as to be exacting in its requirements. So we find Miss Simcox saying that Mrs. Lewes, in her friendships, "had the unconscious exactingness of a full nature. She was intolerant of a vacuum in the mind or character, and she was indifferent to admiration that did not seem to have its root in fundamental agreement with those principles she held to be most 'necessary to salvation.' Where this sympathy existed, her generous affection was given to a fellow-believer, a fellow-laborer, with singularly little reference to the fact that such full sympathy was never unattended with profound love and reverence for herself as a living witness to the truth and power of the principles thus shared. To love her was a strenuous pleasure; for in spite of the tenderness for all human weakness that was natural to her, and the scrupulous charity of her overt judgments, the fact remained that her natural standard was ruthlessly out of reach, and it was a painful discipline for her friends to feel that she was compelled to lower it to suit their infirmities. The intense humility of her self-appreciation, and the unfeigned readiness with which she would even herself with any sinner who sought her counsel, had the same effect upon those who would compare what she condemned in herself with what she tolerated in them. And at the same time, no doubt, this total absence of self-sufficiency had something to do with the passionate tenderness with which commonplace people dared to cherish their immortal friend."

As has already been suggested, her womanliness is a more prominent characteristic of Mrs. Lewes's mind than its great intellectual power. Her sympathy was keen and most sensitive, her modesty and humility were almost excessive, and her tenderness of nature was a woman's own. She gave her sympathy readily and freely to the humble and unfavored. She had no taint of intellectual aristocracy, says one of her friends. Faithful, devoted love; the sacredness of simple duties and plain work; earnest help of other souls, — these were among the daily lessons of her life and teaching. "How strong was the current of her sympathy in the direction of all humble effort," exclaims one of her friends, "how reluctantly she checked presumption! The most ordinary and uninteresting of her friends must feel that had they known nothing of her but her rapid insight into and quick response to their inmost feelings she would still have been a memorable personality to them. This sympathy was extended to the sorrows most unlike anything she could ever by any possibility have known — the failures of life obtained as large a share of her compassion as its sorrows. The wish to console and cheer was indeed rooted in the most vital part of her nature." Another of her friends has said that "she possessed to a marvellous degree the divine gifts of charity, and of attracting moral outcasts to herself, whose devils she cast out, if I may be permitted the expression, by shutting her eyes to their existence. In her presence you felt wrapped round by an all-embracing atmosphere of sympathy and readiness to make the least of all your shortcomings, and the most of any good which might be in you. But great as was her personality, she shrank with horror from intruding it upon you, and, in general society, her exquisitely melodious voice was, unhappily for the outside circles, too seldom raised beyond the pitch of something not much above a whisper. Of the rich vein of humor which runs through George Eliot's works there was comparatively little trace in her conversation, which seldom descended from the grave to the gay. But although she rarely indulged in conversational levity herself, she was most tolerant of it, and even encouraged its ebullition, in others, joining heartily in any mirth which might be going on."

She made her younger admirers feel the deeper influence of her great personality by inspiring them with the largest moral purposes. To awaken and to arouse the moral nature seems always to have been her purpose, and to lead it to the highest attainable results. Earnest young minds never "failed to feel in her presence that they were for the time, at all events, raised into a higher moral level, and none ever left her without feeling inspired with a stronger sense of duty, and positively under the obligation of striving to live up to a higher standard of life." Hence her personal influence was considerable, though she led the close life of a student, and did not go into general society at all. This high moral earnestness made her a prophet to her friends, as in her books it made her a great moral teacher to the world at large. Those who had the privilege of an intimate acquaintance with Mrs. Lewes have pronounced the woman greater than her books. She was not only a great writer but a great woman. Human nature in its largest capacities was represented in her, for she rose above the limitations of sex; and she is thought of less as a great woman than as a large human personality. Hers was a massive nature, emphatic, individual, many-sided. Genius of a very high order, though not the highest, was hers, while she was possessed of a broad culture and great learning. Seldom does genius carry with it talents so varied and well-trained or a culture so full and thorough. And her culture was of that kind which entered into every fibre of her nature and became a part of her own personality. It was thoroughly digested and absorbed into good healthy red blood, and became a quickened, sustained motive to the largest efforts. How vital this love of culture was, may be seen when we are told that "she possessed in an eminent degree that power which has led to success in so many directions, of keeping her mind unceasingly at the stretch without conscious fatigue. She would cease to ponder or to read when other duties called her, but never because she herself felt tired. Even in so complex an effort as a visit to a picture gallery implies, she could continue for hours at the same pitch of earnest interest, and outweary strong men. Nor was this a mere habit of passive reception. In the intervals between her successive compositions her mind was always fusing and combining its fresh stores."

She had culture, moral power and earnestness in a high degree, warmth of sympathy and sensitiveness to all beauty, but she had no saintliness. Profound as was her reverence for moral purity, and lofty as was her moral purpose, she was not a saint, and holiness was not a characteristic of her nature. This clear and high sense of moral truth everywhere appears in her life and thought. "For the lessons most imperatively needed by the mass of men, the lessons of deliberate kindness, of careful truth, of unwavering endeavor, — for these plain themes one could not ask a more convincing teacher than she. Everything in her aspect and presence was in keeping with the bent of her soul. The deeply lined face, the too marked and massive features, were united with an air of delicate refinement, which in one way was the more impressive because it seemed to proceed entirely from within. Nay, the inward beauty would sometimes quite transform the external harshness; there would be moments when the thin hands that entwined themselves in their eagerness, the earnest figure that bowed forward to speak and hear, the deep gaze moving from one face to another with a grave appeal, — all these seemed the transparent symbols that showed the presence of a wise, benignant soul. But it was the voice which best revealed her, a voice whose subdued intensity and tremulous richness seemed to environ her uttered words with the mystery of a world that must remain untold. And then again, when in moments of more intimate converse some current of emotion would set strongly through her soul, when she would raise her head in unconscious absorption and look out into the unseen, her expression was not one to be soon forgotten. It has not, indeed, the serene felicity of souls to whose childlike confidence all heaven and earth are fair. Rather it was the look of a strenuous Demiurge, of a soul on which high tasks are laid, and which finds in their accomplishment its only imagination of joy."

Another side of her influence on persons is expressed by the representative of that publishing house which gave her books to the world. "In addition to the spell which bound the world to her by her genius, she had a personal power of drawing to herself, in ties of sympathy and kindly feeling, all who came under her influence. She never oppressed any one by her talents; she never allowed any one to be sensible of the depth and variety of her scholarship; she knew, as few know, how to draw forth the views and feelings of her visitors, and to make their sympathies her own. There was a charm in her personal character which of itself was sufficient to conciliate deep and lasting regard. Every one who entered her society left it impressed with the conviction that they had been under the influence of a sympathy and tenderness not less remarkable than the force of her mental power. . . . Her deep and catholic love for humanity in its broadest and best sense, which was in itself the strongest quickening motive of her genius, will maintain her influence in the future as in the present."

Hers was a somewhat sensitive, shrinking nature, with no self-assumption, and without the taint of egotism. She had a modest estimate of her own great literary creations, and shrank from all mention of them and from the homage paid to her as an author. After the publication of *Romola* she was one day reading French to a girl companion in the garden of a Swiss hotel, when a lady drew near to listen to the silvery tones of her voice. Noticing this, she said, "Do you understand?" The lady answered, "I do not care for the matter; I only came to listen to your voice." "Do you like it?" was then inquired. When the lady expressed the pleasure it gave her, Mrs. Lewes took her hand and warmly said, "I thank you. I would rather you would compliment my voice than my *Romola*."[1]

It has been truly said of her that above all novelists, with the exception of Goethe, she was supreme in culture. She had a passion for knowledge, and zeal in the pursuit of learning. She was a lover of books, but not a scholar in the technical and exact sense. Delighting in literature, art, music, and all that appeals to the imagination, rather than in mere information, yet she was a thinker of original powers, with a keen appreciation of philosophy, and ability to tread its most difficult paths with firm step. She had an intimate acquaintance with the literatures of Germany, France, Italy and Spain, and she was well read in the classics of Greece and Rome. She was "competently acquainted" with the different systems of philosophy, and she had mastered their problems while thinking out her own conclusions. Having no professional knowledge of the sciences, she

[1] This story is not authenticated; it may be taken for what it is worth, though it appears to be characteristic.

was a diligent reader of scientific books, and was familiar with all the bearings of science on philosophy and religion. Her books show an intimate knowledge of modern thought in many of its phases, as it bears upon physical, economic, historical and intellectual science. With all her learning, however, she retained a woman's sympathy with life, beauty and poetry. Her knowledge was never dry and technical, but warm and imaginative with genius and poetry.[1]

Her culture may be compared with Mrs. Browning's, who was also an extensive reader and widely informed. The poet as well as the novelist acquired her learning because of her thirst for knowledge, and mainly by her own efforts; but she preferred the classics to science, and literature to philosophy. Mrs. Browning was the wiser, George Eliot the more learned. The writings of Mrs. Browning are less affected by her information than George Eliot's; and this is true because she was of a more poetical temperament, because her imagination was more brilliant and creative.

Mrs. Lewes was an enthusiastic lover of art, and especially of music. She never tired in her interest in beholding fine paintings, and music was the continual delight of her life. She was a tireless frequenter of picture galleries, and every fine musical entertainment in London was sure to find her, in company with Mr. Lewes, an enthusiastic listener. Good acting also claimed not a little of her interest, and she carefully studied even the details of the dramatic art, so that she was able to give a critical appreciation to the acting she enjoyed. Indeed, she had given to her mind that rounded fulness of attainment, and developed all her

[1] Her scholarly habits, and her realistic tendencies, usually made George Eliot very painstaking and accurate, but an occasional slip of pen or memory is to be noted in her books. In Theophrastus Such she credited to the Apologia of Plato what is really contained in the Phædo. The motto to chapter seventeen of Daniel Deronda was quoted, in the first edition, as from In Memoriam instead of Locksley Hall. In an early chapter of Felix Holt she made the parson preach from the words, "Break up the fallow ground of your hearts." The words of scripture are, "Break up your fallow ground." In Adam Bede a clergyman is made to take the words of the Prayer Book, "In the midst of life we are in death," for his text.

faculties with that due proportion, which Fichte so earnestly preached as the characteristic of true culture. "Her character," says Edith Simcox, "seemed to include every possibility of action and emotion; no human passion was wanting in her nature, there were no blanks or negations; and the marvellous thing was to see how, in this wealth of impulses and desires, there was no crash of internal discord, no painful collisions with other human interests outside; how, in all her life, passions of volcanic strength were harnessed in the service of those nearest her, and so inspired by the permanent instinct of devotion to her kind, that it seemed as if it were by her own choice they spent themselves there only where their force was welcome. Her very being was a protest against the opposing and yet cognate heresies that half the normal human passions must be strangled in the quest of virtue, and that the attainment of virtue is a dull and undesirable end, seeing that it implies the sacrifice of most that makes life interesting." She had her own temptations and her imperfections. With these she struggled bravely, and set herself to the hard task of correction and discipline. Her culture was not merely one of books, but it was also one of moral discipline and of strenuous spiritual subjection. It was one of stern moral requirements and duties, as well as one of large sympathy with all that is natural and beautiful.

It was a quiet life of continuous study and authorship which Mrs. Lewes led in The Priory, and it was varied from year to year only by her visits to the continent and by her summer residence in Surrey. One of her summer retreats, at the village of Shotter Mill, has been described, as well as her life there. The most picturesque house in the place is known as Brookbank, and here she spent a summer, that of 1871. It is described as "an old two-storied cottage, the front of the house being half-covered with trailing rose-trees. The rooms are low but pleasant, and furnished in a simple, comfortable manner. We have often endeavored," says the writer of this account, "to glean some information regarding George Eliot's life at Shotter Mill, but she and Mr. Lewes lived in such seclusion that there was very little to be told. They seldom crossed their threshold during the day, but wandered over the commons and hills after sundown. They were very anxious to lodge at the picturesque old farm, ten minutes' walk beyond Brookbank, but all available room was then occupied. However, George Eliot would often visit the farmer's wife, and, sitting on a grassy bank just beside the kitchen door, would discuss the growth of fruit and the quality of butter in a manner so quiet and simple the good country folks were astonished, expecting very different conversation from the great novelist. The farmer was employed to drive them two or three times a week. They occasionally visited Tennyson, whose home is only three miles distant, though a rather tedious drive, since it is up hill nearly all the way. George Eliot did not enjoy the ride much, for the farmer told us that, 'withal her being such a mighty clever body, she were very nervous in a carriage — allays wanted to go on a smooth road, and seemed dreadful feared of being thrown out.' George Eliot was writing *Middlemarch* during her summer at Brookbank, and the term for which they had the cottage expired before they wished to return to London. The Squire was away at the time, so they procured permission to use his house during the remainder of the visit. In speaking of them he said, 'I visited Mr. and Mrs. Lewes several times before they went back to town, and found the authoress a very agreeable woman, both in manner and appearance; but her mind was evidently completely absorbed in her work; she seemed to have no time for anything but writing from morning till night. Her hand could hardly convey her thoughts to paper fast enough. It was an exceptionally hot summer, and yet through it all Mrs. Lewes would have artificial heat placed at her feet to keep up the circulation. Why, one broiling day I came home worn out, longing for a gray sky and a cool breeze, and on going into the garden I found her sitting there, her head just shaded by a deodara on the lawn, writing away as usual. I expostulated with her for letting the midday sun pour down on her like that. "Oh," she replied, "I like it. To-day is the first time I have felt warm this summer." So I said no more, and went my way.' And thus nearly all we could learn about George Eliot was that she loved to bask in the sun and liked green peas. She visited some of the cottagers, but only those living in secluded places, who knew nothing of her. Just such people as these she used in her graphic and realistic sketches of peasant life. With regard to the surrounding country, George Eliot said that it pleased her more than any she knew of in England."

In these summer retreats she continued steadily at her work, and she greatly delighted in the quiet and rest. Other summers were spent at Witley, in the same county, where the fine scenery, lovely drives and wide-reaching views from the hill-tops were to her a perpetual delight. At this place a house was bought, and there was a project of giving up the London residence and of visiting the city only for occasional relaxation. This project was not carried out, for soon after their return from Witley in the autumn of 1878, Mr. Lewes was taken ill, and died in November. His death was a great blow to Mrs. Lewes, and he was deeply mourned, so much so as to seriously impair her health. The state of her mind at this trying period is well indicated in a letter written to Prof. David Kaufmann.

THE PRIORY, 21 NORTH BANK, REGENT'S PARK,
April 17, '79.

MY DEAR SIR,—Your kind letter has touched me very deeply. I confess that my mind has more than once gone out to you as one from whom I should like to have some sign of sympathy with my loss. But you were rightly inspired in waiting till now, for during many weeks I was unable even to listen to the letters which my generous friends were continually sending me. Now, at last, I am eagerly interested in every communication that springs out of an acquaintance with my husband and his works.

I thank you for telling me about the Hungarian translation of his *History of Philosophy*, but what would I not have given if the volumes could have come a few days before his death; for his mind was perfectly clear, and he would have felt some joy in that sign of his work being effective. I do not know whether you enter into the comfort I feel that he never knew he was dying, and fell gently asleep after ten days of illness in which the suffering was comparatively mild. . . . .

One of the last things he did at his desk was to despatch a manuscript of mine to the publishers. The book (not a story and not bulky) is to appear near the end of May, and as it contains some words I wanted to say about the Jews, I will order a copy to be sent to you.

I hope that your labors have gone on uninterruptedly for the benefit of others, in spite of public troubles. The aspect of affairs with us is grevious — industry languishing, and the best part of our nation indignant at our having been betrayed into an unjustifiable war (in South Africa).

I have been occupied in editing my husband's MSS., so far as they are left in sufficient completeness to be prepared for publication without the obtrusion of another mind instead of his. A brief volume on *The Study of Psychology* will appear immediately, and a further volume of pyschological studies will follow in the autumn. But his work was cut short while he still thought of it as the happy occupation of far-stretching months. Once more let me thank you for remembering me in my sorrow, and believe me

Yours with high regard,

M. E. Lewes.

Writing to a friend soon after Lewes's death, who had also lost her husband, she said, —

There is but one refuge — the having much to do. Nothing can make the burden to be patiently borne, except the gradual adaptation of your soul to the new conditions.

The much to do she partly found in editing the uncompleted *Problems of Life and Mind*, and in establishing a studentship for original investigation in physiology, known as "The George Henry Lewes Studentship." Its value is about two hundred pounds, and it is open to both sexes. These labors enabled her to do honor to one she had trusted through many years, whose name and fame she greatly revered, and to recover the even poise of her life. She carefully managed the business affairs he had left in her hands, and she provided for his children.

A year and a half after the death of Lewes, May 6, 1880, she was married at the church of St. George's, Hanover Square, to John Walter Cross, the senior partner in a London banking firm, whom she had first met in 1867, and who had been a greatly valued friend both to herself and Lewes. Though much younger than herself, he had many qualities to recommend him to her regard. A visit to the continent after this ceremony lasted for several months, a considerable portion of the time being spent in Venice. On their return to London in the autumn after spending a happy summer in Surrey, they went to live in the house of Mr. Cross at 4 Cheyne Walk, Chelsea. The old habits of her life were taken up, her studies were resumed, a new novel was begun, her friends came as usual on Sunday afternoons, and many years of work seemed before her, for her health had greatly improved. On Friday, December 17, 1880, she attended the presentation of the *Agamemnon* of Æschylus, in the original Greek, with the accompaniments of the ancient theatre, by the undergraduates of Balliol College, Oxford. She was very enthusiastic about this revival of ancient art, and planned to read anew all the Greek dramatists with her husband. The next day she attended a popular concert at St. James Hall, and listened with her usual intense interest. Sitting in a draught, she caught cold, but that evening she played through much of the music she had heard in the afternoon. The next day she was not so well as usual, yet she met her friends in the afternoon. On Monday her larynx was slightly affected, and a physician was called, but no danger was apprehended. Yet her malady gained rapidly. On Tuesday night she was in a dangerous condition, and on Wednesday the pericardium was found to be seriously diseased. Towards midnight of that day, December 22, after a period of unconsciousness, she quietly passed away. She was buried on the 29th, in the unconsecrated portion of Highgate Cemetery, by the side of George Henry Lewes. The funeral services were conducted by the Rev. Dr. Sadler, a radical Unitarian minister, who spoke of her great genius, and quoted her own words about a future life in the life of humanity. His address contained many references to her personal characteristics, such as could only come from an intimate friend. He said, —

"To those who are present it is given to think of the gentleness, and delicate womanly grace and charm, which were combined with 'that breadth of culture and universality of power which,' as one has expressed it, 'have made her known to all the world.' To those who are present it is given to know the diffidence and self-distrust which, notwithstanding all her public fame, needed individual sympathy and encouragement to prevent her from feeling too keenly how far the results of her labors fell below the standard she had set before her. To those who are present too it may be given — though there is so large a number to whom it is not given — to understand how a nature may be profoundly devout, and yet unable to accept a great deal of what is usually held as religious belief. No intellectual difficulties or uncertainties, no sense of mental incapacity to climb the heights of infinitude, could take from her the piety of the affections or 'the beliefs which were the mother-tongue of her soul.' I cannot doubt that she spoke out of the fulness of her own heart when she put into the lips of another the words, 'May not a man silence his awe or his love and take to finding reasons which others demand? But if his love lies deeper than any reasons to be found!' How patiently she toiled to render her work in all its details as little imperfect as might be! How green she kept the remembrance of all those companions to whom she felt that she owed a moulding and elevating influence, especially in her old home, and of him who was its head, her father! How her heart glowed with a desire to help to make a heaven on earth, to be a 'cup of strength' to others, and when her own days on earth should have closed, to have a place among those

> 'Immortal dead who still live on
> In minds made better by their presence; live
> In pulses stirred to generosity,
> In deeds of daring rectitude; in scorn
> For miserable aims that end with self;
> In thoughts sublime that pierce the night like stars,
> And with their mild persistence urge man's search
> To vaster issues.'

How she thus yearned 'to join the choir invisible, whose music is the gladness of the world!' All this is known to those who had the privilege of being near her."

The address was preceded by a simple burial service, and was followed by a prayer, all being given in the chapel of the cemetery. The coffin, covered with the finest floral tributes, was then borne to the grave, where the burial service was completed, and was followed by a prayer and the benediction. Although the day was a disagreeable one and rain was falling, the chapel was crowded, and many not being able to gain admittance stood about the open grave. Beside her personal friends and her family there were present many persons noted for their literary or scientific attainments. On the lid of the coffin was this inscription:

MARY ANN CROSS.
("George Eliot")
Born 22d Nov., 1819; died 22d Dec., 1880.

Quilla fonte
Che spande di parlar si largo fiume.[1]

The novel which had been begun was left a mere fragment, and in accordance with what it was thought would have been her wish, was destroyed by her family. Perhaps it was better that her dislike of unfinished work should be so respected.

[1] From Dante, and has been rendered into English thus:
That fountain
Which spreads abroad so wide a river of speech.

VI.

LITERARY TRAITS AND TENDENCIES.

GEORGE ELIOT was a painstaking, laborious writer. She did not proceed rapidly, so carefully did she elaborate her pages. Her subjects were thoroughly studied before the pen was taken in hand, patiently thought out, planned with much care, and all available helps secured that could be had. She threw her whole life into her work, became a part of the scenes she was depicting; her life was absorbed until the work of writing became a painful process both to body and mind. "Her beautifully written manuscript," says her publisher, "free from blur or erasure, and with every letter delicately and distinctly finished, was only the outward and visible sign of the inward labor which she had taken to work out her ideas. She never drew any of her facts or impressions from second hand; and thus, in spite of the number and variety of her illustrations, she had rarely much to correct in her proof-sheets. She had all that love of doing her work well for the work's sake which she makes prominent characteristics of Adam Bede and Stradivarius."

When a book was completed, so intense had been her application and the absorption of her life in her work, a period of despondency followed. When a correspondent praised *Middlemarch*, and expressed a hope that even a greater work might follow, she replied, "As to the 'great novel' which remains to be written, I must tell you that I never believe in future books." Again, she wrote of the depression which succeeded the completion of each of her works, —

Always after finishing a book I have a period of despair that I can ever again produce anything worth giving to the world. The responsibility of writing grows heavier and heavier — does it not? — as the world grows older and the voices of the dead more numerous. It is difficult to believe, until the germ of some new work grows into imperious activity within one, that it is possible to make a really needed contribution to the poetry of the world — I mean possible to one's self to do it.

Owing probably somewhat to this tendency to take a despondent view concerning her own work, and to distrust of the leadings of her own genius, was her habit of never reading the criticisms made on her books. She adopted this rule, she tells one correspondent, "as a necessary preservative against influences that would have ended by nullifying her power of writing." To another, who had written her in appreciation of her books, she wrote this note, in which she alludes to the same habit of shunning criticism:

My Dear Miss Wellington, — The signs of your sympathy sent to me across the wide water have touched me with the more effect because you imply that you are young. I care supremely that my writing should be some help and stimulus to those who have probably a long life before them.

Mr. Lewes does not let me read criticisms on my writings. He always reads them himself, and gives me occasional quotations, when he thinks that they show a spirit and mode of appreciation which will win my gratitude. He has carefully read through the articles which were accompanied by your kind letter, and he has a high opinion of the feeling and discernment exhibited in them. Some concluding passages which he read aloud to me are such as I register among the grounds of any encouragement in looking backward on what I have written, if not in looking forward to my future writing.

Thank you, my dear young friend, whom I shall probably never know otherwise than in this spiritual way. And certainly, apart from those relations in life which bring daily duties and opportunities of lovingness, the most satisfactory of all ties is this effective invisible intercourse of an elder mind with a younger.

The quotation in your letter from Hawthorne's book offers an excellent type both for men and women in the value it assigns to that order of work which is called subordinate but becomes ennobling by being finely done.[1] Yours, with sincere obligations.

M. E. Lewes.

[1]A reference to Hilda's ceasing to consider herself an original artist in the presence of the great masters. "Beholding the miracles of beauty which the old masters had achieved, the world seemed already rich enough in original designs, and nothing more was so desirable as to diffuse these selfsame beauties more widely among mankind. So Hilda became a copyist."

By the way, Mr. Lewes tells me that you ascribe to me a hatred of blue eyes — which is amusing, since my own eyes are blue-gray. I am not in any sense one of the "good haters;" on the contrary, my weaknesses all verge toward an excessive tolerance and a tendency to melt off the outlines of things.

THE PRIORY.
21 North Bank, Regent's Park, Jan. 16, '73.[1]

Her sensitiveness was great, and contact with an unappreciative and unsympathetic public depressing to a large degree. It was a part of that shrinking away from the world which kept her out of society, and away from all but a select few whose tastes and sympathies were largely in accordance with her own. Besides, she distrusted that common form of criticism which presumes to tell an author how he ought to have written, and assumes to itself an insight and knowledge greater than that possessed by genius itself. Concerning the value of such criticism she wrote these pertinent words:

I get confirmed in my impression that the criticism of any new writing is shifting and untrustworthy. I hardly think that any critic can have so keen a sense of the shortcomings in my works as that I groan under in the course of writing them, and I cannot imagine any edification coming to an author from a sort of reviewing which consists in attributing to him or her unexpressed opinions, and in imagining circumstances which may be alleged as petty private motives for the treatment of subjects which ought to be of general human interest.

To the same correspondent she used even stronger words concerning her dislike of ordinary criticism.

Do not expect "criticism" from me. I hate "sitting in the seat of judgment," and I would rather try to impress the public generally with the sense that they may get the best result from a book without necessarily forming an "opinion" about it, than I would rush into stating opinions of my own. The floods of nonsense printed in the form of critical opinions seem to me a chief curse of our times — a chief obstacle to true culture.

It is not to be forgotten, however, that George Eliot had done much critical work before she became a novelist, and that much of it was of a keen and cutting nature. Severely as she was handled by the critics, no one of

[1] From The Critic of December 31, 1881. This letter was addressed to Miss Alice Wellington, now Mrs. Rollins.

them was more vigorous than was her treatment of Young and Cumming. Even in later years, when she took up the critical pen, the effect was felt. Mr. Lecky did not pass gently through her hands when she reviewed his *Rationalism in Europe.* Her criticisms in *Theophrastus Such* were penetrating and severe.

For the same reason, she read few works of contemporary fiction, that her mind might not be biassed and that she might not be discouraged in her own work. Always busy with some special subject which absorbed all her time and strength, she could give little attention to contemporary literature. To one correspondent she wrote, —

> My constant groan is, that I must leave so much of the greatest writing which the centuries have sifted for me, unread for want of time.

The style adopted by George Eliot is for the most part fresh, vital and energetic. It is pure in form, rich in illustrations, strong and expressive in manner. There are exceptions to this statement, it is true, and she is sometimes turgid and dry, again gaudy and verbose. Sententious in her didactic passages, she is pure and noble in her sentiment, poetical and impressive in her descriptions of nature. Her diction is choice, her range of expression large, and she admirably suits her words to the thought she would present. There is a rich, teeming fulness of life in her books, the canvas is crowded, there is movement and action. An abundance of passion, delicate feeling and fine sensibility is expressed.

The critics have almost universally condemned the plots of George Eliot's novels for their want of unity. They tell us that the flow of events is often not orderly, while improbable scenes are introduced, superfluous incidents are common, the number of characters is too great, and the analysis of character impedes the unity of events. These objections are not always vital, and sometimes they are mere objections rather than genuine criticisms. Instances of failure to follow the best methods may be cited in abundance, one of which is seen in the first two chapters in *Daniel Deronda* being placed out of their natural order. The opening scenes in *The Spanish Gypsy* seem quite unnecessary to the development of the plot, while the last two scenes of the second book are so fragmentary and unconnected with the remainder of the story as to help it but little. In the middle of *Adam Bede* are several chapters devoted to the birthday party, which are quite unnecessary to the development of the action. *Daniel Deronda* contains two narratives which are in many respects almost entirely distinct from each other, and the reader is made to alternate between two worlds that have little in common. There is much of the improbable in the account of the Transome estate in *Felix Holt*, while the closing scenes in the life of Tito Melema in *Romola* are more tragical than natural. Yet these defects are incidental to her method and art rather than actual blemishes on her work. For the most part, her work is thoroughly unitary, cause leads naturally into effect, and there is a moral development of character such as is found in life itself. Her plots are strongly constructed, in simple outlines, are easily comprehended and kept in mind, and the leading motive holds steadily through to the end. Her analytical method often makes an apparent interruption of the narrative, and the unity of purpose is frequently developed through the philosophic purport of the novel rather than in its literary form. Direct narrative is often hindered, it is true, by her habit of studying the remote causes and effects of character, but she never wanders far enough to forget the real purpose had in view. She holds the many elements of her story well under command, she concentrates them upon some one aim, and she gives to her story a tragic unity of great moral splendor and effect. Even the diverse elements, the minute side-studies and the profuse comments, are all woven into the organic structure, and are essential to the unfoldment of the plot. They seem to be quite irrelevant interruptions until we look back upon the completed whole and study the perfected intent of the story. Then we see how essential they are to the epic finish of the novel, and to that total effect which a work of genius creates. Then it is seen that a dramatic unity and well-studied intent hold together every part and make a completed structure of great beauty.

Her dramatic skill is great, and her dialogues thoroughly good. Her characters are full of power and life, and stand out as distinct personalities. The conversation is sprightly, strong and wise. Probably no novelist has created so many clearly cut, positive, intensely personal characters as George Eliot, and this individualism is depicted as acting within social and hereditary limits; hence dramatic action is constantly arising. Shakspere and Browning only surpass her in dramatic power, as in the creation of character. Yet her method of producing character differs essentially from that of Shakspere, Homer and all the great creators. She describes character, while they present it. Homer gives no description of Helen; but of her beauty and her person we learn all the more because we are left to find them out from the influence they produce. We know Hamlet because he lives before us, and impresses his personality upon every feature of the great drama in which he appears. George Eliot's manner is to describe, to minutely portray, and to dissect to the last muscle and nerve.

She has also a rich and racy humor, sensitive and sober, refined and delicate. She does not caricature folly with Dickens, or laugh at weakness with Thackeray; but she shows us the limitations of life in such a manner as to produce the finest humor. She is never repulsive, grotesque or vulgar; but wise, laughter-loving and sympathetic. Her humor is pure and homely as it is delicate and exquisite; and it is invariably human and noble.

She has an intense love and a wonderful appreciation of the ludicrous, sees whatever is incongruous in life, and makes her laughter genial and joyous. Her humor is the very quintessence of human experience, strikes deadly blows at what is unjust and untrue. It is both intellectual and moral, as Professor Dowden suggests. "The grotesque in human character is reclaimed from the province of the humorous by her affections, when that is possible, and is shown to be a pathetic form of beauty. Her humor usually belongs to her entire conception of character, and cannot be separated from it." She laughs at all, but sneers at no one, — for she has keen sympathy with all.

George Eliot is not so good a satirist as she is humorist. Her humor is as fresh and delightful as a morning in May, but her satire is nearly always labored. She is too much in sympathy with human nature to laugh at its follies and its weaknesses. Its joys, its bubbling humor and delight she can appreciate, as well as all the pain and sorrow that come to men and women; and she can fully enter into the life of her characters of every kind, and portray their inmost motives and impulses; but the foibles of the world she cannot treat in the vein of the satirist. In her earlier books she is said to have been under the influence of Thackeray, but her satire is heavy, and lacks his light touch and his tender undertone of compassion. Here is a good specimen of her earlier attempts to be satirical:

> When a man is happy enough to win the affections of a sweet girl, who can soothe his cares with crochet, and respond to all his most cherished ideas with beaded urn-rugs and chair-covers in German wool, he has, at least, a guarantee of domestic comfort, whatever trials may await him out of doors. What a resource it is under fatigue and irritation to have your drawing-room well supplied with small mats, which would always be ready if you ever wanted to set anything on them! And what styptic for a bleeding heart can equal copious squares of crochet-work, which are useful for slipping down the moment you touch them?[1]

[1] Janet's Repentance, chapter III.

Similar to this is the account of Mrs. Pullett's grief.

It is a pathetic sight and a striking example of the complexity introduced into the emotions by a high state of civilization — the sight of a fashionably dressed female in grief. From the sorrow of a Hottentot to that of a woman in large buckram sleeves, with several bracelets on each arm, an architectural bonnet, and delicate ribbon-strings — what a long series of gradations! In the enlightened child of civilization the abandonment characteristic of grief is checked and varied in the subtlest manner, so as to present an interesting problem to the analytic mind. If, with a crushed heart and eyes half-blinded by the mist of tears, she were to walk with a too devious step through a door-place, she might crush her buckram sleeves, too, and the deep consciousness of this possibility produces a composition of forces by which she takes a line that just clears the door-post. Perceiving that the tears are hurrying fast, she unpins her strings and throws them languidly backward — a touching gesture, indicative, even in the deepest gloom, of the hope in future dry moments when cap-strings will once more have a charm. As the tears subside a little, and with her head leaning backward at an angle that will not injure her bonnet, she endures that terrible moment when grief, which has made all things else a weariness, has itself become weary; she looks down pensively at her bracelets, and adjusts their clasps with that pretty studied fortuity which would be gratifying to her mind if it were once more in a calm and healthy state.[1]

In her later books the strained efforts at satire are partially avoided, and though the satirical spirit is not withdrawn in any measure, yet it is more delicately managed. It is less open, less blunt, but hardly more subtle and penetrative. It is still a strained effort, and it is quite too hard and bare in statement. We are told in *Middlemarch* that

Mrs. Bulstrode's *naive* way of conciliating piety and worldliness, the nothingness of this life and the desirability of cut glass, the consciousness at once of filthy rags and the best damask, was not a sufficient relief from the weight of her husband's invariable seriousness.

Such a turning of sentiment into satire as the following is rather jarring, and is a good specimen of that "laborious smartness," as Mr. R. H. Hutton justly calls it, which is found in all of George Eliot's books: —

Young love-making — that gossamer web! Even the points it clings to — the things whence its subtile interlacings are swung —

[1] Mill on the Floss, chapter VII.

are scarcely perceptible: momentary touches of finger-tips, meetings of rays from blue and dark orbs, unfinished phrases, lightest changes of cheek and lip, faintest tremors. The web itself is made of spontaneous beliefs and indefinable joys, yearnings of one life toward another, visions of completeness, indefinite trust. And Lydgate fell to spinning that web from his inward self with wonderful rapidity, in spite of experience supposed to be finished off with the drama of Laure—in spite, too, of medicine and biology; for the inspection of macerated muscle or of eyes presented in a dish (like Santa Lucia's), and other incidents of scientific inquiry, are observed to be less incompatible with poetic love than a native dulness or a lively addiction to the lowest prose.[1]

This introduction of a scientific illustration will serve to bring another tendency of George Eliot's to our attention. She makes a frequent use of her large learning and culture in her novels. In the earlier ones a Greek quotation is to be found here and there, while in the later, German seems to have the preference. In *The Mill on the Floss* she describes Bob Jakin's thumb as "a singularly broad specimen of that difference between the man and the monkey." Such references to recent scientific speculations are not unfrequent. If they serve to show the tendencies of her mind towards knowledge and large thought, they also indicate a too ready willingness to imbibe, and to use in a popular manner, what is not thoroughly assimilated truth. The force of such an illustration as the following must be lost on most novel-readers: —

Although Sir James was a sportsman, he had some other feelings toward women than toward grouse and foxes, and did not regard his future wife in the light of prey, valuable chiefly for the excitements of the chase. Neither was he so well acquainted with the habits of primitive races as to feel that an ideal combat for her, tomahawk in hand, so to speak, was necessary to the historical continuity of the marriage tie.[2]

It is doubtful whether any reader will quite catch the meaning of this sentence:

Has any one ever pinched into its pilulous smallness the cobweb of prematrimonial acquaintanceship?[3]

[1] Middlemarch, chapter XXXVI.
[2] Middlemarch, chapter VI.
[3] Ibid. chapter II.

Many of her critics have asserted that this use of the language of science, and the adoption of the speculative ideas of the time, had largely increased upon George Eliot in her later books; but this is not true. In her *Westminster Review* essays both tendencies are strongly developed. In one of them she says, "The very chyme and chyle of a rector are conscious of the gown and band." Again, she says, —

> The woman of large capacity can seldom rise beyond the absorption of ideas; her physical conditions refuse to support the energy required for spontaneous activity; the voltaic pile is not strong enough to produce crystallization.

It is not just to George Eliot, however, to refer to such mere casual blemishes, without insisting on the largeness of thought, the wealth of knowledge, and the comprehensive understanding of human experience with which her books abound. She often turns aside to discuss the problems suggested by the experiences of her characters, to point out how the effect of their own thoughts and deeds re-act upon them, and to inculcate the highest ethical lessons. In one of her "asides" she seems to reject this method, in referring to Fielding.

> A great historian, as he insisted on calling himself, who had the happiness to be dead a hundred and twenty years ago, and so to take his place among the colossi whose huge legs our living pettiness is observed to walk under, glories in his copious remarks and digressions as the least imitable part of his work, and especially in those initial chapters to the successive books of his history, where he seems to bring his arm-chair to the proscenium, and chat with us in all the lusty ease of his fine English. But Fielding lived when the days were longer (for time, like money, is measured by our needs), when summer afternoons were spacious, and the clock ticked slowly in the winter evenings. We belated historians must not linger after his example; and if we did so, it is probable that our chat would be thin and eager, as if delivered from a camp-stool in a parrot-house. I, at least, have so much to do in unravelling certain human lots, and seeing how they were woven and interwoven, that all the light I can command must be concentrated on this particular web, and not dispersed over that tempting range of relevancies called the universe.[1]

She does not ramble away from her subject, it is true;

[1] Middlemarch, chapter XV.

but she likes to pause often to discuss the doings of her personages, and to pour forth some tender or noble thought. To many of her readers these bits of wisdom and of sentiment are among the most valuable portions of her books, when taken in their true environment in her pages. She has a purpose larger than that of telling a story or of describing the loves of a few men and women. She seeks to penetrate into the motives of life, and to reveal the hidden springs of action; to show how people affect each other; how ideas mould the destinies of the individual. To do all this in that large, artistic spirit she has followed, requires that there shall be something more than narration and conversation. That she has now and then commented unnecessarily, and in a too-learned manner, is a very small detraction from the interest of her books.

In *Adam Bede* she turns aside for a whole chapter to defend her method of depicting accurately, minutely, in the simplest detail, the feelings, motives, actions and surroundings of very commonplace and uninteresting people. Her reasons for this method in novel-writing apply to all her works, and are worthy of the author of *Adam Bede* and *Silas Marner*.

I would not, even if I had the choice, be the clever novelist who could create a world so much better than this, in which we get up in the morning to do our daily work, that you would be likely to turn a harder, colder eye on the dusty streets and the common green fields — on the real breathing men and women, who can be chilled by your indifference or injured by your prejudice; who can be cheered and helped onward by your fellow-feeling, your forbearance, your outspoken, brave justice.

So I am content to tell my simple story, without trying to make things seem better than they were; dreading nothing, indeed, but falsity, which, in spite of one's best efforts, there is reason to dread. Falsehood is so easy, truth so difficult. The pencil is conscious of a delightful facility in drawing a griffin — the longer the claws, and the larger the wings, the better; but that marvellous facility, which we mistook for genius, is apt to forsake us when we want to draw a real unexaggerated lion. Examine your words well, and you will find that, even when you have no motive to be false, it is a very hard thing to say the exact truth, even about your own immediate feelings — much harder than to say something fine about them which is *not* the exact truth.

It is for this rare, precious quality of truthfulness that I delight in many Dutch paintings, which lofty-minded people despise. I find a source of delicious sympathy in these faithful pictures of a monotonous homely existence, which has been the fate of so many more among my fellow-mortals than a life of pomp or of absolute indigence, of tragic suffering or of world-stirring actions. I turn without shrinking, from cloud-borne angels, from prophets, sibyls and heroic warriors, to an old woman bending over her flower-pot, or eating her solitary dinner, while the noonday light, softened, perhaps, by a screen of leaves, falls on her mob-cap, and just touches the rim of her spinning-wheel and her stone jug, and all those cheap, common things which are the precious necessaries of life to her: or I turn to that village wedding, kept between four brown walls, where an awkward bridegroom opens the dance with a high-shouldered, broad-faced bride, while elderly and middle-aged friends look on, with very irregular noses and lips, and probably with quart pots in their hands, but with expression of unmistakable contentment and good-will. "Foh!" says my idealistic friend, "what vulgar details! What good is there in taking all these pains to give an exact likeness of old women and clowns? What a low phase of life! what clumsy, ugly people!"

But, bless us, things may be lovable that are not altogether handsome, I hope? I am not at all sure that the majority of the human race have not been ugly, and even among those "lords of their kind," the British, squat figures, ill-shapen nostrils, and dingy complexions, are not startling exceptions. Yet there is a great deal of family love among us. I have a friend or two whose class of features is such that the Apollo curl on the summit of their brows would be decidedly trying; yet, to my certain knowledge, tender hearts have beaten for them, and their miniatures — flattering, but still not lovely — are kissed in secret by motherly lips. I have seen many an excellent matron who could never in her best days have been handsome, and yet she had a packet of yellow love-letters in a private drawer, and sweet children showered kisses on her sallow cheeks. And I believe there have been plenty of young heroes of middle stature and feeble beards, who have felt quite sure they could never love anything more insignificant than a Diana, and yet have found themselves in middle life happily settled with a wife who waddles. Yes! thank God; human feeling is like the mighty rivers that bless the earth; it does not wait for beauty — it flows with resistless force, and brings beauty with it.

All honor and reverence to the divine beauty of form! Let us cultivate it to the utmost in men, women and children — in our gardens and in our houses; but let us love that other beauty, too, which lies in no secret of proportion, but in the secret of deep sympathy. Paint us an angel, if you can, with a floating violet robe, and a face paled by the celestial light; paint us yet oftener a Madonna, turning her mild face upward, and opening her arms to welcome the divine glory; but do not impose on us any æsthetic rules which shall banish from the regions of Art those old women scraping carrots with their work-worn hands, those heavy clowns taking holiday in a dingy pot-house — those rounded-backs and stupid, weather-beaten faces that have bent over the spade and done the rough work of the world — those homes with their tin pans, their brown pitchers, their rough curs, and their clusters of onions. In this world there are so many of these common, coarse people, who have no picturesque sentimental wretchedness! It is so needful we should remember their existence, else we may happen to leave them quite out of our religion and philosophy, and frame lofty theories which only fit a world of extremes. Therefore let Art always remind us of them; therefore let us always have men ready to give the loving pains of a life to the faithful representing of commonplace things — men who see beauty in these commonplace things, and delight in showing how kindly the light of heaven falls on them.

There are few prophets in the world — few sublimely beautiful women — few heroes. I can't afford to give all my love and reverence to such rarities; I want a great deal of those feelings for my every-day fellow-men, especially for the few in the foreground of the great multitude, whose faces I know, whose hands I touch, for whom I have to make way with kindly courtesy. Neither are picturesque lazzaroni or romantic criminals half so frequent as your common laborer, who gets his own bread, and eats it vulgarly, but creditably, with his own pocket-knife. It is more needful that I should have a fibre of sympathy connecting me with that vulgar citizen who weighs out my sugar in a vilely assorted cravat and waistcoat, than with the handsomest rascal in red scarf and green feathers; more needful that my heart should swell with loving admiration at some trait of gentle goodness in the faulty people who sit at the same hearth with me, or in the clergyman of my own parish, who is, perhaps, rather too corpulent, and in other respects is not an Oberlin or a Tillotson, than at the deeds of heroes whom I shall never know except by hearsay, or at the sublimest abstract of all clerical graces that was ever conceived by an able novelist.[1]

In all her earlier novels George Eliot has shown the artistic possibilities of the humblest lives and situations. In the most ordinary lives, as in the case of the persons described in *Silas Marner*, and in the least picturesque incidents of human existence, there is an interest for us which, when properly brought out, will be sure to absorb our attention. She has abundantly proved that dramatic situations, historic surroundings and heroic attitudes are not necessary for the highest purposes of the novelist. Hers are heart tragedies and spiritual histories; for life has its tragic, pathetic and

[1] Adam Bede, chapter XVII.

humorous elements of the keenest interest under every social condition. Her realism is relieved, as in actual life, by love, helpfulness and pathos; by deep sorrow, sufferings patiently borne, and tender sympathy for others' woes. And if she sometimes sketches with too free a hand the coarse and repulsive features of life, this fault is relieved by her tender sympathy with the sorrows and weaknesses of her characters. She asks her readers not to grudge Amos Barton his lovely wife, that "large, fair, gentle Madonna," with an imposing mildness and the unspeakable charm of gentle womanhood. He was a man of very middling qualities and a quite stupid sort of person, but he loved his wife and made the most he could of such talents as he had. She pleads in his behalf by saying, —

> I have all my life had a sympathy for mongrel ungainly dogs, who are nobody's pets; and I would rather surprise one of them by a pat and a pleasant morsel, than meet the condescending advances of the loveliest Skye-terrier who has his cushion by my lady's chair.

Much the larger number of characters in these novels are of the same unpromising quality. Most of them are ignorant, uncouth and simple-minded; yet George Eliot gives them a warm place in our hearts, and we rejoice to have known them all. This ignorant rusticity is discovered to have charms and attractions of its own. Especially does the reader learn that what is most human and what is most lovely in personal character may be found within these rough exteriors and amid these unpromising circumstances.

Even so fine a character as Adam Bede, one of the best in all her books, was a workman of limited education and little knowledge of the outside world. The author does "not pretend that his was an ordinary character among workmen." Yet such men as he are found among his class, and the noble qualities he possessed are not out of place among workingmen. Her warm sympathy with this class, the class in which she was born and reared, and her earnest desire to do it justice, is seen in what she says of Adam.

> He was not an average man. Yet such men as he are reared here and there in every generation of our peasant artisans — with an inheritance of affections nurtured by a simple family life of common need and common industry, and an inheritance of faculties trained in skilful, courageous labor; they make their way upward, rarely as geniuses, most commonly as painstaking, honest men, with the skill and conscience to do well the tasks that lie before them. Their lives have no discernible echo beyond the neighborhood where they dwelt, but you are almost sure to find there some good piece of road, some building, some application of mineral produce, some improvement in farming practice, some reform of parish abuses, with which their names are associated by one or two generations after them. Their employers were richer for them, the work of their hands has worn well, and the work of their brains has guided well the hands of other men. They went about in their youth in flannel or paper caps, in coats black with coal-dust or streaked with lime and red paint; in old age their white hairs are seen in a place of honor at church and at market, and they tell their well-dressed sons and daughters seated round the bright hearth on winter evenings, how pleased they were when they first earned their twopence a day. Others there are who die poor, and never put off the workman's coat on week-days; they have not had the art of getting rich; but they are men of trust, and when they die before the work is all out of them, it is as if some main screw had got loose in a machine; the master who employed them says, "Where shall I find their like?"[1]

In *Amos Barton* she states her reasons for portraying characters of so little outward interest. Amos had none of the more manly and sturdy qualities of Adam Bede, and yet to George Eliot it was enough that he was human, that trouble and heartache could come to him, and that he must carry his share of the burdens and weaknesses of the world.

> The Rev. Amos Barton, whose sad fortunes I have undertaken to relate, was, you perceive, in no respect an ideal or exceptional character; and perhaps I am doing a bold thing to bespeak your sympathy on behalf of a man who was so very far from remarkable, — a man whose virtues were not heroic, and who had no undetected crime within his breast; who had not the slightest mystery hanging about him, but was palpably and unmistakably commonplace; who was not even in love, but had had that complaint many years ago. "An utterly uninteresting character!" I think I hear a lady reader exclaim, — Mrs. Farthingale, for example,

[1] Chapter XIX.

who prefers the ideal in fiction; to whom tragedy means ermine tippets, adultery and murder; and comedy, the adventures of some personage who is quite a "character."

But, my dear madam, it is so very large a majority of your fellow-countrymen that are of this insignificant stamp. At least eighty out of a hundred of your adult male fellow-Britons returned in the last census are neither extraordinarily silly, nor extraordinarily wicked, nor extraordinarily wise; their eyes are neither deep and liquid with sentiment, nor sparkling with suppressed witticisms; they have probably had no hairbreadth escapes or thrilling adventures; their brains are certainly not pregnant with genius, and their passions have not manifested themselves at all after the fashion of a volcano. They are simply men of complexions more or less muddy, whose conversation is more or less bald and disjointed. Yet these commonplace people — many of them — bear a conscience, and have felt the sublime prompting to do the painful right; they have their unspoken sorrows, and their sacred joys; their hearts have perhaps gone out towards their first-born, and they have mourned over the irreclaimable dead. Nay, is there not a pathos in their very insignificance, — in our comparison of their dim and narrow existence with the glorious possibilities of that human nature which they share?

Depend upon it, you would gain unspeakably if you would learn with me to see some of the poetry and the pathos, the tragedy and the comedy, lying in the experience of a human soul that looks out through dull gray eyes, and that speaks in a voice of quite ordinary tones. In that case, I should have no fear of your not caring to know what further befell the Rev. Amos Barton, or of your thinking the homely details I have to tell at all beneath your attention.

In her hands the novel becomes the means of recording the history of those whom no history takes note of, and of bringing before the world its unnamed and unnoted heroes. Professor Dowden says her sympathy spreads with a powerful and even flow in every direction. In this effort she has been eminently successful; and her loving sympathy with all that is human; her warm-hearted faith in the weak and unfortunate; the graciousness of her love for the common souls who are faithful and true in their way and in their places, will excuse much greater literary faults than any into which she has fallen. The sincere and loving humanity of her books gives them a great charm, and an influence wide-reaching and noble.

No one of her imitators and successors has gained

anything of like power which is given to her novels by her intense sympathy with her characters. Others have described ignorant and coarse phases of life as something to look at and study, but not to bring into the heart and love. George Eliot loves her characters, has an intense affection for them, pours out her motherliness upon them. Not so Daudet or James or Howells, who study crude life on the surface, and because it is the fashion. There is no heart-nearness in their work, little of passionate human desire to do justice to phases of life hitherto neglected. She has in this regard the genius of Scott and Hugo, who live in and with their characters, and so make them living and real. She identifies herself with the life she describes, and never looks at it from without, with curious and cold and critical gaze, simply for the sake of making a novel.

She is more at home among villagers than in the drawing-room. A profound intuition has led her to the very heart of English life among the happier and worthier classes of working-people. There is no squalor in her books, no general misery, but always conscience, respectability and home-comforts. There is something of coarseness in some of her scenes, and a realism too bare and bald; but for the most part she has come far short of what might have been done in picturing the repulsive and sensual side of life. In all her books there is abundant evidence of her painstaking, and of her anxious desire to be truthful. She has studied life on the spot, and gives to it the local coloring. In writing *Romola*, she searched into every corner of Florentine history, custom and thought. She is true to every touch of local incident and manner. In *Daniel Deronda*, she made herself familiar with Jewish life, and has given the race aroma to her portraits and scenes. She is thoroughly a realist, but a realist with a wide and attractive sympathy, a profound insight into motives and impulses, and a strong imagination. She is too great a genius to believe that the novelist can describe life as the geologist describes the strata of the earth. She feels with her characters; she has that form of insight or imagination which enables her to apprehend a mind totally unlike her own. This is what saves the history of Hetty from coarseness and repulsiveness. It is Hetty's own account of her life-woes. Its infinite pathos, and the tenderness and pity it awakens, destroys our concern for the other features of the narrative.

Psychologic analysis seems out of place in a novel, but with George Eliot it is a chief purpose of her writing. She lays bare the soul, opens its inmost secrets, and its anatomy is minutely studied. She devotes more space to the inner life and character of her personalities than to her narratives and conversations. She traces some of her characters through a long process of development, and shows how they are affected by the experiences of life. Her more important characters grow up under her pen, develop under the influence of thought or sorrow. Novelists usually carry their characters through their pages on the same level of mind and life; and George Eliot not only does this with her uncultured characters, but she also shows the soul in the process of unfolding or expanding. None of her leading characters are at the end what they were in the beginning; with the most subtle power she traces the growth of Tito Melema's mind through its perilous descent into selfish corruption, and with equal or even greater skill she unfolds the history of Daniel Deronda's development under the impulse to find for himself a life-mission. In this direction George Eliot is always great. Her skill is remarkable, albeit she has not sounded either the highest or the lowest ranges of human capacity. The range within which her studies are made is a wide one, however, and within it she has shown herself the master of human motives and a consummate artist in portraying the soul. She devotes the utmost care to describing some plain person who appears in her pages for but a moment, and is as much concerned that he shall be truly presented as if he were of the utmost consequence. More than one otherwise very ordinary character acquires under this treatment of hers the warmest interest for the reader. And she describes such persons, because their influence is subtle or momentous as it affects the lives of others. Personages and incidents play a part in her books not for the sake of the plot or to secure dramatic unity, but for the sake of manifesting the soul, in order that the unfoldment of psychologic analysis may go on. The unity she aims at is that of showing the development of the soul under influence of some one or more decisive impulses or as affected by given surroundings. The lesser characters, while given a nature quite their own, help in the process of unfolding the personality which gives central purpose to each of her novels. The influence of opposite natures on each other, the moulding power of circumstances, and especially the bearings of hereditary impulses, all play a prominent part in this process of psychologic analysis.

Through page after page and chapter after chapter she traces the feelings and thoughts of her characters. How each decisive event appears to them is explained at length. Moreover, the most trivial trait of character, the most incidental impulse, is described in all its particularity. Through many pages Hetty's conduct in her own bedroom is laid before the reader, and in no other way could her nature have been so brought to our knowledge. Her shallow lightness of heart and her vanity could not be realized by ordinary intercourse with one so pretty and so bright; but George Eliot describes Hetty's taking out the earrings given her by Arthur, and we see what she is. The author seeks to open before us the inner life of that childish soul, and we see into its nature and realize all its capacities for good and evil.

Oh, the delight of taking out that little box and looking at the earrings! Do not reason about it, my philosophical reader, and say that Hetty, being very pretty, must have known that it did not signify whether she had any ornaments or not; and that, moreover, to look at earrings which she could not possibly wear out of her bedroom could hardly be a satisfaction, the essence of vanity being a reference to the impressions produced on others; you will never understand women's natures if you are so excessively rational. Try rather to divest yourself of all your rational prejudices, as much as if you were studying the psychology of a canary-bird, and only watch the movements of this pretty round creature as she turns her head on one side with an unconscious smile at the earrings nestled in the little box. Ah! you think, it is for the sake of the person who has given them to her, and her thoughts are gone back now to the moment when they were put into her hands. No; else why should she have cared to have earrings rather than anything else? and I know that she had longed for earrings from among all the ornaments she could imagine.

This faculty of soul interpretation may be illustrated by innumerable passages and from characters the most diverse in nature and capacity. As an instance of her ability to interpret uncommon minds, those affected in some peculiar manner, reference may be made to Baldassarre, in *Romola*. The descriptions of this man's sufferings, the giving way of his mind under them, and the purpose of revenge which took complete possession of him, form a study in character unsurpassed. For subtle insight into the action of a morbid mind, and for a majestic conception of human passion, the passage wherein Baldassarre finds he can again read his Greek book is most worthy of attention.

Her ability to delineate a growing mind, and a mind at work under the influence of new and rare experiences, is shown in the case of Daniel Deronda. His quiet love of ease as a boy is described as he sits one day watching the falling rain, and meditates on the possibility which has been suggested to him, that his is not to be the life of a gentleman.

He knew a great deal of what it was to be a gentleman by inheritance, and without thinking much about himself—for he was a boy of active perceptions, and easily forgot his own existence in that of Robert Bruce—he had never supposed that he could be shut out from such a lot, or have a very different part in the world from that of the uncle who petted him . . . But Daniel's tastes were altogether in keeping with his nurture: his disposition was one in which every-day scenes and habits beget not *ennui* or rebellion but delight, affection, aptitudes; and now the lad had been stung to the quick by the idea that his uncle — perhaps his father — thought of a career for him which was totally unlike his own, and which he knew very well was not thought of among possible destinations for the sons of English gentlemen.

The mind of this lad expands; ideal desires awake in him; there is a yearning for a life of noble knight-errantry in some heroic cause. The reader is permitted to watch from step to step the growth of this longing, and to behold each new deed by which it is expressed. He craves for a broader life, but he is surrounded by such a social atmosphere as to make his longing futile. As a young man who is seeking to know what there is in the world for him to do, and who is eager for some task that is to end in a larger life for man, he is again described.

It happened that the very vividness of his impressions had often made him the more enigmatic to his friends, and had contributed to an apparent indefiniteness in his sentiments. His early wakened sensibility and reflectiveness, had developed into a many-sided sympathy, which threatened to hinder any persistent course of action: as soon as he took up any antagonism, though only in thought, he seemed to himself like the Sabine warriors in the memorable story — with nothing to meet his spear but flesh of his flesh, and objects that he loved. His imagination had so wrought itself to the habit of seeing things as they probably appeared to others, that a strong partisanship, unless it were against an immediate oppression, had become an insincerity for him. His plenteous, flexible sympathy had ended by falling into one current with that reflective analysis which tends to neutralize sympathy. Few men were able to keep themselves clearer of vices than he; yet he hated vices mildly, being used to think of them less in the abstract than as a part of mixed human natures having an individual history, which it was the bent of his mind to trace with understanding and pity. With the same innate balance he was fervidly democratic in his feeling for the multitude, and yet, through his affections and imagination, intensely conservative; voracious of speculations on government and religion, yet loath to part with long-sanctioned forms which, for him, were quick with memories and sentiments that no argument could lay dead . . . He was ceasing to care for knowledge — he had no ambition for practice — unless they could both be gathered up into one current with his emotions; and he dreaded, as if it were a dwelling-place of lost souls, that dead anatomy of culture which turns the universe into a mere ceaseless answer to queries, and knows, not everything, but everything else about everything

-- as if one should be ignorant of nothing concerning the scent of violets except the scent itself, for which one had no nostril. But how and whence was the needed event to come? — the influence that would justify partiality, and make him what he longed to be, yet was unable to make himself — an organic part of social life, instead of roaming in it like a yearning disembodied spirit, stirred with a vague, social passion, but without fixed local habitation to render fellowship real? To make a little difference for the better was what he was not contented to live without; but how make it? It is one thing to see your road, another to cut it.

He rescues Mirah and sets out in search of her brother. He finds Mordecai, and gradually a way is opened to him along which his yearning is satisfied. Step by step the reader is permitted to trace the expansion of his mind. A window is opened into his soul, and we see its every movement as Daniel is led on to find the mission which was to be his. When that task is fully accepted he says to Mordecai, —

Since I began to read and know, I have always longed for some ideal task, in which I might feel myself the heart and brain of a multitude — some social captainship, which would come to me as a duty, and not to be striven for as a personal prize.

In her strong tendency to psychologic analysis George Eliot much resembles Robert Browning. It is the life of passion and ideas which both alike delight to describe. They greatly differ, however, in their methods of dissecting the inner life. Browning lays bare the soul in some startling experience, George Eliot by the slow development of the mind through all the stages of growth. He is impersonal, but she is always present to make comments and to expound the causes of growth. Yet her characters are as clear-cut, as individual, as his. His analysis is the more rapid, subtle and complete in immediate expression; hers is the more penetrating, vigorous and interesting. His lightning flash sees the soul through and through in the present moment; her calmer and intenser gaze penetrates the long succession of hidden causes by which the soul is shaped to its earthly destiny.

Any account of George Eliot which dwells only on her humor and sarcasm, her realism and her powers of analysis, does her grave injustice. She has also in rare degree the power of artistic constructiveness, a strong and brilliant imagination and genius of almost the highest range. She can create character as well as analyze it, and with that brilliant command of resources which indicates a high order of genius. She had culture almost equal to Goethe's, and quite equal to Mrs. Browning's; and she had that wide sympathy with life which was his, with an equal capacity for their expression in an artistic reconstruction of human experience. While Mr. R. H. Hutton is justified in saying that "few minds at once so speculative and so creative have ever put their mark on literature," yet the critic needs to beware lest he give the speculative tendency in her mind a place too prominent compared with that assigned to her creative genius. The poet and the novelist are so seldom speculative, so seldom put into their creations the constant burden of great thoughts, that when one appears who does this, it is likely to be dwelt upon too largely by the critics. George Eliot speculates about life and its experiences, and it is evident she had a philosophy of life at her command; but it is quite as true that she soars on pinions free into the heavens of genius, and brings back the song which no other has sung, and which is a true song. She has created characters, she has described the histories of souls, in a manner which will cause some of her books to endure for all time. If she has allied her genius to current culture and speculation, it has in that way been given continuity of purpose and definiteness of aim. The genius is there and cannot be hidden or obscured; and those who love what is great and noble will be profoundly attracted by her books. If a great thinker, she is still more truly a great literary artist; and such is the largeness and gracious power of her genius that those who do not love her speculations will be drawn to her in spite of all objections. Her genius is generous, expansive, illuminative, profound. Her creativeness is an elemental power; new births are to be found in her books; life has grown under her moulding touch.

VII.

THEORY OF THE NOVEL.

BEFORE George Eliot began her career as a novelist she had already turned her attention to what is good and bad in fiction-writing, and had given expression to her own theory of the novel. What she wrote on this subject is excellent in itself, but it now has an additional interest in view of her success as a novelist, and as throwing light on her conception of the purposes to be followed in the writing of fiction. In what she wrote on this subject two ideas stand out distinctly, that women are to find in novel-writing a literary field peculiarly adapted to their capacities, and that the novel should be a true portraiture of life.

She was a zealous advocate of woman's capacity to excel as a novelist, and she saw in this form of literature a field especially adapted to her greater powers of emotion and sympathy. Very generous and appreciative are her references to the lady novelists whom she defends, the excellence of whose work she maintains entitles them to the highest places as literary artists. In the article on "Lady Novelists" she has drawn attention both to those qualities in which woman may excel and to those in which she may fail. In writing later of "Silly Novels by Lady Novelists" she criticised unsparingly those women who write novels without comprehending life or any of its problems, and who write in a merely artificial manner. The width of her own culture, the vigor of her critical talent, the largeness of her conception of life and its interests, are well expressed in these essays. Only a large mind could have so truly conceived the real nature of woman's relations to literature, and expressed them in a spirit so intelligent and comprehensive. She would have the whole of life portrayed, and she believes only a woman can truly speak for women. But her faith in woman seems not to have been of the revolutionary character. She rather preferred that women should achieve a higher social condition by deeds than by words. A great intellectual career like her own, which places a woman in the front rank of literary creators, does more to elevate the position of women than any amount of agitation in favor of suffrage. That she sought for the highest intellectual achievement, and that she labored to attain the widest results of scholarship, is greatly to her credit; but more to her credit is it, that she made no claim upon the public as a woman, but only as a literary artist. She asked that her work should be judged on its literary merits, as the product of intellect, and not with reference to her sex. While believing that woman can do her work best by being true to the instincts, sympathies and capacities of her sex, yet she would have the same standard of literary judgment applied to women as to men. Its truthfulness, its reality, its power to widen our sympathies and enlarge our culture, its measure of genius and moral power, is the true test to be applied to any literary work. Such being her conception of the manner in which women should be judged when becoming literary creators, she had no excuses to offer for those who make use of prejudices and a false culture in their own behalf. She says that

> The most mischievous form of feminine silliness is the literary form, because it tends to confirm the popular prejudice against the solid education of women.

That she believed in the solid education of women is apparent in her own efforts towards obtaining it for herself, and her conception of what is to be done with it was large and generous. Mere learning she did not hold to be an adornment in a woman. The culture must be transmuted into life-power, and be poured forth, not as oracular wisdom in silly novels, but as sympathy and enlarged comprehension of the daily duties of life. When educated women "mistake vagueness for depth, bombast for eloquence, and affectation for originality," she is not surprised that men regard rhodomontade as the native accent of woman's intellect, or that they come to the conclusion that "the average nature of women is too shallow and feeble a soil to bear much tillage."

> It is true that the men who come to such a decision on such very superficial and imperfect observation may not be among the wisest in the world; but we have not now to contest their opinion — we are only pointing out how it is unconsciously encouraged by many women who have volunteered themselves as representatives of the feminine intellect. We do not believe that a man was ever strengthened in such an opinion by associating with a woman of true culture, whose mind had absorbed her knowledge instead of being absorbed by it. A really cultured woman, like a really cultured man, is all the simpler and the less obtrusive for her knowledge; it has made her see herself and her opinions in something like just proportions; she does not make it a pedestal from which she flatters herself that she commands a complete view of men and things, but makes it a point of observation from which to form a right estimate of herself. . . . She does not write books to confound philosophers, perhaps because she is able to write books that delight them. In conversation she is the least formidable of women, because she understands you, without wanting to make you aware that you *can't* understand her. She does not give you information, which is the raw material of culture, — she gives you sympathy, which is its subtlest essence.

After this estimate of the value of culture to women, it is interesting to turn to George Eliot's words concerning the legitimate work which women can perform in literature. What she says on this subject shows that she not only had culture, but also the wisdom which is its highest result. She saw that while a woman is to ask for no leniency towards her work because she is a woman, yet that she is not to imitate men or to ignore her sex. She is to portray life as a woman sees it, with a woman's sympathies and experiences. To interpret the feminine side of life is her legitimate province as a literary artist.

If we regard literature as the expression of the emotions, the whims, the caprices, the enthusiasms, the fluctuating idealisms which move each epoch, we shall not be far wrong; and inasmuch as women necessarily take part in these things, they ought to give them *their* expression. And this leads us to the heart of the question, what does the literature of women mean? It means this: while it is impossible for men to express life otherwise than as they know it—and they can only know it profoundly according to their own experience—the advent of female literature promises woman's view of life, woman's experience; in other words, a new element. Make what distinctions you please in the social world, it still remains true that men and women have different organizations, consequently different experiences. To know life you must have both sides depicted. Let him paint what he knows. And if you limit woman's sphere to the domestic circle, you must still recognize the concurrent necessity of domestic life finding its homeliest and truest expression in the woman who lives it.

Keeping to the abstract heights we have chosen, too abstract and general to be affected by exceptions, we may further say that the masculine mind is characterized by the predominance of the intellect, and the feminine by the predominance of the emotions. According to this rough division, the regions of philosophy would be assigned to men, those of literature to women. We need scarcely warn the reader against too rigorous an interpretation of this statement, which is purposely exaggerated the better to serve as a sign-post. It is quite true that no such absolute distinction will be found in authorship. There is no man whose mind is shrivelled up into pure intellect; there is no woman whose intellect is completely absorbed by her emotions. But in most men the intellect does not move in such inseparable alliance with the emotions as in most women, and hence, although often not so great as in women, yet the intellect is more commonly dominant. In poets, artists, and men of letters, *par excellence*, we observe this feminine trait, that their intellect habitually moves in alliance with their emotions; and one of the best descriptions of poetry was that given by Professor Wilson, as the "intellect colored by the feelings."

Woman, by her greater affectionateness, her greater range and depth of emotional experience, is well fitted to give expression to the emotional facts of life, and demands a place in literature corresponding to that she occupies in society; and that literature must be greatly benefited thereby, follows from the definition we have given of literature.

But hitherto, in spite of illustrations, the literature of woman has fallen short of its function, owing to a very natural and a very explicable weakness—it has been too much a literature of imitation. To write as men write, is the aim and besetting sin of women; to write as women, is the real office they have to perform. Our definition of literature includes this necessity. If writers are bound to express what they have really known, felt and suffered, that very obligation imperiously declares they shall not quit their own point of view for the point of view of others. To imitate is to abdicate. We are in no need of more male writers; we are in need of genuine female experience. The prejudices, notions, passions and conventionalisms of men are amply illustrated; let us have the same fulness with respect to women. Unhappily the literature of women may be compared with that of Rome: no amount of graceful talent can disguise the internal defect. Virgil, Ovid and Catullus were assuredly gifted with delicate and poetic sensibility; but their light is, after all, the light of moons reflected from the Grecian suns, and such as brings little life with its rays. To speak in Greek, to think in Greek, was the ambition of all cultivated Romans, who could not see that it would be a grander thing to utter their pure Roman natures in sincere originality. So of women. The throne of intellect has so long been occupied by men, that women naturally deem themselves bound to attend the court. Greece domineered over Rome; its intellectual supremacy was recognized, and the only way of rivalling it seemed to be imitation. Yet not *so* did Rome vanquish Pyrrhus and his elephants; not by employing elephants to match his, but by Roman valor.

Of all departments of literature, fiction is the one to which, by nature and by circumstance, women are best adapted. Exceptional women will of course be found competent to the highest success in other departments; but speaking generally, novels are their forte. The domestic experiences which form the bulk of woman's knowledge finds an appropriate form in novels; while the very nature of fiction calls for that predominance of sentiment which we have already attributed to the feminine mind. Love is the staple of fiction, for it "forms the story of a woman's life." The joys and sorrows of affection, the incidents of domestic life, the aspirations and fluctuations of emotional life, assume typical forms in the novel. Hence we may be prepared to find women succeeding better in *finesse* of detail, in pathos and sentiment, while men generally succeed better in the construction of plots and the delineation of character. Such a novel as *Tom Jones* or *Vanity Fair* we shall not get from a woman, nor such an effort of imaginative history as *Ivanhoe* or *Old Mortality;* but Fielding, Thackeray and Scott are equally excluded from such perfection in its kind as *Pride and Prejudice*, *Indiana* or *Jane Eyre*. As an artist Jane Austen surpasses all the male novelists that ever lived; and for eloquence and depth of feeling no man approaches George Sand.

We are here led to another curious point in our subject, viz., the influence of sorrow upon female literature. It may be said without exaggeration that almost all literature has some remote connection with suffering. "Speculation," said Novalis, "is disease." It certainly springs from a vague disquiet. Poetry is analogous to the pearl which the oyster secretes in its malady.

"Most wretched men
Are cradled into poetry by wrong,
They learn in suffering what they teach in song."

What Shelley says of poets, applies with greater force to women.

If they turn their thoughts to literature, it is — when not purely an imitative act — always to solace by some intellectual activity the sorrow that in silence wastes their lives, and by a withdrawal of the intellect from the contemplation of their pain, or by a transmutation of their secret anxieties into types, they escape from the pressure of that burden. If the accidents of her position make her solitary and inactive, or if her thwarted affections shut her somewhat from that sweet domestic and maternal sphere to which her whole being spontaneously moves, she turns to literature as to another sphere. We do not here simply refer to those notorious cases where literature was taken up with the avowed and conscious purpose of withdrawing thoughts from painful subjects; but to the unconscious, unavowed influence of domestic disquiet and unfulfilled expectations, in determining the sufferer to intellectual activity. The happy wife and busy mother are only forced into literature by some hereditary organic tendency, stronger even than the domestic; and hence it is that the cleverest women are not those who have written books.

In the later essay on "Silly Novels" her powers of sarcasm were fully displayed. It showed keen critical powers, and a clear insight into the defects inherent in most novel-writing. She spared no faults, had no mercy for presumption, and condemned unsparingly the pretence of culture. She described four kinds of silly novels, classing them as being of *the mind-and-millinery*, *the oracular*, *the white-neck-cloth*, and *the modern-antique* varieties. All her powers of analysis and insight shown in her novels appeared in this article.

Severe as her criticism is, it is always just. It aims at the presentation of a truer conception of the purpose of novel-writing, and women are judged simply as literary workers. This criticism is based on the clearest apprehension of why it is that women fail as novel-writers; that it is not because they are women, but because they are false to nature and to the simplest conditions of literary art. These women write poor novels because they aim at fine writing, and believe they must be learned and grandiloquent. They ignore what they see about them every day, and which, if they were to describe it in simple language, would give them real power. It is this falsity in thought, method and purpose which is so severely condemned. And it is the very justness of the criticism which makes it severe, which gives to a true description of these novels the nature of a stinging sarcasm. That these women are praised by the critics she justly regards as a sure indication of their incapacity, or a sign of man's chivalry towards the other sex, which does not permit him to speak the truth about what he knows to be so false and immature. She also sees that what women need is to be told the truth, and to be compelled to accept the just consequences of their work.

The standing apology for women who become writers without any special qualification is. that society shuts them out from other spheres of occupation. Society is a very culpable entity, and has to answer for the manufacture of many unwholesome commodities. from bad pickles to bad poetry. But society, like "matter" and her Majesty's Government. and other lofty abstractions. has its share of excessive blame as well as excessive praise. Where there is one woman who writes from necessity. we believe there are three who write from vanity; and besides, there is something so antiseptic in the mere healthy fact of working for one's bread, that the most trashy and rotten kind of literature is not likely to have been produced under such circumstances. "In all labor there is profit;" but ladies' silly novels, we imagine, are less the result of labor than of busy idleness.

Happily we are not dependent on argument to prove that fiction is a department of literature in which women can, after their kind, fully equal men. A cluster of great names, both living and dead, rush to our memories in evidence that women can produce novels not only fine, but among the very finest; — novels, too, that have a precious specialty, lying quite apart from masculine aptitudes and experience. No educational restrictions can shut women out from the materials of fiction, and there is no species of art which is so free from rigid requirements. Like crystalline masses, it may take any form and yet be beautiful; we have only to pour in the right elements — genuine observation, humor and passion. But it is precisely this absence of rigid requirement which constitutes the fatal seduction of novel-writing to incompetent women. Ladies are not wont to be very grossly deceived as to their power of playing on the piano; here certain positive difficulties of execution have to be conquered, and incompetence inevitably breaks down. Every art which has its absolute *technique* is, to a certain extent, guarded from the intrusions of mere left-handed imbecility. But in novel-writing there are no barriers for incapacity to stumble against, no external criteria to prevent a writer from mistaking foolish facility for mastery. And so we have again and again the old story of La Fontaine's ass. who puts his nose to the flute, and, finding that he elicits some sound, exclaims, "Moi, aussi, je joue de la flute;" — a fable which we commend, at parting, to the consideration of any feminine reader who is in danger of adding to the number of "silly novels by lady novelists."

Her praise of the great novelists is as enthusiastic as her condemnation of the silly ones is severe. It is interesting to note that in the first of these papers she selects Jane Austen and George Sand as the chiefest among women novelists, and that she praises them for the truthfulness of their portraitures of life, nor is she any the less aware of the defects of these masters than of the deficiencies of silly women who write novels. She finds that Jane Austen never penetrates into the deeper spiritual experiences of life, and that George Sand lacks in that moral poise and purity which is so necessary to the finest literary effort. Her sketches of these women are as truthful as they are interesting.

First and foremost let Jane Austen be named, the greatest artist that has ever written, using the term to signify the most perfect mastery over the means to her end. There are heights and depths in human nature Miss Austen has never scaled nor fathomed, there are worlds of passionate existence into which she has never set foot; but although this is obvious to every reader, it is equally obvious that she has risked no failures by attempting to delineate that which she has not seen. Her circle may be restricted, but it is complete. Her world is a perfect orb and vital. Life, as it appears to an English gentlewoman peacefully yet actively engaged in her quiet village, is mirrored in her works with a purity and fidelity that must endow them with interest for all time. To read one of her books is like an actual experience of life; you know the people as if you had lived with them, and you feel something of personal affection towards them. The marvellous reality and subtle distinctive traits noticeable in her portraits has led Macaulay to call her a prose Shakspere. If the whole force of the distinction which lies in that epithet *prose* be fairly appreciated, no one, we think, will dispute the compliment; for out of Shakspere it would be difficult to find characters so typical yet so nicely demarcated within the limits of their kind. We do not find such profound psychological insight as may be found in George Sand (not to mention male writers), but taking the type to which the characters belong, we see the most intimate and accurate knowledge in all Miss Austen's creations.

Only cultivated minds fairly appreciate the exquisite art of Miss Austen. Those who demand the stimulus of effects, those who can only see by strong lights and shadows, will find her tame and uninteresting. We may illustrate this by one detail. Lucy Steele's bad English, so delicately and truthfully indicated, would in the hands of another have been more obvious, more "effective" in its exaggeration, but the loss of this comic effect is more than replaced to the cultivated reader by his relish of the nice discrimination visible in its truthfulness. And so of the rest. *Strong* lights are unnecessary, *true* lights being at command. The incidents, the characters, the dialogue—all are of every-day life, and so truthfully presented that to appreciate the art we must try to imitate it, or carefully compare it with that of others.

We are but echoing an universal note of praise in speaking thus highly of her works, and it is from no desire of simply swelling that chorus of praise that we name her here, but to call attention to the peculiar excellence, at once womanly and literary, which has earned this reputation. Of all imaginative writers she is the most *real*. Never does she transcend her own actual experience, never does her pen trace a line that does not touch the experience of others. Herein we recognize the first quality of literature. We recognize the second and more special quality of womanliness in the tone and point of view; they are novels written by a woman, an Englishwoman, a gentlewoman; no signature could disguise that fact; and because she has so faithfully (although unconsciously) kept to her own womanly point of view, her works are durable. There is nothing of the *doctrinaire* in Jane Austen; not a trace of woman's "mission;" but as the most truthful, charming, humorous, pure-minded, quick-witted and unexaggerated of writers, female literature has reason to be proud of her.

And this is her suggestive portrait of the other, drawn with that skill which is only displayed when one genius interprets another through community of feeling and purpose.

Of greater genius, and incomparably deeper experience, George Sand represents woman's literature more illustriously and more obviously. In her, quite apart from the magnificent gifts of nature, we see the influence of sorrow as a determining impulse to write, and the abiding consciousness of the womanly point of view as the subject matter of her writings. In vain has she chosen the mask of a man: the features of a woman are everywhere visible. Since Goethe no one has been able to say with so much truth, "My writings are my confessions." Her biography lies there, presented, indeed, in a fragmentary shape and under wayward disguises, but nevertheless giving to the motley groups the strong and unmistakable charm of reality. Her grandmother, by whom she was brought up, disgusted at her not being a boy, resolved to remedy the misfortune as far as possible by educating her like a boy. We may say of this, as of all the other irregularities of her strange and exceptional life, that whatever unhappiness and error may be traceable thereto, its influence on her writings has been beneficial, by giving a greater range to her experience. It may be selfish to rejoice over the malady which secretes a pearl, but the possessor of the pearl may at least congratulate himself that at any rate the pearl has been produced; and so of the unhappiness of genius. Certainly few women have had such profound and varied experience as George Sand; none have turned it to more account. Her writings contain many passages that her warmest admirers would wish unwritten; but although severe criticism may detect the weak places, the severest criticism must conclude with the admission of her standing among the highest minds of literature. In the matter of eloquence, she surpasses everything France has yet produced. There has been no style at once so large, so harmonious, so expressive, and so unaffected: like a light shining through an alabaster vase, the ideas shine through her diction; while as regards rhythmic melody of phrase, it is a style such as Beethoven might have written had he uttered in words the melodious passion that was in him.

But deeper than all eloquence, grander than all grandeur of phrase, is that forlorn splendor of a life of passionate experience painted in her works. There is no man so wise but he may learn from them, for they are the utterances of a soul in pain, a soul that has been tried. No man could have written her books, for no man could have had her experience, even with a genius equal to her own. The philosopher may smile sometimes at her philosophy, for *that* is only the reflex of some man whose ideas she has adopted; the critic may smile sometimes at her failure in delineating men; but both philosopher and critic must perceive that those writings of hers are *original* and genuine, are transcripts of experience, and as such fulfil the primary condition of all literature.

This clear, intellectual apprehension of what woman can effect in literature, had much to do with George Eliot's own success. Yet it is doubtful if she was so true, in some directions, to the instincts of her sex as was George Sand, Mrs. Browning or Charlotte Brontë. Hers was in large measure an intellect without sex; and though she was a woman in all the instincts of her heart, yet intellectually she occupied the human rather than the woman's point of view. With a marvellous insight into the heart of woman, and great skill in portraying womanly natures, she had a man's way, the logical and impersonal manner, of viewing the greater problems of human existence. Charlotte Brontë more truly represents the woman's way of viewing life; the trustful way of one educated in the conventional views of religion. She has given a correcter interpretation of the meaning of love to woman than George Eliot has been able to present, and simply because she thought and lived more nearly as other women think and live. Hers was the genius of spontaneous insight and emotion, that vibrated to every experience and was moved by every sentiment. Life played upon her heart like the wind upon an æolian harp, and she reflected its every movement of joy and sorrow. George Eliot studied life, probed into it, cut it in pieces, constructed a theory of it, and then told us what it means. In this she was unlike other women who have made a deep impression on literature. Mrs. Browning had nearly as much culture, was as thoughtful as she, but more genuinely feminine at the heart-core. Love she painted in a purer and happier fashion than that adopted by George Eliot, and she had the warmer impulses of a woman's tenderness. Her account of life is the truer, because it is the more ideal; and this may be said for Charlotte Brontë also. George Eliot had the larger intellect, the keener mind, was a profounder thinker; but her realism held her back from that instinctive conception of life which realizes its larger ideal meanings. It is not enough to see what is; man desires to know what ought to be. The poet is the seer, the one who apprehends, who has that finer eye for facts by which he is able to behold what the facts give promise of. This ideal vision Mrs. Browning had, and in so far she was the superior of George Eliot. The same may be said for George Sand, who, with all her wildness and impurity, was a woman through and through. She was all heart, all impulse, lived in her instincts and emotions. She had the abandon, enthusiasm and spontaneity which George Eliot lacked. If the one represents the head, the other expresses the heart of woman. George Eliot, as a woman, thought, reasoned, philosophized; George Sand felt, gave every emotion reign, lived out all her impulses. What the one lacks the other had; where one was weak the other was strong. With somewhat of George Sand's idealism and emotional zeal for wider and freer life, George Eliot would have been a greater writer. Could she have moulded Dorothea with what is best in Consuelo, she would have been the rival of the greatest literary artists among men. Yet, with her limitations, it must be said that George Eliot is the superior of all other women in her literary accomplishments. If others are her superiors in some directions, in the totality of her powers she surpasses all. Even as an interpreter of woman's nature and the feminine side of life, she does not fail to keep well ahead of the best of feminine writers. She is more thoroughly the master of her powers, is more self-centred, looks out upon human experience more calmly and with a more penetrating gaze. Foremost of the half-dozen women who during the present century have sought to interpret the feminine side of life, she has done much for her sex. Daring more than others, she has given a greater promise than any other of what woman is to accomplish when her nature blossoms out into all its possibilities.

The chief rule for novel-writing laid down by George Eliot in these essays is, that the novel shall be the result of experience and true to nature. She emphasizes the importance of this condition, and says that the novelist is bound to use actual experience as his material, and that alone, or else keep silent. Weak and silly novels are the result of an effort to break away from this rule; but the writer who ventures to disregard it never can be other than silly or weak. Novelists, she says, may either portray experience outwardly through observation, or inwardly through sentiment, or through a combination of both.

> Observation without sentiment usually leads to humor or satire; sentiment without observation to rhetoric and long-drawn lachrymosity. The extreme fault of the one is flippant superficiality, that of the other is what is called sickly sentimentality.

All true literature, she says, is based on fact, describes life as it is lived by men and women, touches and is fragrant with reality. This cardinal principle of literary art she has defined and illustrated in her own strong and expressive manner in this *Review* article.

All poetry, all fiction, all comedy, all *belles lettres*, even to the playful caprices of fancy, are but the expression of experiences and emotions; and these expressions are the avenues through which we reach the sacred *adytum* of humanity, and learn better to understand our fellows and ourselves. In proportion as these expressions are the forms of universal truths, of facts common to all nations or appreciable by all intellects, the literature which sets them forth is permanently good and true. Hence the universality and immortality of Homer, Shakspere, Cervantes, Molière. But in proportion as these expressions are the forms of individual, peculiar truths, such as fleeting fashions or idiosyncrasies, the literature is ephemeral. Hence tragedy never grows old, for it arises from elemental experience; but comedy soon ages, for it arises from peculiarities. Nevertheless, even idiosyncrasies are valuable as side glances; they are aberrations that bring the natural orbit into more prominent distinctness.

It follows from what has been said, that literature, being essentially the expression of experience and emotion — of what we have seen, felt and thought — that only *that* literature is effective, and to be prized accordingly, which has *reality for its basis* (needless to say that emotion is as real as the three-per-cents), *and effective in proportion to the depth and breadth of that basis.*

In writing of the authors of *Jane Eyre* and *Mary Barton*, she shows how important to her mind it is that the novel should have its basis in actual experience, and that it should be an expression of reality.

They have both given imaginative expression to actual experience — they have not invented, but reproduced; they have preferred the truth, such as their own experience testified, to the vague, false, conventional notions current in circulating libraries. Whatever of weakness may be pointed out in their works will, we are positive, be mostly in those parts where experience is deserted, and the supposed requirements of fiction have been listened to; whatever has really affected the public mind is, we are equally certain, the transcript of some actual incident, character or emotion. Note, moreover, that beyond this basis of actuality these writers have the further advantage of deep feeling united to keen observation.

Especially severe is her condemnation of the tendency to introduce only fashionable or learned people into novels. She says the silly novelists rarely make us acquainted with "any other than very lofty and fashionable society," and very often the authors know nothing of such society except from the reading of other such novels.

It is true that we are constantly struck with the want of verisimilitude in their representations of the high society in which they seem to live; but then they betray no closer acquaintance with any other form of life. If their peers and peeresses are improbable, their literary men. tradespeople and cottagers are impossible; and their intellect seems to have the peculiar impartiality of reproducing both what they *have* seen and heard, and what they have *not* seen and heard, with equal faithfulness.

What is simple, natural, unaffected, she pleads for as the true material of fiction. How she would apply this idea may be seen in her condemnation of a novelist who devoted her pages to a defence of Evangelicalism. This writer is "tame and feeble" because she attempts to depict a form of society with which she is not familiar. That the common phases of religious life are capable of affording the richest material for the novelist, George Eliot has abundantly shown, and what she says of their value in this discussion of "Silly Novelists" is of great interest in view of her own success in this kind of portraiture. What she suggested as a fine field for the novelist was to be the one she herself was so well to occupy. Her success proved how clearly she comprehended the nature of novel-writing, and how well she understood the character of the material with which the best results can be attained.

It is less excusable in an Evangelical novelist than any other, gratuitously to seek her subjects among titles and carriages. The real drama of Evangelicalism — and it has abundance of fine drama for any one who has genius enough to discern and reproduce it — lies among the middle and lower classes; and are not Evangelical opinions understood to give an especial interest in the weak things of the earth, rather than in the mighty? Why, then, cannot our Evangelical novelists show us the operation of their religious views among people (there really are many such in the world) who keep no carriage, "not so much as a brass-bound gig," who even manage to eat their dinner without a silver fork, and in whose mouths the authoress's questionable English would be strictly consistent? Why can we not have pictures of religious life among the industrial classes in England as interesting as Mrs. Stowe's pictures of religious life among the negroes?

Was this question a prophecy? It indicates that the writer's attention had already been directed to the richness of this material for the purposes of the novelist. After reading these words we see why she took up the common life of the English village as she had herself been familiar with it from childhood. In order to be true to her own conception of the novel, there was no other field she could occupy. That she understood the picturesqueness of this form of life no reader of her novels will doubt, or that she saw and understood its capacities for artistic delineation. The opening paragraphs of her *Westminster Review* article on the "Natural History of German Life" afford further evidence of her insight and wisdom on this subject. They also afford evidence of her hatred of the conventional and the artificial in art, literature and life. The spirit of imitation and mannerism common to the eighteenth century was in every way repugnant to her. She could have had only contempt for the literary art of a Pope or a Boileau. The nature of her realism, and the conception she had of its importance, may be understood from these paragraphs, for in them she has unfolded her theory more clearly than in anything else she has written, and with that genius for sympathetic description which is so marked in her novels.

How little the real characteristics of the working-classes are known to those who are outside them, how little their natural history has been studied, is sufficiently disclosed by our art as well as by our political and social theories. Where, in our picture exhibitions, shall we find a group of true peasantry? What English artist even attempts to rival in truthfulness such studies of popular life as the pictures of Teniers or the ragged boys of Murillo? Even one of the greatest painters of the pre-eminently realistic school, while in his picture of "The Hireling Shepherd" he gave us a landscape of marvellous truthfulness, placed a pair of peasants in the foreground who were not much more real than the idyllic swains and damsels of our chimney ornaments. Only a total absence of acquaintance and sympathy with our peasantry could give a moment's popularity to such a picture as "Cross Purposes," where we have a peasant girl who looks as if she knew L. E. L.'s poems by heart, and English rustics whose costumes seem to indicate that they are meant for ploughmen with exotic features that remind us of a handsome *primo tenore*. Rather than such cockney sentimentality as this as an education for the taste and sympathies, we prefer the most crapulous group of boors that Teniers ever painted. But even thóse among our painters who aim at giving the rustic type of features, who are far above the effeminate feebleness of the "Keepsake" style, treat their subjects under the influence of traditions and prepossessions rather than of direct observation. The notion that peasants are joyous, that the typical moment to represent a man in a smock-frock is when he is cracking a joke and showing a row of sound teeth, that cottage matrons are usually buxom, and village children necessarily rosy and merry, are prejudices difficult to dislodge from the artistic mind, which looks for its subjects into literature instead of life. The painter is still under the influence of idyllic literature, which has always expressed the imagination of the cultivated and town-bred, rather than the truth of rustic life. Idyllic ploughmen are jocund when they drive their team afield; idyllic shepherds make bashful love under hawthorn bushes; idyllic villagers dance in the chequered shade, and refresh themselves, not immoderately, with spicy nut-brown ale. But no one who has seen much of actual ploughmen thinks them jocund; no one who is well acquainted with the English peasantry can pronounce them merry. The slow gaze, in which no sense of beauty beams, no humor twinkles,—the slow utterance and the heavy slouching walk, remind one rather of that melancholy animal, the camel, than of the sturdy countryman with striped stockings, red waistcoat, and hat aside, who represents the traditional English peasant. Observe a company of haymakers, when you see them at a distance, tossing up the forkfuls of hay in the golden light, while the wagon creeps slowly with its increasing burthen over the meadow, and the bright green space which tells of work done gets larger and larger, you pronounce the scene "smiling," and you think that these companions in labor must be as bright and cheerful as the picture to which they give animation. Approach nearer, and you will certainly find that haymaking time is a time of joking, especially if there are women among the laborers; but the coarse laugh that bursts out every now and then, and expresses the triumphant taunt, is as far as possible from your idyllic conception of idyllic merriment. That delicious effervescence of the mind which we call fun has no equivalent for the northern peasant, except tipsy revelry; the only realm of fancy and imagination for the English clown exists at the bottom of the third quart-pot.

The conventional countryman of the stage, who picks up pocket-books and never looks into them, and who is too simple even to know that honesty has its opposite, represents the still lingering mistake that an unintelligible dialect is a guarantee for ingenuousness, and that slouching shoulders indicate an upright disposition. It is quite true that a thresher is likely to be innocent of any adroit arithmetical cheating, but he is not the less likely to carry home his master's corn in his shoes and pocket; a reaper is not given to writing begging letters, but he is quite capable of cajoling the dairy-maid into filling his small-beer bottle with ale. The selfish instincts are not subdued by the sight of buttercups, nor is integrity in the least established by that classic rural occupation, sheep-washing. To make men moral, something more is requisite than to turn them out to grass.

Opera peasants, whose unreality excites Mr. Ruskin's indignation, are surely too frank an idealization to be misleading; and since popular chorus is one of the most effective elements of the opera, we can hardly object to lyric rustics in elegant laced bodices and picturesque motley, unless we are prepared to advocate a chorus of colliers in their pit costume, or a ballet of charwomen and stocking-weavers. But our social novels profess to represent the people as they are, and the unreality of their representations is a grave evil. The greatest benefit we owe to the artist, whether painter, poet or novelist, is the extension of our sympathies. Appeals founded on generalizations and statistics require a sympathy ready-made, a moral sentiment already in activity; but a picture of human life such as a great artist can give, surprises even the trivial and the selfish into that attention to what is apart from themselves, which may be called the raw material of moral sentiment. When Scott takes us into Luckie Mucklebackit's cottage, or tells the story of The Two Drovers,— when Wordsworth sings to us the reverie of Poor Susan, — when Kingsley shows us Alton Locke gazing yearningly over the gate which leads from the highway into the first wood he ever saw, — when Harnung paints a group of chimney-sweepers, — more is done towards linking the higher classes with the lower, towards obliterating the vulgarity of exclusiveness, than by hundreds of sermons and philosophical dissertations. Art is the nearest thing to life; it is a mode of amplifying experience and extending our contact with our fellow-men beyond the bounds of our personal lot. All the more sacred is the task of the artist when he undertakes to paint the life of the people. Falsification here is far more pernicious than in the more artificial aspects of life. It is not so very serious that we should have false ideas about evanescent fashions — about the manners and conversation of beaux and duchesses; but it *is* serious that our sympathy with the perennial joys and struggles, the toil, the tragedy and the humor in the life of our more heavily laden fellow-men, should be perverted, and turned towards a false object instead of the true one.

This perversion is not the less fatal because the misrepresentation which gives rise to it has what the artist considers a moral end. The thing for mankind to know is, not what are the motives and influences which the moralist thinks *ought* to act on the laborer or the artisan, but what are the motives and influences which *do* act on him. We want to be taught to feel, not for the heroic artisan or the sentimental peasant, but for the peasant in all his coarse apathy, and the artisan in all his suspicious selfishness.

We have one great novelist who is gifted with the utmost power of rendering the external traits of our town population; and if he could give us their psychological character — their conceptions of life, and their emotions — with the same truth as their idiom and manners, his books would be the greatest contribution art has ever made to the awakening of social sympathies. But while he can copy Mrs. Plornish's colloquial style with the delicate accuracy of a sun-picture, while there is the same startling inspiration in his description of the gestures and phrases of "Boots," as in the speeches of Shakspere's mobs or numskulls, he scarcely ever passes from the humorous and external to the emotional and tragic, without becoming as transcendent in his unreality as he was a moment before in his artistic truthfulness. But for the precious salt of his humor, which compels him to reproduce external traits that serve, in some degree, as a corrective to his frequently false psychology, his preternaturally virtuous poor children and artisans, his melodramatic bootmen and courtesans, would be as noxious as Eugene Sue's idealized proletaires in encouraging the miserable fallacy that high morality and refined sentiment can grow out of harsh social relations, ignorance and want; or that the working-classes are in a condition to enter at once into a millennial state of *altruism*, wherein every one is caring for every one else, and no one for himself.

If we need a true conception of the popular character to guide our sympathies rightly, we need it equally to check our theories, and direct us in their application. The tendency created by the splendid conquests of modern generalization, to believe that all social questions are merged in economical science, and that the relations of men to their neighbors may be settled by algebraic equations, — the dream that the uncultured classes are prepared for a condition which appeals principally to their moral sensibilities, — the aristocratic dilettantism which attempts to restore the "good old times" by a sort of idyllic masquerading, and to grow feudal fidelity and veneration as we grow prize turnips, by an artificial system of culture, — none of these diverging mistakes can co-exist with a real knowledge of the people, with a thorough study of their habits, their ideas, their motives. The landholder, the clergyman, the mill-owner, the mining agent, have each an opportunity for making precious observations on different sections of the working-class, but unfortunately their experience is too often not registered at all, or its results are too scattered to be available as a source of information and stimulus to the public mind generally. If any man of sufficient moral and intellectual breadth, whose observations would not be vitiated by a foregone conclusion, or by a professional point of view, would devote himself to studying the natural history of our social classes, especially of the small shop-keepers, artisans and peasantry, — the degree in which they are influenced by local conditions, their maxims and habits, the points of view from which they regard their religious teachers, and the degree in which they are influenced by religious doctrines, the interaction of the various classes on each other, and what are the tendencies in their position towards disintegration or towards development, — and if, after all this study, he would give us the result of his observations in a book well nourished with specific facts, his work would be a valuable aid to the social and political reformer.

The estimates given in these essays of the writings of Jane Austen, George Sand, Charlotte Brontë and

Thackeray, show the soundness of George Eliot's critical judgment. She fully appreciated Jane Austen's artistic skill, as she did George Sand's impassioned love of liberty and naturalness. She also saw how tame are Miss Austen's scenes, how humanly imperfect are Thackeray's characters. Her own work is wanting in Jane Austen's artistic skill and finish, but there is far more of originality and character in her books, more of thought and purpose. Miss Austen tells her story wonderfully well, but her books are all on the same level of social mediocrity and flatness. No fresh, strong, natural, aspiring life is to be found in one of them. George Eliot has not Jane Austen's artistic skill, but she has thought, depth of purpose, originality of expression and conception, and a marvellous creative insight into character. She is less passionate and bold than George Sand, not the same daring innovator, more rational and sensible. She is not so much a poet, has little of George Sand's power of improvisation, much less of eloquence and abandon. She has more literary skill than Charlotte Brontë, less originality, but none of her crudeness. She has not so much of the subtle element of genius, but more of solidity and thought.

Her theories concerning the novel place George Eliot fully in sympathy with what may very properly be called the British school of fiction. The natural history of man is the subject matter used by this school; and to describe accurately, minutely, some portion of the human race, some social community, is its main object. Richardson, Fielding, Miss Austen and Thackeray are the masters in this school, who have given direction to its aims and methods. They have sought to accomplish in novel-writing somewhat the same results as those aimed at by Wordsworth and Browning in poetry, to follow the natural, to make much of the common, to describe things as they are. They are realists both in method and philosophy, though differing widely from the minuteness and coarseness of Tourguénief and Zola, in that they show a large element of the ideal interfused with the real. This school is seldom coarse, vulgar or sensuous, does not mistake the depraved and beastly for the natural. Its members delight in simple scenes, plain life, common joys; the scenes, life and joys which are open to every Englishman. They have made use of the facts lying immediately about them, those with which they were the most familiar. They have broken away from the traditional theories of life, the manners of books of etiquette and the rules of fashionable society, for the life which is natural and instinct with impulses of its own. The life of the professions is described, local dialects and provincialisms appear, places and scenery are carefully painted, and the disagreeable and painful become elements in these novels, because common to humanity.

To this special theory of the novel, as it had been worked out by the English masters of prose-poetry, George Eliot added nothing essential. Thackeray, Mrs. Gaskell, Miss Austen, Miss Mitford, Fielding and Richardson had preceded her along the way she was to follow. Their methods became hers, she accepted their influence, and her work was done in the spirit they had so ably illustrated. In one direction, however, she far surpassed any one of her masters, and gave to the novel a richness of power and fulness of aim it had not attained to with any of her predecessors. George Eliot combined other methods with that of naturalism, not adhering rigidly to the purpose of painting life as it appears on the surface. Not only from the pre-Raphaelites, but from such romanticists as Scott, did she learn much. Past scenes became natural, and history was discovered to be a vast element in the thought of the present. Scott's power of reviving the past in all its romantic and picturesque features, which gave him such capacity for re-creating the life that had once passed away, was not possessed by George Eliot. Still, if not a romancist, she realized how mighty is the shaping power of the past over the present. For this reason, she endeavored to recast old scenes, to revive in living shapes the times that had gone by. The living movements of the present, its efforts at reform, its cries for liberty, its searchings after a freer and purer life, also became a prominent element in her novels. If in this tendency she somewhat enlarged upon the methods of her masters, yet she was quite in sympathy with many who came just before her, and with many more who were her contemporaries. In another direction she kept along the way followed by many of her co-workers, and brought philosophy and socialistic speculation to the aid of the naturalistic method. Indeed, she so far departed from that method, and from the soundest theories of art, as to become to some extent a *doctrinaire*.

Her novels, like much of the poetry of the same period, are eclectic in spirit, combining with the naturalistic methods those of the historic, socialistic, culture and speculative schools. Art and culture for their own sake combined in her novels with the purpose to use history and social life obedient to a distinct conception of their meanings. To describe life accurately there must be a clear conception of what life means. Genius never works aimlessly ; and in seeing life as it is, always sees that it has a tendency and direction. A mind so thoughtful as George Eliot's, with so strong a love of speculative interest in it, was likely to give to novel-writing done by her a large philosophic element. Yet her philosophy is nearly always subject to her imagination and to her naturalism. Her love of nature, her intimate interest in life and its elemental problems, her passionate sympathy with all human passions and experiences, saves her from becoming a mere *doctrinaire*, and gives to her speculations a pathetic, living interest. The poetic elements of her novels are so many as to subordinate the philosophic to the true purposes of art.

In one direction George Eliot departed from the methods of her predecessors, and to so great an extent as to be herself the originator of a new school of fiction. She followed the bent of her time for analysis and psychologic interpretation. It is here more than anywhere else she differs from Charlotte Brontë and George Sand. These two great novelists create character by direct representation, by making their persons live and act. George Eliot shows her characters to the reader by analyzing their motives and by giving the history of their development. The disadvantages of the analytic method are apparent when George Eliot is compared with Scott. Unique, personal and human are his creations, instinct with all human emotions, and profoundly real. It is only the poetic side of life which he sees, not its philosophic. George Eliot wanted to know the meanings of things, and this very desire brings a largeness into her books which is not found in Scott's. She was much the more thoughtful of the two, the one who tried to realize to the intellect what life means. Yet her method of doing this is not always the best one for the poet or the novelist. Scott was no realist, and yet George Eliot has not been more accurate than he. Indeed, he is far more truly accurate in so far as he paints the soul as well as the body of life. The sad endings of her novels grew out of a false theory, and from her inability to see anything of spiritual reality beyond the little round of man's earthly destiny. She did not accept the doctrine that art is to be cultivated only for art's sake, for art was always to her the vehicle of moral or philosophic teaching. The limitations of her art largely lay in the direction of her agnosticism. Scott and George Sand gain for their work a great power and effect by their acceptance of the spiritual as real. There is a light, a subtle aroma, a width of vision, a sense of reality, in their work from this source, which is wanting in George Eliot's. The illimitable mystery beyond the region of the real is the greatest fact man has presented to him, and that region is a reality in all the effects it works on humanity. No poet can ignore it or try to limit it to humanity without a loss to his work. It is this subtle, penetrative, aromatic and mystic power of the ideal which is most to be felt as lacking in the works of George Eliot. Much as we may praise her, we can but feel this limitation. Great as is our admiration, we can but feel that there is a higher range of poetic and artistic creation than any she reached.

The quotations presented from her early writings prove that George Eliot began her career as a novelist with a fully elaborated conception of the purposes of the novel and of the methods to be followed in its production. She had thoroughly studied the subject, had read many of the best works of the best writers, and had formed a carefully digested theory of the novel. That she could do this is rather an indication of critical than of creative power. Her novels everywhere betray the greatness of her reasoning powers, that she was a thinker, that she had strong powers of intellectual analysis, and that she had a logical, accurate mind. Had her mind taken no other direction than this, however, she never could have become a great novelist. These essays indicated something beside powers of reasoning and psychological analysis. They also indicated her capacity for imaginative insight into the motives and impulses of human nature, and an intuitive comprehension of what is most natural to human thought and action. They showed appreciation of sympathy and feeling, and delicate perception of the finer cravings and tendencies of even the commonest souls. They gave promise of so much creative power, her friends saw that in novel-writing she was to find the true expression of her large qualities of mind and heart. The person who could so skilfully point out the faults in the poor novels rapidly issuing from the press, and realize the true indications of a master's power in the creations of the literary artists, might herself possess the genius necessary to original work of her own. Her early essays are now chiefly of value for this promise they give of larger powers than those which could be fully expressed in such work. They prophesied the future, and made her friends zealous to overcome her own reluctance to enter upon a larger work. She doubted her own genius, but it was not destined to remain unfruitful.

VIII.

POETIC METHODS.

HAD George Eliot written nothing else than the poems which bear her name, she would have been assigned a permanent place among the poets. Having first attained her rank in the highest order of novelists, however, her poetry suffers in comparison with her prose. The critics tell us that no person gifted with supreme excellence in one form of creative expression has ever been able to attain high rank in another. They forget that Goethe was great both in prose and poetry; that his *Wilhelm Meister* is of scarcely inferior genius to his *Faust*. They also forget that Victor Hugo holds the first place among the French poets of the present century, at the same time that he is the greatest of all French novelists. It would be well for them also to remember that Scott held high rank as a poet before he began his wonderful career as a novelist. A contemporary of George Eliot's, to name a single instance of another kind, was equally excellent as poet and painter. Dante Rossetti made for himself a lasting place in both directions, and in both he did work of a high order.

In reality, the novel much resembles the narrative or epic poem; and if a work of true genius, it is difficult to distinguish it from the poem except as they differ in external form. The novel has for its main elements those qualities of imagination, description, high-wrought purpose, which are also constituents of much of the best poetry. The novel is more expansive than the poem, one of the chief characteristics of which is condensation;

its theme may take a wider range, and it may embrace those cruder and more common features of life which are inappropriate to the poem. The novelist can make a greater use of humor, he can give more detail to description, and portrayal of character can be carried to a much greater extent, than is usual with the poet. The poet requires a subject more sublime, inspiring and naturally beautiful than the novelist, who seeks what is the more human, nearer the level of daily social existence, and full of the affecting even if ruder interests and passions of life. The novel is so similar to the poem, and in so many ways requires such similar qualities of mind for its production, that there is no inherent reason why the same person cannot do equally good work in both. The supposition is that the poet may become a novelist, or the novelist a poet, in all cases except where there is some outward disqualification. The novelist may not have the sense of rhythmical form and of metrical expression; and the poet may not possess that constructive faculty which builds up plots, incidents and characters. In nearly all respects but these the two forms of creative genius so nearly assimilate each other, it is to be expected a novelist may turn poet if he have a large imagination and a stimulating capacity for metrical expression.

Novelists of strong imagination and a ready command of expressive words, barely escape writing poetry when they only purpose to write prose. This is true of Hugo, Auerbach, Dickens and George Eliot, again and again. The glow of creation, the high-wrought impulse of imagination, the ideal conception of life, all move the novelist in the direction of poetry. With much effort he keeps meter and rhyme out of his prose, but simile and metaphor, condeused expression, unusual words, poetic compounds, alliteration, sublime and picturesque expression, will intrude themselves. Dickens even permits meter and rhyme to conquer him, and weakens his style in consequence. He grows sentimental, and the real strength of pure prose is lost. George Eliot is often poetical in expression, touches the very borders of poetry continually, but she seldom permits herself to lapse from the strong, energetic and impressive prose which she almost uniformly writes. Specimens of this noble poetic-prose may be found very often in her pages. While it would be difficult by any transposition of words to turn it into poetry, as may often be done in the case of Dickens's prose, yet it contains most of the elements of a high order of poetry. In the account of the death of Maggie and Tom is to be found a fine specimen of her style, the last words being good iambics.

The boat reappeared, but brother and sister had gone down in an embrace never to be parted; living through again, in one supreme moment, the days when they *had clasped their little hands in love, and roamed the daisied fields together.*

In the first paragraph of the thirty-third chapter of *Adam Bede* is a sentence which makes a successful stanza in iambics by the addition of a single word.

The woods behind the chase,
And all the hedgerow trees,
Took on a solemn splendor *then*
Under the dark low-hanging skies.

It is very seldom, however, that George Eliot permits anything like meter in her prose, and she is usually very reticent of rhythm. There is fervor and enthusiasm, imagination and poetic insight, but all kept within the limits of robust and manly prose. This capacity of prose to serve most of the purposes of poetry may be seen in a marked degree in all of George Eliot's novels. In the account of Adam Bede's love for Hetty this subtle power of words and ideas to give the charm and impression of poetry without rhythm or rhyme is exhibited in a characteristic manner.

I think the deep love he had for that sweet, rounded, blossom-like, dark-eyed Hetty, of whose inward self he was really very ignorant, came out of the very strength of his nature, and not out of any inconsistent weakness. Is it any weakness, pray, to be wrought on by exquisite music? to feel its wondrous harmonies searching the subtlest windings of your soul, the delicate fibres of life where no memory can penetrate, and binding together your whole being, past and present, in one unspeakable vibration; melting you in one moment with all the tenderness, all the love that has been scattered through the toilsome years, concentrating in one emotion of heroic courage or resignation all the hard-learned lessons of self-renouncing sympathy, blending your present joy with past sorrow, and your present sorrow with all your past joy? If not, then neither is it a weakness to be so wrought upon by the exquisite curves of a woman's cheek and neck and arms, by the liquid depths of her beseeching eyes, or the sweet childish pout of her lips. For the beauty of a lovely woman is like music; what can one say more? Beauty has an expression beyond and far above the one woman's soul that it clothes, as the words of genius have a wider meaning than the thought that prompted them; it is more than a woman's love that moves us in a woman's eyes — it seems to be a far-off, mighty love that has come near to us, and made speech for itself there; the rounded neck, the dimpled arm, move us by something more than their prettiness — by their close kinship with all we have known of tenderness and peace.[1]

Love, music and beautiful landscapes continually inspire the poetic side of her nature; and these themes, which are constantly recurring in her chapters, draw forth her imagination and give fervor and enthusiasm to her expression. Her love of nature is deep and most appreciative of all its transformations and beauties. This sensitiveness to the changes of the outward world is a large element in her mind, and indicates the reality of her poetic gifts. This may be seen in a passage such as the following: —

The ride to Stone Court, which Fred and Rosamond took the next morning, lay through a pretty bit of midland landscape, almost all meadows and pastures, with hedgerows still allowed to grow in bushy beauty, and to spread out coral fruit for the birds. Little details gave each field a particular physiognomy, dear to the eyes that have looked on them from childhood; the pool in the corner where the grasses were dank and trees leaned whisperingly; the great oak shadowing a bare place in mid-pasture; the high bank where the ash-trees grew; the sudden slope of the old marl-pit making a red background for the burdock; the huddled roofs and ricks of the homestead without a traceable way of approach; the gray gate and fences against the depths of the bordering wood; and the stray hovel, its old, old thatch full of mossy hills and valleys, with wondrous modulations of light and shadow, such as

[1]Adam Bede, chapter XXXIII.

we travel far to see in later life, and see larger, but not more beautiful. These are the things that made the gamut of joy in landscape to midland-bred souls — the things they toddled among, or perhaps learned by heart, standing between their father's knees while he drove leisurely.[1]

It is nature as affecting man, and man as transformed into a creature of feeling and passion by the mysterious conditions of his existence, which oftenest arouses the poetic fervor in her. The enthusiasm of high resolves, yearnings after the pure and beautiful, and love's regenerating power, give to her themes which kindle poetic expression to a glow. The vision of Mordecai on Blackfriars' bridge affords a fine example of her love of the ideal in moral purpose, and shows how stimulating it is to her imagination. It is a poetic picture of the finest quality she has given in this chapter, one that could easily have been made to find expression in verse of great beauty; but it is poetry in thought and spirit alone, not in form or structure. It is true prose in form, strong in its fulness of detail, knit together with words of the right texture, built up into a true prose image of beauty in thought.

Mordecai's mind wrought so constantly in images that his coherent trains of thought often resembled the significant dreams attributed to sleepers by waking persons in their most inventive moments; nay, they often resembled genuine dreams in their way of breaking off the passage from the known to the unknown. Thus, for a long while, he habitually thought of the Being answering to his need as one distinctly approaching or turning his back toward him, darkly painted against a golden sky. The reason of the golden sky lay in one of Mordecai's habits. He was keenly alive to some poetic aspects of London; and a favorite resort of his, when strength and leisure allowed, was to some one of the bridges, especially about sunrise or sunset. Even when he was bending over watch-wheels and trinkets, or seated in a small upper room looking out on dingy bricks and dingy cracked windows, his imagination spontaneously planted him on some spot where he had a far-stretching scene; his thought went on in wide spaces, and whenever he could, he tried to have in reality the influences of a large sky. Leaning on the parapet of Blackfriars' bridge, and gazing meditatively, the breadth and calm of the river, with its long vista half hazy, half luminous, the grand dim masses or tall forms of buildings which were the signs of world-commerce, the on-coming of boats and barges from

[1] Middlemarch, chapter XII.

the still distance into sound and color, entered into his mood and blent themselves indistinguishably with his thinking, as a fine symphony to which we can hardly be said to listen, makes a medium that bears up our spiritual wings. Thus it happened that the figure representative of Mordecai's longing was mentally seen darkened by the excess of light in the aerial background. But in the inevitable progress of his imagination toward fuller detail he ceased to see the figure with its back toward him. It began to advance, and a face became discernible; the words youth, beauty, refinement, Jewish birth, noble gravity, turned into hardly individual but typical form and color: gathered from his memory of faces seen among the Jews of Holland and Bohemia, and from the paintings which revived that memory. Reverently let it be said of this mature spiritual need that it was akin to the boy's and girl's picturing of the future beloved; but the stirrings of such young desire are feeble compared with the passionate current of an ideal life straining to embody itself, made intense by resistance to imminent dissolution. The visionary form became a companion and auditor, keeping a place not only in the waking imagination, but in those dreams of lighter slumber of which it is truest to say, "I sleep, but my heart is awake" — when the disturbing trivial story of yesterday is charged with the impassioned purpose of years.[1]

Many times in her prose George Eliot has recognized the true character of poetry, and she has even given definitions of it which show how well she knew its real nature. She makes Will Ladislaw say that —

To be a poet is to have a soul so quick to discern that no shade of quality escapes it, and so quick to feel that discernment is but a hand playing with finely ordered variety on the chords of emotion — a soul in which knowledge passes instantaneously into feeling, and feeling flashes back as a new organ of knowledge.[2]

She thinks poetry and romance are as plentiful in the world as ever they were, that they exist even amidst the conditions created by invention and science; and if we do not find them there it is only because poetry and romance are absent from our own minds. If we have not awe and tenderness, wonder and enthusiasm, poetry cannot come near us, and we shall not be thrilled and exalted by it.[3] Yet it is not difficult to see that George Eliot is not a poet in the fullest sense, because hers is not thoroughly and always a poetic

[1] Daniel Deronda, chapter XXXVIII.
[2] Middlemarch, chapter XXII.
[3] Daniel Deronda, chapter XIX.

mind, because she reasons about things too much. The poet is impressed, moved, thrilled and exalted, and pours out his song from his feelings and transfused with emotion. George Eliot was given to speculation, loved exactness of expression, and kept too close to the real. She had not that lightness of touch, that deftness and flexibility of expression, and that versatility of imaging forth her ideas, which the real poet possesses. Her mind moved with a ponderous tread, which needed a prose style large and stately as its true medium of expression. While she had poetic ideas in abundance, and an imaginative discernment of nature and life, she had not the full gift of poetic speech. She lacked inspiration as well as flexibility of thought, her imagination was not sufficiently rich, and she had not the full sense of rhythmic harmony.

George Eliot first began to write in verse, as was to be expected of one gifted with an imagination vigorous as hers. Her love of music, her keen perception of the beauties of nature, her love of form and color, gave added attraction and impetus in the same direction. That she did not continue through many years to write poetry seems to have been partly the result of her intense interest in severer studies. The speculative cast of her mind predominated the poetical so nearly as to turn her away from the poetic side of life to find a solution for its graver and more intricate problems. Her return to the poetic form of expression may be accounted for partly as the result of a greater confidence in her own powers which came from success, and partly from a desire for a new and richer medium of utterance.

So far as can be judged from the dates of her poems, as appended to many of them, "How Lisa Loved the King" was the earliest written. This was written in the year of the publication of *Romola*, and was followed the next year by the first draft of *The Spanish Gypsy*. The poetical mottoes of *Felix Holt*, however, were the first to be published; and not until these appeared did the public know of her poetic gifts. *The Spanish Gypsy* was not published until 1868, and "How Lisa Loved the King" appeared the following year.

The original mottoes in *Felix Holt* gave good hint of George Eliot's poetic gifts. They are solid with thought, pregnant with the ripe wisdom of daily experience, significant for dramatic expression, or notable for their humor. They are rather heavy and ponderous in style, though sonorous in expression. A stately tread, a largeness of expression, an air of weighty meaning, appear in nearly all these mottoes. As a specimen of the more philosophic, the following will indicate the truthfulness of this description: —

Truth is the precious harvest of the earth,
But once, when harvest waved upon a land,
The noisome cankerworm and caterpillar,
Locusts, and all the swarming, foul-born broods,
Fastened upon it with swift, greedy jaws,
And turned the harvest into pestilence,
Until men said, What profits it to sow?

Her capacity for dramatic expression, in which a rich comprehension of life is included, may be seen in these lines:

1st Citizen. Sir, there's a hurry in the veins of youth
That makes a vice of virtue by excess.
2d Citizen. What if the coolness of our tardier veins
Be loss of virtue?
1st Citizen. All things cool with time —
The sun itself, they say, till heat shall find
A general level, nowhere in excess.
2d Citizen. 'Tis a poor climax, to my weaker thought,
That future middlingness.

Wisdom alloyed with humor appears in another motto:

It is a good and soothfast saw;
Half-roasted never will be raw;
No dough is dried once more to meal.
No crock new-shapen by the wheel;
You can't turn curds to milk again
Nor Now, by wishing, back to Then;
And having tasted stolen honey,
You can't buy innocence for money.

Mr. Buxton Forman says, that "in the charming headings to the chapters of *Felix Holt* it seemed as though the strong hand which had, up to that point, exercised masterly control over the restive tendency of high prose to rear up into verse, had relaxed itself just for the sake of a holiday, and no more. These headings did not bear the stamp of original poetry upon them. Forcible as were some, admirable in thought and applicability to the respective chapters as were all, none bore traces of that clearly defined individuality of style betrayed by all great and accomplished practitioners of verse, in even so small a compass as these headings. Some of them possess the great distinctive technical mark of poetry, — condensation; but this very condensation is compassed not in an original and individual method, but in the method of some pre-existent model; and it is hardly necessary to enforce that power of assimilation or reproduction, however large, is no infallible index of self-existent poetical faculty." This critic finds traces of Shakspere, Wordsworth and Mrs. Browning in these mottoes, and thinks they are all imitative, even when they are best. It is too easy, however, to dispose of a piece of literary work in this manner, and such criticism is very apt to have little meaning in it. George Eliot has proven herself far too original, both in prose and poetry, to make such a criticism of much value. Even if the charge of imitation is a valid one, it is far more probable that it was conscious and purposed, than that George Eliot's poetic gifts could only be exercised when impelled by the genius of some other. To give the impression of quotation may have been a part of George Eliot's purpose in writing these mottoes, which are original enough, and thoughtful enough, to have been attributed to any of the great poets. The real defects of her poetry lie in quite another direction than that of a lack of originality. She has enough to say that is fresh and interesting, she has no need to consult others for what she is to utter; but she has not the fervor of expression, the impressive touch, which separates poetry from prose. There is intellectual power enough, thought even in excess, but she does not soar and sing. She walks steadily, majestically along on the ground, she has no wings for the clear ether. Indeed, she is too much a realist to breathe in that upper air of pure song; it is too fine and delicate for one who loves the solid facts of earth so well as she.

If George Eliot often wrote prose which is almost poetry, she also wrote poetry which is almost prose. The concentrated, image-bearing phrases of poetry are wanting oftentimes in her verse. There is meter but no other quality of poetry, and not a few passages could be printed as prose with scarce a suspicion to the reader that they were intended for poetry. Mr. Buxton Forman has given a passage from *The Spanish Gypsy* in this way, adding only six insignificant words, and restoring *i* to *is* in two instances. He rightly says that the passage printed in prose "would surely be read by any one who saw it for the first time, without any suspicion that it merely required the excision of six little words and two letters to transform it to verse; no single expression betraying the secret that the passage is from a poem."

Do you hear the trumpet! There *is* old Ramon's blast. No bray but his can shake the air so well. He takes his trumpeting as solemnly as *an* angel charged to wake the dead; thinks war was made for trumpeters, and *that* their great art *was* made solely for themselves who understand it. His features have all shaped themselves to blowing, and when his trumpet *is either* bagged or left at home he seems *like* a chattel in a broker's booth, a spoutless watering-can, a promise to pay no sum particular!

George Eliot had not full command of poetic expression. This frequently appears, not only in the fact that many lines are simply prose in thought, but in the defects of the poetic form. Some lines are too short and others too long, some having four and some six feet. An instance of the former is to be found in these words between Don Silva and the Prior, forming one line:

> Strong reasons, father.
>
> Ay, but good?

Of the latter:

> And starry flashing steel and pale vermilion.

Still more suggestive are the expedients she resorts to in order to complete the line. Lopez is made to say, —

> Santiago! Juan, thou art hard to please.
> I speak not for my own delighting, I.
> I can be silent, I.

Very near this, Lopez is spoken of in this line:

> That was not what he drew his sword at — he!

Such defects as these are not, certainly, of vital importance, and may doubtless be found in even the greatest poets; but they are noticeable here because of one texture with that which limits the quality of her poetic art. The principal criticism to be made on her poetry is that it was composed and did not create itself out of a full poetic mind. It was wrought out, was the result of study and composition, is wanting in spontaneity and enthusiasm. The most serious defect of her poetry is also the most marked defect of her prose, and this is a want of the ideal element. She was a realist by nature, and could not free herself from the tendency to look at the world on its surface only.

In her poetry George Eliot is much more a *doctrinaire* than in her novels. All her poems, except a few of the shorter ones, are devoted to the inculcation of some moral or philosophic teaching. The very effort she was obliged to make to give herself utterance in poetry predisposed her to intellectual subjects and those of a controversial nature. For this reason her verse has a special interest for those who are attracted to her teachings. Her pen was freer, more creative, in her great novels than in her poems. In fact, her novels, especially *Adam Bede* and *The Mill on the Floss*, are much more poetical than much she did in verse. In her verse she tried to present the more spiritual side of life, to make living and effective her own conceptions of the unseen and eternal. Yet she was burdened constantly in this effort by the fact that she had a new theory of the spiritual and ideal side of life to interpret. The poets who win the homage of mankind, and conquer all hearts to themselves, take the accepted interpretations of the great spiritual problems of life as the basis of their work and give those a larger, loftier meaning through their poetic and ideal insight and capacity of interpretation. They shun theories which must be expounded and interpretations for which no one is prepared. It is here George Eliot is seriously at fault as a poet, however much she may be commended as a teacher and reformer. Perhaps the truest piece of poetic work she did was *Agatha*, in which, however, there is a greater reliance than in most of her poems, on the accepted interpretations of spiritual beliefs. In portraying the trust, childlike and simple, of an old woman, and in endeavoring to realize the poetic elements of that trust and simplicity, she was very effective. In such work as this she would have been much more successful, from the strictly poetic point of view, than she has been, if she had not attempted to give her theories a clothing in verse. In her "Brother and Sister" she was also very successful, but especially so in the "Two Lovers." There is an exquisite charm and power in some of these minor poems. Where the heart was free, and the intellect was not dominant and insistent on the importance of its theories, there was secured a genuine poetic beauty. There is true poetry in these lines:

Two lovers by a moss-grown spring:
They lean soft cheeks together there,
Mingled the dark and sunny hair,
And heard the wooing thrushes sing.
Oh budding time!
Oh love's blest prime!

Two wedded from the portal stept:
The bells made happy carrollings,
The air was soft as passing wings,
White petals on the pathway slept.
Oh pure-eyed bride!
Oh tender pride!

There is a beauty and majesty in the poem on subjective immortality which is likely to make it, as it has already become, the one popular poem among all she wrote. There is a stimulus, enthusiasm and abandon about it which is attained but seldom in her other verses. The love of humanity, its passionate longing to sacrifice self for the good of all, is acceptable to much of the thought and purpose of the present time; and its spirit of sacrifice is one which may commend it to all earnest souls. In the more extended poems there is genuine accomplishment just in proportion as the leading purpose was artistic rather than philosophic or moral.

Difficult as it was for a successful novelist to secure applause as a poet, George Eliot overcame the distrust of her admirers and gained also a not unmerited place as a poet. Her verse has been a real addition to her work, and is likely to command an increasing interest in the future. That it is not always successful from the merely artistic point of view, that it is not to be placed by the side of the best poetry of the time, is no reason why it will not appeal to many minds and enlist its own company of admirers. Next after the universal poets are those who appeal to a select circle and charm a particular class of minds. Among these George Eliot will stand as one of the foremost and one of those most worthy of homage. As the poet of positivism, she will long delight those in sympathy with her teachings. It would be extravagant praise to call her a second Lucretius, and yet that which has given the Roman author his place among poets will also give George Eliot rank in the same company. With all his merits as a poet, it has not been his poetic power, or his love of nature, or his worth as an interpreter of human nature, which has given Lucretius his reputation as a poet. With real poetic power, — for he would have been a much smaller man without this, — he combined a philosophic mind and a daring genius for speculation. The poetry gave charm and ideal grandeur to the speculations, and the philosophy made the poetry full of meaning and earnest intellectual purpose. He read life and nature with a keener eye and a more profound penetration than others of his time; he tried to grasp the secret of the universe, and because of it he left behind the touch of a strong mind. In some such way as this, George Eliot's poetry is likely to be read in the future. As poetry merely, it cannot take high rank; but for the sake of its philosophy, which is conceived as a poet would conceive it, there is promise that its future is to be one that is lasting. Even for poetry there must be thought, and the larger, profounder it is the better for the poetry, if it is imaginatively conceived and expressed. It is not thought, or even philosophy, which annuls poetry, but want of ideal and creative insight. To Goethe, Wordsworth or Browning there was a gain by enlargement of intellectual materials, but these were suffused in true poetic fire, and came forth a new creation. In so far as George Eliot has attained this result is she a poet, and is she sure of the future suffrages of those who accept her philosophy. At the least, her admirers must rejoice at the enlarged range of expression she secured by the use of the poetic form.

IX.

PHILOSOPHIC ATTITUDE.

GEORGE ELIOT was pre-eminently a novelist and a poet; but she is also the truest literary representative the nineteenth century has yet afforded of its positivist and scientific tendencies. What Comte and Spencer have taught in the name of philosophy, Tyndall and Hæckel in the name of science, she has applied to life and its problems. Their aims, spirit and tendencies have found in her a living embodiment, and re-appear in her pages as forms of genius, as artistic creations. They have experimented, speculated, elaborated theories of the universe, drawn out systems of philosophy; but she has reconstructed the social life of man through her creative insight. What they mean, whither they lead, is not to be discovered nearly so plainly in their books as in hers. She is their interpreter through that wonderful insight, genius and creative power which enabled her to see what they could not themselves dis cover, — the effect of their teachings on man as an individual and as a social being.

Whoever would know what the agnostic and evolution philosophy of the time has to teach about man, his social life, his moral responsibilities, his religious aspirations, should go to the pages of George Eliot in preference to those of any other. The scientific spirit, the evolution philosophy, live in her pages, reveal themselves there in all their strength and in all their weakness. She was a thinker equal to any of those whose names stand forth as the representatives of the philosophy she accepted, she was as competent as they to think out the problems of life and to interpret social existence in accordance with their theories of man and nature. Competent to grasp and to interpret the positive philosophy in all its details and in all its applications, she also had that artistic spirit of reconstruction which enabled her to apply to life what she held in theory. Along with the calm philosophic spirit which thinks out "the painful riddle of the earth," she had the creative spirit of the artist which delights in portraying life in all its endeavors, complexities and consequences. She not only accepted the theory of hereditary transmission as science has recently developed it, and as it has been enlarged by positivism into a shaping influence of the past upon the present, but she made this law vital with meaning as she developed its consequences in the lives of her characters. To her it was not merely a theory, but a principle so pregnant with meaning as to have its applications in every phase of human experience. Life could not be explained without it; the thoughts, deeds and aspirations of men could be understood only with reference to it; much that enters into human life of weal and woe is to be comprehended only with reference to this law. In regard to all the other evolution problems and principles her knowledge was as great, her insight as clear, and her constructive use of them as original.

A new theory of life and the universe may be intellectually accepted as soon as its teachings are comprehended; but the absorption of that theory into the moral tissues, so that it becomes an active and constant impulse and motive in feeling and conduct, is a long and difficult process. It takes generations before it can associate itself with the instinctive impulses of the mind. It is one thing to accept the theory of universal law as an intellectual explanation of the sequences of phenomena, but it is quite another to be guided by that theory in all the most spontaneous movements of feeling, conscience and thought. A few minds are able to make such a theory at once their own by virtue of genius of a very instinctive and subtle order; but for the great majority of mankind this result can only be reached after generations of instruction. The use made of such theories by the poets and novelists is a sure test of their popular acceptance. When the poets accept such a theory, and naturally express themselves in accordance with its spirit, the people may soon feel and think according to its meaning.

The theory of evolution will not easily adjust the human mind to its conclusions and methods. It is therefore very remarkable that George Eliot, the contemporary of Comte, Spencer, Darwin, Lewes and Tyndall, should be able to give a true literary expression to their speculations. She has not only been able to follow these men, to accept their theories and to understand them in all their implications and tendencies, but she has so absorbed these theories into her mind, and so made them a part of all its processes, that she has painted life thoroughly in accordance with their spirit. Should the teachings of the evolutionists of to-day be finally accepted, and after a few generations become the universally received explanations of life and the universe, it is not likely any poet or novelist will more genuinely and entirely express their spirit than George Eliot has done. The evolutionary spirit and ways of looking at life became instinctive to her; she saw life and read its deepest experiences wholly in the light shed by this philosophy. For this reason her writings are of great value to those who would understand the evolution philosophy in its higher phases.

George Eliot accepted the intellectual conclusions of evolution, and the outline thus afforded she filled in with feeling and poetry. She interpreted the pathos, the tragedy, the aspirations of life in the light of this philosophy. Accepting with a bold and undismayed intellect the implications and consequences of evolution, rejecting or abating no least portion of it, she found in it a place for art, poetry and religion; and she tried to show how it touches and moulds and uplifts man. She shrank from nothing which would enable her to reveal how man is to live in such a universe as she believed in; she saw all its hardness, cruelty, anguish and mystery, and resolutely endeavored to show how these enter into and help to form his destiny. In doing this she followed the lead of the positivists in the acceptance of feeling as the basis and the true expression of man's inner life. The emotional life is made the essential life; and all its phases of manifestation in art, poetry and religion are regarded as of great importance. George Eliot viewed the higher problems of life from this point of view, giving to the forms in which the emotional side of man's nature is expressed a supreme importance. Religion, as the response of feeling to the mystery of existence, occupied a most important place in her philosophy. That her interpretation of the emotional elements of life is the true one, that she has discovered their source or their real ideal significance, may well be doubted; but there is every reason for believing that she realized their great value, and she certainly tried in an earnest spirit to make them helpful in the life of ideal beauty and truthfulness.

All that agnostic science and the evolution philosophy had to teach, George Eliot accepted, its doctrine of descent, its new psychology, and its theories of society and human destiny. Its doctrine of experience, its ethical theories, were equally hers. Yet into her interpretation of existence went a woman's heart, the widest and tenderest sympathy, and a quick yearning purpose to do what good she could in the world. She saw with the lover's eyes, motherhood revealed itself in her soul, the child's trust was in her heart. The new philosophy she applied to life, revealed its relations to duty, love, sorrow, trial and death. To her it had a deep social meaning, a vital connection with the heart, its hopes and its burdens, and for her it touched the spiritual content of life with reality. It was in this way she became the truest interpreter of the evolution philosophy, the best apostle of the ethics taught by agnostic science. She not only speculated, she also felt and lived. Philosophy was to her more than an abstract theory of the universe; into it entered a tender sympathy for all human weakness, a profound sense of the mystery of existence, and a holy purpose to make life pure and true to all she could reach. This larger comprehension gives a new significance to her interpretation of evolution. It makes it impossible that this philosophy should be fully understood without a study of her books.

It is because George Eliot was not a mere speculative thinker that her teachings become so important. The true novelist, who is gifted with genius, who creates character and situation with a master's hand, must have some theory of life. He must have some notion of what life means, what the significance of the pathos and tragedy of human experience, and why it is that good and evil in conduct do not produce the same results. Such a theory of life, if firmly grasped and worked out strongly, becomes a philosophy. Much depends with the novelist on that philosophy, what it places foremost, what it sees destiny to mean. It will affect his insight, give shape to his plots, decide his characters, guide his ethical interpretations, fix his spiritual apprehension. It was because George Eliot adopted a new and remarkable philosophy, one that teaches much which the instincts of the race have rejected, and repudiates much which the race has accepted as necessary to its welfare, that her teachings become so noteworthy. Genius first of all she had, and the artist's creative power; but the way she used these, and the limitations she put upon them by her philosophy, give her books an interest which not even her wonderful genius could alone produce. That philosophy is in debate; and it is not yet decided whether it is mainly false because growing out of wrong methods, or if it be in reality a true explanation of existence. Its revolutionary character, its negative spirit, its relations to ethics and religion, make it remarkable, and even startling. Profound thinkers, men of commanding philosophic apprehension and power of generalization, have accepted it; physical science has largely lent its aid to the support of its conclusions. Yet on its side genius, imagination, creative instinct, artistic apprehension, have not given their aid. Without them it is defective, and cannot command the ideal sentiments and hopes of the race. First to fill this gap came George Eliot, and she yet remains its only great literary ally and coadjutor. Tyndall, Hæckel and DuBois Raymond can give us science; but this is not enough. Comte, Mill and Spencer can give us philosophy; but that is inadequate. They have also essayed, one and all, to say some true word about morals, religion and the social ideals; but they have one and all failed. They are too speculative, too far away from the vital movements of life, know too little of human experience as it throbs out of the heart and sentiments. They can explain their theories in terms of science, ethics and philosophy; but George Eliot explains them in terms of life. They have speculated, she has felt; they have made philosophies, she has created ideal characters and given us poetry; they have studied nature, she has studied experience and life; they have tried to resolve the mind into its constituent elements, she has entered into the heart and read its secrets; they have looked on to see what history meant, she has lived all heart tragedies and known all spiritual aspirations.

George Eliot was not a mere disciple of any of the great teachers of evolution. Though of their school, and largely in accord and sympathy with them, yet she often departed from the way they went, and took a position quite in opposition to theirs. Her standpoint in philosophy was arrived at quite independently of their influence, and in many of its main features her philosophy was developed before she had any acquaintance either with them or their books. She wrote concerning John Stuart Mill,[1] —

> I never had any personal acquaintance with him, never saw him to my knowledge except in the House of Commons; and though I have studied his books, especially his *Logic* and *Political Economy* with much benefit, I have no consciousness of their having made any marked epoch in my life.

Concerning another leading positivist she has said,—

> Of [Herbert Spencer's] friendship I have had the honor and advantage for twenty years, but I believe that every main bias of my mind had been taken before I knew him. Like the rest of his readers, I am, of course, indebted to him for much enlargement and clarifying of thought.

Not long previous to her death, in reading Bridges' version of *The General View of Positivism*, she expressed her dissent more often than her assent, and once she said, —

> I cannot submit my intellect or my soul to the guidance of Comte.

George Eliot did not take up her residence in London until her thirty-second year, and previous to that time her acquaintance with the positivist leaders must have been slight. Before that age the opinions of most persons are formed, and such was the case with George Eliot. It is likely her opinions underwent many changes after this date, but only in the direction of those already established and in modification of the philosophy already accepted. She became an evolutionist without the aid of those men who are supposed to be the originators of this theory. Every new idea or new way of interpreting nature and life grows into form gradually, and under the influence of many different minds. The evolution philosophy was long accepted before it became a doctrine or was formulated

[1] Elizabeth Stuart Phelps' "Last words from George Eliot," in Harper's Magazine for March, 1882. The names of Mill and Spencer are not given in this article, but the words from her letters so plainly refer to them that they have been quoted here as illustrating her relations to these men.

into a philosophy. The same influences worked in many quarters to produce the same conclusions. It was given to George Eliot to come under a set of influences which led her to accept all the leading ideas of evolution before she had any opportunity to know that philosophy as it has been elaborated by the men whose names are most often connected with it. A brief account of the successive philosophic influences which most directly and personally touched her mind will largely help towards the comprehension of her teachings.

The most intimate friend of her youth, who gave her a home when trouble came with her family, and stimulated her mind to active inquiry after truth, was a philosopher of no mean ability. Charles Bray not only was the first philosopher she knew, but her opinions of after years were mainly in the direction he marked out for her. In his *Philosophy of Necessity*, published in 1841, he maintained that the only reality is the *Great Unknown* which we name God, that all natural laws are actions of the first cause. He taught that the world is created in our own minds, the result of some unknown cause without us, which we call matter; but it is thus God mirrors himself to us. "All we see is but the vesture of God, and what we call laws of nature are but attributes of Deity." Matter is known to us only as the cause of sensations, while the soul is the principle of sensation, dependent upon the nervous system; the nervous system depending upon life, and life upon organization. All knowledge comes to man through the action of the external world upon the senses; all truth, all progress, come to us out of experience. "Reason is dependent for its exercise upon experience, and experience is nothing more than the knowledge of the invariable order of nature, of the relations of cause and effect." All acts of men are ruled by necessity. Pain produces our ideas of right and wrong, and happiness is the test of all moral action. There are no such things as sin and evil, only pains and pleasures. Evil is the natural and necessary limitation of our faculties, and our consequent liability to error; and pain, which we call evil, is its corrective. Nothing, under the circumstances, could have happened but that which did happen; and the actions of men, under precisely the same circumstances, must always issue in precisely the same results. Death, treated of in a separate chapter, is shown to be good, and a necessary aid to progress. Society is regarded as an organism, and man is to find his highest life in the life of others. "The great body of humanity (considered as an individual), with its soul, the principle of sensation, is ever fresh and vigorous and increasing in enjoyment. Death and birth, the means of renewal and succession, bear the same relation to this body of society as the system of waste and reproduction do to the human body; the old and useless and decayed material is carried out, and fresh substituted, and thus the frame is renovated and rendered capable of ever-increasing happiness. . . . The minds, that is to say, the ideas and feelings of which they were composed, of Socrates, Plato, Epicurus, Galileo, Bacon, Locke, Newton, are thus forever in existence, and the immortality of the soul is preserved, not in individuals, but in the great body of humanity. . . . To the race, though not to individuals, all beautiful things are preserved forever; all that is really good and profitable is immortal."

Nearly every idea here presented was accepted by George Eliot and re-appears in her writings. In Bray's later books much also is to be found which she embraced. He therein says that all outside of us is a delusion of the senses.[1] The senses conspire with the intellect to impose upon us. The constitution of our faculties forces us to believe in an external world, but it has no more reality than our dreams. Each creature is the creator of its own separate, different world. The

[1] This summary of Bray's philosophy is condensed from an article in the Westminster Review for April, 1879.

unity of outward things is imposed on them by the faculty of individuality, and is a mere fiction of the mind. Matter is a creature of the imagination, and is a pure assumption. It is the centre of force, as immaterial as spirit, as ethereal and unsubstantial. As centres of force imply locality, and locality space, so space must have an extension of its own. Not so; it is a pure creation of the mind. The same holds true of time. The world of mind, the moral world as well, are our own creations. Man has no power over himself; nothing could have been otherwise than as it is. Repentance and remorse are foolish regrets over what could not have been otherwise. All actions and motives are indifferent; only in their consequences can any distinction be observed between them. Such as minister to man's pleasure he calls good; such as produce pain he calls evil. There is no good but pleasure, and no evil but pain. Hence there is no distinction between moral and physical evil. Morality is the chemistry of the mind, its attractions and repulsions, likes and dislikes. God is an illusion, as are all moral conclusions based on his existence. Nor has man any reality; he is the greatest illusion and delusion of all. The faculty of individuality gives us all our ideas and feelings, and creates for us what we call our minds. A mind is an aggregate of a stream of consciousness. Ideas, feelings, states of consciousness, do not inhere in anything; each is a distinct entity. "Thinking is," is what we should say, not "I think." Here we are at the ground fact of what constitutes being, on solid footing; consciousness cannot deceive us. Thinking is, even if mind and matter, self and not-self, are illusory. It is, even if we deny both the external and internal causes of consciousness. We know our own consciousness, that alone. All is inference beside. When we consider what inferences are most probable, we are led to build up a constructive philosophy. Consciousness says we have a body, body a brain, and pressure on the brain stops consciousness; hence a close connection between the brain and consciousness. The two go together, and in the brain we must lay the foundation of our philosophy. The mental faculties create the world of individual consciousness, it the outside world. We know only what is revealed in consciousness. Matter and mind are one. Life and mind are correlates of physical force; they are the forms assumed by physical force when subjected to organic conditions. Yet there is no such thing as mere physical force. Every atom of matter acts intelligently; it has so acted always. The conscious intel ligence of the universe has subsided into natural law, and acts automatically. This universal agent of life in all things is God. All consciousness and physical force are but "the varied God." There is in reality no agent but mind, conscious or unconscious. God is nature; matter is mind solidified. Matter is force as revealed by the senses. It is the body, force is the soul. In nature, as in man, body and soul are one and indivisible. Mind builds up organisms. There is a living will, conscious or unconscious, in all things. The One and All requires the resignation of the individual and personal, of all that is selfish, to the Infinite whole.

The basis of Bray's philosophy was idealism and pantheism, assuming form under the influence of modern science. He quoted Emerson frequently, and the school of thought Emerson represents affected him greatly. On the other hand, he was then a strong phrenologist, had imbibed much of the teaching of Combe's *Constitution of Man*, and he eagerly embraced those notions of the relations of body and mind which have been propagated in the name of physical science.

The same double influence is to be seen at work upon the next thinker who was destined to give direction to George Eliot's philosophy. Feuerbach was a disciple of Hegel, whose influence is deeply marked through all his earlier writings. He also was affected by physical science, and he found in sensationalism an element for his system. To him all thought is the product of experience; he founded his ideas on materials which can be appropriated only through the activity of the senses. The external world affects the senses and generates feeling, feeling produces ideas. Feeling re-acts upon the external world, interprets it according to its own wants. Feeling is thus the source of all knowledge; feeling is the basis alike of religion and philosophy. Feuerbach, as well as Bray, finds that man creates the outward world in consciousness; all that is out of man which he can know, is but a reflection of what is in him. This conception of consciousness, this pure idealism, becomes the source of Feuerbach's philosophy of religion. He says that religion is based on the differences between man and the brute; man has consciousness, which is only present in a being to whom his species, his essential nature, is an object of thought. Man thinks, converses with himself, is at once I and Thou, can put himself in the place of another. Religion is identical with self-consciousness, and expresses man's sense of the infinitude of his own faculties. Man learns about himself through what is objective to him, but the object only serves to bring out what is in him; his own nature becomes the absolute to him. Consciousness marks the self-satisfaction, self-perfection of man, that all truth is in him. As feeling is the cause of the outward world, or of that notion of it man has, it becomes the organ of religion. The nature of God is nothing else than an expression of the nature of feeling. As man lives mainly in feeling, finds there the sources of all his mental and moral life, he comes to regard feeling as the divinest part of his nature, the noblest and most excellent; so it becomes to him the organ of the divine. When man thinks what is infinite he in reality does nothing more than to perceive and affirm that to him feeling has an infinite power. If you feel the infinite, you feel and affirm the infinitude of the power of feeling. The object of the intellect is intellect objective to itself; the object of feeling is feeling objective to itself. God is pure, unlimited, free feeling. In religion, consciousness of the object and self-consciousness coincide. The object of any subject is nothing else than the subject's own nature taken objectively. God is like our thoughts and dispositions; consciousness of God is self-consciousness, knowledge of God is self-knowledge. Religion is the unveiling of a man's hidden treasures, the revelation of his intimate thoughts, the open confession of his love secrets. It is to the understanding Feuerbach attributes man's capacity for objectifying himself or of attributing to the outward world those qualities which really exist only within. Man's consciousness cf God is nothing else than his consciousness of his species. "Man has his highest being, his God, in himself; not in himself as an individual, but in his essential nature, his species. No individual is an adequate representative of his species, but only the human individual is conscious of the distinction between the species and the individual. In the sense of this distinction lies the root of religion. The yearning of man after something above himself is nothing else than the longing after the perfect type of his nature, the yearning to be free from himself, *i.e.*, from the limits and defects of his individuality. Individuality is the self-conditioning, the self-limitation of the species. Thus man has cognizance of nothing above himself, of nothing beyond the nature of humanity; but to the individual man this nature presents itself under the form of an individual man. All feelings which man experiences towards a superior man, nay, in general, all moral feelings which man has towards man, are of a religious nature. Man feels nothing towards God which he does not also feel towards man." The dogmas of Christianity are interpreted by Feuerbach from this standpoint of conceiving religion as a projection of feeling upon the outward world. So he explains the incarnation as man's love for man, man's yearning to help his fellows, the renunciation and suffering man undergoes for man. The passion of Christ represents freely accepted suffering for others in love of them. The trinity typifies the participated, social life of the species; it shows the father, mother and son as the symbols of the race. The *logos* or son is the nature of the imagination made objective, the satisfaction of the need for mental images, the reflected splendor of the imagination. Faith in providence is faith in one's own worth; it indicates the divine reality and significance of our own being. Prayer is an expression of the power of feeling, a dialogue of man with his own heart. Faith is confidence in the reality of the subjective in opposition to the limitations or laws of nature and reason. Its specific object is miracle; faith and miracle are absolutely inseparable. That which is objectively miracle is subjectively faith. Faith is the miracle of feeling; it is nothing else than belief in the absolute reality of subjectivity. The power of miracle is the power of the imagination, for imagination corresponds to personal feeling; it sets aside all limits, all laws painful to the feelings, and thus makes objective to man the immediate, absolutely unlimited satisfaction of his subjective wishes. The belief in miracle accepts wishes as realities. In fact, the fundamental dogmas of Christianity are simply realized wishes of the heart. This is true, because the highest law of feeling is the immediate unity of will and deed, of wishing and reality. To religion, what is felt or wished is regarded as real. In the Redeemer this is realized, wish becomes fact. All things are to be wrought, according to religion, by belief. Thus the future life is a life where feeling realizes every desire. Its whole import is that of the abolition of the discordance which exists between wish and reality. It is the realization of a state which corresponds to the feelings, in which man is in unison with himself. The other world is nothing more than the reality of a known idea, the satisfaction of a conscious desire, the fulfilment of a wish. "The sum of the future life is happiness, the everlasting bliss of personality, which is here limited and circumscribed by nature. Faith in the future life is therefore faith in the freedom of subjectivity from the limits of nature; it is faith in the eternity and infinitude of personality, and not of personality viewed in relation to the idea of the species, in which it forever unfolds itself in new individuals, but of personality as belonging to already existing individuals; consequently, it is the faith of man in himself. But faith in the kingdom of heaven is one with faith in God; the context of both ideas is the same; God is pure absolute subjectivity released from all natural limits; he is what individuals ought to be and will be; faith in God is therefore the faith of man in the infinitude and truth of his own nature; the Divine Being is the subjective human being in his absolute freedom and uulimitedness."

It is not probable that George Eliot confined her philosophic studies to the writings of Charles Bray and Feuerbach, but it is quite certain that in their books which she did faithfully study, are to be found some of the leading principles of her philosophy. What gives greater confirmation to the supposition that her philosophy was largely shaped under their influence is the fact that her intimate friend, Sara Hennell, drew from the same sources for the presentation of theories quite identical with hers. Sara Hennell's *Thoughts in Aid of Faith*, published in 1860, is an attempt to show that the religious sentiments may be retained when the doctrines of theology are intellectually rejected, that a disposition of the heart akin to Paul's may be present though conviction be extinct. In securing this result, she too takes Feuerbach as her guide, and his teachings she claims are fully corroborated by the philosophy of Herbert Spencer. Religion she regards as the result of the tendency of man's mind towards philosophy, the outgrowth of the activity of his mental faculties seeking satisfaction for themselves in explaining the world given for his contemplation and study. "The growth of religion in the human intelligence (thereby distinguished from mere blind emotion), is coincident with, or rather immediately consequent upon, the power of forming abstract ideas; that is to say, it is a generalization effected by the operation of the intellect upon the sentiments and emotions, when these have attained to so great extent and distinctness as to become self-conscious." Man early objectifies the qualities he finds in himself and his fellows, regards them as entities, is prostrated in awe and worship before them, conceives them to be gods. He attributes to outward objects his subjective states, and regards them as like himself, only infinitely more powerful. His emotions he believes are caused by these objective beings, and he thinks he is inspired, that the gods are at work within him. Feeling becomes the voice of God, the revelator of religions and theologies. Christianity Miss Hennell regards as "the form in which the religious affections, struggling against earthly limitations, have created for themselves the satisfaction they demand, and, therefore, in so far, real, just as the affections are real." Feeling, she says, is real as logic, and must equally have its real foundation. That is, feeling gives us the truth, actually answers to the realities of things as man can know them. She is here an ontologist, and she is convinced that feeling is a direct witness of the deeper knowledge and reality which man seeks in religion. The permanency and validity of religion she believes in, and she testifies to its wholesome and ennobling effect upon the race. "Christianity, having formed an actual portion of the composition both of our own individual experience and of the world's history, can no more be annihilated out of them than the sum of what we learned during a certain number of years of our childhood, from the one, or the effects of any notable occurrence, such as the fall of the Roman Empire, or the Norman invasion, from the other; — Christianity on every view, whether of its truth or falsity, and consequently of its good or bad effect, has undoubtedly contributed to make us what we are; without it we should have grown into something incalculably different from our present selves. . . . And how can it be otherwise than real to us, this belief that has nourished the souls of us all, and seems to have moulded actually anew their internal constitution, as well as stored them up with its infinite variety of external interests and associations? What other than a very real thing has it been in the life of the world, sprung out of, and again causing to spring forth, such volumes of human emotion? making a current, as it were, of feeling, that has drawn within its own sphere all the moral vitality of so many ages. In all this reality of influence there is indeed the testimony of Christianity having truly formed an integral portion of the organic life of humanity."

Though Miss Hennell is so earnest a believer in Christianity, yet she totally rejects the idea of any objective reality corresponding to its dogmas. This conclusion is based on the philosophic notion, which she shares with Bray, Feuerbach, George Eliot, Spencer and Lewes, that man has no real knowledge whatever except that which is given in consciousness. This philosophy, shared in common by these persons, is called by Lewes "reasoned realism," and by Spencer "transfigured realism." It accepts the reality of an outward world, but says that all man knows of it is, that it produces impressions on his senses which are transmuted into sensations. Sensations produce feelings, and feelings become ideas. According to Spencer, the steps of knowledge are three: the co-ordinating of sensations in a living organism; the registering of impressions within the organism in such a way as to build up a store of experiences; the transmission of the organism and its susceptibilities to offspring. Miss Hennell accepts Spencer's theory that feeling is the source of all our knowledge. Not only, as she says, does it "constitute the essential and main vitality of our nature," but when it is stored up in the human organism and inherited, it becomes the vital source out of which all moral and religious truth is built up. Experience, transformed into inherited feeling, takes on the form of those intuitions which "are the only reliable ground of solid belief." "These sentiments which are born within us, slumbering as it were in our nature, ready to be awakened into action immediately they are roused by hint of corresponding circumstances, are drawn out of the whole of previous human existence. They constitute our treasured inheritance out of all the life that has been lived before us, to which no age, no human being who has trod the earth and laid himself to rest with all his mortal burden upon her maternal bosom, has failed to add his contribution. No generation has had its engrossing conflict, surely battling out the triumphs of mind over material force, and through forms of monstrous abortions concurrent with its birth, too hideous for us now to bear in contemplation, moulding the early intelligence by every struggle, and winning its gradual powers, — no single soul has borne itself through its personal trial, — without bequeathing to us of its fruit. There is not a religious thought that we take to ourselves for secret comfort in our time of grief, that has not been distilled out of the multiplicity of the hallowed tears of mankind; not an animating idea is there for our fainting courage that has not gathered its inspiration from the bravery of the myriad armies of the vorld's heroes. All this best of humanity's hard earnings has been hoarded with generous care by our *alma natura naturans;* so that at last, in our rich ages, the *mens naturata* opens its gaze with awful wonder upon its environment of spiritual possessions."

The intimate sympathy of George Eliot and Miss

Hennell indicates that they followed much the same studies, and it is certain they arrived at very similar conclusions. That the one was directly influenced or led by the other there seem to be no reasons for believing. All that is probable is, that there was a close affinity of thought and purpose between them, and that they arrived at similar philosophical conclusions. The same is to be said in regard to George Eliot's relations to George Henry Lewes. Her theories of life, as has been already clearly indicated, were firmly fixed before she knew him, and her philosophical opinions were formed. The similarity of their speculative opinions doubtless had something to do with bringing them together; and it is certain that the tenor of their thoughts, their views about life, and their spiritual aspirations, were very much alike, giving promise of a most thorough sympathy in all their intellectual and moral pursuits. If she was influenced by him, he was quite as much influenced by her. Lewes accepted the philosophical side of Comte's Positive Philosophy, but the religious side of it he rejected and strongly condemned. In his *History of Philosophy*, he says, "Antagonism to the method and certain conclusions of the *Politique positive* led me for many years to regard that work as a deviation from the Positive Philosophy in every way unfortunate. My attitude has changed now that I have learned (from the remark of one very dear to me) to regard it as an Utopia, presenting hypotheses rather than doctrines, suggestions for inquirers rather than dogmas for adepts — hypotheses carrying more or less of truth, and serviceable as a provisional mode of colligating facts, to be confirmed or contradicted by experience." It is altogether probable, as in this case, that George Eliot gave Lewes the suggestive aid of her acute mind. If she was aided by him, it was only as one strong mind aids another, by collision and suggestion rather than by direct teaching.

Lewes may have had the effect to deepen and establish firmly the conclusions already reached by George Eliot, and a consideration of his philosophy must confirm this conjecture. He, too, makes feeling the basis of all knowing. From this point, however, he diverges widely from Herbert Spencer and the other English empiricists. Spencer regards matter and mind as two phases of an underlying substance, which he presents as the unknown and unknowable. Lewes at once denies the duality implied in the words matter and mind, motion and feeling, and declares these are one and the same thing, objectively or subjectively presented. Feeling is motion, and motion is feeling; mind is the spiritual aspect of the material organism, and matter is the objective aspect of feeling. Feeling is not the cause of motion, as idealism would suggest; and motion does not cause or turn into feeling, as materialism teaches. The two are absolutely identical; there is no dualism or antithesis. In the same way, cause and effect are but two aspects of one phenomenon; there is no separation between them, but one and the same thing before and after. He applies this idea to the conception of natural law, and declares it to be only the persistence of phenomena; that is, the persistence of feeling. He denies that there is any absolute behind phenomena; the absolute is in the phenomena, which is the only reality. The phenomenal universe is simply a group of relations, nothing more; and what seems to be, really exists, because the relations are real.

It is not necessary here to enter into a full presentation of Lewes's philosophy, but his theories about the functions of feeling are of importance, in view of George Eliot's acceptance of them. They have been summarized into the statement that "all truths are alike feelings, ideally distinguishable according to the aspects under which they are viewed. There is no motion apart from feeling, for the motion *is* the feeling; there is no force apart from matter which compels it to move, for the force *is* the matter, as matter is motion — differently viewed; there is no essence or substance which determines the properties, for the substance is the whole group of properties; there are no causes outside of effects, no laws outside the processes, no reality outside the phenomena, no absolute outside the relative, which determine things to be as they are and not otherwise, for all these are but different sides of one and the same thing." The central thought presented by Lewes is, that "for us there is nothing but feeling, whose subjective side is sensations, perceptions, memories, reasonings, the ideal constructions of science and philosophy, emotions, pleasures, pains; whose objective side is motion, matter, force, cause, the absolute." The outcome of this theory is, it enables Lewes to believe that the inner and outer practically agree, that our feelings give a sufficiently correct picture of the universe. In reality, the two do not agree, and even "science is in no respect a plain transcript of reality;" but so intimate are feeling and the outer world, that the inward report is to be regarded as practically a correct one.

In many ways Lewes differed from his contemporaries, disagreeing again and again with Spencer, Bain and Huxley. He often seems much nearer Schelling than Hæckel. He differs from Schelling in his demand for verification and the inductive method, and in claiming that all his conclusions are the result of scientific experiments and deductions. He agrees with Schelling in his rejection of mechanical processes and in his acceptance of a vital, organic method in nature and in social development. He differs from many of the other leaders of speculative science in his rejection of reflex action, maintaining that the brain is not the only seat of sensation, and that all cerebral processes are mental processes. With equal vigor he rejects the theory of animal automatism, and the assertion that animal actions can be completely expressed and accounted for in terms of nervous matter and motion. The laws of the mind, he maintained, are not to be deduced from physiological processes, but with them must be joined the psychical processes of the individual and the social man. He separates man by an impassable barrier from the lower animals, this gulf between them being due to human society and to the social acquisition of language. In the social factor he finds an important element of psychology, and one that must always come in to overturn any mechanical theories of mental activity.

It has been very truly said, that Lewes must be credited with the doctrine of the dependence of the human mind on the social medium. Others had hit upon this idea, and it had been very well developed by Spencer and Comte; but Lewes gave it a wider and profounder interpretation than any other. One of his critics says that Lewes "has the sort of claim to have originated this theory that Bacon has to be considered the discoverer of the inductive method." He not only held with Spencer and other evolutionists, that the human mind is the product of experience in contact with the outer world, that experience transmitted by heredity and built up into mental processes and conclusions; but he maintained that the social medium is a much greater and more important factor. The past makes the present; the social life develops the individual. Our language, our thought, as individuals, are the product of the collective life of the race. "We are to seek in the social organism for all the main conditions of the higher functions, and in the social medium of beliefs, opinions, institutions, &c., for the atmosphere breathed by the intellect. Man is no longer to be considered simply as an assemblage of organs, but also as an organ in a collective organism. From the former he derives his sensations, judgments, primary impulses; from the latter, his conceptions, theories and virtues. This is very clear when we learn how the intellect draws both its inspiration and its instrument from the social needs. All the materials of intellect are images and symbols, all its processes are operations on images and symbols. Language — which is wholly a social product for a social need — is the chief vehicle of symbolical operation, and the only means by which abstraction is affected. . . . Language is the creator and sustainer of that ideal world in which the noblest part of human activity finds a theatre, the world of thought and spiritual insight, of knowledge and duty, loftily elevated above that of sense and appetite. Into this ideal world man absorbs the universe as in a transfiguration. It is here that he shapes the programme of his existence; and to that programme he makes the real world conform. It is here he forms his highest rules of conduct. It is here he plants his hopes and joys. It is here he finds his dignity and power. The ideal world becomes to him the supreme reality." Lewes said that what a man thinks "is the necessary product of his organism and external conditions." The "organism itself is the product of its history; it is what it has become; it is a part of the history of the race." Because man is a creature of feeling he is susceptible to the influences of the outer world, and from the influences and experiences thus received the foundations of his mental life are laid. The structure erected on this foundation, however, is the product of man's social environment. As a social being, he inherits mental capacities, and all the instruments of mental, moral and social development, as these have been produced in the past. The social structure takes up and preserves the results of individual effort; and social capacity enlarges mental and moral power quite beyond what mere inheritance produces.

Lewes assigned as high a value to introspection as to observation in psychology, and said that whatever place is assigned to the one in scientific method must be assigned to the other. He therefore accorded a high value to imagination and intuition, and to all ideal constructions of life and its meanings which are based on science. All knowledge grows out of feeling, and must be expressible again in feeling, if it is to have any value. Accordingly, man's life is of little value apart from sentiment, and the emotional nature must always be satisfied. As Lewes begins his philosophy in feeling, he holds that the final object of philosophy is to develop feeling into a perfect expression, in accordance with the ideal wants of man's nature. In other words, the final and supreme object of philosophy is the expression of religion and the founding of a moral and spiritual system of life. He believed that religion will continue to regulate the evolution of humanity, and in "a religion founded on science and expressing at each stage what is known of the world and of man." As much as any zealous Christian believer he accepted man's need of spiritual culture and religious development. At the same time, his philosophy rejected a substantive absolute, or any other spiritual realities or existences apart from the universe given in feeling and consciousness. Accordingly, man must find his ideal satisfactions, his spiritual realities and moral ideals, within the limits of the universe as known to philosophy, and in the organic life of the race.

George Eliot was also largely influenced by the teachings of Auguste Comte. The place he assigned to positive knowledge and the inductive method, to feeling, to development and the influence of the past upon the present, were all accepted by her in an enthusiastic spirit. Altruism commanded her hearty belief, and to its principles she devoted her life. Comte's conceptions in regard to sentiment, and the vital importance of religion and social organization, had her entire assent. She differed from him in regard to spiritual and social organization, and she could not accept his arbitrary and artificial methods. One of the leaders of positivism in England[1] has given this account

[1] Some Public Aspects of Positivism, the annual address before the Positivist Society, London, January 1, 1881, by Professor E. G. Beesley, of University College.

of her relations to its organized movements and to its founder:

"Her powerful intellect had accepted the teaching of Auguste Comte, and she looked forward to the reorganization of belief on the lines which he had laid down. Her study of his two great works was diligent and constant. The last time I saw her — a few days before her death — I found that she had just been reading over again, with closest attention, that wonderful treatise, *The General View of Positivism*, a book which always seems full of fresh wisdom, however often one comes back to it. She had her reservations, no doubt. There were details in Comte's work which did not satisfy her. But all who knew her were aware — and I speak from an acquaintance of eighteen years — that she had not only cast away every shred of theology and metaphysics, but that she had found refuge from mere negativism in the system of Comte. She did not write her positivism in broad characters on her books. Like Shakspere, she was first an artist and then a philosopher; and I imagine she thought it to be her business as an artist rather to paint humanity as it is than as she would have it to be. But she could not conceal her intellectual conviction, and few competent persons read her books without detecting her standpoint. If any doubt could have existed, it was set at rest by that noble poem on 'Subjective Immortality,' the clearest, and at the same time the most beautiful, expression that has yet been given to one of the most distinctive doctrines of positivism; a composition of which we can already say with certainty that it will enter into the positivist liturgies of all countries and through all time. Towards positivism as an organization, a discipline, — in short, as a church, — her attitude must be plainly stated. She had much sympathy with it, as she showed by regularly subscribing to positivist objects, as, for instance, to the fund of the central organization in Paris presided over by M. Laffitte.

But she sought membership neither in that nor any other church. Like most of the stronger and thoroughly emancipated minds in this period of transition and revolutionary disturbance, she looked not beyond her own conscience for guidance and authority, but judged for herself, appealing to no external tribunal from the solitary judgment-seat within. I do not for a moment suppose that she looked on the organization of a church as unattainable; but she did not regard it as attained."

Another of her friends[1] has indicated very clearly the nature and extent of her dissent from Comte. He remarks that "her apologetic representation of the *Politique* as an *Utopia* evinces that she did not admit the cogency of its reasoning, or regard the entire social reconstruction of Comte as demonstrably valid. Her dissatisfaction with some of his speculations, as expressed to ourselves in the spring of 1880, was very decided. . . . All membership with the positivist community she steadily rejected. That a philosophy originally so catholic as that of Comte should assume a sectarian character, was a contingency she foreboded and deprecated." In this last remark we doubtless have the explanation of George Eliot's dissent from Comte. She believed in an organic, vital development of a higher social structure, which will be brought about in the gradual evolution of humanity. Comte's social structure was artificial, the conception of one mind, and therefore as ill adapted to represent the wants of mankind as any other system devised by an individual thinker. His philosophy proper, his system of positive thought, she accepted with but few reservations. Her views in this direction, as in many others, were substantially those presented by Lewes in his many works bearing on positivism. She was profoundly indebted to Comte, although in her later years she largely passed beyond his influence to the acceptance of the new evolution philosophy. In fact, she belonged to

[1] W. M. W. Call in the Westminster Review for July, 1881.

that school of English positivists which has only accepted the positive philosophy of Comte, and which has rejected his later work in the direction of social and religious construction. Lewes was the earliest of English thinkers to look at Comte in this way; but other representative members of the school are John Stuart Mill, George Eliot, Frederic Harrison and John Morley. Zealously accepting Comte's position that philosophy must limit itself to positive data and methods, they look upon the "Religion of Humanity," with Prof. Tyndall, as Catholicism minus Christianity, and reject it.

She certainly came nearer to Comte in some directions than to Herbert Spencer, for the latter has not so fully recognized those elements of the mental and social life which most attracted her attention. Her theory of duty is one which he does not accept. He insists in his *Data of Ethics* that duty will become less and less *obligatory* and necessary in the future, because all action will be in harmony with the impulses of the inner man and with the conditions of the environment. This conclusion is entirely opposed to the moral theory of George Eliot, and is but one instance of their wide divergence. He insists, in his *Study of Sociology*, that the religious consciousness will not change its lines of evolution. He distinctly rejects the conclusion arrived at by George Eliot, that there is no Infinite Reality knowable to man, and that the substance and reality of religion is purely subjective. "That the object-matter of religion," he says, "can be replaced by another object-matter, as supposed by those who think the 'religion of humanity' will be the religion of the future, is a belief countenanced neither by induction nor by deduction. However dominant may become the moral sentiment enlisted on behalf of humanity, it can never exclude the sentiment alone properly called religious, awakened by that which is behind humanity and behind all other things." George Eliot was content with humanity, and believed that all religion arises out of the subjective elements of human life. At the same time that she made religion a development from feeling, she limited the moral law to emotional sanctions. On the contrary, Spencer is much more a rationalist, and insists on the intellectual basis both of morals and of religion. He makes less of feeling than she; and in this fact is to be found a wide gulf of separation between them. She could have been no more content with his philosophy than she was indebted to it in the construction of her own. As much one as they are in their philosophic basis and general methods, they are antagonistic in their conceptions about man and in the place assigned to nature in the development of religion. To George Eliot, religion is the development of feeling. To Spencer, it is the result of our "*thought* of a power of which humanity is but a small and fugitive product." In these, as in other directions, they were not in sympathy. Her realism, her psychologic method, her philosophic theories, her scientific sympathies, she did not derive from him, diligently as she may have studied his books.

George Eliot agreed with Comte and all other positivists in setting aside every inquiry into causes, and limiting philosophy to the search after laws. The idea of causes is idealistic, and a cause of any kind whatever is, according to these thinkers, not to be found. "The knowledge of laws," says Comte, "is henceforth to take the place of the search after causes." In other words, it is impossible for man to find out *why* anything is, he can only know *how* it is. George Eliot entirely agreed with Comte as to the universal dominion of law. She also followed him in his teachings about heredity, which he held to be the cause of social unity, morality, and the higher or subjective life. His conception of feeling as the highest expression of human life confirmed the conclusions to which she had already arrived from the study of Feuerbach. She was an enthusiastic believer in the Great Being, Humanity; she worshipped at that shrine. More to her than all other beliefs was her belief that we are to live for others. With Comte she said, "Altruism alone can enable us to live in the highest and truest sense." She would have all our doctrines about *rights* eliminated from morality and politics. They are as absurd, says Comte, as they are immoral.

George Eliot had a strong tendency towards philosophical speculations. While yet a student she expressed an ardent desire that she might live to reconcile the philosophy of Locke with that of Kant. In positivism, as developed and modified by Lewes, she found that reconciliation. She went far towards accepting the boldest speculations of the agnostic science of the time, but she modified it again and again to meet the needs of her own broader mind and heart. Yet it is related of her that in parting with one of the greatest English poets, probably Tennyson, when he said to her, "Well, good-by, you and your molecules," she replied, "I am quite content with my molecules." Her speculations led to the rejection of anything like a positive belief in God, to an entire rejection of faith in a personal immortality, and to a repudiation of all idealistic conceptions of knowledge derived from supersensuous sources. Her theories are best represented by the words environment, experience, heredity, development, altruism, solidarité, subjective immortality. These speculations confront the reader in nearly every chapter of her novels, and they gave existence to all but a very few of her poems.

X.

DISTINCTIVE TEACHINGS.

SCIENCE was accepted by George Eliot as furnishing the method and the proof for her philosophic and religious opinions. She was in hearty sympathy with Spencer and Darwin in regard to most of their speculations, and the doctrine of evolution was one which entirely approved itself to her mind. All her theories were based fundamentally on the hypothesis of universal law, which she probably interpreted with Lewes, in his *Foundations of a Creed*, as the uniformities of Infinite Activity. Not only in the physical world did she see law reigning, but also in every phase of the moral and spiritual life of man. In reviewing Lecky's *Rationalism in Europe*, she used these suggestive words concerning the uniformity of sequences she believed to be universal in the fullest sense:

> The supremely important fact that the gradual reduction of all phenomena within the sphere of established law, which carries as a consequence the rejection of the miraculous, and has its determining current in the development of physical science, seems to have engaged comparatively little of his attention; at least he gives it no prominence. The great conception of uniform regular sequence, without partiality and without caprice — the conception which is the most potent force at work in the modification of our faith, and of the practical form given to our sentiments — could only grow out of that patient watching of external fact, and that silencing of preconceived notions, which are urged upon the mind by the problems of physical science.[1]

The uniformities of nature have the effect upon man, through his nervous organization, of developing a responsive feeling and action. He learns to respond to

[1] Fortnightly Review, May, 1865.

that uniformity, to conform his actions to it. The habits thus acquired are inherited by his children, and moral conduct is developed. Heredity has as conspicuous a place in the novels of George Eliot as in the scientific treatises of Charles Darwin. She has attempted to indicate the moral and social influences of heredity, that it gives us the better part of our life in all directions. Heredity is but one phase of the uniformity of nature and the persistence of its forces. That uniformity never changes for man; his life it entirely ignores. He is crushed by its forces; he is given pain and sorrow through its unpitying disregard of his tender nature. Not only the physical world, but the moral world also, is unfailing in the development of the legitimate sequences of its forces. There is no cessation of activity, no turning aside of consequences, no delay in the transformation of causes into necessary effects.

George Eliot never swerves from this conception of the universe, physical and moral; everywhere cause is but another name for effect. The unbending order adopts man into its processes, helps him when he conforms to them, and gives him pain when he disregards them. The whole secret of man's existence is to be found in the agreement of his life with the invariable sequences of nature and moral activity; harmony with them brings true development, discord brings pain and sorrow. The unbending nature of law, and man's relations to it, she has portrayed in "Mr. Gilfil's Love Story," when describing Tina's sorrows.

While this poor little heart was being bruised with a weight too heavy for it, Nature was holding on her calm inexorable way, in unmoved and terrible beauty. The stars were rushing in their eternal courses; the tides swelled to the level of the last expectant weed; the sun was making brilliant day to busy nations on the other side of the expectant earth. The stream of human thought and deed was hurrying and broadening onward. The astronomer was at his telescope; the great ships were laboring over the waves; the toiling eagerness of commerce, the fierce spirit of revolution, were only ebbing in brief rest, and sleepless statesmen were dreading the possible crisis of the morrow. What were our little Tina and her trouble in this mighty torrent, rushing from one awful unknown to another? Lighter than the smallest centre of quivering-life in the water-drop, hidden and uncared for as the pulse of anguish in the breast of the tiniest bird that has fluttered down to its nest with the long-sought food, and has found the nest torn and empty.

The effect of the uniformities of nature upon man, as George Eliot regarded them, is not quite that which would be inferred from these words alone. While she believed that nature is as unbending and pitiless as is here indicated, yet that unbending uniformity, which never changes its direction for man, is a large influence towards the development of his higher life. It has the effect on man to develop feeling which is the expression of all that is best and most human in his life.

George Eliot believed that the better and nobler part of man's life is to be found in feeling. It is the first expression which he makes as a sentient being, to have emotions; and his emotions more truly represent him than the purely intellectual processes of the mind. She would have us believe that feeling is rather to be trusted than the intellect, that it is both a safer and a surer guide. In *Middlemarch* she says that "our good depends on the quality and breadth of our emotions." Her conception of the comparative worth of feeling and logic is expressed in *Romola* with a characteristic touch.

After all has been said that can be said about the widening influence of ideas, it remains true that they would hardly be such strong agents unless they were taken in a solvent of feeling. The great world-struggle of developing thought is continually foreshadowed in the struggle of the affections, seeking a justification for love and hope.

In *Daniel Deronda*, when considering the causes which prevent men from desecrating their fathers' tombs for material gain, she says, "The only check to be alleged is a sentiment, which will coerce none who do not hold that sentiments are the better part of the world's wealth." To the same effect is her saying in *Theophrastus Such*, that "our civilization, considered as a splendid material fabric, is helplessly in peril without the spiritual police of sentiments or ideal feelings." She expresses the conviction in *Adam Bede*, that "it is possible to have very erroneous theories and very sublime feelings;" and she does not hesitate through all her writings to convey the idea, that sublime feelings are much to be preferred to profound thoughts or the most perfect philosophy. She makes Adam Bede say that "it isn't notions sets people doing the right thing — it's feelings," and that "feeling's a sort o' knowledge." Feeling gives us the only true knowledge we have of our fellow-men, a knowledge in every way more perfect than that which is to be derived from our intellectual inquiries into their natures and wants. In *Janet's Repentance* this power of feeling to give us true knowledge of others, to awaken us to the deeper needs of our own souls, when we come in contact with those who are able to move and inspire us, is eloquently presented.

> Blessed influence of one true loving human soul on another! Not calculable by algebra, not deducible by logic, but mysterious, effectual, mighty as the hidden process by which the tiny seed is quickened, and bursts forth into tall stem and broad leaf, and glowing tasselled flower. Ideas are often poor ghosts; our sun-filled eyes cannot discern them; they pass athwart us in thin vapor, and cannot make themselves felt. But sometimes they are made flesh; they breathe upon us with warm breath; they touch us with soft responsive hands; they look at us with sad, sincere eyes, and speak to us in appealing tones; they are clothed in a living human soul, with all its conflicts, its faith and its love. Then their presence is a power; then they shake us like a passion, and we are drawn after them with gentle compulsion, as flame is drawn to flame.[1]

She returns to the same subject when considering the intellectual theories of happiness and the proportion of crime there is likely to occur in the world. She shows her entire dissent from such a method of dealing with human woe, and she pleads for that sympathy and love which will enable us to feel the pain of others as our

[1] Chapter XIX.

own. This fellow-feeling gives us the most adequate knowledge we can have.

It was probably a hard saying to the Pharisees, that "there is more joy in heaven over one sinner that repenteth than over ninety and nine just persons that need no repentance." And certain ingenious philosophers of our own day must surely take offence at a joy so entirely out of correspondence with arithmetical proportion. But a heart that has been taught by its own sore struggles to bleed for the woes of another — that has "learned pity through suffering" — is likely to find very imperfect satisfaction in the "balance of happiness," "doctrine of compensations," and other short and easy methods of obtaining thorough complacency in the presence of pain; and for such a heart that saying will not be altogether dark. The emotions I have observed are but slightly influenced by arithmetical considerations: the mother, when her sweet lisping little ones have all been taken from her one after another, and she is hanging over her last dead babe, finds small consolation in the fact that the tiny dimpled corpse is but one of a necessary average, and that a thousand other babes brought into the world at the same time are doing well, and are likely to live; and if you stood beside that mother — if you knew her pang and shared it — it is probable you would be equally unable to see a ground of complacency in statistics. Doubtless a complacency resting on that basis is highly rational; but emotion, I fear, is obstinately irrational; it insists on caring for individuals; it absolutely refuses to adopt the quantitative view of human anguish, and to admit that thirteen happy lives are a set-off against twelve miserable lives, which leaves a clear balance on the side of satisfaction. This is the inherent imbecility of feeling, and one must be a great philosopher to have got quite clear of all that, and to have emerged into the serene air of pure intellect, in which it is evident that individuals really exist for no other purpose than that abstractions may be drawn from them — abstractions that may rise from heaps of ruined lives like the sweet savor of a sacrifice in the nostrils of philosophers, and of a philosophic Deity. And so it comes to pass that for the man who knows sympathy because he has known sorrow, that old, old saying about the joy of angels over the repentant sinner outweighing their joy over the ninety-nine just, has a meaning which does not jar with the language of his own heart. It only tells him that for angels too there is a transcendent value in human pain which refuses to be settled by equations; that the eyes of angels too are turned away from the serene happiness of the righteous to bend with yearning pity on the poor erring soul wandering in the desert where no water is; that for angels too the misery of one casts so tremendous a shadow as to eclipse the bliss of ninety-nine.[1]

Again, she says in the same story, —

Surely, surely the only true knowledge of our fellow-man is that

[1] Chapter XXII.

which enables us to feel with him — which gives us a fine ear for the heart-pulses that are beating under the mere clothes of circumstance and opinion. Our subtlest analogies of schools and sects must miss the essential truth, unless it be lit up by the love that sees in all forms of human thought and work the life-and-death struggles of separate human beings.

George Eliot would have us believe, that until we can feel with man, enter sympathetically into his emotions and yearnings, we cannot know him. It is because we have common emotions, common experiences, common aspirations, that we are really able to understand man; and not because of statistics, natural history, sociology or psychology. The objective facts have their place and value, but the real knowledge we possess of mankind is subjective, grows out of fellow-feeling.

The mental life of man, according to George Eliot, is simply an expansion of the emotional life. At first the mental life is unconscious, it is instinctive, simply the emotional response of man to the sequences of nature. This instinctive life of the emotions always remains a better part of our natures, and is to be trusted rather than the more formal activities of the intellectual faculties. In the most highly developed intellects even, there is a subconscious mental activity, an instinctive life of feeling, which is rather to be trusted than reason itself. This is a frequently recurring statement, which George Eliot makes in the firmest conviction of its truthfulness. It appears in such a sentence as this, in *The Mill on the Floss:* "Watch your own speech, and notice how it is guided by your less conscious purposes." In *Daniel Deronda* it finds expression in the assertion that "there is a great deal of unmapped country within us which would have to be taken into account in an explanation of our gusts and storms." It is more explicitly presented in *Adam Bede.*

Do we not all agree to call rapid thought and noble impulses by the name of inspiration? After our subtlest analysis of the mental process, we must still say that our highest thoughts and our best deeds are all given to us.

George Eliot puts into the mouth of Mordecai the assertion that love lies deeper than any reasons which are to be found for its exercise. In the same way, she would have us believe that feeling is safer than reason. Daniel Deronda questions Mordecai's visions, and doubts if he is worth listening to, except for pity's sake. On this the author comments, in defence of the visions, as against reason.

Suppose he had introduced himself as one of the strictest reasoners: do they form a body of men hitherto free from false conclusions and illusory speculations? The driest argument has its hallucinations, too hastily concluding that its net will now at last be large enough to hold the universe. Men may dream in demonstrations, and cut out an illusory world in the shape of axioms, definitions and propositions, with a final exclusion of fact signed Q. E. D. No formulas for thinking will save us mortals from mistake in our imperfect apprehension of the matter to be thought about. And since the unemotional intellect may carry us into a mathematical dream-land where nothing is but what is not, perhaps an emotional intellect may have absorbed into its passionate vision of possibilities some truth of what will be — the more comprehensive massive life feeding theory with new material, as the sensibility of the artist seizes combinations which science explains and justifies. At any rate, presumptions to the contrary are not to be trusted.[1]

As explicit is a passage in *Theophrastus Such*, wherein imagination is regarded as a means of knowledge, because it rests on a subconscious expression of experience.

It is worth repeating that powerful imagination is not false outward vision, but intense inward representation, and a creative energy constantly fed by susceptibility to the veriest minutiæ of experience, which it reproduces and constructs in fresh and fresh wholes; not the habitual confusion of probable fact with the fictions of fancy and transient inclination, but a breadth of ideal association which informs every material object, every incidental fact, with far-reaching memories and stored residues of passion, bringing into new light the less obvious relations of human existence.[2]

Imagination, feeling and the whole inward life are being constantly shaped by our actions. Experience gives new character to the inward life, and at the same time determines its motives and its inclinations The

[1] Chapter XLI [2] Chapter XIII.

muscles develop as they are used; what has been once done it is easier to do again. In the same way, our deeds influence our lives, and compel us to repeat our actions. At least this is George Eliot's opinion, and one she is fond of re-affirming. After Arthur had wronged Hetty, his life was changed, and of this change wrought in his character by his conduct, George Eliot says,—

> Our deeds determine us, as much as we determine our deeds; and until we know what has been or will be the peculiar combination of outward with inward facts which constitute a man's critical actions, it will be better not to think ourselves wise about his character. There is a terrible coercion in our deeds which may at first turn the honest man into a deceiver, and then reconcile him to the change; for this reason — that the second wrong presents itself to him in the guise of the only practicable right. The action which before commission has been seen with that blended common sense and fresh untarnished feeling which is the healthy eye of the soul, is looked at afterward with the lens of apologetic ingenuity, through which all things that men call beautiful and ugly are seen to be made up of textures very much alike. Europe adjusts itself to a *fait accompli*, and so does an individual character — until the placid adjustment is disturbed by a convulsive retribution.[1]

What we have done, determines what we shall do, even in opposition to our wills. After Tito Melema had done his first act towards denying his foster-father, we have this observation of the author's:

> Our deeds are like children that are born to us; they live and act apart from our own will. Nay, children may be strangled, but deeds never; they have an indestructible life both in and out of our consciousness; and that dreadful vitality of deeds was pressing hard on Tito for the first time.

When Tito had openly denied that father, at an unexpected moment, we hear the ever-present chorus repeating this great ethical truth:

> Tito was experiencing that inexorable law of human souls, that we prepare ourselves for sudden deeds by the reiterated choice of good or evil that gradually determines character.

As a river moves in the channel made for it, as a plant grows towards the sunlight, so man does again

[1] Chapter XXIX.

what he has once done. The impression of his act is left upon his nature, it is taken up into his motives, it leads to feeling and impulse, it repeats itself in future conduct. His deed lives in memory, it lives in weakness or strength of impulse, it lives in disease or in health, it lives in mental listlessness or in mental vigor. What is done, determines our natures in their character and tendency for the future. "A man can never separate himself from his past history," says George Eliot in one of the mottoes of *Felix Holt*. We cannot rid ourselves of the effects of our actions; they follow us forever. This truth takes shape in *Romola* in these words:

Our lives make a moral tradition for our individual selves, as the life of mankind at large makes a moral tradition for the race; and to have once acted greatly, seems a reason why we should always be noble. But Tito was feeling the effect of an opposite tradition: he had now no memories of self-conquest and perfect faithfulness from which he could have a sense of falling.

A motto in *Daniel Deronda* reiterates this oft-repeated assertion.

Deeds are the pulse of Time, his beating life,
And righteous or unrighteous, being done,
Must throb in after-throbs till Time itself
Be laid in stillness, and the universe
Quiver and breathe upon no mirror more.

Feeling is to be preferred to logic, according to George Eliot, because it brings us the results of long-accumulating experiences, because it embodies the inherited experiences of the race. She was an earnest believer in "far-reaching memories and stored residues of passion," for she was convinced that the better part of all our knowledge is brought to us by inheritance. The deeds of the individual make the habits of his life, they remain in memory, they guide the purposes of the will, and they give motives to action. Deeds often repeated give impulse and direction to character, and these appear in the offspring as predispositions of body and mind. In this way our deeds "throb in after-throbs" of our children; and in the same manner the deeds of a people live in the life of the race and become guiding motives in its future deeds. As the deeds of a person develop into habits, so the deeds of a people develop into national tendencies and actions.

George Eliot was a thorough believer in the Darwinian theories of heredity, and she has in all her books shown the effects of hereditary conditions on the individual and even upon a people. Family and race are made to play a very important part in her writings. Other novelists disregard the conditions and limitations imposed by heredity, and consider the individual as unrestricted by other laws than those of his own will; but George Eliot gives conspicuous prominence to the laws of heredity, both individual and social. Felix Holt never ceases in her pages to be the son of his mother, however enlarged his ideas may become and broad his culture. Rosamond Vincy also has a parentage, and so has Mary Garth. Daniel Deronda is a Jew by birth, the son of a visionary mother and a truth-seeking father. This parentage expresses itself throughout his life, even in boyhood, in all his thought and conduct. Heredity shapes the destiny of Tito Melema, Romola, Fedalma, Maggie Tulliver, Will Ladislaw, Gwendolen Harleth and many another character in George Eliot's novels. It is even more strongly presented in her poems. In *The Spanish Gypsy* she describes Fedalma as a genuine daughter of her father, as inheriting his genius and tendencies, which are stronger than all the Spanish culture she had received. When Fedalma says she belongs to him she loves, and that love

> is nature too,
> Forming a fresher law than laws of birth, —

Zarca replies, —

> Unmake yourself, then, from a Zincala —
> Unmake yourself from being child of mine!
> Take holy water, cross your dark skin white;

Round your proud eyes to foolish kitten looks;
Walk mincingly, and smirk, and twitch your robe:
Unmake yourself — doff all the eagle plumes
And be a parrot, chained to a ring that slips
Upon a Spaniard's thumb, at will of his
That you should prattle o'er his words again!

Fedalma cannot unmake herself; she has already danced in the plaza, and she is soon convinced that she is a Zincala, that her place is with her father and his tribe. The Prior had declared, —

That maiden's blood
Is as unchristian as the leopard's,

and it so proves. His statement of reasons for this conviction expresses the author's own belief.

What! Shall the trick of nostrils and of lips
Descend through generations, and the soul
That moves within our frame like God in worlds —
Convulsing, urging, melting, withering —
Imprint no record, leave no documents,
Of her great history? Shall men bequeath
The fancies of their palates to their sons,
And shall the shudder of restraining awe,
The slow-wept tears of contrite memory,
Faith's prayerful labor, and the food divine
Of fasts ecstatic — shall these pass away
Like wind upon the waters, tracklessly?
Shall the mere curl of eyelashes remain,
And god-enshrining symbols leave no trace
Of tremors reverent?

This larger or social heredity is that which claims much the larger share of George Eliot's attention, and it is far more clearly and distinctively presented in her writings. She gives a literary expression here to the teachings of the evolutionists, shows the application to life of what has been taught by Spencer, Hæckel and Lewes. In his *Foundations of a Creed*, Lewes has stated this theory in discussing "the limitations of knowledge." "It is indisputable," he says, "that every particular man comes into the world with a heritage of organized forms and definite tendencies, which will determine his feeling and thinking in certain definite ways, whenever the suitable conditions are present.

And all who believe in evolution believe that these forms and tendencies represent ancestral experiences and adaptations; believe that not only is the pointer born with an organized tendency to point, the setter to set, the beaver to build, and the bird to fly, but that the man is born with a tendency to think in images and symbols according to given relations and sequences which constitute logical laws, that *what* he thinks is the necessary product of his organism and the external conditions. This organism itself is a product of its history; it *is* what it has *become;* it is a part of the history of the human race; it is also specially individualized by the particular personal conditions which have distinguished him from his fellow-men. Thus resembling all men in general characters, he will in general feel as they feel, think as they think; and differing from all men in special characters, he will have personal differences of feeling and shades of feeling, thought and combinations of thought. . . . The mind is built up out of assimilated experiences, its perceptions being shaped by its pre-perceptions, its conceptions by its pre-conceptions. Like the body, the mind is shaped through its history." In other words, experience is inherited and shapes the mental and social life. What some philosophers have called intuitions, and what Kant called the categories of the mind, Lewes regarded as the inherited results of human experience. By a slow process of evolution the mind has been produced and shaped into harmony with its environment; the results of inherited experience take the form of feelings, intuitions, laws of thought and social tendencies. Its intuitions are to be accepted as the highest knowledge, because the transmitted results of all human experience.

As the body performs those muscular operations most easily to which it is most accustomed, so men as social beings perform those acts and think those thoughts most easily and naturally to which the race has been longest accustomed. Man lives and thinks as man has lived and thought; he inherits the past. In his social life he is as much the child of the past as he is individually the son of his father. If he inherits his father's physiognomy and habits of thought, so does he socially inherit the characteristics of his race, its social and moral life. George Eliot was profoundly convinced of the value of this fact, and she has presented it in her books in all its phases. In her *Fortnightly Review* essay on "The Influence of Rationalism," she says all large minds have long had "a vague sense" "that tradition is really the basis of our best life." She says, "Our sentiments may be called organized traditions; and a large part of our actions gather all their justification, all their attractions and aroma, from the memory of the life lived, of the actions done, before we were born." Tradition is the inherited experience of the race, the result of its long efforts, its many struggles, after a larger life. It lives in the tendencies of our emotions, in the intuitions and aspirations of our minds, as the wisdom which our minds hold dear, as the yearnings of our hearts after a wider social life. These things are not the results of our own reasonings, but they are the results of the life lived by those who have gone before us, and who, by their thoughts and deeds, have shaped our lives, our minds, to what they are. Tradition is the inherited experience, feeling, yearning, pain, sorrow and wisdom of the ages. It furnishes a great system of customs, laws, institutions, ideas, motives and feelings into which we are born, which we naturally adopt, which gives shape and strength to our growing life, which makes it possible for us to take up life at that stage it has reached after the experiences of many generations. George Eliot says in *Middlemarch* that "a kind Providence furnishes the limpest personality with a little gum or starch in the form of tradition." We come into a world made ready for us, and find prepared for our immediate use a vastcomplex of customs and duties and ideas, the results of the world's experience. George Eliot believed, with Comte, that with each generation the influence of the past over the present becomes greater, and that men's lives are more and more shaped by what has been. In *The Spanish Gypsy* she makes Don Silva say that

> The only better is a Past that lives
> On through an added Present, stretching still
> In hope unchecked by shaming memories
> To life's last breath.

This deep conviction of the blessed influence of the past upon us is well expressed in the little poem on "Self and Life," one of the most fully autobiographical of all her poems, where she makes Life bid Self remember

> How the solemn, splendid Past
> O'er thy early widened earth
> Made grandeur, as on sunset cast
> Dark elms near take mighty girth.
> Hands and feet were tiny still
> When we knew the historic thrill,
> Breathed deep breath in heroes dead,
> Tasted the immortals' bread.

In expressive sentences, in the development of her characters, and in many other ways, she affirms this faith in tradition. In one of the mottoes in *Felix Holt* she uses a fine sentence, which is repeated in "A Minor Prophet."

> Our finest hope is finest memory.

The finest hope of the race is to be found in memory of its great deeds, as its saddest loss is to be found in forgetfulness of a noble past. In *The Mill on the Floss*, when describing St. Ogg's, she attributes its sordid and tedious life to its neglect of the past and its inspiring memories.

> The mind of St. Ogg's did not look extensively before or after. It inherited a long past without thinking of it, and had no eyes for the spirits that walk the streets. Since the centuries when St. Ogg with his boat, and the Virgin Mother at the prow, had been seen on

the wide water, so many memories had been left behind, and had gradually vanished like the receding hill-tops! And the present time was like the level plain where men lose their belief in volcanoes and earthquakes, thinking to-morrow will be as yesterday, and the giant forces that used to shake the earth are forever laid to sleep. The days were gone when people could be greatly wrought upon by their faith, still less change it: the Catholics were formidable because they would lay hold of government and property, and burn men alive; not because any sane and honest parishioner of St. Ogg's could be brought to believe in the Pope. One aged person remembered how a rude multitude had been swayed when John Wesley preached in the cattle-market; but for a long while it had not been expected of preachers that they should shake the souls of men. An occasional burst of fervor in Dissenting pulpits on the subject of infant baptism was the only symptom of a zeal unsuited to sober times when men had done with change. Protestantism sat at ease, unmindful of schisms, careless of proselytism; Dissent was an inheritance along with a superior pew and a business connection; and Churchmanship only wondered contemptuously at Dissent as a foolish habit that clung greatly to families in the grocery and chandlering lines, though not incompatible with prosperous wholesale dealing.[1]

This faith in tradition, as giving the basis of all our best life, is perhaps nowhere so expressively set forth by George Eliot as in *The Spanish Gypsy*. It is distinctly taught by all the best characters in the words they speak, and it is emphatically taught in the whole purpose and spirit of the poem. Zarca says his tribe has no great life because it has no great national memories. He calls his people

> Wanderers whom no God took knowledge of
> To give them laws, to fight for them, or blight
> Another race to make them ampler room;
> Who have no whence or whither in their souls,
> No dimmest lure of glorious ancestors
> To make a common breath for piety.

As his people are weak because they have no traditional life, he proposes by his deeds to make them national memories and hopes and aims.

> No lure
> Shall draw me to disown them, or forsake
> The meagre wandering herd that lows for help —
> And needs me for its guide, to seek my pasture
> Among the well-fed beeves that graze at will.

[1] Chapter XII.

Because our race has no great memories,
I will so live, it shall remember me
For deeds of such divine beneficence
As rivers have, that teach men what is good
By blessing them. I have been schooled — have caught
Lore from Hebrew, deftness from the Moor —
Know the rich heritage, the milder life,
Of nations fathered by a mighty Past.

The way in which such a past is made is suggested by Zarca, in answer to a question about the Gypsy's faith; it is made by a common life of faith and brotherhood, that gives origin to a common inheritance and memories.

O, it is a faith
Taught by no priest, but by their beating hearts
Faith to each other: the fidelity
Of fellow-wanderers in a desert place
Who share the same dire thirst, and therefore share
The scanty water: the fidelity
Of men whose pulses leap with kindred fire,
Who in the flash of eyes, the clasp of hands,
The speech that even in lying tells the truth
Of heritage inevitable as birth,
Nay, in the silent bodily presence feel
The mystic stirring of a common life
Which makes the many one: fidelity
To that deep consecrating oath our sponsor Fate
Made through our infant breath when we were born
The fellow-heirs of that small island, Life,
Where we must dig and sow and reap with brothers.
Fear thou that oath, my daughter — nay, not fear,
But love it; for the sanctity of oaths
Lies not in lightning that avenges them,
But in the injury wrought by broken bonds
And in the garnered good of human trust.
And you have sworn — even with your infant breath
You too were pledged.

George Eliot's faith in tradition, as furnishing the basis of our best life, and the moral purpose and law which is to guide it, she has concentrated into one question asked by Maggie Tulliver.

If the past is not to bind us, where can duty lie? We should have no law but the inclination of the moment.

Although this question is asked in regard to an indi

vidual's past, the answer to it holds quite as good for the race as for the individual. She repudiates all theories which give the individual authority to follow inclination, or even to follow some inner or personal guide. The true wisdom is always social, always grows out of the experiences of the race, and not out of any personal inspiration or enlightenment. Tradition furnishes the materials for reason to use, but reason does not penetrate into new regions, or bring to us wisdom apart from that we obtain through inherited experiences. George Eliot compares these two with each other in *The Spanish Gypsy* in the words of Sephardo.

I abide
By that wise spirit of listening reverence
Which marks the boldest doctors of our race.
For Truth, to us, is like a living child
Born of two parents: if the parents part
And will divide the child, how shall it live?
Or, I will rather say: Two angels guide
The path of man, both aged and yet young,
As angels are, ripening through endless years.
On one he leans: some call her Memory,
And some, Tradition; and her voice is sweet,
With deep mysterious accords: the other,
Floating above, holds down a lamp which streams
A light divine and searching on the earth,
Compelling eyes and footsteps. Memory yields,
Yet clings with loving check, and shines anew
Reflecting all the rays of that bright lamp
Our angel Reason holds. We had not walked
But for Tradition; we walk evermore
To higher paths, by brightening Reason's lamp.

Man leans on tradition, it is the support of his life, by its strength he is able to move forward. Reason is a lamp which lights the way, gives direction to tradition; it is a beacon and not a support. Tradition not only brings us the wisdom of all past experience, but it develops into a spiritual atmosphere in which we live, move and have our being. This was Comte's idea, that the spiritual life is developed out of tradition, that the world's experiences have produced for us intangible hopes, yearnings and aspirations; awe, reverence and sense of subtle mystery; mystic trust, faith in invisible memories, joy in the unseen power of thought and love; and that these create for us a spiritual world most real in its nature, and most powerful in its influence. On every hand man is touched by the invisible, mystical influences of the past, spiritual voices call to him out of the ages, unseen hands point the way he is to go. He breathes this atmosphere of spiritual memories, he is fed on thoughts other men have made for his sustenance, he is inspired by the heroisms of ages gone before. In an article in the *Westminster Review* in July, 1856, on "The Natural History of German Life," in review of W. H. Riehl's books on the German peasant, and on land and climate, she presents the idea that a people can be understood only when we understand its history. Society, she says, has developed through many generations, and has built itself up in many memories and associations. To change it we must change its traditions. Nothing can be done *de novo;* a fresh beginning cannot be had. The dream of the French Revolution, that a new nation, a new life, a new morality, was to be created anew and fresh out of the cogitations of philosophers, is not in any sense to be realized. Tradition forever asserts itself, the past is more powerful than all philosophers, and new traditions must be made before a new life can be had for society. These ideas are well expressed by George Eliot in her review of Riehl's books.

He sees in European society ***incarnate history***, and any attempt to disengage it from its historical elements must, he believes, be simply destruction of social vitality. What has grown up historically can only die out historically, by the gradual operation of necessary laws. The external conditions which society has inherited from the past are but the manifestation of inherited internal conditions in the human beings who compose it; the internal conditions and the external are related to each other as the organism and its medium, and development can take place only by the gradual consentaneous development of both. As a necessary preliminary to a purely rational society, you must obtain purely rational men, free from the sweet and bitter prejudices of hereditary affection and antipathy; which is as easy as to get running streams without springs, or the leafy shade of the forest without the secular growth of trunk and branch.

The historical conditions of society may be compared with those of language. It must be admitted that the language of cultivated nations is in anything but a rational state; the great sections of the civilized world are only approximately intelligible to each other, and even that, only at the cost of long study; one word stands for many things, and many words for one thing; the subtle shades of meaning, and still subtler echoes of association, make language an instrument which scarcely anything short of genius can wield with definiteness and certainty. Suppose, then, that the effort which has been again and again made to construct a universal language on a rational basis has at length succeeded, and that you have a language which has no uncertainty, no whims of idiom, no cumbrous forms, no fitful shimmer of many-hued significance, no hoary archaisms "familiar with forgotten years,"—a patent deodorized and non-resonant language, which effects the purpose of communication as perfectly and rapidly as algebraic signs. Your language may be a perfect medium of expression to science, but will never express *life*, which is a great deal more than science. With the anomalies and inconveniences of historical language, you will have parted with its music and its passion, with its vital qualities as an expression of individual character, with its subtle capabilities of wit, with everything that gives it power over the imagination; and the next step in simplification will be the invention of a talking watch, which will achieve the utmost facility and despatch in the communication of ideas by a graduated adjustment of ticks, to be represented in writing by a corresponding arrangement of dots. A "melancholy language of the future!" The sensory and motor nerves that run in the same sheath are scarcely bound together by a more necessary and delicate union than that which binds men's affections, imagination, wit and humor with the subtle ramifications of historical language. Language must be left to grow in precision, completeness and unity, as minds grow in clearness, comprehensiveness and sympathy. And there is an analogous relation between the moral tendencies of men and the social conditions they have inherited. The nature of European men has its roots intertwined with the past, and can only be developed by allowing those roots to remain undisturbed while the process of development is going on, until that perfect ripeness of the seed which carries with it a life independent of the root. . . .

It has not been sufficiently insisted on, that in the various branches of social science there is an advance from the general to the special, from the simple to the complex, analogous with that which is found in the series of the sciences, from mathematics to biology. To the laws of quantity comprised in mathematics and physics are superadded, in chemistry, laws of quality; to those again are added, in biology, laws of life; and lastly, the conditions of life in general branch out into its special conditions, or natural history, on the one hand, and into its abnormal conditions, or pathology, on the other. And in this series or ramification of the sciences, the more general science will not suffice to solve the problems of the more special. Chemistry embraces phenomena which are not explicable by physics; biology embraces phenomena which are not explicable by chemistry; and no biological generalization will enable us to predict the infinite specialties produced by the complexity of vital conditions. So social science, while it has departments which in their fundamental generality correspond to mathematics and physics, namely, those grand and simple generalizations which trace out the inevitable march of the human race as a whole, and, as a ramification of these, the laws of economical science, has also, in the departments of government and jurisprudence, which embrace the conditions of social life in all their complexity, what may be called its biology, carrying us on to innumerable special phenomena which outlie the sphere of science, and belong to natural history. And just as the most thorough acquaintance with physics, or chemistry, or general physiology, will not enable you at once to establish the balance of life in your private vivarium, so that your particular society of zoophytes, molluscs and echinoderms may feel themselves, as the Germans say, at ease in their skins; so the most complete equipment of theory will not enable a statesman or a political and social reformer to adjust his measures wisely, in the absence of a special acquaintance with the section of society for which he legislates, with the peculiar characteristics of the nation, the province, the class whose well-being he has to consult. In other words, a wise social policy must be based not simply on abstract social science but on the natural history of social bodies.

Her conception of the corporate life of the race has been clearly expressed by George Eliot in the concluding essay in *Theophrastus Such*. In that essay she writes of the powerful influence wrought upon national life by "the divine gift of memory which inspires the moments with a past, a present and a future, and gives the sense of corporate existence that raises man above the otherwise more respectable and innocent brute." The nations which lead the world on to a larger civilization are not merely those with most genius, originality, gift of invention or talent for scientific observation, but those which have the finest traditions. As a member of such a nation, the individual can be noble and great. We should almost be persuaded, reading George Eliot's eloquent rhetoric on this subject, that personal genius is of little moment in comparison with a rich inheritance of national memories. It is indeed true that Homer, Virgil, Dante, Milton and Shakspere have used the traditions of their people for the materials of their immortal works, but what would those traditions have been without the genius of the men who deal with the traditions in a fashion quite their own, giving them new meaning and vitality! The poet, however, needs materials for his song, and memories to inspire it. The influence of these George Eliot well understands in calling them "the deep suckers of healthy sentiment."

The historian guides us rightly in urging us to dwell on the virtues of our ancestors with emulation, and to cherish our sense of a common descent as a bond of obligation. The eminence, the nobleness of a people, depends on its capability of being stirred by memories, and for striving for what we call spiritual ends—ends which consist not in an immediate material possession, but in the satisfaction of a great feeling that animates the collective body as with one soul. A people having the seed of worthiness in it must feel an answering thrill when it is adjured by the deaths of its heroes who died to preserve its national existence; when it is reminded of its small beginnings and gradual growth through past labors and struggles, such as are still demanded of it in order that the freedom and well-being thus inherited may be transmitted unimpaired to children and children's children; when an appeal against the permission of injustice is made to great precedents in its history and to the better genius breathing in its institutions. It is this living force of sentiment in common which makes a national consciousness. Nations so moved will resist conquest with the very breasts of their women, will pay their millions and their blood to abolish slavery, will share privation in famine and all calamity, will produce poets to sing "some great story of a man," and thinkers whose theories will bear the test of action. An individual man, to be harmoniously great, must belong to a nation of this order, if not in actual existence yet existing in the past—in memory, as a departed, invisible, beloved ideal, once a reality, and perhaps to be restored. . . . Not only the nobleness of a nation depends on the presence of this national consciousness, but also the nobleness of each individual citizen. Our dignity and rectitude are proportioned to our sense of relationship with something great, admirable, pregnant with high possibilities, worthy of sacrifice, a continual inspiration to self-repression and discipline by the presentation of aims larger and more attractive to our generous part than the securing of personal ease or prosperity.[1]

Zealous as is George Eliot's faith in tradition, she is broad-minded enough to see that it is limited in its influence by at least two causes,—by reason and by the spirit of universal brotherhood. We have already seen

[1] Theophrastus Such, chapter XVIII.

that she makes reason one of man's guides. In *Romola* the right of the individual to make a new course for action is distinctly expressed. Romola had "the inspiring consciousness," we are told, "that her lot was vitally united with the general lot which exalted even the minor details of obligation into religion," and so "she was marching with a great army, she was feeling the stress of a common life." Yet she began to feel that she must not merely repeat the past; and the influence of Savonarola, in breaking with Rome for the sake of a pure and holy life, inspired her.

> To her, as to him, there had come one of those moments in life when the soul must dare to act on its own warrant, not only without external law to appeal to, but in face of a law which is not unarmed with divine lightnings — lightnings that may yet fall if the warrant has been false.

It is reason's lamp by which "we walk evermore to higher paths;" and by its aid, new deeds are to be done, new memories created, fresher traditions woven into feeling and hope. National memories are to be superseded by the spirit of brotherhood, for, as the race advances, nations are brought closer to each other, have more in common, and development is made of world-wide traditions. Theophrastus Such, in the last of his essays, tells us that "it is impossible to arrest the tendencies of things towards the quicker or slower fusion of races."

The environment of her characters George Eliot makes of very great importance. She dwells upon the natural scenery which they love, but especially does she magnify the importance of the social environment, and the perpetual influence it has upon the whole of life. Mr. James Sully has clearly interpreted her thought on this subject, and pointed out its engrossing interest for her.

"A character divorced from its surroundings is an abstraction. A personality is only a concrete living whole, when we attach it by a network of organic filaments to its particular environment, physical and social. Our author evidently chooses her surroundings with strict regard to her characters. She paints nature less in its own beauty than in its special aspect and significance for those whom she sets in its midst. 'The bushy hedgerows,' 'the pool in the corner of the field where the grasses were dank,' 'the sudden slope of the old marl-pit, making a red background for the burdock'— these things are touched caressingly and lingered over because they are so much to the 'midland-bred souls' whose history is here recorded; so much because of cumulative recollection reaching back to the time when they 'toddled among' them, or perhaps 'learnt them by heart standing between their father's knees while he drove leisurely.' And what applies to the natural environment applies still more to those narrower surroundings which men construct for themselves, and which form their daily shelter, their work-shop, their place of social influence. The human interest which our author sheds about the mill, the carpenter's shop, the dairy, the village church, and even the stiff, uninviting conventicle, shows that she looks on these as having a living continuity with the people whom she sets among them. Their artistic value is but a reflection of all that they mean to those for whom they have made the nearer and habitually enclosing world." The larger influence in the environment of any person, according to George Eliot, is that which arises from tradition. Cut off from the sustenance given by tradition, the person loses the motives, the supports of his life. This is well shown in the case of Silas Marner, who had fled from his early home and all his life held dear. George Eliot describes the effect of such a change of environment.

Even people whose lives have been made various by learning, sometimes find it hard to keep a fast hold on their habitual views of life, on their faith in the Invisible — nay, on the sense that their past joys and sorrows are a real experience, when they are suddenly transported to a new land, where the beings around them know nothing of their history, and share none of their ideas — where their mother earth shows another lap, and human life has other forms than those on which their souls have been nourished. Minds that have been unhinged from their old faith and love, have perhaps sought this Lethean influence of exile, in which the past becomes dreamy because its symbols have all vanished, and the present too is dreamy because it is linked with no memories.[1]

She delights to return again and again to the influences produced upon us by the environment of childhood. In *The Mill on the Floss* she tells us how dear the earth becomes by such associations.

We could never have loved the earth so well if we had had no childhood in it,—if it were not the earth where the same flowers come up again every spring that we used to gather with our tiny fingers as we sat lisping to ourselves on the grass—the same hips and haws on the autumn hedgerows—the same redbreasts that we used to call "God's birds," because they did no harm to the precious crops. What novelty is worth that sweet monotony where everything is known, and *loved* because it is known?

The wood I walk in on this mild May day, with the young yellow-brown foliage of the oaks between me and the blue sky, the white star-flowers, and the blue-eyed speedwell, and the ground-ivy at my feet—what grove of tropic palms, what strange ferns or splendid broad-petalled blossoms, could ever thrill such deep and delicate fibres within me as this home-scene? These familiar flowers, these well-remembered bird-notes, this sky with its fitful brightness, these furrowed and grassy fields, each with a sort of personality given to it by the capricious hedgerows—such things as these are the mother tongue of our imagination, the language that is laden with all the subtle inextricable associations the fleeting hours of our childhood left behind them. Our delight in the sunshine on the deep-bladed grass to-day might be no more than the faint perception of wearied souls, if it were not for the sunshine and the grass in the far-off years, which still live in us, and transform our perception into love.[2]

In the backward glance of *Theophrastus Such* this anchorage of the life in familiar associations is described as a source of our faith in the spiritual, even when all the childhood thoughts about those associations cannot be retained.

The illusions that began for us when we were less acquainted with evil have not lost their value when we discern them to be illusions. They feed the ideal better, and in loving them still, we strengthen the precious habit of loving something not visibly, tangibly existent, but a spiritual product of our visible, tangible selves.

[1] Chapter II. [2] Chapter V.

In the evolution philosophy she found the reconciliation between Locke and Kant which she so earnestly desired to discover in girlhood. The old school of experimentalists did not satisfy her with their philosophy; she saw that the dictum that all knowledge is the result of sensation was not satisfactory, that it was shallow and untrue. On the other hand, the intellectual intuition of Schelling was not acceptable, nor even Kant's categories of the mind. She wished to know why the mind instinctively throws all experiences and thoughts under certain forms, and why it must think under certain general methods. She found what to her was a perfectly satisfactory answer to these questions in the theory of evolution as developed by Darwin and Spencer. Through the aid of these men she found the reconciliation between Locke and Kant, and discovered that both were wrong and both right. So familiar has this reconciliation become, and so wide is its acceptance, that no more than a mere hint of its meaning will be needed here. This philosophy asserts, with Locke, that all knowledge begins in sensation and experience; but with Kant, it affirms that knowledge passes beyond experience and becomes intuitional. It differs from Kant as to the source of the intuitions, pronouncing them the results of experience built up into legitimate factors of the mind by heredity. Experience is inherited and becomes intuitions. The intuitions are affirmed to be reliable, and, to a certain extent, sure indications of truth. They are the results, to use the phrase adopted by Lewes, of "organized experience;" experience verified in the most effective manner in the organism which it creates and modifies. According to this philosophy, man must trust the results of experience, but he can by no means be certain that those results correspond with actuality. They are actual for him, because it is impossible for him to go beyond their range. Within the little round created by "organized experience," which is also Lewes's definition of science, man may trust his knowledge, because it is consistent with itself; but beyond that strict limit he can obtain no knowledge, and even knows that what is without it does not correspond with what is within it. In truth, man knows only the relative, not the absolute; he must rely on experience, not on creative reason.

George Eliot would have us believe that the sources of life are not inward, but outward; not dependent on the deep affirmations of individual reason, or on the soul's inherent capacity to see what is true, but on the effects of environment and the results of social experience. Man is not related to an infinite world of reason and spiritual truth, but only to a world of universal law, hereditary conditions and social traditions. Invariable law, heredity, feeling, tradition; these words indicate the trend of George Eliot's mind, and the narrow limitations of her philosophy. Man is not only the product of nature, but, according to this theory, nature limits his moral capacity and the range of his mental activity. Environment is regarded as all-powerful, and the material world as the *source* of such truth as we can know. In her powerful presentation of this philosophy of life George Eliot indicates her great genius and her profound insight. At the same time, her work is limited, her genius cramped, and her imagination crippled, by a philosophy so narrow and a creed so inexpansive.

XI.

RELIGIOUS TENDENCIES.

AS a great literary creator, George Eliot holds a singular position in reference to religious beliefs. To most literary artists religion is a vital part of life, which enters as a profound element into their teachings or into their interpretations of character and incident. Religion deeply affects the writings of Tennyson, Browning and Ruskin; its problems, its hopes, its elements of mystery and infinity touch all their pages. In an equal degree, though with a further departure from accredited beliefs, and with a greater effect from philosophical or humanitarian influences, has it wrought itself into the genius of Goethe, Carlyle and Hugo. Even the pages of Voltaire, Shelley and Heine have been touched by its magic influence; their words glow with its great interests, and bloom into beauty through its inspiration. None of these is more affected by religion than George Eliot has been; nor does it form a greater element in their writings than in hers.

What is singular about George Eliot's position is, that she both affirms and denies; she is deeply religious and yet rejects all religious doctrines. No writer of the century has given religion a more important relation to human interests or made it a larger element in his creative work; and yet no other literary artist has so completely rejected all positive belief in God and immortality. In her books she depicts every phase of religious belief and life, and with sympathy and appreciation. A very large proportion of her characters are clergymen or other religious persons, who are described with accuracy and sympathy. Her own faith, the theory of religion she accepts, is not given to any of her characters. What she believes, appears only in her comments, and in the general effect which life produces on the persons she describes. She believed Christianity is subjectively true, that it is a fit expression of the inner nature and of the spiritual wants of the soul. She did not propagate the pantheism of Spinoza or the theism of Francis Newman, because she did not regard them as so near the truth as the Christianity of Paul. As intellectual theories they may have been preferable to her, but from the outlook of feeling which she ever occupied, Paul was the truer teacher, and especially because his teachings are linked with the spiritual desires and outpourings of many generations. The spontaneous movements of the human mind, which have taken possession of vast numbers of people through long periods of time, have a depth of meaning which the speculations of no individual theorizer can ever possess. Especially did she regard Christianity as a pure and noble expression of the soul's inner wants and aspirations. It is an objective realization of feeling and sentiment, it gives purpose and meaning to man's cravings for a diviner life, it links generation to generation in a continued series of beautiful traditions and noble inspirations. Her intellectual view of the subject was expressed to a friend in these words:

> Deism seems to me the most incoherent of all systems, but to Christianity I feel no objection but its want of evidence.

She also expressed more sympathy with the simple faith of the multitude than with the intellectual speculations of philosophers and theologians; and again, she said that she felt more sympathy with than divergence from the narrowest and least cultivated believer in Christianity. As a vehicle of the accumulated hopes and traditions of the world's feeling and sorrow she appreciated Christianity, saw its beauty, felt deeply in sympathy with its spirit of renunciation, accepted its ideal of a divine life. She learned from Feuerbach that religion, that Christianity, gives fit expression to the emotional life and spiritual aspirations of man, and that what it finds within in no degree corresponds with that which surrounds man without.

Barren and lifeless as this view must seem to most persons, it was a source of great confidence and inspiration to George Eliot. It enabled her to appreciate the religious experiences of men, to portray most accurately and sympathetically a great variety of religious believers, and to give this side of life its place and proportion. At the same time, it was a personal satisfaction to her to be able to keep in unbroken sympathy with the religious experiences of her childhood and youth while intellectually unable to accept the beliefs on which these experiences rested. More than this, she believed that religion and spirituality of life are necessary elements of human existence, that man can never cast them off, and that man will lead a happy and harmonious life only when they have a true and fitting expression in his culture and civilization. She maintained, with Sara Hennell, that we may retain the religious sentiments in all their glow and in all their depth of influence, at the same time that the doctrines of theology and all those conceptions of nature and man on which they rest are rejected; that we may have a disposition of the heart akin to that of the prophets and saints of religion, while we intellectually cast aside all which gave meaning to their faith and devotion. According to George Eliot, religion rests upon feeling and the relations of man to humanity, as well as upon his irreversible relations to the universe. In *The Mill on the Floss* she has given a definition of it, in speaking of Maggie's want of

> that knowledge of the irreversible laws within and without her, which, governing the habits, becomes morality, and developing the feelings of submission and dependence, becomes religion.[1]

[1] Book IV., chapter III.

It is the human side of religion which interests George Eliot, its influence morally, its sympathetic impulse, its power to comfort and console. Its supernatural elements seem to have little influence over her mind, at least only so far as they serve the moral aims of life. It is humanity which attracts her mind, inspires her ideal hopes, kindles her enthusiasms. Religion, apart from human encouragement and elevation, the suppression of human sin and sorrow, and the increase of human sympathy and joy, has little attraction for her. She takes no ground of opposition to the beliefs of others, expresses no contempt for any form of belief in God; but she measures all beliefs by their moral influence and their power to enkindle the enthusiasm of humanity.

The pantheistic theism defended by Lewes in his book on Comte, in 1853, seems to have been also accepted by George Eliot. We are told that her mind long wavered between the two, though pantheism was less acceptable than theism, on account of its moral indifference. It was undoubtedly the moral bearings of the subject which all the time had the greatest weight with her, and probably Kant's position had not a little effect on her opinions. She came, at least, to find final satisfaction in agnosticism, to believe that all intellectual speculations on the subject are in vain. At the same time, her moral convictions grew stronger, and she believed in the power of moral activity to work out a solution of life when no other can be found. At this point she stood with Kant rather than with Comte, in accepting the moral nature as a true guide. She very zealously believed with Fichte in a moral order of the world, approving of the truth which underlies the words of Fichte's English disciple, Matthew Arnold, when he discourses of "the Eternal, not ourselves, which makes for righteousness." Her positive convictions and beliefs on the subject lie in this direction, and she firmly accepted the idea of a moral order and purpose.

So much she thought we can know and rely on; beyond this she believed we can know nothing. Her later convictions on this subject have been expressed in a graphic manner by one of her friends. "I remember now," says this person, "at Cambridge, I walked with her once in the Fellows' Garden, of Trinity, on an evening of rainy May; and she, stirred somewhat beyond her wont, and taking as her text the three words which have been used so often as the inspiring trumpet-calls of man, — the words *God, Immortality, Duty,* — pronounced, with terrible emphasis, how inconceivable was the *first*, how unbelievable the *second*, and yet how peremptory and absolute the *third*. Never, perhaps, have sterner accents affirmed the sovereignty of impersonal and unrecompensed law. I listened, and night fell; her grave, majestic countenance turned towards me like a sibyl's in the gloom; it was as though she withdrew from my grasp, one by one, the two scrolls of promise, and left me the third scroll only, awful with inevitable fates."[1] All her later writings, at least, confirm this testimony to her assertion of the inconceivableness of God, and her open denial of faith in theism. She cannot have gone so far as to assert the non-existence of God, affirming only that she could not conceive of such a being as actually existing. She could not believe in a personal God, but Lewes's conception of a dynamic life was doubtless acceptable.

With as much emphasis she pronounced immortality unbelievable. She early accepted the theory of Charles Bray and Sara Hennell, that we live hereafter only in the life of the race. The moral bearings of the subject here also were most effective over her mind, for she felt that what we ought most of all to consider is our relations to our fellow-men, and that another world can have little real effect upon our present living. In her *Westminster Review* article on "Evangelical Teach-

[1] F. W. H. Myers in The Century Magazine for November, 1881.

ing" as presented in Young's *Night Thoughts*, she criticises the following declaration : —

> "Who tells me he denies his soul immortal,
> What'er his boast, has told me he's a knave.
> His duty 'tis to love himself alone,
> Nor care though mankind perish, if he smiles."

Her comments on these lines of Young's are full of interest, in view of her subsequent teachings, and they open an insight into her tendencies of mind very helpful to those who would understand her fully. Her interest in all that is human, her craving for a more perfect development of human sympathy and co-operation, are very clearly to be seen.

> We may admit that if the better part of virtue consists, as Young appears to think, in contempt for mortal joys, in "meditation of our own decease," and in "applause" of God in the style of a congratulatory address to Her Majesty — all which has small relation to the well-being of mankind on this earth — the motive to it must be gathered from something that lies quite outside the sphere of human sympathy. But, for certain other elements of virtue, which are of more obvious importance to untheological minds, — a delicate sense of our neighbor's rights, an active participation in the joys and sorrows of our fellow-men, a magnanimous acceptance of privation or suffering for ourselves when it is the condition of good to others, — in a word, the extension and intensification of our sympathetic nature, — we think it of some importance to contend that they have no more direct relation to the belief in a future state than the interchange of gases in the lungs has to the plurality of worlds. Nay, to us it is conceivable that in some minds the deep pathos lying in the thought of human mortality — that we are here for a little while and then vanish away, that this earthly life is all that is given to our loved ones and to our many suffering fellow-men — lies nearer the fountains of moral emotion than the conception of extended existence. And surely it ought to be a welcome fact, if the thought of *mortality*, as well as of immortality, be favorable to virtue. Do writers of sermons and religious novels prefer that we should be vicious in order that there may be a more evident political and social necessity for printed sermons and clerical fictions? Because learned gentlemen are theological, are we to have no more simple honesty and good-will? We can imagine that the proprietors of a patent water-supply have a dread of common springs; but, for our own part, we think there cannot be too great security against a lack of fresh water or of pure morality. To us it is a matter of unmixed rejoicing that this latter necessary of healthful life is independent of theological ink,

and that its evolution is insured in the interaction of human souls as certainly as the evolution of science or art, with which, indeed, it is but a twin ray, melting into them with undefinable limits.

The considerations here presented are very effective ones, and quite as truthful as effective. There are human supports for morality of the most important and far-reaching character, and such as are outside of any theological considerations. We ought, as George Eliot so well says, to rejoice that the reasons for being moral are manifold, that sympathy with others, as well as the central fires of personality, or the craving to be in harmony with the Eternal, is able to conduce to a righteous conduct. Her objections to Young's narrow and selfish defence of immortality are well presented and powerful, but they do not touch such high considerations as those offered by Kant. The craving for personal freedom and perfection is as strong and as helpful to the race as sympathy for others and yearning to lift up the weak and fallen. When the sense of personality is gone, man loses much of his character; and personality rests on a deep spiritual foundation which does not mean egotism merely, but which does mean for the majority a conviction of a continued existence. The tendency of the present time is to dwell less upon the theological and more upon the human motives to conduct; but it is to be doubted if the highest phases of morality can be retained without belief in God and a future life. The common virtues, the sympathetic motives to conduct, the spirit of helpfulness, may be retained intact, and even increased in power and efficiency, by those motives George Eliot presents; but the loftier virtues of personal heroism and devotion to truth in the face of martyrdom of one form or another, the saintly craving for purity and holiness, and the sturdy spirit of liberty which will suffer no bonds to exist, can be had in their full development only with belief that God calls us to seek for perfect harmony with himself. Kant's view that a divine law within, the living word of God, calls ever to us as personal beings to attain the perfection of our natures in the perfection of the race, and in conformity to the eternal law of righteousness, is far nobler and truer than that which George Eliot accepted.

She was not a mere unbeliever, however, for she did not thrust aside the hope of immortality with a contemptuous hand. This problem she left where she left that concerning God, in the background of thought, among the questions which cannot be solved. She believed that the power to contribute to the future good of the race is hope and promise enough. At the same time, she was very tender of the positive beliefs of others, and especially of that yearning so many feel after personal recognition and development. Writing to one who passionately clung to such a hope, she said, —

I have no controversy with the faith that cries out and clings from the depths of man's need. I only long, if it were possible to me, to help in satisfying the need of those who want a reason for living in the absence of what has been called consolatory belief. But all the while I gather a sort of strength from the certainty that there must be limits or negations in my own moral powers and life experience which may screen from me many possibilities of blessedness for our suffering human nature. The most melancholy thought surely would be that we in our own persons had measured and exhausted the sources of spiritual good. But we know the poor help the poor.

These words seem to be uttered in quite another tone than that in which she asserted the unbelievableness of immortality, though they do not indicate anything more than a tender yearning for human good and a belief that she could not herself measure all the possibilities of such good. The consolation of which she writes, comes only of human sympathy and helpfulness. In writing to a friend suffering under the anguish of a recent bereavement, she said, —

For the first sharp pangs there is no comfort; — whatever goodness may surround us, darkness and silence still hang about our pain. But slowly the clinging companionship with the dead is linked with our living affections and duties, and we begin to feel our sorrow as a solemn initiation preparing us for that sense of loving, pitying fellowship with the fullest human lot which, I must think, no one who has tasted it will deny to be the chief blessedness of our life. And especially to know what the last parting is, seems needful to give the utmost sanctity of tenderness to our relations with each other. It is that above all which gives us new sensibilities to "the web of human things, birth and the grave, that are not as they were." And by that faith we come to find for ourselves the truth of the old declaration, that there is a difference between the ease of pleasure and blessedness, as the fullest good possible to us wondrously mixed mortals.

In these words she suggests that sorrow for the dead is a solemn initiation into that full measure of human sympathy and tenderness which best fits us to be men. Looking upon all human experience through feeling, she regarded death as one of the most powerful of all the shaping agents of man's destiny in this world. She speaks of death, in *Adam Bede*, as "the great reconciler" which unites us to those who have passed away from us. In the closing scenes of *The Mill on the Floss* it is presented as such a reconciler, and as the only means of restoring Maggie to the affections of those she had wronged. It is in *The Legend of Jubal*, however, that George Eliot has expressed her thought of what death has been in the individual and social evolution of mankind. The descendants of Cain

in glad idlesse throve,
Nor hunted prey, nor with each other strove;

but all was peace and joy with them. There were no great aspirations, no noble achievements, no tending toward progress and a higher life. On an evil day, Lamech, when engaged in athletic sport, accidentally struck and killed his fairest boy. All was then changed, the old love and peace passed away; but good rather than evil came, for man began to lead a larger life.

And a new spirit from that hour came o'er
The race of Cain: soft idlesse was no more,
But even the sunshine had a heart of care.
Smiling with hidden dread — a mother fair
Who folding to her breast a dying child
Beams with feigned joy that but makes sadness mild.

Death was now lord of Life, and at his word
Time, vague as air before, new terrors stirred,
With measured wing now audibly arose
Throbbing through all things to some unknown close.
Now glad Content by clutching Haste was torn,
And Work grew eager, and Devise was born.
It seemed the light was never loved before,
Now each man said, "'Twill go and come no more."
No budding branch, no pebble from the brook,
No form, no shadow, but new dearness took
From the one thought that life must have an end;
And the last parting now began to send
Diffusive dread through love and wedded bliss,
Thrilling them into finer tenderness.
Then Memory disclosed her face divine,
That like the calm nocturnal lights doth shine
Within the soul, and shows the sacred graves,
And shows the presence that no sunlight craves,
No space, no warmth, but moves among them all;
Gone and yet here, and coming at each call,
With ready voice and eyes that understand,
And lips that ask a kiss, and dear responsive hand.
Thus to Cain's race death was tear-watered seed
Of various life and action-shaping need.
But chief the sons of Lamech felt the stings
Of new ambition, and the force that springs
In passion beating on the shores of fate.
They said, "There comes a night when all too late
The mind shall long to prompt the achieving hand,
The eager thought behind closed portals stand,
And the last wishes to the mute lips press
Buried ere death in silent helplessness.
Then while the soul its way with sound can cleave,
And while the arm is strong to strike and heave,
Let soul and arm give shape that will abide
And rule above our graves, and power divide
With that great god of day, whose rays must bend
As we shall make the moving shadows tend.
Come, let us fashion acts that are to be,
When we shall lie in darkness silently,
As our young brother doth, whom yet we see
Fallen and slain, but reigning in our will
By that one image of him pale and still."

Death brings discord and sorrow into a world once happy and unaspiring, but it also brings a spiritual eagerness and a divine craving. Jabal began to tame the animals and to cultivate the soil, Tubal-Cain began to use fire and to work metals, while Jubal discovered song and invented musical instruments. Out of the longing and inner unrest which death brought, came the great gift of music. It had power to

> Exult and cry, and search the inmost deep
> Where the dark sources of new passion sleep.

Jubal passes to other lands to teach them the gift of song, but at last returns an old man to share in the affections of his people. He finds them celebrating with great pomp the invention of music, but they will not accept him as the Jubal they did honor to and believed dead. Then the voice of his own past instructs him that he should not expect any praises or glory in his own person; it is enough to live in the joy of a world uplifted by music. Thus instructed, his broken life succumbs.

> Quitting mortality, a quenched sun-wave,
> The All-creating Presence for his grave.

In this poem George Eliot regards death as a means of drawing men into a deeper and truer sympathy with each other. The same thought is more fully presented when she exultingly sings, —

> O may I join the choir invisible
> Of those immortal dead who live again
> In minds made better by their presence: live
> In pulses stirred to generosity,
> In deeds of daring rectitude, in scorn
> For miserable aims that end with self,
> In thoughts sublime that pierce the night like stars,
> And with their mild persistence urge man's search
> To vaster issues.

Death teaches us to forget self, to live for others, to pour out unstinted sympathy and affection for those whose lives are short and difficult. It is the same thought as that given in reply to Young; mortal sorrows and pains should move us as hopes of immortality cannot. There accompanies this idea the larger one, that our future life is to be found in the better life we make for those who come after us. George Eliot believed with Comte, that we are to live again in minds made better by what we have done and been, that an influence goes out from every helpful and good life which makes the lives of those who come after us fairer and grander.

She rests this belief on no sentimental or ideal grounds. Its justification is to be found in science, in the law of hereditary transmission. Darwin and Spencer base the great world-process of evolution on the two laws of transmission and variation. The fittest survives, and the world advances. The survival of every fit and positive form of life in the better forms which succeed it is in accordance with a process or a law which holds true up into all the highest and subtlest expressions of man's inner life. Heredity is as true morally and spiritually as physically, and our moral and spiritual offspring will partake of our own qualities; and, standing on the vantage ground of our lives, will rise higher than we. What George Eliot regards as the positive teaching of science becomes also an inspiring religious belief to her.

George Eliot accepted the belief of an immortality in the race with a deep and earnest conviction. It gave a great impulse to her life, it satisfied her craving for closer harmony and sympathy with her fellows, it satisfied her longing for the power to assuage sorrow and to comfort pain.

> So to live is heaven;
> To make undying music in the world,

and to have an influence for good result from our lives far down the future. Through the beneficent influences we can awake in the world

> All our rarer, better, truer self,
> That sobbed religiously in yearning song,
> That watched to ease the burthen of the world,
> . . . . shall live till human time
> Shall fold its eyelids, and the human sky
> Be gathered like a scroll within the tomb
> Unread forever.

It was this belief, so satisfying to her and so ardently entertained, which inspired the best and noblest of her poems. With an almost exultant joy, with the enthusiasm of an old-time devotee, she sings of that immortality which consists in renouncing all which is personal. The diffusive good which sweetens life for others through all time is the real heaven she sought.

> This is life to come,
> Which martyred men have made more glorious
> For us who strive to follow. May I reach
> That purest heaven, be to other souls
> The cup of strength in some great agony,
> Enkindle generous ardor, feed pure love,
> Beget the smiles that have no cruelty —
> Be the sweet presence of a good diffused,
> And in diffusion ever more intense.
> So shall I join the choir invisible
> Whose music is the gladness of the world.

Believing that humanity represents an organic life and development, it was easy for George Eliot to accept the idea of immortality in the race. She reverenced the voice of truth

> Sent by the invisible choir of all the dead.

It was to her a divine voice, full of tenderness, sympathy and strength. She was fascinated by this thought of the solemn, ever-present and all-powerful influence of the dead over the living; there was mystery and inspiration in this belief for her. All phases of religious history, all religious experiences, were by her interpreted in the light of this conception. The power of Jesus's life is, that his trancendent beauty of soul lives in the "everlasting memories" of men, and that the cross of his shame has become

> The sign
> Of death that turned to more diffusive life

His influence, his memory, has lifted up the world with a great effect, and made his life, spirit and ideas an inherent part of humanity. He has been engrafted into the organic life of the race, and lives there a mighty and an increasing influence. What has happened in his case happens in the case of all the gifted and great. According to what they were living they enter into the life of the world for weal or woe. To become an influence for good in the future, to leave behind an undying impulse of thought and sympathy, was the ambition of George Eliot; and this was all the immortality she desired.

The religious tendencies of George Eliot's mind are rather to be noted in her conception of renunciation than in her beliefs about God and immortality. These latter beliefs were of a negative character as she entertained them, but her doctrine of renunciation was of a very positive nature. The central motive of that belief was not faith in God, but faith in man. It gained all its charm and power for her out of her conception of the organic life of the race. Her thought was, that we should live not for self, but for humanity. What so many ardent souls have been willing to do for the glory of God she was willing to do for the uplifting of man. The spirit of renunciation with her took the old theologic form of expression to a considerable extent, associated itself in her thought with the lofty spiritual consecration and self-abnegation of other ages. So ardently did she entertain this doctrine, so fully did she clothe it with the old forms of expression, that many have been deceived into believing her a devoted Christian. A little book was published in 1879 for the express purpose of showing that "the doctrine of the cross" is the main thought presented throughout all George Eliot's books.[1] This book was read by George Eliot with much delight, and was regarded by her as the only criticism of her works which did full justice to her purpose in writing them. She is presented in that book as the writer of fiction who "stands out as the deepest, broadest and most catholic illustrator of the true ethics

[1] The Ethics of George Eliot's Works. By the late John Crombie Brown Edinburgh: William Blackwood and Sons, 1879.

of Christianity; the most earnest and persistent expositor of the true doctrine of the cross, that we are born and should live to something higher than love of happiness." "Self-sacrifice as the divine law of life, and its only true fulfilment; self-sacrifice, not in some ideal sphere sought out for ourselves in the vain spirit of self-pleasing, but wherever God has placed us, amid homely, petty anxieties, loves and sorrows; the aiming at the highest attainable good in our own place, irrespective of all results of joy or sorrow, of apparent success or failure — such is the lesson" that is conveyed in all her books. George Eliot is presented as a true teacher of the doctrine which admonishes us to love not pleasure but God, to forsake all things else for the sake of obedience and devotion, to shun the world and to devote ourselves perpetually to God's service. The Christian doctrine of renunciation has always bidden men put their eyes on God, forget everything beside, and seek only for that divine life which is spiritual union with the Eternal.

That doctrine was not George Eliot's. Christianity bids men renounce the world for the sake of a perfect union with God; George Eliot desires men to renounce selfishness for the sake of humanity. The Christian idea includes the renunciation of all self-seeking, it bids us give ourselves for others, it even teaches us that others are to be preferred to ourselves. Yet all this is to be done, not merely for the sake of the present, but in view of an eternal destiny, and because we can thus only fulfil God's will and attain to holy oneness with him. George Eliot did, however, throughout her writings, identify the altruist impulse to live for others with the Christian doctrine of the cross. To her, the life of devotion to humanity, which she has so beautifully presented in the poem, "O may I join the Choir Invisible," was the true interpretation of the Christian doctrine of self-sacrifice. She accepted this world-old religious belief, consecrated with all the tears and sacrifices and martyrdoms of the world, as a true expression of a want of the soul, as the poetic expression of emotions and aspirations which ever live in man. It is a beautiful symbolism of that need of his fellows man ever has, of the conviction which is growing stronger, that man must live for the race and not for himself. The individual is nothing except as he identifies himself with the corporate body of humanity; the true fulfilment of life comes only to those who in some way recognize this fact, and give themselves for the good of the world. George Eliot even goes so far in her willingness to renounce self that she says in *Theophrastus Such*, "I am really at the point of finding that this world would be worth living in without any lot of one's own. Is it not possible for me to enjoy the scenery of earth without saying to myself, I have a cabbage-garden in it?"

The relations of the individual to the past and the present of the race make duties and burdens and woes for him which he has not created, but which are given him to bear. The sins of others bring pain and sorrow to us; we are a part of all the good and evil of the world. The present is determined by the past; we must accept the lot created for us by those who have gone before us. "He felt the hard pressure of our common lot, the yoke of that mighty, resistless destiny laid upon us by the past of other men," says George Eliot of one of her characters. The past brings us burdens and sorrows difficult to bear; it also brings us duties. We owe to it many things; our debt to the race is an immense one. That debt can only be discharged by a life of devotion and loyalty, by doing what we can to make humanity better. The Christian idea of a debt owed to God, which we can only repay by perfect loyalty and self-abnegation, becomes to George Eliot a debt owed to humanity, which we can only repay in the purest altruistic spirit.

The doctrine of renunciation has been presented

again and again by George Eliot; her books are full of it. It is undoubtedly the central theme of all her teaching. In the conversation between Romola and Savonarola when she is escaping from her home and is met by him, it is vividly expressed. Savonarola speaks as a Christian, as a Catholic, as a monk; but the words he uses quite as well serve to express George Eliot's convictions. The Christian symbolism laid aside, and all was true to her; yet her feelings, her sense of corporate unity with the past, would not even suffer her to lay aside the symbolism in presenting her thoughts on this subject. Romola pleads that she would not have left Florence as long as she could fulfil a duty to her father; but Savonarola reminds her that there are other duties, other ties, other burdens.

"If your own people are wearing a yoke, will you slip from under it, instead of struggling with them to lighten it? There is hunger and misery in our streets, yet you say, 'I care not; I have my own sorrows; I will go away, if peradventure I can ease them.' The servants of God are struggling after a law of justice, peace and charity, that the hundred thousand citizens among whom you were born may be governed righteously; but you think no more of that than if you were a bird, that may spread its wings and fly whither it will in search of food to its liking. And yet you have scorned the teaching of the Church, my daughter. As if you, a wilful wanderer, following your own blind choice, were not below the humblest Florentine woman who stretches forth her hands with her own people, and craves a blessing for them; and feels a close sisterhood with the neighbor who kneels beside her, and is not of her own blood; and thinks of the mighty purpose that God has for Florence; and waits and endures because the promised work is great, and she feels herself little."

She then asserts her purpose not to go away to a life of ease and self-indulgence, but rather to one of hardship; but that plea is not suffered to pass.

"You are seeking your own will, my daughter. You are seeking some good other than the law you are bound to obey. But how will you find good? It is not a thing of choice: it is a river that flows from the foot of the Invisible Throne, and flows by the path of obedience. I say again, man cannot choose his duties. You may choose to forsake your duties, and choose not to have the sorrow they bring. But you will go forth; and what will you find, my daughter? Sorrow without duty — bitter herbs, and no bread with them."

Savonarola bids her draw the crucifix from her bosom, which she secretly carries, and appeals to her by that symbol of devotion and self-sacrifice to remain true to her duties, to accept willingly the burdens given her to bear, not to think of self, but only of others. He condemns the pagan teaching she had received, of individual self-seeking, and the spirit of culture, refinement and ease which accompanied that teaching. She looks on the image of a suffering life, a life offered willingly as a sacrifice for others' good, and he says, —

"Conform your life to that image, my daughter; make your sorrow an offering; and when the fire of divine charity burns within you, and you behold the need of your fellow-men by the light of that flame, you will not call your offering great. You have carried yourself proudly, as one who held herself not of common blood or of common thoughts; but you have been as one unborn to the true life of man. What! you say your love for your father no longer tells you to stay in Florence? Then, since that tie is snapped, you are without a law, without religion; you are no better than a beast of the field when she is robbed of her young. If the yearning of a fleshly love is gone, you are without love, without obligation. See, then, my daughter, how you are below the life of the believer who worships that image of the Supreme Offering, and feels the glow of a common life with the lost multitude for whom that offering was made, and beholds the history of the world as the history of a great redemption, in which he is himself a fellow-worker, in his own place and among his own people! If you held that faith, my beloved daughter, you would not be a wanderer flying from suffering, and blindly seeking the good of a freedom which is lawlessness. You would feel that Florence was the home of your soul as well as your birthplace, because you would see the work that was given you to do there. If you forsake your place, who will fill it? You ought to be in your place now, helping in the great work by which God will purify Florence and raise it to be the guide of the nations. What! the earth is full of iniquity — full of groans — the light is still struggling with a mighty darkness, and you say, 'I cannot bear my bonds; I will burst them asunder; I will go where no man claims me?' My daughter, every bond of your life is a debt: the right lies in the payment of that debt; it can lie nowhere else. In vain will you wander over the earth; you will be wandering forever away from the right."

Romola hesitates, she pleads that her brother Dino forsook his home to become a monk, and that possibly Savonarola may be wrong. He then appeals to her conscience, and assures her that she has assumed relations and duties which cannot be broken from on any plea. The human ties are forever sacred; there can exist no causes capable of annulling them.

"You are a wife. You seek to break your ties in self-will and anger, not because the higher life calls upon you to renounce them. The higher life begins for us, my daughter, when we renounce our own will to bow before a Divine law. That seems hard to you. It is the portal of wisdom, and freedom, and blessedness. And the symbol of it hangs before you. That wisdom is the religion of the cross. And you stand aloof from it; you are a pagan; you have been taught to say, 'I am as the wise men who lived before the time when the Jew of Nazareth was crucified.' And that is your wisdom! To be as the dead whose eyes are closed, and whose ear is deaf to the work of God that has been since their time. What has your dead wisdom done for you, my daughter? It has left you without a heart for the neighbors among whom you dwell, without care for the great work by which Florence is to be regenerated and the world made holy; it has left you without a share in the Divine life which quenches the sense of suffering self in the ardors of an ever-growing love. And now, when the sword has pierced your soul, you say, 'I will go away; I cannot bear my sorrow.' And you think nothing of the sorrow and the wrong that are within the walls of the city where you dwell; you would leave your place empty, when it ought to be filled with your pity and your labor. If there is wickedness in the streets, your steps should shine with the light of purity; if there is a cry of anguish, you, my daughter, because you know the meaning of the cry, should be there to still it. My beloved daughter, sorrow has come to teach you a new worship; the sign of it hangs before you."

This teaching of renunciation is no less distinctly presented in *The Mill on the Floss*, the chief ethical aim of which is its inculcation. It is also there associated with the Catholic form of its expression, through Maggie's reading of *The Imitation of Christ*, a book which was George Eliot's constant companion, and was found by her bedside after her death. It was the spirit of that book which attracted George Eliot, not its doctrines. Its lofty spirit of submission and renunciation she admired; and she believed that altruism can be made real only through tradition, only as associated with past heroisms and strivings and ideals. As an embodiment of man's craving for perfect union with humanity, for full and joyous submission to his lot, the old forms of faith are sacred. They carry the hopes of ages; they are a pictured poem of man's inward strivings. To break away from these memories is to forsake one's home, is to repudiate one's mother. We cannot intellectually accept them, we cannot assent to the dogmas associated with them; but the forms are the spontaneous expressions of the heart, while the dogmas are an after-thought of the inquiring intellect. The real meaning of the cross of Christ is self-sacrifice for humanity's sake; that was its inspiration, that has ever been its true import. It was this view of the subject which made George Eliot so continuously associate her new teachings with the old expressions of faith.

In altruism she believes is to be found the hope of the world, the cure of every private pain and grief. Altruism means living for and in the race, as a willing member of the social organic life of humanity, as desiring not one's own good but the welfare of others. That doctrine she applies to Maggie's case. This young girl was dissatisfied with her life, out of harmony with her surroundings, and could not accept the theories of life given her.

She wanted some explanation of this hard, real life; the unhappy-looking father, seated at the dull breakfast-table; the childish, bewildered mother; the little sordid tasks that filled the hours, or the more oppressive emptiness of weary, joyless leisure; the need of some tender, demonstrative love; the cruel sense that Tom didn't mind what she thought or felt, and that they were no longer playfellows together; the privation of all pleasant things that had come to *her* more than to others — she wanted some key that would enable her to understand, and in understanding endure, the heavy weight that had fallen on her young heart. If she had been taught "real learning and wisdom, such as great men knew," she thought she should have held the secrets of life; if she had only books, that she might learn for herself what wise men knew! Saints and martyrs had never interested Maggie so much as sages and poets. She knew little of saints and martyrs, and had gathered, as a general result of her teaching, that they were a temporary provision against the spread of Catholicism, and had all died at Smithfield.

Into the darkness of Maggie's life a light suddenly comes in the shape of the immortal book of Thomas à Kempis. Why that book; why along such a way should the light come? The answer is, that George Eliot meant to teach certain ideas. It is this fact which justifies her reader in taking these scenes of her novels, these words spoken in the interludes, as genuine reflections and transcripts of her own mind. Maggie turns over a parcel of books brought her by Bob Jakin, to find little in them —

but *Thomas à Kempis*. The name had come across her in her reading, and she felt the satisfaction, which every one knows, of getting some ideas to attach to a name that strays solitary in the memory. She took up the little old clumsy book with some curiosity; it had the corners turned down in many places, and some hand, now forever quiet, had made at certain passages strong pen-and-ink marks, long since browned by time. Maggie turned from leaf to leaf, and read where the quiet hand pointed. "Know that the love of thyself doth hurt thee more than anything in the world. . . . If thou seekest this or that, and wouldst be here or there to enjoy thy own will and pleasure, thou shalt never be quiet nor free from care; for in everything somewhat will be wanting, and in every place there will be some that will cross thee. . . . Both above and below, which way soever thou dost turn thee, everywhere thou shalt find the cross; and everywhere of necessity thou must have patience, if thou wilt have inward peace, and enjoy an everlasting crown. . . . If thou desire to mount unto this height, thou must set out courageously, and lay the axe to the root, that thou mayest pluck up and destroy that hidden inordinate inclination to thyself, and unto all private and earthly good. On this sin, that a man inordinately loveth himself, almost all dependeth, whatsoever is thoroughly to be overcome; which evil being once overcome and subdued, there will presently ensue great peace and tranquillity. . . . It is but little thou sufferest in comparison of them that have suffered so much, were so strongly tempted, so grievously afflicted, so many ways tried and exercised. Thou oughtest therefore to call to mind the more heavy sufferings of others, that thou mayest the easier bear thy little adversities. And if they seem not little unto thee, beware lest thy impatience be the cause thereof. . . . Blessed are those ears that receive the whispers of the divine voice, and listen not to the whisperings of the world. Blessed are those ears which hearken not unto the voice which soundeth outwardly, but unto the Truth which teacheth inwardly."

A strange thrill of awe passed through Maggie while she read, as if she had been wakened in the night by a strain of solemn music, telling of beings whose souls had been astir while hers was in stupor. She went on from one brown mark to another, where the quiet hand seemed to point, hardly conscious that she was reading — seeming rather to listen while a low voice said, —

"Why dost thou here gaze about, since this is not the place of thy rest? In heaven ought to be thy dwelling, and all earthly things are to be looked on as they forward thy journey thither.

All things pass away, and thou together with them. Beware thou cleave not unto them lest thou be entangled and perish. . . . If a man should give all his substance, yet it is as nothing. And if he should do great penances, yet are they but little. And if he should attain to all knowledge, he is yet far off. And if he should be of great virtue and very fervent devotion, yet is there much wanting; to wit, one thing which is most necessary for him. What is that? That having left all, he leave himself, and go wholly out of himself, and retain nothing of self-love. . . . I have often said unto thee, and now again I say the same. Forsake thyself, resign thyself, and thou shalt enjoy much inward peace. . . . Then shall all vain imaginations, evil perturbations and superfluous cares fly away; then shall immoderate fear leave thee, and inordinate love shall die."

Maggie drew a long breath and pushed her heavy hair back, as if to see a sudden vision more clearly. Here, then, was a secret of life that would enable her to renounce all other secrets—here was a sublime height to be reached without the help of outward things—here was insight, and strength, and conquest, to be won by means entirely within her own soul, where a supreme Teacher was waiting to be heard. It flashed through her like the suddenly apprehended solution of a problem, that all the miseries of her young life had come from fixing her heart on her own pleasure, as if that were the central necessity of the universe; and for the first time she saw the possibility of shifting the position from which she looked at the gratification of her own desires, of taking her stand out of herself, and looking at her own life as an insignificant part of a divinely guided whole. She read on and on in the old book, devouring eagerly the dialogues with the invisible Teacher, the pattern of sorrow, the source of all strength; returning to it after she had been called away, and reading until the sun went down behind the willows. With all the hurry of an imagination that could never rest in the present, she sat in the deepening twilight forming plans of self-humiliation and entire devotedness, and, in the ardor of first discovery, renunciation seemed to her the entrance into that satisfaction which she had so long been craving in vain. She had not perceived—how could she until she had lived longer?—the inmost truth of the old monk's outpourings, that renunciation remains sorrow, though a sorrow borne willingly. Maggie was still panting for happiness, and was in ecstasy because she had found the key to it. She knew nothing of doctrines and systems—of mysticism or quietism; but this voice out of the far-off middle ages was the direct communication of a human soul's belief and experience, and came to Maggie as an unquestioned message. I suppose that is the reason why the small, old-fashioned book, for which you need only pay sixpence at a book-stall, works miracles to this day, turning bitter waters into sweetness, while expensive sermons and treatises, newly issued, leave all things as they were before. It was written down by a hand that waited for the heart's promptings; it is the chronicle of a solitary hidden anguish, struggle, trust and triumph,—not written on velvet cushions to teach endurance to those who are treading with bleeding feet on the stones. And so it remains to all time a lasting record of human needs and human consolations; the voice of a brother who, ages ago, felt, and suffered, and renounced, — in the cloister, perhaps, with serge gown and tonsured head, with much chanting and long fasts, and with a fashion of speech different from ours,— but under the same silent, far-off heavens, and with the same passionate desires, the same strivings, the same failures, the same weariness.[1]

Life now has a meaning for Maggie, its secret has been in some measure opened. Only by bitter experiences does she at last learn the full meaning of that word; but all her after-life is told for us in order that the depth and breadth and height of that meaning may be unfolded. Very soon Maggie is heard saying,

"Our life is determined for us — and it makes the mind very free when we give up wishing, and only think of bearing what is laid upon us, and doing what is given us to do."

It is George Eliot who really speaks these words; hers is the thought which inspires them.

Yet Maggie has not learned to give up wishing; and the sorrow, the tragedy of her life comes in consequence. She is pledged in love to Philip, the son of the bitter enemy of her family, and is attracted to Stephen, the lover of her cousin Lucy. A long contest is fought out in her life between attraction and duty; between individual preferences and moral obligations. The struggle is hard, as when Stephen avows his love, and she replies, —

"Oh, it is difficult — life is very difficult. It seems right to me sometimes that we should follow our strongest feeling; but, then, such feelings continually come across the ties that all our former life has made for us — the ties that have made others dependent on us — and would cut them in two. If life were quite easy and simple, as it might have been in Paradise, and we could always see that one being first toward whom — I mean, if life did not make duties for us before love comes, love would be a sign two people ought to belong to each other. But I see — I feel that it is not so now; there are things we must renounce in life; some of us must resign love. Many things are difficult and dark to me, but I see one thing quite clearly — that I must not, cannot seek my own happiness by sacrificing others. Love is natural; but surely

[1] The Mill on the Floss, Book IV., chapter III.

pity, and faithfulness and memory are natural too. And they would live in me still and punish me if I did not obey them. I should be haunted by the suffering I had caused. Our love would be poisoned."

Against her will she elopes with Stephen, or her departure with him is so understood; but as soon as she realizes what she has done, her better nature asserts itself, and she refuses to go on. Stephen pleads that the natural law which has drawn them together is greater than every other obligation; but Maggie replies, —

"If we judged in that way, there would be a warrant for all treachery and cruelty. We should justify breaking the most sacred ties that can ever be formed on earth."

He then asks what is outward faithfulness and constancy without love. Maggie pleads the better spirit.

"That seems right — at first; but when I look further, I'm sure it is *not* right. Faithfulness and constancy mean something else besides doing what is easiest and pleasantest to ourselves. They mean renouncing whatever is opposed to the reliance others have in us — whatever would cause misery to those whom the course of our lives has made dependent on us. If we — if I had been better, nobler, those claims would have been so strongly present with me — I should have felt them pressing on my heart so continually, just as they do now in the moments when my conscience is awake, that the opposite feeling would never have grown in me as it has done: it would have been quenched at once. I should have prayed for help so earnestly — I should have rushed away as we rush from hideous danger. I feel no excuse for myself — none. I should never have failed toward Lucy and Philip as I have done, if I had not been weak, selfish and hard — able to think of their pain without a pain to myself that would have destroyed all temptation. Oh, what is Lucy feeling now? She believed in me — she loved me — she was so good to me! Think of her!"

She can see no good for herself which is apart from the good of others, no joy which is the means of pain to those she holds dear. The past has made ties and memories which no present love or future joy can take away; she must be true to past obligations as well as present inclinations.

"There are memories and affections, and longing after perfect goodness, that have such a strong hold on me, they would never quit me for long; they would come back and be pain to me — repentance. I couldn't live in peace if I put the shadow of a wilful sin between myself and God. I have caused sorrow already — I know — I feel it; but I have never deliberately consented to it; I have never said, 'They shall suffer that I may have joy.'"

And again, she says, —

"We can't choose happiness either for ourselves or for another; we can't tell where that will lie. We can only choose whether we will indulge ourselves in the present moment, or whether we will renounce that, for the sake of obeying the divine voice within us — for the sake of being true to all the motives that sanctify our lives. I know this belief is hard; it has slipped away from me again and again; but I have felt that if I let it go forever I should have no light through the darkness of this life."

In these remarkable passages from *Romola* and *The Mill on the Floss*, George Eliot presented her own theory of life. One of her friends, in giving an account of her moral influence, speaks of "the impression she produced, that one of the greatest duties of life was that of resignation. Nothing was more impressive as exhibiting the power of feelings to survive the convictions which gave them birth, than the earnestness with which she dwelt on this as the great and real remedy for all the ills of life. On one occasion she appeared to apply it to herself in speaking of the short space of life that lay before her, and the large amount of achievement that must be laid aside as impossible to compress into it — and the sad, gentle tones in which the word *resignation* was uttered, still vibrate on the ear."[1] Not only renunciation but resignation was by her held to be a prime requisite of a truly moral life. Man must renounce many things for the sake of humanity, but he must also resign himself to endure many things because the universe is under the dominion of invariable laws. Much of pain and sorrow must come to us which can in no way be avoided. A true resignation and renunciation will enable us to turn pain and sorrow into the means of a higher life. In *Adam Bede* she says that "deep, unspeakable suffering may well be called a bap-

[1] Contemporary Review, February, 1881.

tism, a regeneration, the initiation into a new state." She teaches that man can attain true unity with the race only through renunciation, and renunciation always means suffering. Self-sacrifice means hardship, struggle and sorrow; but the true end of life can only be attained when self is renounced for that higher good which comes through devotion to humanity. Her noblest characters, Maggie Tulliver, Romola, Jubal, Fedalma, Armgart, attain peace only when they have found their lives taken up in the good of others. To her the highest happiness consists in being loyal to duty, and it "often brings so much pain with it that we can only tell it from pain by its being what we would choose before everything else, because our souls see it is good."

George Eliot's religion is without God, without immortality, without a transcendent spiritual aim and duty. It consists in a humble submission to the invariable laws of the universe, a profound love of humanity, a glorification of feeling and affection, and a renunciation of personal and selfish desires for an altruistic devotion to the good of the race. Piety without God, renunciation without immortality, mysticism without the supernatural, everywhere finds eloquent presentation in her pages. Offering that which she believes satisfies the spiritual wants of man, she yet rejects all the legitimate objects of spiritual desire. Even when her characters hold to the most fervent faith, and use with the greatest enthusiasm the old expressions of piety, it is the human elements in that faith which are made to appear most prominently. We are told that no radiant angel came across the gloom with a clear message for Romola in her moment of direst distress and need. Then we are told that many such see no angels; and we are made to realize that angelic voices are to George Eliot the voices of her fellows.

In those times, as now, there were human beings who never saw angels or heard perfectly clear messages. Such truth as came to them was brought confusedly in the voices and deeds of men not at all like the seraphs of unfailing wing and piercing vision — men who believed falsities as well as truths, and did the wrong as well as the right. The helping hands stretched out to them were the hands of men who stumbled and often saw dimly, so that these beings unvisited by angels had no other choice than to grasp that stumbling guidance along the path of reliance and action which is the path of life, or else to pause in loneliness and disbelief, which is no path, but the arrest of inaction and death.

The same thought is expressed in *Silas Marner*, that man is to expect no help and consolation except from his fellow-man.

In old days there were angels who came and took men by the hand and led them away from the city of destruction. We see no white-winged angels now. But yet men are led away from threatening destruction: a hand is put into theirs, which leads them forth gently towards a calm and bright land, so that they look no more backward; and the hand may be a little child's.

Even more explicit in its rejection of all sources of help, except the human, is the motto to "The Lifted Veil."

Give me no light, great Heaven, but such as turns
To energy of human fellowship;
No powers beyond the growing heritage
That makes completer manhood.

The purpose of this story is to show that supernatural knowledge is a curse to man. The narrator of the story is gifted with the power of divining even the most secret thoughts of those about him, and of beholding coming events. This knowledge brings him only evil and sorrow. His spiritual insight did not save him from folly, and he is led to say, —

"There is no short cut, no patent tram-road to wisdom. After all the centuries of invention, the soul's path lies through the thorny wilderness, which must be still trodden in solitude, with bleeding feet, with sobs for help, as it was trodden by them of old time."

He also discourses of the gain which it is to man that the future is hidden from his knowledge.

"So absolute is our soul's need of something hidden and uncertain for the maintenance of that doubt and hope and effort which are the breath of its life, that if the whole future were laid bare to us beyond to-day, the interest of all mankind would be bent on the hours that lie between; we should pant after the uncertainties of our one morning and our one afternoon; we should rush fiercely to the exchange for our last possibility of speculation, of success, of disappointment; we should have a glut of political prophets foretelling a crisis or a no-crisis within the only twenty-four hours left open to prophecy. Conceive the condition of the human mind if all propositions whatsoever were self-evident except one, which was to become self-evident at the close of a summer's day, but in the mean time might be the subject of question, of hypothesis, of debate. Art and philosophy, literature and science, would fasten like bees on that one proposition that had the honey of probability in it, and be the more eager because their enjoyment would end with sunset. Our impulses, our spiritual activities, no more adjust themselves to the idea of their future reality than the beating of our heart, or the irritability of our muscles."

All is hidden from man that does not grow out of human experience, and it is better so. Such is George Eliot's method of dealing with our craving for a higher wisdom and a direct revelation. Such wisdom and such revelation are not to be had, and they would not help man if he had them. The mystery of existence rouses his curiosity, stimulates his powers, develops art, religion, sympathy, and all that is best in human life. In her presentations of the men and women most affected by religious motives she adheres to this theory, and represents them as impelled, not by the sense of God's presence, but by purely human considerations. She makes Dorothea Brooke say,—

"I have always been thinking of the different ways in which Christianity is taught, and whenever I find one way that makes it a wider blessing than any other, I cling to that as the truest—I mean that which takes in the most good of all kinds, and brings in the most people as sharers in it."

Of the same character is the belief which comforts Dorothea, and takes the place to her of prayer.

"That by desiring what is perfectly good, even when we don't quite know what it is and cannot do what we would, we are a part of the divine power against evil—widening the skirts of light and making the struggle with darkness narrower."

Mr. Tryan, in *Janet's Repentance*, is a most ardent disciple of Evangelicalism, and accepts all its doctrines; but George Eliot contrives to show throughout the book, that all the value of his work and religion consisted in the humanitarian spirit of renunciation he awakened.

George Eliot does not entirely avoid the supernatural, but she treats it as unexplainable. Instances of her use of it are to be found in Adam Bede's experience while at work on his father's coffin, in the visions of Savonarola, and in Mordecai's strange faith in a coming successor to his own faith and work. For Adam Bede's experience there is no explanation given, nor for that curious power manifest in the "Lifted Veil." On the other hand, the spiritual power of Savonarola and Mordecai have their explanation, in George Eliot's philosophy, in that intuition which is inherited insight. In her treatment of such themes she manifests her appreciation of the great mystery which surrounds man's existence, but she shows no faith in a spiritual world which impinges on the material, and ever manifests itself in gleams and foretokenings.

It is to be noted, however, that many traces of mysticism appear in her works. This might have been expected from her early love of the transcendentalists, as well as from her frequent perusal of Thomas à Kempis. More especially was this to be expected from her conception of feeling as the source of all that is best in man's life. The mystics always make feeling the source of truth, prefer emotion to reason. All thinkers who lay stress on the value of feeling are liable to become mystics, even if materialists in their philosophy. Here and there in her pages this tendency towards mysticism, which manifests itself in some of the more poetic of the scientists of the present time, is to be seen in George Eliot. Some of her words about love, music and nature partake of this character. Her sayings about altruism and renunciation touch the border of the mystical occasionally. Had she been less thoroughly a rationalist she would doubtless have become a mystic in fact. Her tendency in this direction hints at the close affinity between the evolutionists of to-day and the idealists of a century ago. They unite in making matter and mind identical, and in regarding feeling as a source of truth. These are the two essential thoughts on which all mysticism rests. As modern science becomes the basis of speculation about religion, and gives expression to these doctrines, it will develop mysticism. Indeed, it is difficult to know wherein much that George Eliot wrote differs from mysticism. Her subjective immortality derived much of its acceptableness and beauty from those poetic phases given to it by idealistic pantheism. Her altruism caught the glow of the older humanitarianism. Her conception of feeling and emotional sympathy is touched everywhere with that ideal glamour given it by the mystical teachings of an earlier generation. Had she lived half a century earlier she might have been one of Fichte's most ardent disciples, and found in his subjective idealism the incentive to a higher inspiration than that attained to under the leadership of Comte. Her religion would then have differed but little from what it did in fact, but there would have been a new sublimity and a loftier spirit at the heart of it.

George Eliot retains the traditional life, piety and symbolism of Christianity, but she undertakes to show they have quite another meaning than that usually given them. Her peculiarity is that she should wish to retain the form after the substance is gone. Comte undertook to give a new outward expression to those needs of the soul which lead to worship and piety; but George Eliot accepted the traditional symbolisms as far better than anything which can be invented. If we would do no violence to feeling and the inner needs of life, we must not break with the past, we must not destroy the temple of the soul. The traditional worship, piety and consecration, the poetic expression of feeling and sentiment, must be kept until new traditions, a new symbolism, have developed themselves out of the experiences of the race. God is a symbol for the great mystery of the universe and of being, the eternity and universality of law. Immortality is a symbol for the transmitted impulse which the person communicates to the race. The life and death of Christ is a symbol of that altruistic spirit of renunciation and sorrow willingly borne, by which humanity is being lifted up and brought towards its true destiny. Feeling demands these symbols, the heart craves for them. The bare enunciation of principles is not enough; they must be clothed upon by sentiment and affection. The Christian symbols answer to this need, they most fitly express this craving of the soul for a higher and purer life. The spontaneous, creative life of humanity has developed them as a fit mode of voicing its great spiritual cravings, and only the same creative genius can replace them. The inquiring intellect cannot furnish substitutes for them; rationalism utterly fails in all its attempts to satisfy the spiritual nature.

Such is George Eliot's religion. It is the "Religion of Humanity" as interpreted by a woman, a poet and a genius. It differs from Comte's as the work of a poet differs from that of a philosopher, as that of a woman differs from that of a man. His *positive religion* gives the impression of being invented; it is artificial, unreal. Hers is, at least, living and beautiful and impressive; it is warm, tender and full of compassion. He invents a new symbolism, a new hierarchy, and a new worship; that is, he remodels Catholicism to fit the Religion of Humanity. She is too sensible, too wise, or rather too poetic and sympathetic, to undertake such a transformation, or to be satisfied with it when accomplished by another. She gives a new poetic and spiritual meaning to the old faith and worship; and in doing this makes no break with tradition, rejects nothing of the old symbolism.

It was her conviction that nothing of the real meaning and power of religion escaped by the transformation she made in its spiritual contents. She believed that she had dropped only its speculative teachings, while all that had ever made it of value was retained. That she was entirely mistaken in this opinion scarcely needs to be said; or that her speculative interpretation, if generally accepted, would destroy for most persons even those elements of religion which she accepted. A large rich mind, gifted with genius and possessed of wide culture, as was hers, could doubtless find satisfaction in that attenuated substitute for piety and worship which she accepted. There certainly could be no Mr. Tryan, no Dinah Morris, no Savonarola, no Mordecai, if her theories were the common ones; and it would be even less possible for a Dorothea, a Felix Holt, a Daniel Deronda, or a Romola to develop in such an atmosphere. What her intellectual speculations would accomplish when accepted as the motives of life, is seen all too well in the case of those many radical thinkers whom this century has produced. Only the most highly cultivated, and those of an artistic or poetic temperament, could accept her substitute for the old religion. The motives she presents could affect but a few persons; only here and there are to be found those to whom altruism would be a motive large enough to become a religion. To march in the great human army towards a higher destiny for humanity may have a strong fascination for some, and is coming to affect and inspire a larger number with every century; but it is not enough to know that the race is growing better. What is the end of human progress? we have a right to ask. Does that progress go on in accordance with some universal purpose, which includes the whole universe? We must look not only for a perfect destiny for man, but for a perfect destiny for all worlds and beings throughout the infinitude of God's creative influence. A progressive, intellectual religion such as will answer to the larger needs of modern life, must give belief in a universal providence, and it must teach man to trust in the spiritual capacities of his own soul. Unless the universe means something which is intelligible, and unless it has a purpose and destiny progressive and eternal, it is impossible that religion will continue to inspire men. That is, only a philosophy which gives such an interpretation to the universe can be the basis of an enduring and progressive religion.

If religion is to continue, it is also necessary that man should be able to believe in the soul as something more than the product of environment and heredity. It is not merely the belief in immortality which has inspired the greatest minds, but the inward impulse of creative activity, resting on the conviction that they were working with God for enduring results. Absorption into the life of humanity can be but a feeble motive compared with that which grows out of faith in the soul's spiritual eternity in co-operation with God.

George Eliot's religion is highly interesting, and in many ways it is suggestive and profitable. Her insistence on feeling and sympathy as its main impulses is profoundly significant; but that teaching is as good for Theism or Christianity as for the Religion of Humanity, and needs everywhere to be accepted. In like manner, her altruistic spirit may be accepted and realized by those who can find no sympathy for her intellectual speculations. Love of man, self-sacrifice for human good, cannot be urged by too many teachers. The greater the number of motives leading to that result, the better foı man.

XII.

ETHICAL SPIRIT.

WHATEVER may be said of George Eliot's philosophy and theology, her moral purpose was sound and her ethical intent noble. She had a strong passion for the ethical life, her convictions regarding it were very deep and earnest, and she dwelt lovingly on all its higher accomplishments. Her books are saturated with moral teaching, and her own life was ordered after a lofty ethical standard. She seems to have yearned most eagerly after a life of moral helpfulness and goodness, and she has made her novels the teachers of a vigorous morality.

Her friends bear enthusiastic testimony to the nobleness of her moral life and to her zeal for ethical culture. We are told by one of them that "she had upbuilt with strenuous pains a resolute virtue," conquering many faults, and gaining a lofty nobleness of spirit. Another has said, that "precious as the writings of George Eliot are and must always be, her life and character were yet more beautiful than they." Her zeal for morality was very great; she was an ethical prophet; the moral order of life roused her mind to a lofty inspiration. If she could not conceive of God, if she could not believe in immortality, yet she accepted duty as peremptory and absolute. Her faith in duty and charity seemed all the more vigorous and confident because her religion was so attenuated and imperfect. Love of man with her grew into something like that mighty and absorbing love of God which is to be seen in some of the greatest souls. Morality became to her a religion, not so intense as with saints and prophets, but more sympathetic and ardent than with most ethical teachers. She was no stoic, no teacher of moral precepts, no didactic debater about moral duties, no mere *dilettante* advocate of human rights. She was a warm, tender, yearning, sympathetic, womanly friend of individuals, who hoped great things for humanity, and who believed that man can find happiness and true culture only in a moral life.

She was distinctively a moral teacher in her books. The novel was never to her a work of art alone. The moral purpose was always present, always apparent, always clear and emphatic. There was something to teach for her whenever she took the pen in hand; some deep lesson of human experience, some profound truth of human conduct, some tender word of sympathy for human sorrow and suffering. She seems to have had no sympathy with that theory which says that the poet and the novelist are to picture life as it is, without regard to moral obligations and consequences. In this respect she was one of the most partisan of all partisans, an absolute dogmatist; for she never forgot for a moment the moral consequences of life. She was one of the most ardent of modern preachers, her books are crowded with teaching of the most positive character. In her way she was a great believer, and when she believed she never restrained her pen, but taught the full measure of her convictions. She did not look upon life as a scene to be sketched, but as an experience to be lived, and a moral order to be improved by sympathy and devotedness. Consequently the artist appears in the teacher's garb, the novelist has become an ethical preacher. She does not describe life as something outside of herself, nor does she regard human sorrows and sufferings and labors merely as materials for the artist's use; but she lives in and with all that men do and suffer and aspire to. Hers is not the manner of Homer and Scott, who hide their personality behind the wonderful distinctness of their personalities, making the reader forget the author in the strength and power of the characters described. It is not that of Shakspere, of whom we seem to get no glimpse in his marvellous readings of human nature, who paints other men as no one else has done, but who does not paint himself. Hers is rather the manner of Wordsworth and Goethe, who have a theory of life to give us, and whose personality appears on every page they wrote. She has a philosophy, a morality and a religion to inculcate. She had a vast subjective intensity of conviction, and a strong individualism of purpose, which would not hide itself behind the scenes. Her philosophy impregnates with a strong personality all her classic utterances; her ethics present a marked purpose in the development of her plots and in her presentation of the outcome of human experience; and her religion glows in the personal ardor and sympathy of her noblest characters, and in their passion for renunciation and altruism.

Her ethical passion adds to the strength and purpose of George Eliot's genius. No supreme literary creator has been devoid of this characteristic, however objective and impersonal he may have been. Homer, Virgil, Dante, Cervantes, Shakspere, Scott, were all earnest ethical teachers. The moral problems of life impressed them profoundly, and they showed a strong personal preference for righteousness. The literary masters of all times and countries have loved virtue, praised purity, and admired ethical uprightness. Any other attitude than this argues something less than genius, though genius may be far from didactic and not given to preaching. The moral intent of life is so inwoven with all its experiences, that the failure of any mind to be impressed with it, and profoundly affected, proves it wanting in insight, poetic vision and genius. George Eliot is entirely in harmony, in this respect, with all the masters of the literary art. Her ethical passion is a clear sign of her genius, and proves the vigor of her intellectual vision. No one who rightly weighs the value of her books, and fairly estimates the nature of her teaching, can regret that she had so keen a love of ethical instruction. The vigor, enthusiasm and originality of her teaching compensate for many faults.

Her teachings have a special interest because they afford a literary embodiment of the ethical theories of the evolution philosophy. They indicate the form which is likely to be given to ethics if theism and individualism are discarded, and the peculiar effects upon moral life which will be induced by agnosticism. She applied agnosticism to morals, by regarding good and evil as relative, and as the results of man's environment. For her, ethics had no infinite sanctions, no intuitive promulgation of an eternal law; but she regarded morality as originating in and deriving its authority from the social relations of men to each other. Our intuitive doing of right, or sorrow for wrong, is the result of inherited conditions. In *Romola* she speaks of Tito as affected by —

> the inward shame, the reflex of that outward law which the great heart of mankind makes for every individual man, a reflex which will exist even in the absence of the sympathetic impulses that need no law, but rush to the deed of fidelity and pity as inevitably as the brute mother shields her young from the attack of the hereditary enemy.[1]

This teaching is often found in her pages, and in connection with the assertion of the relativity of morals. There is no absolute moral law for her, no eternal ideal standard; but what is right is determined by the environment. Instead of Kant's categorical imperative of the moral law, proclaimed as a divine command in every soul, George Eliot found in the conscience and in the moral intuitions simply inherited experiences. In *Daniel Deronda* she says, "Our consciences are not all of the same pattern, an inner

[1] Chapter IX

deliverance of fixed laws; they are the voice of sensibilities as various as our memories."

George Eliot's rejection of any absolute standard of moral conduct or of happiness continually asserts itself in her pages. We must look at the individual, his inherited moral power, his environment, his special motives, if we would judge him aright. In the last chapters of *The Mill on the Floss*, when writing of Maggie's repentance, this idea appears. Maggie is not to be tried by the moral ideal of Christianity, nor by any such standard of perfection as Kant proposed, but by all the circumstances of her place in life and her experience. We are accordingly told that —

> Moral judgments must remain false and hollow unless they are checked and enlightened by a perpetual reference to the special circumstances that mark the individual lot.

George Eliot says in one of the mottoes in *Felix Holt* that moral happiness is "mainly a complex of habitual relations and dispositions." Even more explicit is her assertion, in one of the mottoes of *Daniel Deronda*, of the relativity of moral power.

> Looking at life in the growth of a single lot, who having a practised vision may not see that ignorance of the true bond between events, and false conceit of means whereby sequences may be compelled — like that falsity of eyesight which overlooks the gradations of distance, seeing that which is afar off as if it were within a step or a grasp — precipitate the mistaken soul on destruction?

She does not teach, however, that man is a mere victim of circumstances, that he is a creature ruled by fate. His environment includes his own moral heredity, which may overcome the physical circumstances which surround him. In *Middlemarch* she says, "It always remains true that if we had been greater, circumstances would have been less strong against us." The same thought appears in Zarca's appeal to Fedalma to be his true daughter, in one of the most effective scenes of *The Spanish Gypsy*. Moral devotedness is the strongest of all forces, he argues, even when it fails of its immediate aim; and even in failure the inherited life of the race is enlarged.

> No great deed is done
> By falterers who ask for certainty.
> No good is certain, but the steadfast mind,
> The undivided will to seek the good:
> 'Tis that compels the elements, and wrings
> A human music from the indifferent air.
> The greatest gift the hero leaves his race
> Is to have been a hero. Say we fail! —
> We feed the high tradition of the world,
> And leave our spirit in our children's breasts.

George Eliot never goes so far as to say that man may, by virtue of his inward life, rise superior to all circumstances, and maintain the inviolable sanctity of his own moral nature. She does not forget that defeat is often the surest victory, that moral faithfulness may lead to disgrace and death; but even in these cases it is for the sake of the race we are to be faithful. The inward victory, the triumph of the soul in unsullied purity and serenity, she does not dwell upon; and it may be doubted if she fully recognized such a moral result. Her mind is so occupied with the social results of conduct as to overlook the individual victories which life ever brings to those who are faithful unto death. George Eliot has put her theory of morality into the mouth of Guildenstern, one of the characters in "A College Breakfast Party."

> Where get, you say, a binding law, a rule
> Enforced by sanction, an Ideal throned
> With thunder in its hand? I answer, there
> Whence every faith and rule has drawn its force
> Since human consciousness awaking owned
> An Outward, whose unconquerable sway
> Resisted first and then subdued desire
> By pressure of the dire impossible
> Urging to possible ends the active soul
> And shaping so its terror and its love.
> Why, you have said it — threats and promises
> Depend on each man's sentence for their force:
> All sacred rules, imagined or revealed,
> Can have no form or potency apart
> From the percipient and emotive mind.

God, duty, love, submission, fellowship,
Must first be framed in man, as music is,
Before they live outside him as a law.
And still they grow and shape themselves anew,
With fuller concentration in their life
Of inward and of outward energies
Blending to make the last result called Man,
Which means, not this or that philosopher
Looking through beauty into blankness, not
The swindler who has sent his fruitful lie
By the last telegram: it means the tide
Of needs reciprocal, toil, trust and love —
The surging multitude of human claims
Which make "a presence not to be put by"
Above the horizon of the general soul.
Is inward reason shrunk to subtleties,
And inward wisdom pining passion-starved? —
The outward reason has the world in store,
Regenerates passion with the stress of want,
Regenerates knowledge with discovery,
Shows sly rapacious self a blunderer,
Widens dependence, knits the social whole
In sensible relation more defined.

As these words would indicate, George Eliot's faith in the moral meaning and outcome of the world is very strong. All experience is moral, she would have us believe, and capable of teaching man the higher life. That is, all experience tends slowly to bring man into harmony with his environment, and to teach him that certain actions are helpful, while others are harmful. This teaching is very definite and emphatic in her pages, often rising into a lofty eloquence and a rich poetic diction, as her mind is wrought upon by the greatness and the impressiveness of the moral lessons of life.

However effective the outward order of nature may be in creating morality, it is to be borne in mind that ethical rules can have no effect "apart from the percipient and emotive mind." It is, in reality, the social nature which gives morality its form and meaning. It is a creation of the social organism. Its basis is found, indeed, in the invariable order of nature, but the superstructure is erected out of and by society. "Man's individual functions," says Lewes, "arise in relations to the cosmos; his general functions arise in relations to the social medium; thence moral life emerges. All the animal impulses become blended with human emotions. In the process of evolution, starting from the merely animal appetite of sexuality, we arrive at the purest and most far-reaching tenderness. The social instincts tend more and more to make sociality dominate animality, and thus subordinate personality to humanity. . . . The animal has sympathy, and is moved by sympathetic impulses, but these are never altruistic; the ends are never remote. Moral life is based on sympathy; it is feeling for others, working for others, aiding others, quite irrespective of any personal good beyond the satisfaction of the social impulse. Enlightened by the intuition of our community of weakness, we share ideally the universal sorrows. Suffering harmonizes. Feeling the need of mutual help, we are prompted by it to labor for others."[1] Morality is social, not personal; the result of those instincts which draw men together in community of interests, sympathies and sufferings. Its sanctions are all social; its motives are purely human; its law is created by the needs of humanity. There is no outward coercive law of the divine will or of invariable order which is to be supremely regarded; the moral law is human need as it changes from age to age. The increase of human sympathies in the process of social evolution gives the true moral ideal to be aspired after. What will increase the social efficiency of the race, what will promote altruism, is moral.

Alike because of the invariable order of nature, and the social dependence of men on each other, are the effects of conduct wrought out in the individual. George Eliot believes in "the orderly sequence by which the seed brings forth a crop after its kind." All evil is injurious to man, destructive of the integrity of

[1] Foundations of a Creed, vol. I., pp. 147, 153.

his life. She teaches the doctrine of Nemesis with as much conviction, thoroughness and eloquence as the old Greek dramatists, making sin to be punished, and wrong-doing to be destructive. Sometimes she presents this doctrine with all the stern, unpitying vigor of an Æschylus, as a dire effect of wrong that comes upon men with an unrelenting mercilessness. In *Janet's Repentance* she says, —

> Nemesis is lame, but she is of colossal stature, like the gods; and sometimes, while her sword is not yet unsheathed, she stretches out her huge left arm and grasps her victim. The mighty hand is invisible, but the victim totters under the dire clutch.

Her doctrine of Nemesis resembles that of the old Greeks more than that of the modern optimists and theists. Hers is not the idealistic conception of compensation, which measures out an exact proportion of punishment for every sin, and of happiness for every virtuous action. Wrong-doing injures others as well as those who commit the evil deed, and moral effects reach far beyond those who set them in operation. Very explicitly is this fact presented in *The Mill on the Floss*.

> So deeply inherent is it in this life of ours that men have to suffer for each other's sins, so inevitably diffusive is human suffering, that even justice makes its victims, and we can conceive no retribution that does not spread beyond its mark in pulsations of unmerited pain.

In *Adam Bede*, Parson Irwine says to Arthur, —

> Consequences are unpitying. Our deeds carry their terrible consequences quite apart from any fluctuations that went before — consequences that are hardly ever confined to ourselves.

Yet wrong-doing does not go unpunished, for the law of moral cause and effect ever holds good. This is the teaching of the first chapter of *Felix Holt*.

> There is seldom any wrong-doing which does not carry along with it some downfall of blindly climbing hopes, some hard entail of suffering, some quickly satiated desire that survives, with the life in death of old paralytic vice, to see itself cursed by its woeful progeny — some tragic mark of kinship in the one brief life to the

far-stretching life that went before, and to the life that is to come after, such as has raised the pity and terror of men ever since they began to discern between will and destiny. But these things are often unknown to the world, for there is much pain that is quite noiseless; and vibrations that make human agonies are often a mere whisper in the roar of hurrying existence. There are glances of hatred that stab and raise no cry of murder; robberies that leave man or woman forever beggared of peace and joy, yet kept secret by the sufferer — committed to no sound except that of low moans in the night, seen in no writing except that made on the face by the slow months of suppressed anguish and early morning tears. Many an inherited sorrow that has marred a life has been breathed into no human ear.

In the same novel we are told, that —

To the end of men's struggles a penalty will remain for those who sink from the ranks of the heroes into the crowd for whom the heroes fight and die.

The same teaching is to be found in the motto of *Daniel Deronda*, where we are bidden to fear the evil tendencies of our own souls.

Let thy chief terror be of thine own soul:
There, 'mid the throng of hurrying desires
That trample o'er the dead to seize their spoil,
Lurks vengeance, footless, irresistible
As exhalations laden with slow death,
And o'er the fairest troop of captured joys
Breathes pallid pestilence.

The manner in which George Eliot believes Nemesis works out her results has already been indicated. Her effects do not appear in any outward and palpable results, necessarily; her method is often unknown to men, hidden even from the keenest eyes. Evil causes produce evil results, that is all; and these are shown in the most subtle and secret results of what life is. One of her methods is indicated in *Adam Bede*.

Nemesis can seldom forge a sword for herself out of our consciences — out of the suffering we feel in the suffering we may have caused; there is rarely metal enough there to make an effective weapon. Our moral sense learns the manners of good society, and smiles when others smile; but when some rude person gives rough names to our actions, she is apt to take part against us.

The Mill on the Floss reflects this thought.

Retribution may come from any voice; the hardest, cruelest, most imbruted urchin at the street-corner can inflict it.

More effective still is that punishment which comes of our own inward sense of wrong-doing. George Eliot makes Parson Irwine say that "the inward suffering is the worst form of Nemesis." This is well illustrated in the experience of Gwendolen, who, after the death of her husband at Geneva, is anxious to leave that place.

For what place, though it were the flowery vale of Enna, may not the inward sense turn into a circle of punishment where the flowers are no better than a crop of flame-tongues burning the soles of our feet?

Even before this, Gwendolen had come to realize the dire effects of selfish conduct in that dread and bitterness of spirit which subdued her and mocked all her hopes and joys.

Passion is of the nature of seed, and finds nourishment within, tending to a predominance which determines all currents toward itself, and makes the whole life its tributary. And the intensest form of hatred is that rooted in fear, which compels to silence and drives vehemence into a constructive vindictiveness, an imaginary annihilation of the deserted object, something like the hidden rites of vengeance with which the persecuted have made a dark vent for their rage, and soothed their suffering into dumbness. Such hidden rites went on in the secrecy of Gwendolen's mind, but not with soothing effect — rather with the effect of a struggling terror. Side by side with the dread of her husband had grown the self-dread which urged her to flee from the pursuing images wrought by her pent-up impulse. The vision of her past wrong-doing, and what it had brought on her, came with a pale ghastly illumination over every imagined deed that was a rash effort at freedom, such as she had made in her marriage.[1]

The way in which wrong-doing affects us to our hurt is suggested also in *Romola*, where its results upon the inward life are explicitly revealed.

Under every guilty secret there is hidden a brood of guilty wishes, whose unwholesome infecting life is cherished by the darkness. The contaminating effect of deeds lies less in the commission than in the consequent adjustment of our desires — the enlistment of our self-interest on the side of falsity; as, on the other

[1] Chapter LIV.

hand, the purifying effect of public confession springs from the fact that by it the hope in lies is forever swept away, and the soul recovers the noble attitude of simplicity.

In the same novel the effect of wrong-doing is regarded as an inward and subduing fear of the consequences of our conduct. This dread so commonly felt, and made a most effective motive by all religions, George Eliot regards as the soul's testimony to the great law of retribution. Experience that moral causes produce moral effects, as that law is every day taught us, takes hold of feeling, and becomes a nameless dread of the avenging powers.

Having once begun to explain away Baldassarre's claim, Tito's thought showed itself as active as a virulent acid, eating its rapid way through all the tissues of sentiment. His mind was destitute of that dread which has been erroneously decried as if it were nothing higher than a man's animal care for his own skin; that awe of the divine Nemesis which was felt by religious pagans, and, though it took a more positive form under Christianity, is still felt by the mass of mankind simply as a vague fear at anything which is called wrong-doing. Such terror of the unseen is so far above mere sensual cowardice that it will annihilate that cowardice: it is the initial recognition of a moral law restraining desire, and checks the hard bold scrutiny of imperfect thought into obligations which can never be proved to have any sanctity in the absence of feeling. "It is good," sing the old Eumenides, in Æschylus, "that fear should sit as the guardian of the soul, forcing it into wisdom—good that men should carry a threatening shadow in their hearts under the full sunshine; else how shall they learn to revere the right?" That guardianship may become needless; but only when all outward law has become needless—only when duty and love have united in one stream and made a common force.[1]

Another form in which Nemesis punishes us is described in the essay on "A Half-Breed" in *The Impressions of Theophrastus Such*. Mixtus was a man with noble aims, but he was fascinated by Scintilla, and realized none of his ideals. He was captivated by her prettiness, liveliness and music, and then he was captured on his worldly side. She did not believe in "notions" and reforms, and he succumbed to her wishes. As a result, his life was crippled, he was always un-

[1] Chapter XI.

satisfied with himself. Of this form of retribution George Eliot says, —

> An early deep-seated love to which we become faithless has its unfailing Nemesis, if only in that division of soul which narrows all newer joys by the intrusion of regret and the established presentiment of change. I refer not merely to the love of a person, but to the love of ideas, practical beliefs and social habits. And faithlessness here means not a gradual conversion dependent on enlarged knowledge, but a yielding to seductive circumstance; not a conviction that the original choice was a mistake, but a subjection to incidents that flatter a growing desire. In this sort of love it is the forsaker who has the melancholy lot; for an abandoned belief may be more effectively vengeful than Dido. The child of a wandering tribe, caught young and trained to polite life, if he feels a hereditary yearning, can run away to the old wilds and get his nature into tune. But there is no such recovery possible to the man who remembers what he once believed without being convinced that he was in error, who feels within him unsatisfied stirrings toward old beloved habits and intimacies from which he has far receded without conscious justification or unwavering sense of superior attractiveness in the new. This involuntary renegade has his character hopelessly jangled and out of tune. He is like an organ with its stops in the lawless condition of obtruding themselves without method, so that hearers are amazed by the most unexpected transitions — the trumpet breaking in on the flute, and the oböe confounding both.

With a strong and eloquent energy, George Eliot teaches the natural consequences of conduct. Every feeling, thought and deed has its effect, comes to fruition. Desire modifies life, shapes our destiny, moulds us into the image of its own nature. Actions become habits, become controlling elements in our lives, and tend to work out their own legitimate results. The whole of George Eliot's doctrine of retribution is, that human causes, as much as any other, lead to their appropriate effects. Her frequent use of the word *Nemesis* indicates the idea she had of the inevitableness of moral consequences, that a force once set in motion can never be recalled in its effects, which make a permanent modification of human life in its present and in its past. It was not the old doctrine of fate which she presented, not any arbitrary inflictment from supernatural powers. The inevitableness of moral consequences influenced her as a solemn and fearful reality which man must strictly regard if he would find true manhood.

The doctrine of retribution is very clearly taught by George Eliot in her comments. With a still greater distinctness it is taught in the development of her characters. As we follow the careers of Hetty, Maggie, Tito, Fedalma, Lydgate and Gwendolen we see how wonderful was George Eliot's insight into the moral issues of life. Not only with these, but with all her characters, we see a righteous moral unfoldment of character into its effects. There is no compromise with evil in her pages; all selfishness, wrong and crime comes to its proper results. The vanity and selfishness of Hetty leads to what terrible crime and shame for her, and what misery for others! Tito's selfishness and want of resolute purpose carries him inevitably downward to a hideous end. What is so plain in the case of these characters is as true, though not so palpable, in that of many others in her books. Dorothea's conduct is clearly shown to develop into consequences (as did Lydgate's) which were the natural results of what she thought, did and was. Maggie's misery was the product of her conduct, the legitimate outcome of it.

George Eliot goes beyond the conduct of any one person and its results, and attempts to show how it is affected by the person's environment. It was Maggie's family, education, social standing and personal qualities of mind and heart which helped to determine for her the consequences of her conduct. It was Dorothea's education and social environment which largely helped to shape her career and to leave her bereaved of the largest possibilities of which her life was capable. Gwendolen's life was largely determined by her early training and by her social surroundings. Yet with all these, life has its necessary issues, and Nemesis plays its part. Retribution is for all; it is ever stern, just and inevitable. Just, however, only in the sense that wrong-doing cannot escape its own effects, but not just in the sense that the guiltless must often share the fate of the guilty. Wrong-doing drags down to destruction many an innocent person. It is to be said of George Eliot, however, that she never presents any of her characters as doomed utterly by the past. However strong the memories of the ages lay upon them, they are capable of self-direction. Not one of her characters is wholly the victim of his environment. There is no hint in *Middlemarch* that Dorothea was not capable of heroism and self-consecration. Her environment gave a wrong direction to her moral purpose; but that purpose remained, and the moral nobleness of her mind was not destroyed. Still, it is largely true, that in her books the individual is sacrificed to his social environment. He is to renounce his own personality for the sake of the race. Consequently his fate is linked with that of others, and he must suffer from other men's deeds.

With all its limitations and defects, George Eliot's teaching concerning the moral effects of conduct is wholesome and healthy. It rests on a solid foundation of experience and scientific evidence. Her books are full of moral stimulus and strengthening, because of the profound conviction with which she has presented her conception of moral cause and effect. With her, we must believe that moral sequences are as inevitable as the physical.

It would be very unjust to George Eliot to suppose that she left man in the hands of a relentless moral order which manifests no tenderness and which is incapable of pity and mercy. She did not believe in an Infinite Father, full of love and forgiveness; that faith was not for her. Yet she did believe in a providence which can assuage man's sorrows and deal tenderly with his wrong-doing. While nature is stern and the moral sequences of life unbending, man may be sympathetic and helpful Man is to be the providence of man humanity is to be his tender forgiving Friend. A substitute so poor for the old faith would seem to have little power of moral renovation or sympathetic impulse in it; but it quickened George Eliot's mind with enthusiasm and ardor. The "enthusiasm of humanity" filled her whole soul, was a luminous hope in her heart and an inspiring purpose to her mind. With Goethe and Carlyle she found in work for humanity the substitute for all faith and the cure for all doubt. Faust finds for his life a purpose, and for the universe a solution, when he comes to labor for the practical improvement of humanity. This was George Eliot's own conclusion, that it is enough for us to see the world about us made a little better and more orderly by our efforts. All her noblest characters find in altruism a substitute for religion, and they find there a moral anchorage. She says very plainly in *Middlemarch*, that every doctrine is capable of "eating out our morality if unchecked by the deep-seated habit of direct fellow-feeling with individual fellow-men." To the same effect is her saying in *Romola*, that "with the sinking of the high human trust the dignity of life sinks too; we cease to believe in our own better self, since that also is a part of the common nature which is degraded in our thought; and all the finer impulses of the soul are dulled." In *Janet's Repentance* she has finely presented this faith in sympathetic humanitarianism, showing how Janet found peace in the sick-room where all had been doubt and trial before.

Day after day, with only short intervals of rest, Janet kept her place in that sad chamber. No wonder the sick-room and the lazaretto have so often been a refuge from the tossings of intellectual doubt — a place of repose for the worn and wounded spirit. Here is a duty about which all creeds and all philosophies are at one: — here, at least, the conscience will not be dogged by doubt — the benign impulse will not be checked by adverse theory: here you may begin to act without settling one preliminary question. To moisten the sufferer's parched lips through the long night-watches, to bear up the drooping head, to lift the helpless limbs, to divine the want that can find no utterance beyond the feeble motion of the hand or beseeching glance of the eye — these are offices that demand no self-questionings, no casuistry, no assent to propositions, no weighing of consequences. Within the four walls where the stir and glare of the world are shut out, and every voice is subdued,— where a human being lies prostrate, thrown on the tender mercies of his fellow, — the moral relation of man to man is reduced to its utmost clearness and simplicity: bigotry cannot confuse it, theory cannot pervert it, passion, awed into quiescence, can neither pollute nor perturb it. As we bend over the sick-bed all the forces of our nature rush towards the channels of pity, of patience and of love, and sweep down the miserable choking drift of our quarrels, our debates, our would-be wisdom, and our clamorous, selfish desires. This blessing of serene freedom from the importunities of opinion lies in all simple, direct acts of mercy, and is one source of that sweet calm which is often felt by the watcher in the sick-room, even when the duties there are of a hard and terrible kind.[1]

The basis of such sympathetic helpfulness she finds in the common sorrows and trials of the world. All find life hard, pain comes to all, none are to be found unacquainted with sorrow. These common experiences draw men together in sympathy, unite them in a common purpose of assuagement and help. The sorrow of Adam Bede made him more gentle and patient with his brother.

It was part of that growing tenderness which came from the sorrow at work within him. For Adam, though you see him quite master of himself, working hard and delighting in his work after his inborn inalienable nature, had not outlived his sorrow — had not felt it slip from him as a temporary burden, and leave him the same man again. Do any of us? God forbid! It would be a poor result of all our anguish and our wrestling if we won nothing but our old selves at the end of it — if we could return to the same blind loves, the same self-confident blame, the same light thoughts of human suffering, the same frivolous gossip over blighted human lives, the same feeble sense of that Unknown toward which we have sent forth irrepressible cries in our loneliness. Let us rather be thankful that our sorrow lives in us as an indestructible force, only changing its form, as forces do, and passing from pain into sympathy — the one poor word which includes all our best insight and our best love. Not that this transformation of pain into sympathy had completely taken place in Adam yet; there was still a great remnant of pain, which he felt would subsist as long as *her* pain was not a memory, but an existing thing, which he must think of as renewed with the light of every morning. But we get accustomed to mental as well as bodily pain, without, for all that, losing our sensibility to it; it becomes a habit of our lives, and we

[1] Chapter XXIV.

cease to imagine a condition of perfect ease as possible for us. Desire is chastened into submission; and we are contented with our day when we are able to bear our grief in silence, and act as if we were not suffering. For it is at such periods that the sense of our lives having visible and invisible relations beyond any of which either our present or prospective self is the centre, grows like a muscle that we are obliged to lean on and exert.

Armgart finds that "true vision comes only with sorrow." Sorrow and suffering create a sympathy which sends us to the relief of others. "Pain must enter into its glorified life of memory before it can turn into compassion," we are told in *Middlemarch*. In the trying hours of Maggie Tulliver's life she came to know —

that new sense which is the gift of sorrow — that susceptibility to the bare offices of humanity which raises them into a bond of loving fellowship.

Again, she learns that "more helpful than all wisdom is one draught of simple human pity that will not forsake us." Man is in this way brought to live for man, to suffer in his sufferings, to be mercifully tender and pitiful with him in his temptations and trials. Sympathy builds up the moral life, gives an ethical meaning to man's existence. Thus humanity becomes a providence to man, and it is made easier for him to bear his sufferings and to be comforted in his sorrows. Nemesis is stern, but man is pitiful; retribution is inexorable, but humanity is sympathetic. Nature never relents, and there is no God who can so forgive us our sins as to remove their legitimate effects; but man can comfort us with his love, and humanity can teach us to overcome retribution by righteous conduct.

All idealistic rights are to be laid aside, according to her theory, all personal claims and motives are to be renounced. In the duties we owe to others, life is to find its rightful expression. In *Janet's Repentance* she says, —

The idea of duty, that recognition of something to be lived for beyond the mere satisfaction of self, is to the moral life what the addition of a great central ganglion is to animal life. No man can begin to mould himself on a faith or an idea without rising to a higher order of experience: a principle of subordination, of self-mastery, has been introduced into his nature; he is no longer a mere bundle of impressions, desires and impulses.

To live for self, George Eliot seems to regard as immoral; self is to be ignored except in so far as it can be made to serve humanity. As rights are individual they are repudiated, and the demand for them is regarded as revolutionary and destructive.

That man is a moral being because he is a social being she carries to its farthest extreme in some of her teachings, as when she makes public opinion the great motive power to social improvement. Felix Holt pronounces public opinion — the ruling belief in society about what is right and what is wrong, what is honorable and what is shameful — to be the greatest power under heaven. In the "Address to Working Men, by Felix Holt," published in *Blackwood's Magazine*, Felix is made to say to his fellows, —

> Any nation that had within it a majority of men — and we are the majority — possessed of much wisdom and virtue, would not tolerate the bad practices, the commercial lying and swindling, the poisonous adulteration of goods, the retail cheating and the political bribery which are carried on boldly in the midst of us. A majority has the power of creating a public opinion. We could groan and hiss before we had the franchise: if we had groaned and hissed in the right place, if we had discerned better between good and evil, if the multitude of us artisans and factory hands and miners and laborers of all sorts had been skilful, faithful, well-judging, industrious, sober — and I don't see how there can be wisdom and virtue anywhere without these qualities — we should have made an audience that would have shamed the other classes out of their share in the national vices. We should have had better members of Parliament, better religious teachers, honester tradesmen, fewer foolish demagogues, less impudence in infamous and brutal men; and we should not have had among us the abomination of men calling themselves religious while living in splendor on ill-gotten gains. I say it is not possible for any society in which there is a very large body of wise and virtuous men to be as vicious as our society is — to have as low a standard of right and wrong, to have so much belief in falsehood, or to have so degrading, barbarous a notion of what pleasure is, or of what justly raises a man above his fellows. Therefore let us have done with this nonsense about our being much better than the rest of our countrymen, or the pretence that that was a reason why we ought to have such an extension of the franchise as has been given to us.

The essay on "Moral Swindlers," in *Theophrastus Such*, clearly indicates George Eliot's point of view in ethics. She makes those moral traits which are social of greater importance than those which are personal. She complains that a man who is chaste and of a clean personal conduct is regarded as a moral man when his business habits are not good. To her, his relations to his fellows in all the social and business affairs of life are of higher importance than his personal habits or his family relations. She rebels against that deep moral instinct of the race which identifies morality with personal character, and is indignant that the altruism she so much believed in is not everywhere made identical with ethics. To her, the person is nothing; the individual is thought of only as a member of a community. She forgot that any large and noble moral life for a people must rest upon personal character, upon a pure and healthy state of the moral nature in individuals. Nations cannot be moral, but persons can. Public corruption has its foundation in personal corruption. The nation cannot have a noble moral life unless the individuals of which it is composed are pure in character and noble in conduct. She complains that sexual purity is made identical with morality, while business integrity is not. Every social and moral bond we have, she says, "is a debt; the right lies in the payment of that debt; *it can lie nowhere else*." It is a debt owed, not to God, but to humanity; it is therefore to be paid, not by personal holiness, but by human sympathy and devotion.

The higher social morality, that which inspires nations with great and heroic purposes, George Eliot believes, is mainly due, as she says in the essay on "The Modern Hep, Hep, Hep!" "to the divine gift of a memory which inspires the moments with a past, a present and a future, and gives the sense of corporate existence that raises man above the otherwise more respectable and innocent brute." The memories of the past lie mainly in the direction of national movements, and hence the higher moral life of the present must be associated with national memories. The glorious commonplaces of historic teaching, as well as of moral inspiration, are to be found in the fact "that the preservation of national memories is an element and a means of national greatness, that their revival is a sign of reviving nationality, and that every heroic defender, every patriotic restorer, has been inspired by such memories and has made them his watchword." To reject such memories, such social influences, she regards as "a blinding superstition," and says that the moral visions of a nation are an effective bond which must be accepted by all its members. Two of her most characteristic books are written to inculcate this teaching. In *The Spanish Gypsy* we learn that there is no moral strength and purpose for a man like Don Silva, who repudiates his country, its memories and its religion. The main purpose of *Daniel Deronda* is to show how binding and inspiring is the vision of moral truth and life which comes from association even with the national memories of an outcast and alien people.

She wished to see individuals helped and good done in the present. She makes Theophrastus Such, in the essay on "Looking Backward," speak her own mind.

> "All reverence and gratitude for the worthy dead on whose labors we have entered, all care for the future generations whose lot we are preparing; but some affection and fairness for those who are doing the actual work of the world, some attempt to regard them with the same freedom from ill-temper, whether on private or public grounds, as we may hope will be felt by those who will call us ancient! Otherwise, the looking before and after, which is our grand human privilege, is in danger of turning to a sort of other-worldliness, breeding a more illogical indifference or bitterness than was ever bred by the ascetic's contemplation of heaven."

Again, she says that "the action by which we can do the best for future ages is of the sort which has a certain beneficence and grace for contemporaries." And this was not merely the teaching of her books, it was the practice of her life. Miss Edith Simcox has made it clear that she was zealously anxious to help men and women by personal effort. She tells us that "George Eliot's sympathies went out more readily towards enthusiasm for the discharge of duties than for the assertion of rights. It belonged to the positive basis of her character to identify herself more with what people wished to do themselves than with what they thought somebody else ought to do for them. Her indignation was vehement enough against dishonest or malicious oppression, but the instinct to make allowance for the other side made her a bad hater in politics, and there may easily have been some personal sympathy in her description of Deronda's difficulty about the choice of a career. She was not an inviting auditor for those somewhat pachydermatous philanthropists who dwell complacently upon 'cases' and statistics which represent appalling depths of individual suffering. Her imagination realized these facts with a vividness that was physically unbearable, and unless she could give substantial help, she avoided the fruitless agitation. At the same time, her interest in all rational good works was of the warmest, and she was inclined to exaggerate rather than undervalue the merits of their promoters, with one qualification only. 'Help the millions, by all means,' she has written; 'I only want people not to scorn the narrower effect.' Charity that did not begin at home repelled her as much as she was attracted by the unpretentious kindness which overlooked no near opportunity; and perhaps we should not be far wrong in guessing that she thought for most people the scrupulous discharge of all present and unavoidable duties was nearly occupation enough. Not every one was called to the high but difficult vocation of setting the world to rights. But on the other hand, it must be remembered that her standard of exactingness was high, and some of the things that in her eyes it was merely culpable to leave undone might be counted by others among virtues of supererogation. Indeed, it is within the limits of possibility that a philanthropist wrapped in over-much conscious virtue might imagine her cold to the objects proposed, when she only failed to see uncommon merit in their pursuit. No one, however, could recognize with more generous fervor, more delighted admiration, any genuine unobtrusive devotion in either friends or strangers, whether it were spent in making life easier to individuals, or in mending the conditions among which the masses live and labor." This writer gives us further insight into George Eliot's character when we are told that "she came as a very angel of consolation to those persons of sufficiently impartial mind to find comfort in the hint that the world might be less to blame than they were as to those points on which they found themselves in chronic disagreement with it. But she had nothing welcome for those whose idea of consolation is the promise of a *deus ex machinâ* by whose help they may gather grapes of thorns and figs of thistles. She thought there was much needed doing in the world, and criticism of our neighbors and the natural order might wait at all events until the critic's own character and conduct were free from blame." She had faith in ordinary lives, and these she earnestly desired to help and encourage. Those who themselves struggle with difficulties are best capable, she thought, of helping others out of theirs. In *Daniel Deronda* she said, "Our guides, we pretend, must be sinless; as if those were not often the best teachers who only yesterday got corrected for their mistakes."

George Eliot's interest in the present amelioration of human conditions was strengthened by her faith in the future of the race. She expected no rapid improvement, no revolutionizing development; but she believed the past of mankind justifies faith in a gradual attainment of perfect conditions. This conviction was expressed when she said, —

What I look to is a time when the impulse to help our fellows shall be as immediate and irresistible as that which I feel to grasp something firm if I am falling.

She saw too much evil and suffering to be an optimist; she could not see that all things are good or tending towards what is good. Yet her faith in the final outcome was earnest, and she looked to a slow and painful progress as the result of human struggles. When called an optimist, she responded, "I will not answer to the name of optimist, but if you like to invent Meliorist, I will not say you call me out of my name." She trusted in that gradual development which science points out as the probable result of the survival of the fittest in human life. In "A Minor Prophet" she has presented her conception of human advancement, and tenderly expressed her sympathy with all humble, imperfect lives.

Bitterly
I feel that every change upon this earth
Is bought with sacrifice. My yearnings fail
To reach that high apocalyptic mount
Which shows in bird's-eye view a perfect world,
Or enter warmly into other joys
Than those of faulty, struggling human kind.
That strain upon my soul's too perfect wing
Ends in ignoble floundering: I fall
Into short-sighted pity for the men
Who, living in those perfect future times,
Will not know half the dear imperfect things
That move my smiles and tears — will never know
The fine old incongruities that raise
My friendly laugh; the innocent conceits
That like a needless eyeglass or black patch
Give those who wear them harmless happiness;
The twists and cracks in our poor earthenware,
That touch me to more conscious fellowship
(I am not myself the finest Parian)
With my coevals. So poor Colin Clout,
To whom raw onions give prospective zest,
Consoling hours of dampest wintry work,
Could hardly fancy any regal joys
Quite unimpregnate with the onion's scent:
Perhaps his highest hopes are not all clear
Of waftings from that energetic bulb:
'Tis well that onion is not heresy.
Speaking in parable, I am Colin Clout.

A clinging flavor penetrates my life —
My onion is imperfectness: I cleave
To nature's blunders, evanescent types
Which sages banish from Utopia.
"Not worship beauty?" say you. Patience, friend!
I worship in the temple with the rest;
But by my hearth I keep a sacred nook
For gnomes and dwarfs, duck-footed waddling elves
Who stitched and hammered for the weary man
In days of old. And in that piety
I clothe ungainly forms inherited
From toiling generations, daily bent
At desk, or plough, or loom, or in the mine,
In pioneering labors for the world.
Nay, I am apt, when floundering confused
From too rash flight, to grasp at paradox,
And pity future men who will not know
A keen experience with pity blent,
The pathos exquisite of lovely minds
Hid in harsh forms — not penetrating them
Like fire divine within a common bush
Which glows transfigured by the heavenly guest,
So that men put their shoes off; but encaged
Like a sweet child within some thick-walled cell,
Who leaps and fails to hold the window-bars;
But having shown a little dimpled hand,
Is visited thenceforth by tender hearts
Whose eyes keep watch about the prison walls.
A foolish, nay, a wicked paradox!
For purest pity is the eye of love,
Melting at sight of sorrow; and to grieve
Because it sees no sorrow, shows a love
Warped from its truer nature, turned to love
Of merest habit, like the miser's greed.
But I am Colin still: my prejudice
Is for the flavor of my daily food.
Not that I doubt the world is growing still,
As once it grew from chaos and from night;
Or have a soul too shrunken for the hope
Which dawned in human breasts, a double morn,
With earliest watchings of the rising light
Chasing the darkness; and through many an age
Has raised the vision of a future time
That stands an angel, with a face all mild,
Spearing the demon. I, too, rest in faith
That man's perfection is the crowning flower
Towards which the urgent sap in life's great tree
Is pressing — seen in puny blossoms now,
But in the world's great morrows to expand
With broadest petal and with deepest glow.

With no disgust toward the crude and wretched life

man everywhere lives to-day, but with pity and tenderness for all sorrow, suffering and struggle, she yet believed that the world is being shaped to a glorious and a mighty destiny. This faith finds full and clear expression in the concluding lines of the poem just quoted.

The faith that life on earth is being shaped
To glorious ends, that order, justice, love,
Mean man's completeness, mean effect as sure
As roundness in the dewdrop — that great faith
Is but the rushing and expanding stream
Of thought, of feeling, fed by all the past.
Our finest hope is finest memory,
As they who love in age think youth is blest
Because it has a life to fill with love.
Full souls are double mirrors, making still
An endless vista of fair things before
Repeating things behind: so faith is strong
Only when we are strong, shrinks when we shrink.
It comes when music stirs us, and the chords
Moving on some grand climax shake our souls
With influx new that makes new energies.
It comes in swellings of the heart and tears
That rise at noble and at gentle deeds —
At labors of the master-artist's hand
Which, trembling, touches to a finer end,
Trembling before an image seen within.
It comes in moments of heroic love,
Unjealous joy in love not made for us —
In conscious triumph of the good within,
Making us worship goodness that rebukes.
Even our failures are a prophecy,
Even our yearnings and our bitter tears
After that fair and true we cannot grasp;
As patriots who seem to die in vain
Make liberty more sacred by their pangs,
Presentiment of better things on earth
Sweeps in with every force that stirs our souls
To admiration, self-renouncing love,
Or thoughts, like light, that bind the world in one:
Sweeps like the sense of vastness, when at night
We hear the roll and dash of waves that break
Nearer and nearer with the rushing tide,
Which rises to the level of the cliff
Because the wide Atlantic rolls behind,
Throbbing respondent to the far-off orbs.

George Eliot did all that could be done to make the morality she taught commendable and inspiring. In her own direct teachings, and in the development of her characters and her plots, she has done much to make it acceptable. Her strong insistence on the social basis of morality is to be admired, and the truth presented is one of great importance. Even more important is her teaching of the stern nature of retribution, that every thought, word and deed has its effect. There is need of such teaching, and it can be appropriated into the thought and life of the time with great promise of good. Yet the outcome of George Eliot's morality was rather depressing than otherwise. While she was no pessimist, yet she made her readers feel that life was pessimistic in its main tendencies. She makes on the minds of very many of her readers the impression that life has not very much light in it. This comes from the whole cast of her mind, and still more because the light of true ideal hopes was absent from her thought. A stern, ascetic view of life appears throughout her pages, one of the results of the new morality and the humanitarian gospel of altruism. Unbending, unpitiful, does the universe seem to be when the idea of law and Nemesis is so strongly presented, and with no relief from it in the theory of man's free will. Not less depressing to the moral nature is an unrelieved view of the universe under the omnipotent law of cause and effect, which is not lighted by any vision of God and a spiritual order interpenetrating the material. Her teaching too often takes the tone of repression; it is hard and exacting. She devotes many pages to showing the effects of the law of retribution; she gives comparatively few to the correlative law that good always has its reward. Renunciation is presented as a moral force, and as duty of supreme importance; life is to be repressed for the sake of humanity. The spontaneous tendencies of the mind and heart, the importance of giving a free and healthy development to human nature, is not regarded. Her morality is justly to be criticised for its ascetic and pessimistic tendencies.

XIII.

EARLIER NOVELS.

THE first four novels written by George Eliot form a group by themselves; and while all similar to each other in their main characteristics, are in important respects different from her later works. This group includes *Clerical Scenes*, *Adam Bede*, *The Mill on the Floss* and *Silas Marner*. With these may also be classed "Brother Jacob." They are all alike novels of memory, and they deal mainly with common life. Her own life and the surroundings of her childhood, the memories and associations and suggestions of her early life, are drawn upon. The simple surroundings and ideas of the midland village are seldom strayed away from, and most of the characters are farmers and their laborers, artisans or clergymen. *The Mill on the Floss* offers a partial exception to this statement, for in that book we touch upon the border of a different form of society, but we scarcely enter into it, and the leading characters are from the same class as those in the other books of this group. "Mr. Gilfil's Love Story" alone enters wholly within the circle of aristocratic society. There is more of the realism of actual life in these novels than in her later ones, greater spontaneity and insight, a deeper sympathy and a more tender pathos. They came more out of her heart and sympathies, are more impassioned and pathetic.

Throughout the *Scenes of Clerical Life* are descriptions of actual scenes and incidents known to George Eliot in her girlhood. Mrs. Hackit is a portrait of her own mother. In the first chapter of "Amos Barton," Shepperton Church is that at Chilvers Coton, which she attended throughout her childhood. It is from memory, and with an accurate pen, she describes —

> Shepperton Church as it was in the old days with its outer court of rough stucco, its red-tiled roof, its heterogeneous windows patched with desultory bits of painted glass, and its little flight of steps with their wooden rail running up the outer wall, and leading to the school-children's gallery. Then inside, what dear old quaintnesses! which I began to look at with delight, even when I was so crude a member of the congregation that my nurse found it necessary to provide for the re-inforcement of my devotional patience by smuggling bread-and-butter into the sacred edifice. There was the chancel, guarded by two little cherubims looking uncomfortably squeezed between arch and wall, and adorned with the escutcheons of the Oldinport family, which showed me inexhaustible possibilities of meaning in their blood-red hands, their death's-heads and cross-bones, their leopards' paws and Maltese crosses. There were inscriptions on the panels of the singing-gallery, telling of benefactions to the poor of Shepperton, with an involuted elegance of capitals and final flourishes which my alphabetic erudition traced with ever-new delight. No benches in those days; but huge roomy pews, round which devout church-goers sat during "lessons," trying to look everywhere else than into each others' eyes. No low partitions allowing you, with a dreary absence of contrast and mystery, to see everything at all moments; but tall dark panels, under whose shadow I sank with a sense of retirement through the Litany, only to feel with more intensity my burst into the conspicuousness of public life when I was made to stand up on the seat during the psalms or the singing.

Not only is this description of Shepperton Church accurate in every particular, but a subject of neighborhood gossip is made the basis of the story of "Amos Barton." When George Eliot was about a dozen years old a strange lady appeared at the Coton parsonage, and became a subject of much discussion on the part of the parishioners. Much pity was felt for the wife of the curate, an intimate friend of Marian Evans's mother, whose poverty, seven children and poor health made her burdens far from easy. She died not long after, and her grave may be seen at Chilvers Coton. The Knebley Church of "Mr. Gilfil's Love Story" is located only a short distance from Chilvers Coton, and is the chancel of the collegiate church founded by Sir Thomas de Astley in the time of Edward III. Its spire was very high, and served as a landmark to travellers through the forest of Arden, and was called "The lanthorn of Arden." The spire fell in the year 1600, but was rebuilt later. The present church was repaired by the patron of George Eliot's father, Sir Roger Newdigate. She describes it in the first chapter of "Mr. Gilfil's Love Story" as —

a wonderful little church, with a checkered pavement which had once rung to the iron tread of military monks, with coats of arms in clusters on the lofty roof, marble warriors and their wives without noses occupying a large proportion of the area, and the twelve apostles with their heads very much on one side, holding didactic ribbons, painted in fresco on the walls.

A delightful lane, overshadowed with noble trees, that ran by Griff House, the birthplace of George Eliot, led to the lodge of Arbury Hall, the home of Sir Roger Newdigate. Arbury Hall was situated in the midst of a fine old forest, and it was originally a large quadrangular brick house. Sir Roger rebuilt it, acting as his own architect, and made it into a modern dwelling of the commodious gothic order. This house and its owner appear in "Mr. Gilfil's Love Story" as Cheverel Manor and Sir Christopher Cheverel. In the fourth chapter the reader is told that, —

For the next ten years Sir Christopher was occupied with the architectural metamorphosis of his old family mansion, thus anticipating through the prompting of his individual taste that general re-action from the insipid imitation of the Palladian style towards a restoration of the Gothic, which marked the close of the eighteenth century. This was the object he had set his heart on, with a singleness of determination which was regarded with not a little contempt by his fox-hunting neighbors. . . . "An obstinate, crotchety man," said his neighbors. But I, who have seen Cheverel Manor as he bequeathed it to his heirs, rather attribute that unswerving architectural purpose of his, conceived and carried out through long years of systematic personal exertion, to something of the fervor of genius.

In this story an incident in the life of Sir Roger Newdigate may have been made use of by George Eliot. He was childless, and adopted a cottager's child he and his wife heard singing at its father's door one day. They educated the child, who proved to have a fine voice and a passionate love of music.

Janet's Repentance also has its scenes from actual life. Dr. Dempster was thought to be recognized by his neighbors as a well-known person in Nuneaton. Milby and its High street are no other than Nuneaton and its market-place. The character of the town and the manner of life there are all sketched from the Nuneaton of George Eliot's childhood. The school she attended was very near the vicarage. While she was attending this school, when about nine years old, a young curate from a neighboring hamlet was permitted by the Bishop to give Sunday-evening lectures in the Nuneaton church, with the results described in *Janet's Repentance.*

In *Adam Bede* there is also a considerable element of actual history. The heroine, Dinah Morris, is, in some slight particulars at least, sketched from Elizabeth Evans, an aunt of George Eliot's. Elizabeth Evans was born at Newbold, Lincolnshire, in 1776.[1] She was a beautiful woman when young, with soft gray eyes and a fine face, and had a very simple and gentle manner. She was a Methodist preacher, lived at Wirksworth, Derbyshire, and preached wherever an opportunity occurred. When it was forbidden that women should preach, she continued to exhort in the cottages, and to visit the poor and the sick in their homes. She married Samuel Evans, who was born in Boston, and was a carpenter. He had a brother William, who was a joiner and builder. Their father was a village carpenter and undertaker, honest and respectable, but who took to drink in his later years. He was at an ale-

[1] This subject has been fully worked out in a book published by Blackwood, "George Eliot in Derbyshire: a volume of gossip about passages in the novels of George Eliot," by Guy Roslyn. Reprinted from London Society, with alterations and additions, and an introduction by George Barnett Smith. Its statements are mainly based on a small book published in London in 1859, by Talbot & Co., entitled "Seth Bede, the Methody: his Life and Labors." Guy Roslyn is a pseudonym for Joshua Hatton.

house very late one night, and the next morning was found dead in a brook near his house. Samuel became a Methodist and a preacher, but was teased about it by his brother, who criticised his blunders in prayer and preaching. He was gentle and very considerate at home, and was greatly attached to his brother, though they could not agree in matters of religion. While they were partners in business they prospered, but Samuel did not succeed when by himself. Samuel and Elizabeth were married at St. Mary's Church, Nottingham. In company with a Miss Richards, Elizabeth attended, in 1801 or 1802, a Mary Voce who had poisoned her child. They visited her in jail, and were with her when she was hung in Nottingham. Elizabeth wrote an account of her own life, especially of her conversion and her early work in the ministry. Concerning the execution of Mary Voce, she gives this account: "At seven o'clock [on the morning of the execution] we all knelt down in prayer, and at ten minutes before eight o'clock the Lord in mercy spoke peace to her soul. She cried out, 'Oh, how happy I am! the Lord has pardoned all my sins, and I am going to heaven.' She never lost the evidence for one moment, and always rejoiced in the hope of glory. Is it not by grace we are saved through faith? And is not the Saviour exalted at the Father's right hand to give repentance to Israel and forgiveness of sins? If salvation were by works who would be saved? The vilest and worst may come unto Him. None need despair. None ought to presume. Miss Richards and I attended her to the place of execution. Our feelings on this occasion were very acute. We rode with her in the cart to the awful place. Our people sang with her all the way, which I think was a mile and a half. We were enabled to lift up our hearts unto the Lord in her behalf, and she was enabled to bear a public testimony that God in mercy had pardoned all her sins. When the cap was drawn over her face, and she was about to be turned off, she cried, 'Glory! glory! glory! the angels are waiting around me.' And she died almost without a struggle. At this awful spot I lost a great deal of the fear of man, which to me had been a great hindrance for a long time. I felt if God would send me to the uttermost parts of the earth I would go, and at intervals felt I could embrace a martyr's flame. Oh, this burning love of God, what will it not endure? I could not think I had an enemy in the world. I am certain I enjoyed that salvation that if they had smote me on one cheek, I could have turned to them the other also. I lived

'The life of heaven above,
All the life of glorious love.'

"I seemed myself to live between heaven and earth. I was not in heaven because of my body, nor upon earth because of my soul. Earth was a scale to heaven, and all I tasted was God. I could pray without ceasing, and in everything give thanks. I felt that the secret of the Lord is with them that fear Him. If I wanted to know anything I had only to ask, and it was given, generally in a moment. Whether I was in the public street, or at my work, or in my private room, I had continued intercourse with my God; and many, I think I may say hundreds of times, He shone upon His Word, and showed me the meaning thereof, that is, texts of scripture, so as to furnish me with sufficient matter to speak to poor sinners for a sufficient length of time."

The life of Elizabeth Evans was only a hint to the mind of the author of *Adam Bede*. Dinah was not intended as a portrait, and the resemblances between the two were probably not the result of a conscious purpose on the part of George Eliot. Soon after the publication of *Adam Bede*, when gossip had begun to report that Dinah Morris was an accurate sketch of Elizabeth Evans, and even that her sermon and prayers had been copied from the writings of the aunt, George Eliot wrote a letter to her intimate friend, Miss Sara Hennell, in which she explained to what extent she was indebted to Elizabeth Evans for the portrait of Dinah Morris.

HOLLY LODGE, Oct. 7, 1859.

Dear Sara. — I should like, while the subject is vividly present with me, to tell you more exactly than I have ever yet done, *what* I knew of my aunt, Elizabeth Evans. My father, you know, lived in Warwickshire all my life with him, having finally left Staffordshire first, and then Derbyshire, six or seven years before he married my mother.[1] . . .

As to my aunt's conversation, it is a fact that the only two things of any interest I remember in our lonely sittings and walks are her telling me one sunny afternoon how she had, with another pious woman, visited an unhappy girl in prison, stayed with her all night, and gone with her to execution, and one or two accounts of supposed miracles in which she believed — among the rest, *the face with the crown of thorns seen in the glass*. In her account of the prison scenes, I remember no word she uttered — I only remember her tone and manner, and the deep feeling I had under the recital. Of the girl she knew nothing, I believe — or told me nothing — but that she was a common coarse girl, convicted of child-murder. The incident lay in my mind for years on years as a dead germ, apparently, till time had made my mind a nidus in which it could fructify; it then turned out to be the germ of *Adam Bede*.

I saw my aunt twice after this. Once I spent a day and a night with my father in the Wirksworth cottage, sleeping with my aunt, I remember. Our interview was less interesting than in the former time: I think I was less simply devoted to religious ideas. And once again she came with my uncle to see me — when father and I were living at Foleshill; *then* there was some pain, for I had given up the form of Christian belief, and was in a crude state of free-thinking. She stayed about three or four days, I think. This is all I remember distinctly, as matter I could write down, of my dear aunt, whom I really loved. You see how she suggested Dinah; but it is not possible you should see as I do how her entire individuality differed from Dinah's. How curious it seems to me that people should think Dinah's sermon, prayers and speeches were *copied* — when they were written with hot tears as they surged up in my own mind!

As to my indebtedness to facts of *locale*, and personal history of a small kind connected with Staffordshire and Derbyshire — you may imagine of what kind that is when I tell you that I never remained in either of those counties more than a few days together, and of only two such visits have I more than a shadowy, interrupted recollection. The details which I knew as facts and have made use of for my picture were gathered from such imperfect allusion and narrative as I heard from my father in his occasional talk about old times.

As to my aunt's children or grandchildren saying, if they *did* say, that Dinah is a good portrait of my aunt — that is simply the

[1] What is here omitted of this letter will be found on page 12.

vague, easily satisfied notion imperfectly instructed people always have of portraits. It is not surprising that simple men and women without pretension to enlightened discrimination should think a generic resemblance constitutes a portrait, when we see the great public so accustomed to be delighted with *mis*-representations of life and character, which they accept as representations, that they are scandalized when art makes a nearer approach to the truth.

Perhaps I am doing a superfluous thing in writing all this to you, but I am prompted to do it by the feeling that in future years *Adam Bede* and all that concerns it may have become a dim portion of the past, and I may not be able to recall so much of the truth as I have now told you.

Once more, thanks, dear Sara. Ever your loving

MARIAN.

When, in 1876, a book was published to show the identity of Dinah Morris and Elizabeth Evans, George Eliot wrote to the author to protest against such a conclusion. She said to him that the one was not intended to represent the other, and that any identification of the two would be protested against as not only false in fact and tending to perpetuate false notions about art, but also as a gross breach of social decorum. Yet these declarations concerning Elizabeth Evans have been repeated, and to them has been added the assertion that she actually copied in *Adam Bede* the history and sermons of Dinah Morris.[1] During visits to her aunt in 1842 we are told they spent several hours together each day. "They used to go to the house of one of Mrs. Evans's married daughters, where they had the parlor to themselves and had long conversations. These secret conversations excited some curiosity in the family, and one day Mrs. Evans's daughter said, 'Mother, I can't think what thee and Mary Ann have got to talk about so much.' To which Mrs. Evans replied, 'Well, my dear, I don't know what she wants, but she gets me to tell her all about my life and my religious experience, and she puts it all down in a little book. I can't make out what she wants it for.' While at Wirksworth, Miss Evans made a note of everything people said in

[1] "Dinah Morris and Elizabeth Evans," an article by L. Buckley in The Century for August, 1882.

her hearing; no matter who was speaking, down it went into the note-book, which seemed never out of her hand. These notes she transcribed every night before going to rest. After her departure Mrs. Evans said to her daughter, 'Oh dear, Mary Ann has got one thing I did not mean her to take away, and that is the notes of the first sermon I preached on Ellaston Green.' The sermon preached by Dinah on Hayslope Green has been recognized as one of Mrs. Evans's." The purpose here seems to be to convey the impression that George Eliot actually carried away one of Mrs. Evans's sermons, and that she afterwards copied it into *Adam Bede*. George Eliot's own positive statement on this subject ought to be sufficient to convince any candid mind the sermon was not copied. The evidence brought forward so far in regard to the relations of Dinah Morris to Elizabeth Evans is not sufficient to prove the one was taken from the other. George Eliot's declarations, written soon after *Adam Bede* was published, when all was perfectly fresh in her mind, and after her relatives had made their statements about Mrs. Evans, ought to settle the matter forever. Unless new and far more positive evidence is brought forward, Dinah Morris ought to be regarded as substantially an original creation.

That some features of Elizabeth Evans's character were sketched into that of Dinah Morris seems certain. It is also said that the names of Mrs. Poyser and Bartle Massey were the names of actual persons, the latter being the schoolmaster of her father. As showing her power of local coloring, Miss Mathilde Blind relates this incident: "On its first appearance, *Adam Bede* was read aloud to an old man, an intimate associate of Robert Evans in his Staffordshire days. This man knew nothing concerning either author or subject beforehand, and his astonishment was boundless on recognizing so many friends and incidents of his own youth portrayed with unerring fidelity. He sat up half the night listening to the story in breathless excitement, now and then slapping his knees as he exclaimed, 'That's Robert, that's Robert, to the life.'"

In *Adam Bede*, as well as in the *Clerical Scenes* and *The Mill on the Floss*, she describes types of character instead of actual personages; and yet so much of the realistic is embodied that more than one of her characters has been identified as being in a considerable degree a sketch from life. This is true of *The Mill on the Floss* even more fully than of her previous books. In Maggie she has portrayed one side of her own character, and made use of much of her early experience. Lucy is said to be her sister, and two of her aunts are sketched in the aunts of Maggie — Mrs. Glegg and Mrs. Pullett. Her brother recognized the minute faithfulness of this story, as he did that of *Adam Bede*. The town of St. Ogg's is a good description of the tide-water town of Gainesborough in Lincolnshire. The Hayslope of *Adam Bede* has been identified as the village of Ellaston, four miles from Ashbourne, in Derbyshire. It is near Wirksworth, the home of Elizabeth Evans.

The local exactness of George Eliot's descriptions is another evidence of her realism. "It is not unlikely," suggests Mr. Kegan Paul, "that the time will come when with one or other of her books in their hand, people will wander among the scenes of George Eliot's early youth, and trace each allusion, as they are wont to do at Abbotsford or Newstead, and they will recognize the photographic minuteness and accuracy with which these scenes, so long unvisited, had stamped themselves on the mind of the observant girl." The historical setting of her novels is also faithful in even minute details. The time of "Mr. Gilfil's Love Story" is at the beginning of the last quarter of the eighteenth century, and it well describes the country customs of the earlier years of the present century. *Adam Bede* describes the first decade of the present century, while *Silas Marner* is a little later. With "Amos Barton," and *The Mill on the Floss* we are in the second decade of the century, before hand-looms had gone out or railroads had come in. She has a fondness for these days of rustic simplicity, quiet habits and homely dis-ingenuousness, and she more than once expresses a doubt if much has been gained by the introduction of machinery, suffrage and culture. She regrets that —

Human advancement has no moments when conservative reforming intellect takes a nap, while imagination does a little toryism by the sly, revelling in regret that dear old brown, crumbling, picturesque inefficiency is everywhere giving place to spick-and-span, new-painted, new-varnished efficiency, which will yield endless diagrams, plans, elevations and sections; but, alas! no picture. Mine, I fear, is not a well-regulated mind: it has an occasional tenderness for old abuses; it lingers with a certain fondness over the days of nasal clerks and top-booted parsons, and has a sigh for the departed shades of vulgar errors.[1]

In *Adam Bede*, when describing a leisurely walk home from church in the good old days, she bursts out again into enthusiastic praise of the time before there was so much advancement and culture.

Surely all other leisure is hurry compared with a sunny walk through the fields from "afternoon church" — as such walks used to be in those old leisurely times when the boat, gliding sleepily along the canal, was the newest locomotive wonder; when Sunday books had most of them old brown leather covers, and opened with a remarkable precision always in one place. Leisure is gone — gone where the spinning-wheels are gone, and the pack-horses and the slow wagons and the pedlers who brought bargains to the door on sunny afternoons. Ingenious philosophers tell you, perhaps, that the great work of the steam-engine is to create leisure for mankind. Do not believe them; it only creates a vacuum for eager thought to rush in. Even idleness is eager now — eager for amusement; prone to excursion trains, art museums, periodical literature and exciting novels; prone even to scientific theorizing and cursory peeps through microscopes. Old Leisure was quite a different personage; he only read one newspaper, innocent of leaders, and was free from that periodicity of sensations which we call post-time. He was a contemplative, rather stout gentleman, of excellent digestion — of quiet perceptions, undiseased by hypothesis, happy in his inability to know the causes of things, preferring the things themselves. He lived chiefly in the country, among pleasant seats and homesteads, and was fond of sauntering by the fruit-tree wall, and scenting the apricots when they were warmed by the

[1] Amos Barton, chapter I.

morning sunshine, or of sheltering himself under the orchard boughs at noon when the summer pears were falling. He knew nothing of week-day services, and thought none the worse of the Sunday sermon if it allowed him to sleep from the text to the blessing — liking the afternoon service best, because the prayers were the shortest, and not ashamed to say so; for he had an easy, jolly conscience, broad-backed like himself, and able to carry a great deal of beer or port wine — not being made squeamish by doubts and qualms and lofty aspirations. Life was not a task to him, but a sinecure; he fingered the guineas in his pocket, and ate his dinners and slept the sleep of the irresponsible; for had he not kept up his charter by going to church on the Sunday afternoon? Fine old Leisure! Do not be severe upon him and judge him by our modern standard; he never went to Exeter Hall, or heard a popular preacher, or read *Tracts for the Times* or *Sartor Resartus*.[1]

Her faithfulness to the life she describes is seen in her skilful use of dialect. The sense of local coloring is greatly heightened by the dialogues which speak the language of the people portrayed. When Luke describes his rabbits as *nesh* things, and Mrs. Jerome says little *gells* should be seen and not heard, and Tommy Trounsom mentions his readiness to pick up a *chanch* penny, we are brought closer to the homely life of these people. She has so well succeeded, in Mr. Carson's words, in portraying "what they call the dileck as is spoke hereabout," the reader is enabled to realize, as he could not so well do by any other method, the homeliness and rusticity of the life presented.

George Eliot has not attempted a great variety in the use of dialect, for she has avoided unfamiliar words, and has made use of no expressions which would puzzle her readers in the attempt to understand them. The words not to be found in the dictionary are those which may in almost every instance be heard in the speech of the uncultured wherever the English language is spoken. Among others are these words: chapellin', chanch, coxy, curchey, dawnin', fettle, franzy, gell, megrim, nattering, nesh, overrun, queechy, plash. In a letter to Professor Skeats, published in the *Transactions of the English*

[1] Adam Bede, chapter LII.

Dialect Society, she has explained her methods of using dialect.

It must be borne in mind that my inclination to be as close as I could to the rendering of dialect, both in words and spelling, was constantly checked by the artistic duty of being generally intelligible. But for that check I should have given a stronger color to the dialogue in *Adam Bede*, which is modelled on the talk of North Staffordshire and the neighboring part of Derbyshire. The spelling, being determined by my own ear alone, was necessarily a matter of anxiety, for it would be as possible to quarrel about it as about the spelling of Oriental names. The district imagined as the scene of *Silas Marner* is in North Warwickshire; but here, and in all my other presentations of English life except *Adam Bede*, it has been my intention to give the general physiognomy rather than a close portraiture of the provincial speech as I have heard it in the Midland or Mercian region. It is a just demand that art should keep clear of such specialties as would make it a puzzle for the larger part of its public; still, one is not bound to respect the lazy obtuseness or snobbish ignorance of people who do not care to know more of their native tongue than the vocabulary of the drawing-room and the newspaper.

It may be said of George Eliot's realism that she did not borrow nearly so much from actual observation as was done by Charlotte Brontë, in whose novels, scenes, persons and events are described with great accuracy and fulness. In large measure Charlotte Brontë borrowed her materials from the life about her. Large as was her invention, original as her mind was, and unique in its thought, yet she seems to have been unable to create the plots of her novels without aid from real events and persons. Persons and scenes and events were so vividly portrayed in *Jane Eyre* as to be at once recognized, subjecting the author to much annoyance and mortification. In *Shirley* there is even a larger use of local traditions and manners, the locality of the story being described with great accuracy. George Eliot did not use such materials to nearly so great an extent, being far less dependent on them. Nor had she anything of Scott's need of local traditions. Accurate as she is, she creates her own story, not depending, as he did, on the suggestive help of the stories of the past. Few of his novels are the entire creations of his own mind; but he used every hint and suggestion he could find as the basis of his work. In this, George Eliot is no more a realist than either of her great predecessors. Even Goldsmith and Fielding were no more creative and original than she, for they depended as much as she on the occurrences of real life for their plots. All genuine novelists have drawn their materials from the life about them, and they could not attain success otherwise. All depends, however, on how the material thus used is made to bear its results. If Charlotte Brontë borrowed more from actual life of event and scenery, yet she was not more a realist; rather her power lies in something higher than realism, in that subtle insight and creative power which gives originality to her work. She was an idealist keeping close to the actual; and in this fact is to be found her superiority to George Eliot in certain directions. George Eliot studied life accurately and intimately, but she did not tie herself to any individual occurrences or persons. She had so absorbed the spirit of the life amidst which she lived, as to give a true expression to it under an almost purely fictitious garb.

There is less of distinct teaching in the *Scenes of Clerical Life* than in George Eliot's later novels. Yet even in these earlier stories there is to be found many a clear indication of her thought. In "Amos Barton" she has especially set forth her sympathy with humble life. This fundamental canon of her art is presented more distinctly in this story, and dwelt upon more fully, than in any of her subsequent novels. It would be difficult to discover any special teaching in "Mr. Gilfil's Love Story;" and this is perhaps the only production of George Eliot's pen which has not some distinct object beyond the telling of the story itself. The religious *motif* is strong in *Janet's Repentance*, and not to be mistaken by any attentive reader who now for the first time takes up the story. The value of religion as a reforming force is plainly inculcated, as well as that the main and only value of that force is altruistic. It presents a fine picture of the Evangelical movement and its work, though mainly on its humanitarian side. Its deeper spirit of devotion, its loftier religious ideal, its craving after a more intimate realization of the divine presence, is not portrayed. The real purport of the story is contained in its closing words, where the reader is told that the true memorial left behind him by Edgar Tryan is to be found in a life saved to all noble things by his efforts.

It is Janet Dempster, rescued from self-despair, strengthened with divine hopes, and now looking back on years of purity and helpful labor. The man who has left such a memorial behind him must have been one whose heart beat with true compassion, and whose lips were moved by fervent faith.

These *Scenes of Clerical Life* surpass all George Eliot's later novels in one respect—their pathos. *Adam Bede* comes nearer them in this particular than any of the later works, but even that novel does not equal them in their power to lay hold of feeling and sympathy and in moving the reader to tears. They differ greatly in this respect from another short story, written only a few years later, entitled "Brother Jacob." This story has more of light banter in it than any other novel of George Eliot's, and less of tenderness and pathos. It is but another lesson on her great theme of *retribution*. The author says in the last sentence of the story that "we see in it an admirable instance of the unexpected forms in which the great Nemesis hides herself." The central thought of the story is, that even in the lives of the most ordinary persons, and in the case of even the smallest departures from the right, there is a power of retribution at work bringing us an unfailing punishment for the evil we do.

The literary excellences of the *Scenes from Clerical Life* are many. They are simple, charming stories, full of life, and delightful in tone. Their humor is rare and effective, never coarse, but racy and touching. Their tenderness of tone lays warm hold upon the reader's sympathies and brings him closer to the throbbing hearts of his fellow-men. There is a pure idyllic loveliness and homelikeness about these stories that is exquisite. They all evidently grew out of the tender memories and associations of George Eliot's girlhood.

In *Adam Bede* the author's purpose is concentrated on character and the moral unfoldment of the lives she describes, while the thorough dramatic unity is lacking which such a work demands. It is a delightful picture of country life, and for idyllic loveliness is scarcely equalled, never surpassed, in English literature. The charm of the narrative is only rivalled by the deep human interest the characters have for us. This exquisite picture of rural life is not merely a piece of fine painting; but the deepest problems, the largest human interests, ever appear as a perpetual background of spiritual reality, giving a sublimity to the whole that truly dignifies it. The thoughtful reader soon finds this inweaving of a larger purpose adding greatly to the idyllic loveliness of these scenes. The moral tone is clear and earnest, and the religious element gives a charm and nobility to this delightful picture of rustic simplicity.

Adam Bede has probably delighted a larger number of her readers than any other of George Eliot's books, and even a majority of her critics prefer it to any other. It at once arrests and fixes the attention of the reader. The first chapter has an immediate interest in its wonderful picture of Adam, and its most vivid description of the workshop. The second chapter, with its account of Dinah Morris and her preaching, leaves no possibility of doubt about the genius and power of the book. The reader is brought at once face to face with scenes and persons that act as enchantment on him; and this complete absorption of interest never flags to the end. The elements of this fascination, which is in itself so simple, natural and human, have been pointed out by various critics. They are to be found in the homeliness, pathos and naturalness of the whole story from beginning to end. Little as the critics have noted it, however, much of this fascination comes of the high and pure moral tone of the story, its grasp on the higher motives and interests of life, and its undertone of yearning after a religious motive and ideal adequate to all the problems of human destiny. This religious motive is indeed more than a yearning, for it is a fixed and self-contained confidence in altruism, expressed in sympathy and feeling and pathos most tender and passionate. This novel is full of an eager desire to realize to men their need of each other, and of longing to show them how much better and happier the world would be if we were more sympathetic and had more of fellow-feeling. Life is full of suffering, and this can be lessened only as we help and love each other, only as we can make our feelings so truly tender as to feel the sorrows of others as our own, causing us to live for the good of those who suffer. It is said of Adam Bede that —

> He had too little fellow-feeling with the weakness that errs in spite of foreseen consequences. Without this fellow-feeling, how are we to get enough patience and charity toward our stumbling, falling companions in the long and changeful journey? And there is but one way in which a strong determined soul can learn it — by getting his heart-strings bound round the weak and erring, so that he must share not only the outward consequence of their error but their inward suffering.

This compassion for human suffering is conspicuous throughout, and it is regarded as the most effective means of binding men together in common sympathy and helpfulness. Sorrow is regarded as the true means of man's elevation, as that purifying agent which is indispensable to his true development. This teaching is fully depicted in the chapter headed "The Hidden Dread," and in which Hetty's flight is described. We are told in that chapter that this looks like a very bright world on the surface, but that as we look closer within man's nature we find sorrow and pain untold.

What a glad world this looks like, as one drives or rides along the valleys and over the hills! I have often thought so when, in foreign countries, where the fields and woods have looked to me like our English Loamshire: the rich land tilled with just as much care, the woods rolling down the gentle slopes to the green meadows — I have come on something by the roadside which has reminded me that I am not in Loamshire — an image of a great agony — the agony of the Cross. It has stood, perhaps, by the clustering apple-blossoms, or in the broad sunshine by the corn-field, or at a turning by the wood where a clear brook was gurgling below; and surely, if there came a traveller to this world who knew nothing of the story of man's life upon it, this image of agony would seem to him strangely out of place in the midst of this joyous nature. He would not know that hidden behind the apple-blossoms, or among the golden corn, or under the shrouding boughs of the wood, there might be a human heart beating heavily with anguish — perhaps a young blooming girl, not knowing where to turn for refuge from swift-advancing shame; understanding no more of this life of ours than a foolish lost lamb, wandering farther and farther in the nightfall on the lonely heath, yet tasting the bitterest of life's bitterness. Such things are sometimes hidden among the sunny fields and behind the blossoming orchards; and the sound of the gurgling brook, if you came close to one spot behind a small bush, would be mingled for your ear with a despairing human sob. No wonder man's religion has much sorrow in it; no wonder he needs a Suffering God.

The remedy for this sorrow, even in the pages of *Adam Bede*, is not the atoning love of Christ or the blessedness of a divine forgiveness, but the altruistic compassion of man for man. There is, however, a deeper recognition in this novel of Christian belief than in any other by George Eliot. The prayer and sermon of Dinah Morris have a truly Christian tone and thought. This is not the case with the teachings of Savonarola, who is always much more an altruist than a Christian, and into whose mouth Christian phrases are put, while it is very evident the Christian spirit in its wholeness was not put into his heart. Sorrow and suffering are regarded in *Adam Bede* as the means of baptism into a larger life of sympathy, as the means of purification from selfishness and individual aims. Along with this teaching goes the cognate one, that feeling is the true test of the religious life. A feeling that draws us close to others in helpfulness is worth more than knowledge, culture and refinement of taste.

The doctrine of retribution is presented as distinctly and positively in *Adam Bede* as in any subsequent book George Eliot wrote. It is given the form of distinct statement, and it is developed fully in the working out of the plot. Parson Irwine speaks the thought of the author in these words:

> "There is no sort of wrong deed of which a man can bear the punishment alone; you can't isolate yourself, and say that the evil which is in you shall not spread. Men's lives are as thoroughly blended with each other as the air they breathe; evil spreads as necessarily as disease. I know, I feel the terrible extent of suffering this sin of Arthur's has caused to others; but so does every sin cause suffering to others besides those who commit it."

The tendency of selfishness and wrong to develop misery is fully unfolded. The terrible law of moral cause and effect is made apparent throughout the whole work. The folly of Arthur and the vanity of Hetty work them terrible consequences of evil and bitterness. Many others are made to suffer with them. The fatal Nemesis is unmasked in these revelations of human nature.

If the critics are right in pronouncing *Adam Bede* artistically defective, it is not difficult to see that there is still less of unity in *The Mill on the Floss*. Unconnected and unnecessary scenes and persons abound, while the Tulliver and Dodson families, and their stupidities, are described at a tedious length. Yet the picture of child-life given here compensates for all we might complain of in other directions. Maggie is an immortal child, wonderfully drawn, out of the very heart of nature herself. Her joy in life, her doubts and fears, her conflicts with self, are delineated with a master's hand, and justify — such is their faithfulness to child-life — the supposition that this is George Eliot's own childhood, so delicate and penetrating is the insight of this description. Swinburne has justly said that "no man or woman, outside the order of poets, has ever written of children with such adorable fidelity of affection as the spiritual mother of Totty, Eppie and of Lillo." Nor have the poets surpassed her in truthfulness to child-life and intuitive insight into child-nature. The child Maggie is unsurpassed, not as an ideal being, but as a living child that plays in the dirt, tears her frocks, and clips her hair in an hour of childish anger.

In this novel we first come distinctly upon another element in the writings of George Eliot, and this is a yearning after a fuller, larger life. It does not appear as distinctly developed in *Adam Bede*, where there is more of poise and repose. Maggie represents the restless spirit of the nineteenth century, intense dissatisfaction with self, and a profoundly human passion for something higher and diviner. A passionate restlessness and a profound spiritual hunger are united in this novel to an eager desire for a deeper and fuller life, and for a satisfactory answer to the soul's spiritual thirst. The spiritual repose of Dinah, who has found all the religious cravings of her nature satisfied in Methodism, is abandoned for the inward yearning of Maggie, whose passionate search for spiritual truth ends in disaster.

No other of George Eliot's books has been so severely criticised as this one, except *Daniel Deronda*, and mainly because of Maggie. The apparent fall of the heroine, and the crude tragedy of the ending, have been regarded as serious defects. The moral tone and purpose have been severely condemned. In his essays on foul and fair fiction, Ruskin puts *The Mill on the Floss* into that class of novels which describe life's blotches, burrs and pimples, and calls it "the most striking instance extant of this study of cutaneous disease." He says the personages are picked up from behind the counter and out of the gutter, and he finds "there is not a single person in the book of the smallest importance to anybody in the world but themselves, or whose qualities deserved so much as a line of printer's type in their description." To the same effect is Swinburne's criticism of Maggie's relations to Stephen Guest. He calls it "the hideous transformation by which Maggie is debased." He says that most of George Eliot's admirers would regard this as "the highest and the purest and the fullest example of her magnificent and matchless powers. The first two thirds of the book suffice to compose perhaps the very noblest of tragic as well as of humorous prose idyls in the language; comprising one of the sweetest as well as saddest and tenderest, as well as subtlest examples of dramatic analysis — a study in that kind as soft and true as Rousseau's, as keen and true as Browning's, as full as either's of the fine and bitter sweetness of a pungent and fiery fidelity. But who can forget the horror of inward collapse, the sickness of spiritual re-action, the reluctant, incredulous rage of disenchantment and disgust, with which he came upon the thrice-unhappy third part? The two first volumes have all the intensity and all the perfection of George Sand's best work, tempered by all the simple purity and interfused with all the stainless pathos of Mrs. Gaskell's; they carry such affluent weight of thought, and shine with such warm radiance of humor, as invigorates and illuminates the work of no other famous woman; they have the fiery clarity of crystal or of lightning; they go near to prove a higher claim and attest a clearer right on the part of their author than that of George Sand herself to the crowning crown of praise conferred on her by the hand of a woman ever greater and more glorious than either in her sovereign gift of lyric genius, to the salutation given as by an angel indeed from heaven, of 'large-brained woman and large-hearted man.'" In the momentary lapse of Maggie, Swinburne finds a fatal defect, which no subsequent repentance atones for. He says that "here is the patent flaw, here too plainly is the flagrant blemish, which defaces and degrades the very crown and flower of George Eliot's wonderful and most noble work; no rent or splash on the raiment, but a cancer in the very bosom, a gangrene in the very flesh. It is a radical and mortal plague-spot, corrosive and incurable."

Such criticism has little if any value, because there is no point of sympathy between the critic and his author. That real life contains such errors as Maggie's cannot be doubted, and George Eliot wished to paint no ideal scenes or heroines. To portray a passionate, eager, yearning nature, full of poetry, longing for a diviner spiritual life, surrounded by dull and unpoetic conditions and persons, was her purpose. That the hunger of such a person for the expression of her inward cravings for joy, music and beauty should lead her astray and make a sudden lapse possible, is not to be doubted. The fault of the critics is in supposing that this lapse from moral conduct was that of a physical depravity. Maggie's passion grew wholly out of that inward yearning for a fuller life which made all her difficulties. It was not physical passion but spiritual craving; and in the purpose of the novelist she was as pure after as before.

The cause of what must be regarded as the great defect in *The Mill on the Floss* is not that George Eliot chose to paint life in a diseased state, but that she had not the power to make her characters act what they themselves were. While the delightful inward portraiture of Maggie is in process all are charmed with her, her soul is as pure and sweet as a rose new-blown; but when the time arrives for her to act as well as to meditate and to dream, she is not made equal to herself. Through all her books this is true, that George Eliot can describe a soul, but she cannot make her men and women act quite up to the facts of daily life. In this way Dinah and Adam are not equal to themselves, and settle down to a prosaic life such as is not in keeping with that larger action of which they were capable. George Eliot's characters are greater than their deeds; their inward life is truer and more rounded than their outward life is pure and noble.

The Mill on the Floss fully develops George Eliot's conception of the value of self-renunciation in the life of the individual, and gives a new emphasis to her ideas about the importance of the spiritual life as an element in true culture. It has been said that she intended to indicate the nature of physiological attraction between men and women, and how large an influence it has; but whether that was an aim of hers or not, she undoubtedly did attempt to indicate how altogether important is renunciation to a life of true development, how difficult it is to attain, and that it is the vital result of all human endeavor. She surrounded a tender, sensitive, musical and poetic soul, one quick to catch the tone of a higher spiritual faith, with the common conditions of ordinary social life, to show how such an "environment" cripples and retards a soul full of aspiration and capable of the best things. Maggie saw the way to the light, but the way was hard, beset with difficulties individual and social, and she could neither overcome herself nor the world. She was taken suddenly away, and the novel comes to a hasty conclusion, because the author desired to indicate the causes of spiritual danger to ardent souls, and not to inculcate a formula for their relief. Maggie had learned how difficult it is for the individual to make for himself a new way in life, how benumbing are the conditions of ordinary human existence; and through her death we are to learn that in such difficulties as hers there is no remedy for the individual. Only through the mediation of death could Maggie be reconciled to those she had offended; death alone could heal the social wounds she had made, and restore her as an accepted and ennobled member of the corporate existence of humanity. This seems to be the idea underlying the hurried conclusion of this novel, that the path of renunciation once truly entered on, brings necessarily such difficulties as only death can overcome; and death does overcome them when those we have loved and those we have helped, forget what seem to them our wrong deeds in the loving memories which follow the dead. Over the grave men forget all that separated them from others, and the living are reconciled to those who can offend them no more. All that was good and pure and loving is then made to appear, and memory glorifies the one who in life was neglected or hated. Through death Maggie was restored to her brother, and over her grave came perfect reconciliation with those others from whom she had been alienated. That renunciation may lead to cruel martyrdoms is what George Eliot means; but she would say it has its lofty recompense in that restoration which death brings, when the individual becomes a part of the spiritual influence which surrounds and guides us all. For those who can accept such a conclusion as this the unity of the novel may seem complete.

The poetry of Maggie's nature found itself constantly dragged down to conditions of vulgar prose by the life about her. That life was prosy and hard because those ideal aims which come from a recognition of the past and its traditions were absent from it. Maggie tried to overcome them by renunciation, but by renunciation which did not rest on any genuine sorrow and pain. At last these came, and the real meaning of renunciation was made clear to her. Her bitter sorrow taught her the great lesson which George Eliot ever strives to inculcate, that what is hard, sorrowful and painful in the world should move us to more and more of compassion and help for our fellows who also find life sad and burdensome. At the last Maggie learned this greatest of all lessons which life can give us.

She sat quite still far on into the night, with no impulse to change her attitude, without active force enough even for the mental act of prayer—only waiting for the light that would surely come again. It came with the memories that no passion could long quench: the long past came back to her, and with it the fountains of self-renouncing pity and affection, of faithfulness and resolve. The words that were marked by the quiet hand in the little old book that she had long ago learned by heart, rushed even to her lips, and found a vent for themselves in a low murmur that was quite lost in the loud driving of the rain against the window, and the loud moan and roar of the wind: "I have received the Cross, I have received it from Thy hand; I will bear it, and bear it till death, as Thou hast laid it upon me."

But soon other words rose that could find no utterance but in a sob: "Forgive me, Stephen. It will pass away. You will come back to her."

She took up the letter, held it to the candle, and let it burn slowly on the hearth. To-morrow she would write to him the last word of parting.

"I will bear it, and bear it till death. . . . But how long it will be before death comes! I am so young, so healthy. How shall I have patience and strength? Am I to struggle and fall, and repent again? Has life other trials as hard for me still?" With that cry of self-despair Maggie fell on her knees against the table, and buried her sorrow-stricken face. Her soul went out to the Unseen Pity that would be with her to the end. Surely there was something being taught her by this experience of great need, and she must be learning a secret of human tenderness and long-suffering that the less erring could hardly know. "O God, if my life is to be long, let me live to bless and comfort —"

Then the flood came, and death. Maggie could repent, she could acquire the true spirit of renunciation, she could even give herself to a life of altruism; but death only could restore her to the world. Death, says George Eliot, is the great reconciler.

Silas Marner is the only one of these earlier novels in which there is a continuous unity of purpose and action. Its several parts are thoroughly wrought into each other, the aim of the narrative is adhered to throughout, and there are no superfluous incidents. The plot is simple, cause and effect flow on steadily to the end in the unfoldment of character and action, and the design of the author is easily grasped. One of her critics, himself a novelist of a high order, has said that in its unity of purpose and dramatic expression *Silas Marner* is more nearly a masterpiece than any other of George Eliot's novels; "it has more of that simple, rounded, consummate aspect, that absence of loose ends and gaping issues, which marks a classical work."[1] In this novel, too, her humor flows out with a richer fulness, a racier delight and a more sparkling variety of

[1] Henry James, Jr.

expression than in any other book of hers, not excepting *Adam Bede*. She has here reached the very height of her qualities as a humorist, for in *Silas Marner* her humor is constantly genial and delightful.

Certain ethical ideas appear very distinctly in this novel. It illustrates man's need of social ties and connections. Silas forsook his old life, the life of his childhood and youth, and the world was a blank for him in consequence. With the sundering of the ties which bound him to the traditional environment amidst which he was reared, all the purpose and meaning of his life was gone. The old ties, obligations and associations gone, his life was without anchorage, its ideal aims perished, and he lived a selfish and worthless creature. When new social ties were formed by the young child he found then his life opened up to a larger meaning again, and he recovered the better things in his nature. He was then led back again into his relations to society, he became once more a man, a fresh life was opened to him. This brought a new confidence in religion, a new trust in the moral motives of life. In this way George Eliot presents the social basis of the higher life in man, and her theory that it cannot be broken off from its traditional surroundings without grave injury to the finer elements of our nature. The law of retribution manifests itself clearly in these pages. Godfrey deserts wife and child. In after years he would fain restore the child to its rightful place, but he finds it has grown up under conditions which alienate it from any sympathy with him. He pronounces his own condemnation:

> "There's debts we can't pay like money debts, by paying extra for the years that have slipped by. While I've been putting off and putting off, the trees have been growing — it's too late now. Marner was in the right in what he said about a man's turning away a blessing from his door: it falls to somebody else. I wanted to pass for childless once, Nancy — I shall pass for childless now against my wish."

A pure moral tone, a keen ethical instinct, mark all these earlier novels by George Eliot. Quite as noticeable is their spiritual atmosphere and their high place assigned to the religious life. Their teaching in these directions has a conservative tendency, and it is based on the most vigorous convictions.

XIV.

ROMOLA.

WHATEVER differences there may exist between George Eliot's earlier and later books are due rather to the materials used than to any change in purpose, methods or beliefs. In writing of the distinction drawn between her earlier and later books, she said, —

> Though I trust there is some growth in my appreciation of others and in my self-distrust, there has been no change in the point of view from which I regard our life since I wrote my first fiction, the *Scenes of Clerical Life*. Any apparent change of spirit must be due to something of which I am unconscious. The principles which are at the root of my effort to paint Dinah Morris are equally at the root of my effort to paint Mordecai.

Her later books grow more out of conscious effort and deliberate study than the earlier, are more carefully wrought out, and contain less of spontaneity. The spiritual and ethical purpose, however, is not more distinct and conscious in *Daniel Deronda* than in *The Mill on the Floss*, in *Romola* than in *Adam Bede*. The ethical purpose may be more apparent in *Daniel Deronda* than in *Adam Bede*, more on the surface, and clearer to the view of the general reader, but this is because it takes an unusual form, rather than because it is really any more distinctly present. In *The Mill on the Floss* her teaching first became known to her readers, and in *Romola* this purpose to use the novel as the vehicle for propagating ideas became fully apparent. Her aim having once come clearly to view, it was not difficult to see how large an element it was in her earlier books, where it had not been seen before.

If she had written nothing but *Adam Bede* her teachings might not have come to light, though some of those she has most often insisted on are to be found clearly stated in that book. Her doctrinal aim, however, became more clear and pronounced as she went on in her career as a novelist, and became more thoroughly conscious of her own powers and of the purposes which she wished to work out in her novels. She gained courage to express her ideas, and their importance was more deeply impressed upon her mind and heart.

In *Romola* it was first made clear that George Eliot is to be judged as a moralist as well as a literary artist. That she is a great literary artist, surpassed only by a select few, is to be borne constantly in mind; but as a moralist she surpasses most others in the amount of her teaching, and teaching which is thoroughly incorporated into the literary fibre of her work. She much resembles Wordsworth in this, that while she is an original creator of artistic forms and ideas, her books will be sought for their views of life as well for their qualities as novels. Wordsworth is a poet of vast original powers, but the poetic fire in him often burns low and his verses become mere prose. Yet his ideas about nature, life and morals command for him a place higher than that occupied by any other poet of his time, and a school of thinkers and critics has been developed through his influence. In much the same way, George Eliot is likely to attract attention because of her teachings; and it is probable her books will be resorted to and interpreted largely with reference to her moral and philosophical ideas. Should such a movement as this ever spring up, *Romola* will necessarily become one of the most important of all her books. Some of her principal ideas appear therein more distinctly, in clearer outline, and with a greater fulness of expression, than they obtain in any other of her books. The foreign setting of her story enabled her to give a larger utterance to her thoughts, while there was less of personal and pathetic interest to impede their expression. This is also true of *The Spanish Gypsy*, that it has more of teaching and less of merely literary attraction than any other of her longer poems. The purpose to do justice to the homely life of rustic England was no longer present, and she was free to give her intellectual powers a deliberate expression in the form of a thoughtful interpretation of a great historic period. Mr. Henry James, Jr., has recognized the importance of this effort, and says of *Romola*, that he regards it, "on the whole, as decidedly the most important of her works, — not the most entertaining nor the most readable, but the one in which the largest things are attempted and grasped. The figure of Savonarola, subordinate though it is, is a figure on a larger scale than any which George Eliot has elsewhere undertaken; and in the career of Tito Melema there is a fuller representation of the development of a character. Considerable as are our author's qualities as an artist, and largely as they are displayed in *Romola*, the book is less a work of art than a work of morals. Like all of George Eliot's works, its dramatic construction is feeble; the story drags and halts, — the setting is too large for the picture."

The book lacks in spontaneity, is too deliberate, contemplative and ethical. While its artistic elements are great, and even powerful, it is too consciously moral in its purpose to satisfy the literary requirements of a work of art. It wants the sensuous elements of life and the *abandon* of poetic genius. There is little which is sensational about the book; too little, perhaps, of that vivid imaginative interest which impels the reader headlong through the pages of a novel to the end. It is, however, a high merit in George Eliot, that she does not resort to factitious elements of interest in her books, but works honestly, conscientiously, and with a pure purpose. If the reader is not drawn on by the sensational, he is amply repaid by the more deliberate and natural interest which gives a meaning to every chapter.

George Eliot selected for her book one of the most striking and picturesque periods of modern history, in the great centre of culture and art in the fifteenth century. Florence was the intellectual capital of the world in the renaissance period, and the truest representative of its spirit. It was the time also of that remarkable monk-prophet, Savonarola, whose voice was raised so powerfully against the corruptions of that most corrupt age. This unique character, doubtless, had much to do in causing George Eliot to take this city and time for her story. No one of the reformers of the fifteenth and sixteenth centuries was more in earnest, had a loftier purpose, worked in a nobler spirit, than this Dominican monk of Florence. His opposition to the Medici, his conflict with Rome, his visions and prophecies, his leadership of the politics of Florence, his powerful preaching, his untimely death, all give a romantic and a tragic interest to his life, and conspire to make him one of the most interesting figures in modern history. His moral purpose was conspicuous even when tainted by personal ambition. His political influence was supreme while it lasted, and was wielded in the interests of Florence, for its liberties and its moral regeneration. As a religious teacher he was profoundly in earnest; a prophet in his own belief as well as in the depth of his religious insight, he accepted with the most thorough intensity of conviction the spiritual truths he inculcated. In his own belief he was constantly in communion with the spiritual world, and was guided and taught by it. He swayed the people of Florence as the wind sways the branches of a tree, and they bowed utterly to his will for the moment, when he put forth all his moral and intellectual powers in the pulpit. A puritan in morals, he had a most vivid realization of the terrible evils of his time; and he could make his congregation look at the world with his own faith and moral purpose. His influence on literature and art was also great, and it was felt for many years after his death.

Savonarola spoke in the pulpit with the authority of the profoundest personal conviction, and his hearers were impressed by his preaching with the feeling that they listened to one who knew whereof he spoke. Whenever he preached there was a crowd to hear; people came three or four hours before the time, and they came in throngs from the surrounding country. He held separate services for men, for women, for children, in order that all might hear. And this eagerness to listen to him was not for a few weeks, but it continued for years. The greatest enthusiasm was awakened by his influence, the people were melted into tears, every person listened with bated breath to his words. Thousands were converted, and among them many of the most learned of the poets, artists and statesmen of the time. The most remarkable changes in the modes of life took place, money was restored, and contributed freely to buy bread when famine threatened, and the confessional was daily crowded with penitents. One of his biographers says that "the most remarkable change that was apparent in the manners of the people, in their recreations and amusements, was the abandonment of demoralizing practices, of debauchery of all kinds, of profane songs of a licentious character which the lower grades of the people especially were greatly addicted to; and the growth of a new taste and passion for spiritual hymns and sacred poetry that had succeeded that depraved taste."

On one side of his nature, Savonarola seems to have been of a remarkably pure and noble character, with high aims, noble ambitions and a clear moral insight. Looked at on its better side, his religious reformation was wholesome and salutary, and dictated by a genuine desire to elevate worship and to purify faith. There was a very different side to his life and work, however, and in some features of his character he seems to have been a fanatic and enthusiast of the most dangerous sort. He was credulous, superstitious and visionary. He had no clear, strong and well-reasoned purpose to which he could hold consistently to the end. An earnest Catholic, he only sought to reform the Church, not to supersede it; but his moral aims were not high enough to carry him to the logical results of his position. Involved by his visionary faith in claims of miraculous power and supernatural communication, he had not the intellectual honesty to carry those claims to their legitimate conclusion. Weakness, hesitation and inconsistency marked his character in his later years, and have made him a puzzle to modern students. These inconsistencies of character have led to widely divergent conclusions about the man, his sincerity of purpose and the outcome of his work.

Another influence of the time, more powerful because more permanent, was the renaissance movement, which was at this period working its greatest changes and inspiring the most fervid enthusiasm. A new world had been disclosed to the people of the fifteenth century in the revival of knowledge concerning classic literature and art, and there came to be an absorbing, passionate interest in whatever pertained to the ancients. Manuscripts were eagerly sought after, translations were diligently made, literature was modelled after the classic writers, to quote and to imitate the ancients became the habit of the day. A change the most striking was produced in the modes of thought and of life. The love of nature was revived, and with it a graceful abandonment to the dominion of the senses. Paganism seemed likely to return upon the world again and to reconquer from Christianity all that it had once lost. The pagan spirit revived, its tastes and modes of life came back again. Plato was restored to his old place, and in the minds of the cultured seemed worthier of homage than Christ. With such as Lorenzo Medici and his literary friends, Platonism was regarded as a religion.

The recovery of classic literature came to the men of this period as a revelation. It opened a new world to them, it operated upon them like a galvanic shock, it kindled the most fervid enthusiasms. It also had the effect to restore the natural side of life, to liberate men from a false spiritualism and an excessive idealism. From despising the human faculties, men came back to an acceptance of their dictation, and even to an animal delight in the senses and passions. The natural man was deified; but not in the manner of the Greeks, in simplicity and with a pure love of beauty. An artificial love of nature and the natural in man was the result of the renaissance; a hothouse culture and a corrupting moral development followed. Passion was given loose rein, the senses took every form of indulgence. Yet the Church was even worse, while many of the classic scholars were stoic in their moral purity and earnestness. This movement developed individualism in thought, a selfish moral aim, and intellectual arrogance. The men who came under its influence cared more for culture than for humanity, they were driven away from the common interests of their fellows by their new intellectual sympathies. It was the desire of Savonarola to restore the old Christian spirit of brotherhood and helpfulness. In this his movement was wide apart from that of the renaissance, which gave such tyrants as the Medici a justification for their deliberate attacks on the liberties of the people. He loved man, they loved personal development.

George Eliot shows these two influences in antagonism with each other; on the one hand a reforming Christianity, on the other the renaissance movement. She admirably contrasts them in their spirit and influence, though she by no means indicates all of the tendencies of either. Her purpose is not that of the historical novelist, who wishes simply to give a correct and living picture of the time wherein he lays his plot. She uses this portion of history because it furnishes an excellent opportunity to unfold her ideas about life, rather than because it gives an abundance of picturesque material to the novelist. Her primary object is not the interpretation of Florentine life in the time of Savonarola; and this subordination of the historical material must be kept fully in mind by the reader or he will be misled in his judgment on the book. It has well been said that the historical characters in *Romola* are not so well sketched as the original creations. Savonarola is not so lifelike as Tito. She seems to have been cramped by the details of history; and she has not thoroughly conquered and marshalled subordinate to her thought the mass of local incidents she introduces. Her account of Savonarola is inadequate, because it does not enter fully enough into his history, and because it omits much which is necessary to a full understanding of the man and his influence.

So far as the book has an historical purpose it is that of describing the general life of the time rather than that of portraying Savonarola. Because of this purpose much is introduced into the story which is irrelevant to the plot itself. Not only did the author desire to contrast a man like Savonarola, led by the spirit of self-denial and renunciation, with one like Tito Melema led by the spirit of self-love and personal gratification; but she wished to contrast worldliness and spirituality, or individualism and altruism, as social forces. Lorenzo and the renaissance give one form of life, Savonarola and Christianity give another; and these two appear as affecting every class in society and every phase of the social order. To bring out this contrast requires a broad stage and many scenes. Much which seems quite irrelevant to the plot has its place in this larger purpose, and serves to bring out the final unity of impression which the author sought to produce. Nor is the purpose of the book merely that of contrasting two great phases of thought and of social influence, but rather to show them as permanent elements in human nature and the nature of the effect which each produces.

Romola demands for its thorough appreciation that the reader shall have a considerable acquaintance with Italian history in the fifteenth century and with the social and literary changes of that period. Whether it is read with a keen interest and relish will much depend on this previous information. To the mere novel-reader it may seem dull and too much encumbered by uninteresting learning. To one who is somewhat familiar with the renaissance period, and who can appreciate the ethical intention of the book, it will be found to be a work of genius and profound insight. It will help such a reader to a clearer comprehension of this period than he could well obtain in any other manner, and the ethical purpose will add a new and living interest to the story of Florentine life. He will be greatly helped to comprehend the moral and intellectual life of the time, with its —

> strange web of belief and unbelief; of Epicurean levity and fetichistic dread; of pedantic impossible ethics uttered by rote, and crude passions acted out with childish impulsiveness; of inclination toward a self-indulgent paganism, and inevitable subjection to that human conscience which, in the unrest of a new growth, was filling the air with strange prophecies and presentiments.[1]

The artistic features of this period were many and striking, but George Eliot has not made so large a use of them as could have been wished ; at least they appear in her book too much under the influence of historic information. She could not be content merely to absorb and reflect an historic period ; but her active intellect, full of ideas concerning the causes of human changes, must give an explanation of what was before her. This philosophic tendency mars the artistic effect and blurs the picture which would otherwise have been given. Yet the critic must not be too sure of this, and he must be content simply to note that George Eliot was too energetic a thinker to be willing to portray the picturesque features of Florentine life in the fifteenth century

[1] Proem to Romola.

and to do no more. She had at least three objects, — to give a picture of Florentine life in the fifteenth century, to show the influence of the renaissance in conflict with Christianity, and to inculcate certain ethical ideas about renunciation, tradition and moral retribution. While the book thus gains in breadth and in a certain massive impression which it produces, yet it loses in that concentration of effect which a more limited purpose would have secured. It gives the impression of having been written by a vigorous thinker rather than by a genius of the first order. The critic has no right to complain of this, however, or even to assume that genius might do other work than it has done. Had George Eliot been less thoughtful than she was, she would not have been George Eliot. *Romola* grew out of a genius so large and original that it can well endure the criticisms caused by any defects it may have.

The ideas of the time appear subtly expressed in the influence they produce on the persons who entertain them. Savonarola's mysticism and high moral purpose made him at once a prophet and a reformer, but he was not able to separate the spiritual realities of life from devotion to his party. His courage, purity and holiness cannot but be admired, while his fanaticism is to be deplored. George Eliot has well conceived and expressed the effect produced in all but the very greatest minds by the assumption of supernatural powers. Savonarola was strong and great as a preacher and a reformer, weak only on the side of his visions and his faith that his party represented the kingdom of God. Not that his visions were weak, nor are they assumed to be untrue; but his mysticism clouded his intellect, and his fanaticism led him to overlook the practical truths to be inculcated by a genuine reformer. He is a true type of the mystical churchman of the time, who saw the corruption about him and desired a better order of things, but who hoped to secure it by reviving the past in all its imagined supernatural features. He would have ruled the world by visions to be received by monks, and he would have made Jesus Christ the head of the republic. Yet his visions entangled his clear intellect and perverted his moral purpose.

On the other hand, Tito Melema was intended to represent the renaissance movement on its Greek, or its æsthetic and social side. He was not a bad man at heart, but he had no moral purpose, no ethical convictions. He had the Greek love of ease, enjoyment and unconcern for the morrow; a spirit which the renaissance revived in many of its literary devotees. He lived for the day, for self, in the delight of music, art, social intercourse and sensual enjoyment. He had the renaissance quickness of assuming all parts, its love of wide and pretentious learning, its superficial scholarship, its social and political deftness and flexibility. The dry, minute, unprofitable spirit of criticism is well indicated by Bardo Bardi, which had no originality and no fresh vitality, but which loved to comment on the classic writers at tedious length, and to collate passages for purposes the most foreign from any practical aim life could possibly afford. In the conception of Tito, George Eliot has quite surpassed herself, and in all literature there is no delineation of a character surpassing this. One of her critics says there is no character in her novels "more subtly devised or more consistently developed. His serpentine beauty, his winning graciousness, his æsthetic refinement, his masculine energy of intellect, his insinuating affectionateness, with his selfish love of pleasure and his cowardly recoil from pain, his subdulous serenity and treacherous calm, as of a faithless summer sea, make up a being that at once fascinates and repels, that invites love, but turns our love into loathing almost before we have given it."[1] Mr. R. H. Hutton has expressed his conviction that this is one of the most skilfully painted of all the characters in fictitious literature.

[1] Westminster Review, July, 1881.

He says, "A character essentially treacherous only because it is full of soft placid selfishness is one of the most difficult to paint;" but in sketching Tito's career, "the same wonderful power is maintained throughout, of stamping on our imagination with the full force of a master hand a character which seems naturally too fluent for the artist's purpose. There is not a more masterly piece of painting in English romance than this figure of Tito."

Romola represents the divided interests of one who was affected by both the renaissance and Christianity. Brought up to know only what the renaissance had to teach, to delight in culture and to ignore religion, her contact with Savonarola opened a new world to her mind. Her experience in life led her to seek some deeper moral anchorage than was afforded by the culture of her father and husband, yet she could not follow Savonarola into the region of mystical visions and otherworldliness. Her life having broken loose from the ties of love through the faithlessness of Tito, and from the ties of tradition through the failure of culture to satisfy her heart, she drifts out into the world, to find, under the leadership of the great preacher, that life's highest duty is renunciation. His influence over the noblest souls of his time is indicated in Romola's trust in him, and in her acceptance of him as a master and a guide. When this guide failed, as all human guides must fail, she found peace in the service of others. In living for humanity, her sorrows were turned into strength, and her renunciation became a religion. It is Romola who represents George Eliot in this book, gives voice to her ideas, and who preaches the new gospel she would have the world learn. If Romola has her limitations as a conception of womanly character, is too "passionless and didactic," yet she does admirably represent the influence on a thoughtful woman of a contention between culture and religion, and how such a person may gradually attain to a self-poised life in loving service toward others. She is not an ideal woman. She was given a character which prevents her being quite attractive, because she was made to represent ideas and social tendencies.

The altruistic doctrine of renunciation, and of living for others, is more fully developed in *Romola* than in any other of George Eliot's books except *The Mill on the Floss*. That the truest satisfaction life can afford us is to be found in work done for human good is conspicuously shown in the experiences of Romola. She finds no peace as a follower of Savonarola, she finds no abiding content in philosophy; but toil for others among the sick, suffering and dying, brings heavenly joy and a great calm. She had no special love for this work, her early education had even made it repulsive; but Savonarola had shown her that in this direction lay life's true aim. He communicated to her his own enthusiasm for humanity, and she retained this faith even after her loss of confidence in him had loosened her hold on his religious teachings. She went beyond her teacher and inspirer, learned his lessons better than he did himself, and came to see that a true religion is not of a sect or party, but humanitarian. When she warned him against his fanatical devotion to his party, he attempted to justify his narrow policy by identifying true Christianity with his own work. Romola replied, —

> "Do you then know so well what will further the coming of God's kingdom, father, that you will dare to despise the plea of mercy — of justice — of faithfulness to your own teaching? Take care, father, lest your enemies have some reason when they say that, in your visions of what will further God's kingdom, you see only what will strengthen your own party."
>
> "And that is true!" said Savonarola, with flashing eyes. Romola's voice had seemed to him in that moment the voice of his enemies. "The cause of my party *is* the cause of God's kingdom."
>
> "I do not believe it!" said Romola, her whole frame shaken with passionate repugnance. "God's kingdom is something wider — else let me stand outside it with the beings that I love."
>
> The two faces were lit up, each with an opposite emotion, each with an opposite certitude. Further words were impossible. Romola hastily covered her head and went out in silence.[1]

[1] Chapter LIX.

Savonarola forgot the better spirit of his own teachings, he sought to become a political leader. It was his ruin, for his purpose was vitiated, and his influence waned. George Eliot well says that "no man ever struggled to retain power over a mixed multitude without suffering vitiation; his standard must be their lower needs, and not his own best insight." This was the sad fate of the great Florentine preacher and reformer. He lost his faith, and he spoke without the moment's conviction. When this result came about, all hope for Savonarola as a reformer was gone. He was then only the leader of a party. George Eliot has well painted the effect upon Romola of this fall, and given deep insight into the results of losing our trust in those great souls who have been our guides. All the ties of life had snapped for Romola; her marriage had proved a failure, her friend had become unworthy of her confidence; and she fled.

Romola went away, found herself in the midst of a plague-stricken people, gave her life to an assuagement of suffering and sorrow. Then she could come back to her home purified, calm and noble. In the "Epilogue," we find her speaking the word which gives meaning to the whole book. Tessa's child, whom she had rescued, says to her that he would like to lead a life which would give him a good deal of pleasure. Romola says to him, —

"That is not easy, my Lillo. It is only a poor sort of happiness that could ever come by caring very much about our own narrow pleasures. We can only have the highest happiness, such as goes along with being a great man, by having wide thoughts, and much feeling for the rest of the world as well as ourselves; and this sort of happiness often brings so much pain with it that we can only tell it from pain by its being what we would choose before everything else, because our souls see it is good. There are so many things wrong and difficult in the world that no man can be great — he can hardly keep himself from wickedness — unless he gives up thinking much about pleasures or rewards, and gets strength to endure what is hard and painful. My father had the greatness that belongs to integrity; he chose poverty and obscurity rather than falsehood. And there was Fra Girolamo — you know why I keep to-morrow sacred; *he* had the greatness which belongs to a life spent in struggling against powerful wrong, and in trying to raise men to the highest deeds they are capable of. And so, my Lillo, if you mean to act nobly and seek to know the best things God has put within reach of men, you must learn to fix your mind on that end, and not on what will happen to you because of it. And remember, if you were to choose something lower, and make it the rule of your life to seek your own pleasure and escape from what is disagreeable, calamity might come just the same; and it would be calamity falling on a base mind, which is the one form of sorrow that has no balm in it, and that may well make a man say, 'It would have been better for me if I had never been born.' I will tell you something, Lillo."

Romola paused a moment. She had taken Lillo's cheeks between her hands, and his young eyes were meeting hers.

"There was a man to whom I was very near, so that I could see a great deal of his life, who made almost every one fond of him, for he was young, and clever, and beautiful, and his manners to all were gentle and kind. I believe when I first knew him, he never thought of anything cruel or base. But because he tried to slip away from everything that was unpleasant, and cared for nothing else so much as his own safety, he came at last to commit some of the basest deeds—such as make men infamous. He denied his father, and left him to misery; he betrayed every trust that was reposed in him, that he might keep himself safe and get rich and prosperous. Yet calamity overtook him."

Aside from this altruistic teaching which is developed in connection with the life of Romola, the doctrine of retribution is vigorously unfolded in the history of Tito Melema. The effects of selfishness and personal self-seeking have nowhere been so wonderfully studied by George Eliot as in this character. His career is minutely traced from step to step of his downfall, and with a remarkable faithfulness and courage. The effects of vice and sin are nowhere so finely presented and with such profound ethical insight. A careful study of this character alone will give a clear comprehension of George Eliot's conception of retribution, how the natural laws of life drag us down when we are untrue to ourselves and others. It is a great moral lesson presented in this character, a sermon of the most powerful kind. Nemesis follows Tito ever onward from the first false step, lowers the tone of his mind, corrupts his moral nature, drags him into an ever-widening circle of vice and crime, makes him a traitor, and causes him to be false to his wife. Step by step, as he gives way to evil, we see the degradation of his heart and mind, how the unfailing Nemesis is wreaking its vengeance upon him. He is surely punished, and his death is the fit end of his career. We are shown how his evil deeds affect others, how the great law of retribution involves the innocent in his downfall. Here George Eliot has unfolded for us how true it is that our lives are linked on every side with the lives of our fellows, and how the deeds of any one must affect for good or evil the lives of many others.

Almost every leading thought of George Eliot's philosophy and ethics is unfolded in greater or less degree in this novel. It is full of brave, wholesome teaching, and of clear insight into the consequences of conduct.

Romola is the most thoughtful, the most ambitious, the most philosophical of George Eliot's works; and it is also the most lacking in spontaneity, and more than any other shows the evidences of the artist's labors. Yet by many persons it will be accepted as the greatest of her works, and not without the best of reasons. It contains some of her most original characters, gives a remarkable emphasis to great moral laws, and interprets the spiritual influence of the conflict which is ever waging between tradition and advancing culture as no other has done. It is a thought-provoking book, a book of the highest moral aims.

XV.

FELIX HOLT AND MIDDLEMARCH.

THE scenes of George Eliot's later novels are laid in England, but for the most part among a town rather than a rural population. Instead of Hayslope and Raveloe, Mrs. Poyser and Silas Marner, we have Middlemarch and Treby Magna, Dorothea Brooke and Felix Holt. If Felix Holt is quite as much a workingman as Adam Bede, occupying a social position higher in no respect whatever, yet he is a workingman of a far different type. If Adam is the nobler character, the truer type of man, Felix represents a larger social purpose and has higher moral aims. In *Adam Bede* we find rustic simplicity and contentment, but in *Felix Holt* we touch social aspirations and political ambitions. The horizon has widened, the plane of social life has lifted, there are new motives and larger ideals.

Very many of her readers and critics regard *Middlemarch* as George Eliot's greatest novel. This is said to have been her own opinion. With great unanimity her readers pronounce *Felix Holt* her weakest and least interesting work. So far as the dramatic and artistic execution are concerned, these judgments are not entirely correct. The machinery of *Middlemarch* is clumsy, and the plot desultory in aim and method. On the other hand, *Felix Holt* is strongly thought out and skilfully planned. It has much of passion and enthusiasm in it, and not a little of pure and noble sentiment, while *Middlemarch* is never impassioned, but flows on calmly. The author evidently put herself into *Felix Holt* with the purpose of teaching her own views about moral and social life. She lived in the characters, felt and hoped with them, and wrote out of a deep, spontaneous purpose. The sensational element has been more fully used, and the unity of the plot more thoroughly developed, than in any other of her works, while there is a living, breathing purpose in the story which is absent from her later works. *Felix Holt* is one of the two or three novels by George Eliot which have an affirmative and thoroughly constructive purpose. It is this purpose which makes the chief interest of the work. It is a story of social reform, and is to be read as an embodiment of the author's political ideas. From this point of view it is a story full of interest, and it is the one of George Eliot's novels which will most strongly impress those who are fully in sympathy with her ideas of progress and social regeneration. The purpose of *Middlemarch* is critical, to show how our modern social life cramps the individual, limits his energies, and destroys his power of helpful service to the world. This critical aim runs through the whole work and colors every feature of it. The impression made by the whole work is saddening; and the reader, while admiring the artistic power and the literary finish of the book, is depressed by the moral issue. In strength of imagination, intellectual insight, keen power of analysis, this novel surpasses anything else George Eliot has written.

Felix Holt is a novel with an ethical purpose. It aims to show how social and political reform can be brought about. Felix is George Eliot's ideal workingman, a man who remains true to his own class, seeks his own moral elevation, does not have much faith in the ballot, and who is zealous for the education of his fellows. He is a radical who believes in heredity, who is aware of our debt to the past, and who would use the laws of social inheritance for the elevation of mankind. The account Felix gives of his conversion contains George Eliot's conception of what is to be done by all workingmen who rightly understand what social reform is and how it can be most truly brought about. It is to be secured by each workingman living not for self and pleasure, but to do what good he can in the world.

> "I'm not speaking lightly," said Felix. "If I had not seen that I was making a hog of myself very fast, and that pig-wash, even if I could have got plenty of it, was a poor sort of thing, I should never have looked life fairly in the face to see what was to be done with it. I laughed out loud at last to think of a poor devil like me, in a Scotch garret, with my stockings out at heel and a shilling or two to be dissipated upon, with a smell of raw haggis mounting from below, and old women breathing gin as they passed me on the stairs — wanting to turn my life into easy pleasure. Then I began to see what else it could be turned into. Not much, perhaps. This world is not a very fine place for a good many of the people in it. But I've made up my mind it shan't be the worse for me, if I can help it. They may tell me I can't alter the world — that there must be a certain number of sneaks and robbers in it, and if I don't lie and filch, somebody else will. Well, then, somebody else shall, for I won't. That's the upshot of my conversion, Mr. Lyon, if you want to know it."

When Felix gives Esther an account of his plans, and describes to her his purpose to do what he can to elevate his class, we have George Eliot's own views on the subject of social reform. Felix says, —

> "I want to be a demagogue of a new sort: an honest one, if possible, who will tell the people they are blind and foolish, and neither flatter them nor batten on them. I have my heritage — an order I belong to. I have the blood of a line of handicraftsmen in my veins, and I want to stand up for the lot of the handicraftsmen as a good lot, in which a man may be better trained to all the best functions of his nature, than if he belonged to the grimacing set who have visiting-cards, and are proud to be thought richer than their neighbors."

That the leading aim of *Felix Holt* is to show the nature of true social reform may be seen in the address made by Felix at the election, and even more distinctly in the address put into his mouth in *Blackwood's Magazine* for 1868. In the election speech Felix gives it as his belief that if workingmen "go the right way to work they may get power sooner without votes" than with them, by the use of public opinion, "the greatest power under heaven." The novel points out the social complications of life, the influence of hereditary privileges and abuses, and how every attempt at reform is complicated by many interests, and is likely to fall into the hands of demagogues who use the workingmen for their own purposes. The address of Felix in *Blackwood's* is really a commentary on the novel, or rather a fine and suggestive summary of the moral, social and political ideas it was meant to inculcate.

In *Felix Holt*, George Eliot would teach the world that true social reform is not to be secured by act of Parliament, or by the possession of the ballot on the part of all workingmen. It is but another enforcement of the theory that it is not rights men are to seek after, but duties; that social and political reform is not to be secured by insistence on rights, but by the true and and manly acceptance of altruism. Felix Holt is a social reformer who is not a demagogue, who does not seek office or personal advancement, but who wishes to show by his own conduct how a larger life is to be won. He would introduce universal education; he would teach the great principles of right living, physically and morally; he would inculcate the spirit of helpfulness and mutual service. As a brave, earnest, self-sacrificing, pure-minded lover of humanity, he is an inspiring character. George Eliot evidently wished to indicate in his creation what can be done by workingmen towards the uplifting of their own class. A better social order, she would have us believe, cannot be secured from external sources; but it must be had by an internal impulse moving those whose lives are degraded to seek for higher things because of their own intrinsic good. The demagogue seeks the elevation of workingmen because he can use them for his own advancement; but Felix desires their elevation for the good of the whole social structure. To this end he would inspire in his fellows a greater moral ambition and zeal for the common good. He is a Mazzini,

Castelar or John Bright in his own social order; one who loves his own class, wishes to remain in it, and who desires above all things that it shall do its part in the work of national elevation. His aim is not to oppose the other classes in society, but to make his own necessary to the prosperity of his country. Felix is not an ideal character, for he is rough, uncultured and headstrong; but he is an inspiring personality, with gifts of intellectual fascination and moral courage. George Eliot has created no other character like him, for Deronda and Zarca, whose aims somewhat resemble his, are very different. He is no hero, he is not altogether an attractive person. He has, however, the power, which some of the noblest of George Eliot's characters possess, of attracting and uplifting other persons. He made Esther realize the wide gulf between self-pleasing and duty, he inspired her with moral courage and awakened her mind to the higher aims and satisfactions life has to give us. He was undoubtedly meant for a moral hero of the working class, a prophet to the laborers. With all his limitations he is one of the noblest and most helpful characters in George Eliot's books.

Other distinctive ideas of George Eliot's appear throughout this book. Her theories of heredity, altruism and environment affect the whole development of the story. Perhaps no more striking illustration of the law of retribution is to be found in her books than in the case of Mrs. Transome. This woman's sin corrupted her own life, and helped to darken the lives of others.

The aim had in view in *Middlemarch* is to illustrate the impotence of modern life so far as it relates to moral heroism and spiritual attainment. High and noble action is hindered and baulked by the social conditions in the midst of which we live; and those who would live grandly and purely, and in a supreme unselfishness devote themselves to the world, find that their efforts are in vain. Dorothea has longings after a life of love and service; she would live for high purposes and give herself for others' good. Her hopes end in disaster almost; and she is cramped and baulked on every side. Lydgate would devote himself to science, to patient investigations for the sake of alleviating human misery and disease. His social environment cripples him, and his life comes to nothing compared with what he had aimed at, and what he was capable of attaining. Dorothea is presented as capable of becoming a saint, being of an ardent, heroic nature, a woman who yearned after some lofty conception of the world that was to be made, not merely poetry, but an actual fact about her; who was "enamoured of intensity and greatness," and "likely to seek martyrdom." The difficulties which most beset such a nature are presented in the very first chapter, where these saintly tendencies are considered as probable obstacles to her making a good marriage.

> A young lady of some birth and fortune, who knelt suddenly down on a brick floor by the side of a sick laborer and prayed fervidly, as if she thought herself living in the time of the Apostles — who had strange whims of fasting like a Papist, and of sitting up at night to read old theological books! Such a wife might awaken you some fine morning with a new scheme for the application of her income which would interfere with political economy and the keeping of saddle-horses; a man would naturally think twice before he risked himself in such fellowship.

The social life of Tipton really had no room for such a woman, could not employ her rare gifts, knew not what to make of her yearnings and her charity. And Tipton is the world and modern life, which spurns the heroic, has no place for the poetry of existence, can make nothing of yearnings and longings for high heroism. Because the social order into which she was born could not use her gifts, because the vision of life in her soul was other and higher than that which society had marked out for such as she, her life was wasted in an unhappy marriage. In an earlier age she would have become a St. Theresa, for society then had a place for such souls. Now she bows in reverence to a man of learning, dreams great things of tender service to him; but this proves not to be the place in which she belongs. In the last paragraphs of the book the author gives her own account of Dorothea's failure to reach the good she sought.

Sir James never ceased to regard Dorothea's second marriage as a mistake; and indeed this remained the tradition concerning it in Middlemarch, where she was spoken of to a younger generation as a fine girl who married a sickly clergyman, old enough to be her father, and in little more than a year after his death gave up her estate to marry his cousin — young enough to have been his son, with no property, and not well-born. Those who had not seen anything of Dorothea usually observed that she could not have been "a nice woman," else she would not have married either the one or the other.

Certainly those determining acts of her life were not ideally beautiful. They were the mixed result of young and noble impulse struggling under prosaic conditions. Among the many remarks passed on her mistakes, it was never said in the neighborhood of Middlemarch that such mistakes could not have happened if the society into which she was born had not smiled on propositions of marriage from a sickly man to a girl less than half his own age — on modes of education which make a woman's knowledge another name for motley ignorance — on rules of conduct which are in flat contradiction with its own loudly asserted beliefs. While this is the social air in which mortals begin to breathe, there will be collisions such as those in Dorothea's life, where great feelings take the aspect of error, and great faith the aspect of illusion. For there is no creature whose inward being is so strong that it is not greatly determined by what lies outside it. A new Theresa will hardly have the opportunity of reforming a conventual life, any more than a new Antigone will spend her heroic piety in daring all for the sake of a brother's burial; the medium in which their ardent deeds took place is forever gone. But we insignificant people with our daily words and acts, are preparing the lives of many Dorotheas, some of which may present a far sadder sacrifice than that of the Dorothea whose story we know.

Her finely touched spirit had still its fine issues, though they were not widely visible. Her full nature, like that river of which Alexander broke the strength, spent itself in channels which had no great name on the earth. But the effect of her being on those around her was incalculably diffusive; for the growing good of the world is partly dependent on unhistoric acts; and that things are not so ill with you and me as they might have been is half owing to the number who lived faithfully a hidden life, and rest in unvisited tombs.

The influence of social environment is also presented in *Felix Holt* as a chief determining agent in the lives of individuals. However high the aims and noble the purposes of the individual, he must succumb to those social influences which are more powerful than he. In the third chapter we are told that —

> This history is chiefly concerned with the private lot of a few men and women; but there is no private life which has not been determined by a wider public life, from the time when the primeval milkmaid had to wander with the wanderings of her clan, because the cow she milked was one of a herd which had made the pastures bare. Even in that conservatory existence where the fair Camelia is sighed for by the noble young Pineapple, neither of them needing to care about the frost or rain outside, there is a nether apparatus of hot-water pipes liable to cool down on a strike of the gardeners or a scarcity of coal. And the lives we are about to look back upon do not belong to those conservatory species; they are rooted in the common earth, having to endure all the ordinary chances of past and present weather. As to the weather of 1832, the Zadkiel of that time had predicted that the electrical condition of the clouds in the political hemisphere would produce unusual perturbations in organic existence, and he would perhaps have seen a fulfilment of his remarkable prophecy in that mutual influence of dissimilar destinies which we shall see gradually unfolding itself. For if the mixed political conditions of Treby Magna had not been acted on by the passing of the Reform Bill, Mr. Harold Transome would not have presented himself as a candidate for North Loamshire, Treby would not have been a polling-place, Mr. Matthew Jermyn would not have been on affable terms with a Dissenting preacher and his flock, and the venerable town would not have been placarded with handbills, more or less complimentary and retrospective — conditions in this case essential to the "where" and the "what," without which, as the learned know, there can be no event whatever.

In the case of Lydgate, if the ambition was less noble and pure, the fall was greater, and the disaster sadder to contemplate. He, too, was hindered by his "environment," but it was much more of his own creating, the result of his own nature, than in the case of Dorothea. We are told that "he was fired with the possibility that he might work out the proof of an anatomical conception, and make a link in the chain of discovery." That he was fully capable of achieving such a result is made to appear by the author. The account given of the discovery he wished to make, abundantly confirms this opinion of him; it also shows how large was George Eliot's learning, and how well she could use it for the novelist's purposes.

To show how a person capable of such work could be entangled in the ordinary affairs of life and lose sight of his youthful vision, or at least the power of realizing it, is the purpose developed in the career of Lydgate. There were "spots of commonness" in his nature. These —

lay in the complexion of his prejudices, which, in spite of noble intention and sympathy, were half of them such as are found in ordinary men of the world: that distinction of mind which belonged to his intellectual ardor did not penetrate his feeling and judgment about furniture, or women, or the desirability of its being known (without his telling) that he was better born than other country surgeons.

The egotism of his nature, his incapacity for hard, severe economy and the exclusion of luxury and refined pleasure, proved his destruction. Along with this egotism went a too susceptible impressiveness in the presence of beautiful women of soft, delicate ways. He meant to do great things in science, but he could not endure the discipline, the sacrifice, the long years of waiting, by which the great result was to be attained. Even if he could have done this, he lost the power of doing it through the social environment of marriage. How a man's love for a woman may corrupt the heroic purposes of his life is hinted at in one of the paragraphs in which George Eliot describes Lydgate, and the vision which enamoured his young life until the woman turned all his gold into dross.

We are not afraid of telling over and over again how a man comes to fall in love with a woman and be wedded to her, or else be fatally parted from her. Is it due to excess of poetry or of stupidity that we are never weary of describing what King James called a woman's "makdom and her fairnesse," never weary of listening to the twanging of the old Troubadour strings, and are comparatively uninterested in that other kind of "makdom and fairnesse" which must be wooed with industrious thought and renunciation of small desires? In the story of this passion, too, the development varies: sometimes it is the glorious marriage, sometimes frustration and final parting. And not seldom the catastrophe is wound up with the other passion, sung by the Troubadours. For in the multitude of middle-aged men who go about their vocations in a daily course determined for them much in the same way as the tie of their cravats, there is always a good number who once meant to shape their own deeds and alter the world a little. The story of their coming to be shapen after the average, and fit to be packed by the gross, is hardly ever told even in their consciousness; for perhaps their ardor for generous, unpaid toil cooled as imperceptibly as the ardor of other youthful loves, till one day their earlier self walked like a ghost in its old home and made the new furniture ghastly. Nothing in the world more subtle than the process of their gradual change! In the beginning they inhaled it unknowingly: you and I may have sent some of our breath toward infecting them when we uttered our conforming falsities or drew our silly conclusions; or perhaps it came with the vibration from a woman's glance.

The pathetic and saddening tragedy of a man's failure to realize the possibilities of his own nature was never more clearly and minutely told than in the case of Lydgate. We see all the steps of his fall, we know all the reasons why it came, we comprehend fully what he might have been and done. The bitterness of his own failure made him call his wife a basil plant — "a plant which had flourished wonderfully on a murdered man's brains." His hair never became white, but having won a large practice in his profession, he had his life heavily insured, and died at the age of fifty. He regarded his own life as a failure, though he was outwardly successful and "his skill was relied on by many paying patients." Against his will, by ways and causes he could not foresee, through the tenderness and ease of his own nature, the vision of his youth did not come true.

Perhaps *Middlemarch* is the most perfect example among George Eliot's novels of her purpose to show how we are guided, controlled and modified in our thought and action by the whole society of which the individual forms a single atom. Many characters appear in *Middlemarch*, drawn with wonderful skill and finish, each having some part to perform in the complicated play of life, and each some subtle, scarce-understood influence on all. Tragedy and comedy, selfishness and renunciation, greed and charity, love and jealousy, mingle here as in life. Many of these characters, such as Caleb Garth, Farebrother, Mrs. Cadwallader and Mr. Brooke, are remarkable portraitures, original and well conceived; but they all have their place in the social structure, and serve a purpose in the moral issue to be worked out.

It has been said of *Felix Holt*, and justly, that its characters are too typical, too much representative of a class, and too little personal in their natures and individual in their actions. Yet this method of treating character is consistent with the purpose of the novel, which is quite as much ethical as literary. Here we have imbruted and ignorant workingmen, laborers who would elevate their class, pious Dissenters, typical clergymen of the Church of England, old hereditary families with the smouldering evils which accumulate about them, ambitious and unscrupulous adventurers, and all the other phases of character likely to be found in such a town as Treby Magna. Each person stands for a class; and the aim of the novel is to indicate how the relative position of the classes represented may be changed with as little as possible of disorder and disruption.

It should be borne in mind, however, that the aim of George Eliot is not exclusively ethical. *Felix Holt* and *Middlemarch* are not ethical or socialistic treatises, and the whole purpose does not run in these directions. She ever keeps in mind, however, the great fact that on the ethical basis of right and wrong rests all the tragedy and comedy of the world. Her ideas are made alive with genius, and her ethical purposes take color in the glow of a brilliant imagination. She never did violence to the rule which she stated in her essay on the poet Young.

On its theoretic and perceptive side, morality touches science; on its emotional side, art. Now the products of art are great in proportion as they result from that immediate prompting of innate power which we call genius, and not from labored obedience to a theory or rule; and the presence of genius, or innate prompting, is directly opposed to the perpetual consciousness of a rule. The action of faculty is imperious, and excludes the reflection *why* it should act. In the same way, in proportion as morality is emotional, *i. e.*, has affinity with art, it will exhibit itself in direct sympathetic feeling and action, and not as the recognition of a rule. Love does not say, "I ought to love"—it loves. Pity does not say, "It is right to be pitiful"—it pities. Justice does not say, "I am bound to be just"—it feels justly. It is only where moral emotion is comparatively weak that the contemplation of a rule or theory habitually mingles with its action; and in accordance with this, we think experience, both in literature and life, has shown that the minds which are pre-eminently didactic—which insist on a "lesson," and despise everything that will not convey a moral, are deficient in sympathetic emotion.

The moral and social problems of life seem to fire her creative powers, kindle her imagination, and give rein to her genius. While the thoughtful reader may find in *Felix Holt* and *Middlemarch* more that interests his speculative faculties than of what will satisfy his sentiments and imagination, yet he must keep in mind the fact that these are works depending largely for their effect on the mind to their poetic qualities. There is in them both a large and thoughtful contemplation of life, but with a constant reference to its passion, sentiment and ideal aims. If they are realistic it is not to the exclusion of spiritual elements; and the poetic, sentimental phases of human existence are never ignored.

XVI.

DANIEL DERONDA.

THE purpose of George Eliot's last novel is distinctly constructive. While there is much of criticism in its pages, and criticism of the severest kind, its aim is that of spiritual renewal and upbuilding. It unfolds her conception of social growth, and of the influence of tradition and the national idea, much more completely than any other of her works. Moreover, it is all aglow with moral enthusiasm and spiritual ardor. It indicates a greater spontaneity than any of her books after *The Mill on the Floss*, and gives ample evidence that it possessed and absorbed the author's mind with its purpose and spirit. It is written from a great depth of conviction and moral earnestness. That it is her greatest book, artistically considered, there is no reason for believing; that it has its serious limitations as a literary creation all the critics have said. Yet it remains also to be said, that for largeness of aim, wealth of sentiment, and purity of moral teaching, no other book of George Eliot's surpasses *Daniel Deronda*. Indeed, in its realization of the spiritual basis of life, and in its portrayal of the religious sentiment, as these are understood by positivism, this book surpasses every other, by whomsoever written.

Daniel Deronda is a romance, and hence differs in kind, conception, scope, circumstance and form from her other works. It is less a study of character than most of her other works, has more of adventure and action; and while it is no less realistic, yet it has higher ideal aims, and seeks to interpret what ought to be.

At least three distinct purposes may be seen running through the book, which blend into and confirm each other: to show the all-powerful influence of heredity, that blood will assert itself as more effective than any conditions of social environment or education; to indicate that ideals, subjective feelings and sentiments form the reality and the substance of religion, and that tradition affords the true medium of its expression; and to contrast a form of social life based on individualism with one based on tradition. The aim of *Daniel Deronda*, however, is many-sided, and cannot be expressed in a few phrases. It is too vital with life, touches the emotions and sentiments too often, has an ideal motive too large, to be dismissed with a quickly spoken word of contempt. Professor Dowden, one of her best and most sympathetic critics, has said that it is "an homage to the emotions rather than to the intellect of man. Her feeling finds expression not only in occasional gnomic utterances in which sentiments are declared to be the best part of the world's wealth, and love is spoken of as deeper than reason, and the intellect is pronounced incapable of ascertaining the validity of claims which rest upon loving instincts of the heart, or else are baseless. The entire work possesses an impassioned aspect, an air of spiritual prescience, far more than the exactitude of science. The main forces which operate in it are sympathies, aspirations, ardors; and ideas chiefly as associated with these." The object aimed at is ideal and religious, much more than intellectual and scientific, to show how necessary is religion, how weak and imperfect is man when the ideal side of his nature is undeveloped. It makes clear the author's conviction concerning the importance of religion, that she prized its spiritual hopes, found satisfaction in its enthusiasms and aspirations. When Gwendolen was cast down in utter dejection, all of joy and delight the world had afforded her gone, and she felt the greatest need of something to comfort and sustain her in her distrust of self and the world, Deronda said to her, "The refuge you are needing from personal trouble is the higher, the religious life, which holds an enthusiasm for something more than our own appetites and vanities."

The religion inculcated, to be sure, is not that of faith in a personal God and a personal immortality, but that which is based on the mystery of life and nature, impressed on the sensitive soul of man in fears, sorrows, hopes, aspirations, and built up into great ideals and institutions through tradition. *Daniel Deronda* gives us the gospel of altruism, a new preaching of love to man. *Daniel Deronda* proves as no other writing has ever done, what is the charm and the power of these ideas when dissociated from any spiritual hopes which extend beyond humanity.

In order to give the most adequate expression to her ideas, and to show forth the power of the spiritual life as she conceived it, George Eliot made use of that race and religion which presents so remarkable an illustration of the influence of tradition and heredity. She saw in Judaism a striking confirmation of her theories, and a proof of what ideal interests can do to preserve a nation. To vindicate that race in the eyes of the world, to show what capacity there is in its national traditions, was also a part of her purpose. That this was her aim may be seen in what she said to a young Jew in whom she was much interested.

> I wrote about the Jews because I consider them a fine old race who have done great things for humanity. I feel the same admiration for them as I do for the Florentines.

The same idea is to be seen very clearly in the last essay in the *Impressions of Theophrastus Such*. She regarded the great memories and traditions of this people as a priceless legacy which may and ought to draw all the scattered Israelites together and unite them again in a common national life.

> A people having the seed of worthiness in it must feel an answering thrill when it is adjured by the deaths of its heroes who died to

preserve its national existence; when it is reminded of its small beginnings and gradual growth through past labors and struggles, such as are still demanded of it in order that the freedom and well-being thus inherited may be transmitted unimpaired to children and children's children; when an appeal against the permission of injustice is made to great precedents in its history and to the better genius breathing in its institutions. It is this living force of sentiment in common which makes a national consciousness. Nations so moved will resist conquest with the very breasts of their women, will pay their millions and their blood to abolish slavery, will share privation in famine and all calamity, will produce poets to sing "some great story of a man," and thinkers whose theories will bear the test of action. An individual man, to be harmoniously great, must belong to a nation of this order, if not in actual existence, yet existing in the past, in memory, as a departed, invisible, beloved ideal, once a reality, and perhaps to be restored. A common humanity is not yet enough to feed the rich blood of various activity which makes a complete man. The time is not come for cosmopolitanism to be highly virtuous, any more than for communism to suffice for social energy.

This was one of the favorite ideas of George Eliot, which she has again and again expressed. She was impressed with the conviction that such a national life is necessary to the world's growth and welfare, that the era of a common brotherhood, dissociated from national traditions and hopes, has not yet come. Hence her belief that Judaism ought to speak the voice of a united race, occupying the old home of this people, and sending forth its ideas as a national inheritance and inspiration. This belief inspires the concluding words of her essay, as well as the last chapters of the novel.

There is still a great function for the steadfastness of the Jew: not that he should shut out the utmost illumination which knowledge can throw on his national history, but that he should cherish the store of inheritance which that history has left him. Every Jew should be conscious that he is one of a multitude possessing common objects of piety in the immortal achievements and immortal sorrows of ancestors who have transmitted to them a physical and mental type strong enough, eminent enough in faculties, pregnant enough with peculiar promise, to constitute a new beneficent individuality among the nations, and, by confuting the traditions of scorn, nobly avenge the wrongs done to their fathers.

There is a sense in which the worthy child of a nation that has brought forth illustrious prophets, high and unique among the poets of the world, is bound by their visions.

Is bound?

Yes; for the effective bond of human action is feeling, and the worthy child of a people owning the triple name of Hebrew, Israelite and Jew, feels his kinship with the glories and the sorrows, the degradation and the possible renovation of his national family.

Will any one teach the nullification of this feeling and call his doctrine a philosophy? He will teach a blinding superstition — the superstition that a theory of human well-being can be constructed in disregard of the influences which have made us human.

The purpose of *Daniel Deronda*, however, is not merely to vindicate Judaism. This race and its religion are used as the vehicles for larger ideas, as an illustration of the supreme importance to mankind of spiritual aims concentrated into the form of national traditions and aspirations. Her own studies, and personal intercourse with the Jews, helped to attract her to this race; but the main cause of her use of them in this novel is their remarkable history. Their moral and spiritual persistence, their wonderful devotedness to their own race and its aims, admirably adapted them to develop for her the ideas she wished to express. What nation could she have taken that would have so clearly illustrated her theory of national memories and traditions? In the forty-second chapter of *Daniel Deronda* she has put into the mouth of Mordecai her own theories on this subject. He vindicates his right to call himself a *rational* Jew, one who accepts what is reasonable and true.

"It is to see more and more of the hidden bonds that bind and consecrate change as a dependent growth — yea, consecrate it with kinship; the past becomes my parent, and the future stretches toward me the appealing arms of children. Is it rational to drain away the sap of special kindred that makes the families of man rich in interchanged wealth, and various as the forests are various with the glory of the cedar and the palm?"

He declares that each nation has its own work to do in the world, in the uplifting and maintenance of some special idea which is necessary to the welfare and development of humanity. The place he assigns to Judaism is precisely that which made it dear to George Eliot, because it embodied her conception of religion and its social functions.

"Israel is the heart of mankind, if we mean by heart the core of affection which binds a race and its families in dutiful love, and the reverence for the human body which lifts the needs of our animal life into religion, and the tenderness which is merciful to the poor and weak and to the dumb creature that wears the yoke for us."

Again, he utters words which are simply an expression of George Eliot's own sentiments.

"Where else is there a nation of whom it may be as truly said that their religion and law and moral life mingled as the stream of blood in the heart and made one growth — where else a people who kept and enlarged their spiritual store at the very time when they were hunted with a hatred as fierce as the forest fires that chase the wild beast from his covert? There is a fable of the Roman that, swimming to save his life, he held the roll of his writings between his teeth and saved them from the waters. But how much more than that is true of our race? They struggled to keep their place among the nations like heroes — yea, when the hand was hacked off, they clung with the teeth; but when the plow and the harrow had passed over the last visible signs of their national covenant, and the fruitfulness of their land was stifled with the blood of the sowers and planters, they said, 'The spirit is alive, let us make it a lasting habitation — lasting because movable — so that it may be carried from generation to generation, and our sons unborn may be rich in the things that have been, and possess a hope built on an unchangeable foundation.' They said it and they wrought it, though often breathing with scant life, as in a coffin, or as lying wounded amid a heap of slain. Hooted and scared like the unowned dog, the Hebrew made himself envied for his wealth and wisdom, and was bled of them to fill the bath of Gentile luxury; he absorbed knowledge, he diffused it; his dispersed race was a new Phœnicia working the mines of Greece and carrying their products to the world. The native spirit of our tradition was not to stand still, but to use records as a seed, and draw out the compressed virtues of law and prophecy."

Then Mordecai unfolds his theory of national unity and of a regenerated national life; and it is impossible to read his words attentively without accepting them as an expression of George Eliot's own personal convictions. As an embodiment of her conception of the functions of national life they are full of interest aside from their place in the novel.

"In the multitudes of the ignorant on three continents who observe our rites and make the confession of the Divine Unity, the soul of Judaism is not dead. Revive the organic centre: let the unity of Israel which has made the growth and form of its religion be an outward reality. Looking toward a land and a polity, our dispersed people in all the ends of the earth may share the dignity of a national life which has a voice among the peoples of the East and the West — which will plant the wisdom and skill of our race so that it may be, as of old, a medium of transmission and understanding. Let that come to pass, and the living warmth will spread to the weak extremities of Israel, and superstition will vanish, not in the lawlessness of the renegade, but in the illumination of great facts which widen feeling, and make all knowledge alive as the young offspring of beloved memories. . . . The effect of our separateness will not be completed and have its highest transformation unless our race takes on again the character of a nationality. That is the fulfilment of the religious trust that moulded them into a people, whose life has made half the inspiration of the world. What is it to me that the ten tribes are lost untraceably, or that multitudes of the children of Judah have mixed themselves with the Gentile populations as a river with rivers? Behold our people still! Their skirts spread afar; they are torn and soiled and trodden on; but there is a jewelled breast-plate. Let the wealthy men, the monarchs of commerce, the learned in all knowledge, the skilful in all arts, the speakers, the political counsellors, who carry in their veins the Hebrew blood which has maintained its vigor in all climates, and the pliancy of the Hebrew genius for which difficulty means new device — let them say, 'We will lift up a standard, we will unite in a labor hard but glorious like that of Moses and Ezra, a labor which shall be a worthy fruit of the long anguish whereby our fathers maintained their separateness, refusing the ease of falsehood.' They have wealth enough to redeem the soil from debauched and paupered conquerors; they have the skill of the statesman to devise, the tongue of the orator to persuade. And is there no prophet or poet among us to make the ears of Christian Europe tingle with shame at the hideous obloquy of Christian strife which the Turk gazes at as at the fighting of beasts to which he has lent an arena? There is store of wisdom among us to found a new Jewish polity, grand, simple, just, like the old — a republic where there is equality of protection, an equality which shone like a star on the forehead of our ancient community, and gave it more than the brightness of Western freedom amidst the despotisms of the East. Then our race shall have an organic centre, a heart and brain to watch and guide and execute; the outraged Jew shall have a defence in the court of nations, as the outraged Englishman or American. And the world will gain as Israel gains. For there will be a community in the van of the East which carries the culture and the sympathies of every great nation in its bosom; there will be a land set for a halting-place of enmities, a neutral ground for the East as Belgium is for the West. Difficulties? I know there are difficulties. But let the spirit of sublime achievement move in the great among our people, and the work will begin. . . .

"What is needed is the leaven — what is needed is the seed of fire. The heritage of Israel is beating in the pulses of millions; it lives in their veins as a power without understanding, like the morning exultation of herds; it is the inborn half of memory, moving as in a dream among writings on the walls, which it sees dimly but cannot divide into speech. Let the torch of visible community be lighted! Let the reason of Israel disclose itself in a great outward deed, and let there be another great migration, another choosing of Israel to be a nationality whose members may still stretch to the ends of the earth, even as the sons of England and Germany, whom enterprise carries afar, but who still have a national hearth, and a tribunal of national opinion. Will any say, 'It cannot be'? Baruch Spinoza had not a faithful Jewish heart, though he had sucked the life of his intellect at the breasts of Jewish tradition. He laid bare his father's nakedness and said, 'They who scorn him have the higher wisdom.' Yet Baruch Spinoza confessed he saw not why Israel should not again be a chosen nation. Who says that the history and literature of our race are dead? Are they not as living as the history and literature of Greece and Rome, which have inspired revolutions, enkindled the thought of Europe and made the unrighteous powers tremble? These were an inheritance dug from the tomb. Ours is an inheritance that has never ceased to quiver in millions of human frames. . . .

"I cherish nothing for the Jewish nation, I seek nothing for them, but the good which promises good to all the nations. The spirit of our religious life, which is one with our national life, is not hatred of aught but wrong. The masters have said an offence against man is worse than an offence against God. But what wonder if there is hatred in the breasts of Jews who are children of the ignorant and oppressed — what wonder, since there is hatred in the breasts of Christians? Our national life was a growing light. Let the central fire be kindled again, and the light will reach afar. The degraded and scorned of our race will learn to think of their sacred land not as a place for saintly beggary to await death in loathsome idleness, but as a republic where the Jewish spirit manifests itself in a new order founded on the old, purified, enriched by the experience our greatest sons have gathered from the life of the ages. How long is it? — only two centuries since a vessel carried over the ocean the beginning of the great North American nation. The people grew like meeting waters; they were various in habit and sect. There came a time, a century ago, when they needed a polity, and there were heroes of peace among them. What had they to form a polity with but memories of Europe, corrected by the vision of a better? Let our wise and wealthy show themselves heroes. They have the memories of the East and West, and they have the full vision of a better. A new Persia with a purified religion magnified itself in art and wisdom. So will a new Judæa, poised between East and West — a covenant of reconciliation. Will any say the prophetic vision of your race has been hopelessly mixed with folly and bigotry; the angel of progress has no message for Judaism — it is a half-buried city for the paid workers to lay open — the waters are rushing by it as a forsaken field? I say that the strongest principle of growth lies in human choice. The sons of Judah have to choose, that God may again choose them. The Messianic time is the time when Israel shall will the planting of the national ensign. The Nile overflowed and rushed onward; the Egyptian could not choose the overflow, but he chose to work and make channels for the fructifying waters and Egypt became the land of corn. Shall man, whose soul is set in the royalty of discernment and resolve, deny his rank and say, I am an onlooker, ask no choice or purpose of me? That is the blasphemy of this time. The divine principle of our race is action, choice, resolved memory. Let us contradict the blasphemy, and help to will our own better future and the better future of the world — not renounce our higher gift and say, 'Let us be as if we were not among the populations;' but choose our full heritage, claim the brotherhood of our nation, and carry into it a new brotherhood with the nations of the Gentiles. The vision is there: it will be fulfilled."

These words put into the mouth of Mordecai, indicate how thoroughly George Eliot entered into the spirit of Judaism. She read Hebrew with ease, and had delved extensively in Jewish literature, besides being familiar with the monumental works in German devoted to Jewish history and opinions. The religious customs, the home life, the peculiar social habits of the race, she carefully studied. The accuracy of her information has been pointed out by her Jewish critics, by whom the book has been praised with the utmost enthusiasm. One of these, Prof. David Kaufmann, of Buda-Pesth, in an excellent notice of *Daniel Deronda*, bears testimony to the author's learning and to the faithfulness of her Jewish portraitures. He says that, "led by cordial and loving inclination to the profound study of Jewish national and family life, she has set herself to create Jewish characters, and to recognize and give presentment to the influences which Jewish education is wont to exercise — to prove by types that Judaism is an intellectual and spiritual force, still misapprehended and readily overlooked, but not the less an effective power, for the future of which it is good assurance that it possesses in the body of its adherents a noble, susceptible and pliant material which only awaits its final casting to appear in a glorious form." He also says of the author's learning, that it is loving and exact, that her descriptions of Jewish life are always faithful and her characters true to nature.

"Leader of the present so-called realistic school, our

author keeps up in this work the reputation she has won of possessing the most minute knowledge of the subjects she handles, by the manner in which she has described the Jews — the great unknown of humanity. She has penetrated into their history and literature affectionately and thoroughly; and her knowledge in a field where ignorance is still venial if not expressly authorized, has astonished even experts. In her selection of almost always unfamiliar quotations, she shows a taste and a facility of reference really amazing. When shall we see a German writer exhibiting the courteous kindliness of George Eliot, who makes Deronda study Zunz's *Synagogale Poesie*, and places the monumental words which open his chapter entitled 'Leiden,' at the head of the passage in which she introduces us to Ezra Cohen's family, and at the club-meeting at which Mordecai gives utterance to his ideas concerning the future of Israel? She is familiar with the views of Jehuda-ha-Levi as with the dreams and longings of the cabalists, and as conversant with the splendid names of our Hispano-Arabian epoch as with the moral aphorisms of the Talmud and the subtle meaning contained in Jewish legends. . . . It is by the piety and tenderness with which she treats Jewish customs that the author shows how supreme her cultivation and refinement are; and the small number of mistakes which can be detected in her descriptions of Jewish life and ritual may put to blush even writers who belong to that race." Again this critic says of the visionary Mordecai, who has been pronounced a mere dreamer and untrue to nature, that he is an altogether probable character and portrayed with a true realistic touch. "Mordecai is carved of the wood from which prophets are made, and so far as the supersensuous can be rendered intelligible, it may even be said that in studying him we are introduced into a studio or workshop of the prophetic mind. He is one of the most difficult as well as one of the most successful essays in psychological analysis ever attempted by an author; and in his wonderful portrait, which must be closely studied, and not epitomized or reproduced in extracts, we see glowing enthusiasm united to cabalistic profundity, and the most morbid tension of the intellectual powers united to clear and well-defined hopes. How has the author succeeded in making Mordecai so human and so true to nature? By mixing the gold with an alloy of commoner metal, and by giving the angelic likeness features which are familiar to us all."

Another Jew has borne equally hearty testimony to the faithfulness with which George Eliot has described Jewish life and the spirit of the Jewish religion. "She has acquired," this writer says, "an extended and profound knowledge of the rites, aspirations, hopes, fears and desires of the Israelites of the day. She has read their books, inquired into their modes of thought, searched their traditions, accompanied them to the synagogue; nay, she has taken their very words from their lips, and, like Asmodeus, has unroofed their houses. To say that some slight errors have crept into *Daniel Deronda* is to say that no human work is perfect; and these inaccuracies are singularly few and unimportant."[1] Still another Jewish critic says that in her gallery of portraits she "gives in a marvellously full and accurate way all the many sides of the Jewish complex national character." He also says that Mordecai is a true successor of the prophets and moral leaders of the race, that the national spirit and temper are truly represented in him.[2]

That the main purpose of *Daniel Deronda* is not that of defending Judaism, must be apparent to every attentive reader. The Jewish race is made use of for purposes of illustration, as a notable example in proof of her theories. There is a deeper purpose conspicuous throughout the book, which rests on her conceptions of

[1] James Picciotto, author of "Sketches of Anglo-Jewish History," in the Gentleman's Magazine for November, 1876.

[2] Joseph Jacobs, in Macmillan's Magazine for 1877.

the spiritual life as a development of tradition. This larger purpose also rests on her altruistic conception of the moral and spiritual life. As Professor Kaufmann has pointed out, the story falls into two widely separated portions, in one of which the Jewish element appears, in the other the English. Jewish life and its religious spirit are contrasted with English life and a common type of its religion. This is not a contrast, however, which is introduced for the purpose of disparaging Christianity or English social life, but with the object of comparing those whose life is anchored in the spiritual traditions of a great people, with those who find the centre of their life in egotism and an individualistic spirit. Grandcourt is a type of pure egotism; Gwendolen is a creature who lives for self and with no law outside of her own happiness. This is the spirit of the society in which they both move. On the other hand, Mordecai lives in his race, Deronda gives his life constantly away for others, and Mirah is unselfishness and simplicity itself. So distinctly is this contrast drawn, so clearly are these two phases of life brought over against each other, that the book seems to be divided in the middle, and to be two separate works joined by a slender thread. This artistic arrangement has been severely criticised, but its higher purpose is only understood when this comparison and antagonism is recognized. Then the true artistic arrangement vindicates itself, and the unity of the book becomes apparent. Deronda moves in both these worlds, and their influence on him is finely conceived. He finds no spiritual aim and motive for his life until he is led into the charmed circle of a traditional environment, and learns to live in and for his race. Living for self, the life of Gwendolen is blasted, her hopes crushed, and she finds no peace or promise except in the steadfast spiritual strength yielded her by Deronda. That such a contrasting of the two great phases of life was a part of George Eliot's purpose she has herself acknowledged.

A comparison of the spiritual histories of Gwendolen and Deronda will show how earnest was this purpose of the author. Gwendolen is a type of those souls who have no spiritual anchorage in the religious life and traditions of their people. At the opening of chapter third we are told she had no home memories, that "this blessed persistence in which affection can take root had been wanting in Gwendolen's life." At the end of the sixth chapter we are also told that she had no insight into spiritual realities, that the bonds of spiritual power and moral retribution had not been made apparent to her mind.

> Her ideal was to be daring in speech and reckless in braving dangers, both moral and physical; and though her practice fell far behind her ideal, this shortcoming seemed to be due to the pettiness of circumstances, the narrow theatre which life offers to a girl of twenty, who cannot conceive herself as anything else than a lady, or as in any position which would lack the tribute of respect. She had no permanent consciousness of other fetters, or of more spiritual restraints, having always disliked whatever was presented to her under the name of religion, in the same way that some people dislike arithmetic and accounts: it had raised no other emotion in her, no alarm, no longing; so that the question whether she believed it, had not occurred to her, any more than it had occurred to her to inquire into the conditions of colonial property and banking, on which, as she had had many opportunities of knowing, the family fortune was dependent. All these facts about herself she would have been ready to admit, and even, more or less indirectly, to state. What she unwillingly recognized, and would have been glad for others to be unaware of, was that liability of hers to fits of spiritual dread, though this fountain of awe within her had not found its way into connection with the religion taught her, or with any human relations. She was ashamed and frightened, as at what might happen again, in remembering her tremor on suddenly feeling herself alone, when, for example, she was walking without companionship and there came some rapid change in the light. Solitude in any wide scene impressed her with an undefined feeling of immeasurable existence aloof from her, in the midst of which she was helplessly incapable of asserting herself. The little astronomy taught her at school used sometimes to set her imagination at work in a way that made her tremble; but always when some one joined her she recovered her indifference to the vastness in which she seemed an exile; she found again her usual world, in which her will was of some avail, and the religious nomenclature belonging to this world was no more identified for her with those uneasy impressions of awe than her uncle's surplices seen out of use at the rectory. With human ears and eyes about her, she had always

hitherto recovered her confidence, and felt the possibility of winning empire.

Her difficulties all came out of this egoistic spirit, this want of spiritual anchorage and religious faith. Gradually her bitter experiences awakened in her a desire for a purer life, and the influence of Deronda worked powerfully in the same direction. She is to be regarded, however, as simply a representative of that social, moral and spiritual life bred in our century by the disintegrating forces everywhere at work. No moral ideal, no awe of the divine Nemesis, no spiritual sympathy with the larger life of the race, is to be found in her thought. The radicalism of the time, which neglects religious training, which scorns the life of the past, which lives for self and culture, is destroying all that is best in modern society. Gwendolen is one of the results of these processes, an example of that impoverished life which is so common, arising from religious rebellion and egotism.

Another motive and spirit is represented in the character of Deronda. As a boy, his mind was full of ideal aspirations, he was chivalrous and eager to help and comfort others. He would take no mean advantages in his own behalf, he loved the comradeship of those whom he could help, he was always ready with his sympathy.

He was early impassioned by ideas, and burned his fire on those heights.

He would not regard his studies as instruments of success, but as the means whereby to feed motive and opinion. He had a strong craving for comprehensiveness of opinion, and was not content to store up knowledge that demanded a mere act of memory in its acquisition. He had a craving after a larger life, an ideal aim of the most winning attractiveness. Though Deronda was educated amidst surroundings almost identical with those which helped to form Gwendolen's char acter, yet a very different result was produced in him because of his *inherited* tendencies of mind. After he had seen his mother, learned that he was a Jew, he said to Mordecai, —

"It is you who have given shape to what I believe was an inherited yearning — the effect of brooding, passionate thoughts in my ancestors — thoughts that seem to have been intensely present in my grandfather. Suppose the stolen offspring of some mountain tribe brought up in a city of the plain, or one with an inherited genius for painting, and born blind — the ancestral life would be within them as a dim longing for unknown objects and sensations, and the spell-bound habit of their inherited frames would be like a cunningly wrought musical instrument never played on, but quivering throughout in uneasy, mysterious moanings of its intricate structure that, under the right touch, gives music. Something like that, I think, has been my experience. Since I began to read and know, I have always longed for some ideal task in which I might feel myself the heart and brain of a multitude — some social captainship which would come to me as a duty, and not be striven for as a personal prize. You have raised the image of such a task for me — to bind our race together in spite of heresy."

This inherited sense of a larger life made Deronda what he was, and developed in him qualities absent in Gwendolen. This inherited power made him a new Mazzini, a born leader of men, a new saviour of society, a personal magnet to attract and inspire other souls. A magnetic power of influence drew Gwendolen to him from the first time they met, he shamed her narrow life by his silent presence, and he quickened to life in her a desire for a purer and nobler existence. George Eliot probably meant to indicate in his character her conception of the true social reformation which is needed to-day, and how it is to be brought about. The basis on which it is to be built is the traditional and inherited life of the past, inspired with new energies and meanings by the gifted souls who have inherited a large and pure personality, and who are inspired by a quickened sense of what life ought to be. On the one side a life of altruism, on the other a life of egotism, teach that the finer social and moral qualities come out of an inheritance in the national ideals and conquests of a worthy people, while the coarser qualities come of the neglect of this source of spiritual power and sustenance. Two letters written to Professor David Kaufmann indicate that this was the purpose of the book. At the same time, they show George Eliot's mind on other sides, and give added insights into her character. As an indication of her attitude towards Judaism, and her faith in the work she had done in *Daniel Deronda*, they are of great value.

THE PRIORY, 21 NORTH BANK,
May 31, '77.

MY DEAR SIR, — Hardly, since I became an author, have I had a deeper satisfaction, I may say a more heartfelt joy, than you have given me in your estimate of *Daniel Deronda*.[1]

I must tell you that it is my rule, very strictly observed, not to read the criticisms on my writings. For years I have found this abstinence necessary to preserve me from that discouragement as an artist which ill-judged praise, no less than ill-judged blame, tends to produce in me. For far worse than any verdict as to the proportion of good and evil in our work, is the painful impression that we write for a public which has no discernment of good and evil.

My husband reads any notices of me that come before him, and reports to me (or else refrains from reporting) the general character of the notice, or something in particular which strikes him as showing either an exceptional insight or an obtuseness that is gross enough to be amusing. Very rarely, when he has read a critique of me, he has handed it to me, saying, "*You* must read this." And your estimate of *Daniel Deronda* made one of these rare instances.

Certainly, if I had been asked to choose *what* should be written about my book and *who* should write it, I should have sketched — well, not anything so good as what you have written, but an article which must be written by a Jew who showed not merely sympathy with the best aspirations of his race, but a remarkable insight into the nature of art and the processes of the artistic mind. Believe me, I should not have cared to devour even ardent praise if it had not come from one who showed the discriminating sensibility, the perfect response to the artist's intention, which must make the fullest, rarest joy to one who works from inward conviction and not in compliance with current fashions. Such a response holds for an author not only what is best in "the life that now is," but the promise of "that which is to come." I mean that the usual approximative, narrow perception of what one has been intending and professedly feeling in one's work, impresses one with the sense that it must be poor perishable stuff without

[1] George Eliot and Judaism: an Attempt to Appreciate Daniel Deronda. By Prof. David Kaufmann, of the Jewish Theological Seminary, Buda-Pesth.

roots to take any lasting hold in the minds of men; while any instance of complete comprehension encourages one to hope that the creative prompting has foreshadowed, and will continue to satisfy, a need in other minds.

Excuse me that I write but imperfectly, and perhaps dimly, what I have felt in reading your article. It has affected me deeply, and though the prejudice and ignorant obtuseness which has met my effort to contribute something to the ennobling of Judaism in the conception of the Christian community and in the consciousness of the Jewish community, has never for a moment made me repent my choice, but rather has been added proof to me that the effort has been needed, — yet I confess that I had an unsatisfied hunger for certain signs of sympathetic discernment, which you only have given. I may mention as one instance your clear perception of the relation between the presentation of the Jewish element and those of English social life.

I work under the pressure of small hurries; for we are just moving into the country for the summer, and all things are in a vagrant condition around me. But I wished not to defer answering your letter to an uncertain opportunity. . . .

My husband has said more than once that he feels grateful to you. For he is more sensitive on my behalf than on his own.

Hence he unites with me in the assurance of the high regard with which I remain

Always yours faithfully,

M. E. Lewes.

This first letter was followed a few months later by a second.

The Priory, 21 North Bank, Regent's Park,
Oct. 12, '77.

My dear Sir, — I trust it will not be otherwise than gratifying to you to know that your stirring article on *Daniel Deronda* is now translated into English by a son of Prof. Ferrier, who was a philosophical writer of considerable mark. It will be issued in a handsomer form than that of the pamphlet, and will appear within this autumnal publishing season, Messrs. Blackwood having already advertised it. Whenever a copy is ready we shall have the pleasure of sending it to you. There is often something to be borne with in reading one's own writing in a translation, but I hope that in this case you will not be made to wince severely.

In waiting to send you this news I seem to have deferred too long the expression of my warm thanks for your kindness in sending me the Hebrew translations of Lessing and the collection of Hebrew poems, a kindness which I felt myself rather presumptuous in asking for, since your time must be well filled with more important demands. Yet I must further beg you, when you have an opportunity, to assure Herr Bacher that I was most gratefully touched by the sympathetic verses with which he enriched the gift of his work.

I see by your last letter to my husband that your Theological Seminary was to open on the 4th of this month, so that this too retrospective letter of mine will reach you in the midst of your new duties. I trust that this new institution will be a great good to professor and students, and that your position is of a kind that you contemplate as permanent. To teach the young personally has always seemed to me the most satisfactory supplement to teaching the world through books, and I have often wished that I had such a means of having fresh, living, spiritual children within sight.

One can hardly turn one's thought toward Eastern Europe just now without a mingling of pain and dread; but we mass together distant scenes and events in an unreal way, and one would like to believe that the present troubles will not at any time press on you in Hungary with more external misfortune than on us in England.

Mr. Lewes is happily occupied in his psychological studies. We both look forward to the reception of the work you kindly promised us, and he begs me to offer you his best regards.

Believe me, my dear sir,

Yours with much esteem,

M. E. Lewes.

It was a part of George Eliot's purpose in *Daniel Deronda* to criticise the social life of England in the spirit in which she had criticised it in *Middlemarch*, as being deficient in spiritual power, moral purpose and noble sentiment. If she made it clear in *Middlemarch* that the individual is crippled and betrayed by society, it was her purpose to make it quite as clear in *Daniel Deronda* how society may become the true inspirer of the individual. We may quarrel with her theory of the origin and nature of the spiritual life in man, but she has somewhat truly conceived its vast importance and shown the character of that influence it everywhere has over man's life. As types of spiritual life, and as individual conceptions of human character, the personages of this novel are drawn with marvellous skill. Mr. E. P. Whipple says that Daniel Deronda is "one of the noblest and most original characters among the heroes imagined by poets, dramatists and novelists." With equal or even greater justice can it be said that Gwendolen Harleth is one of the most powerful and grandly conceived of imaginary creations in all literature. In the characters, the situations, and the whole working out of this novel, George Eliot shows herself one of the great masters of literary creation.

When the prejudices aroused by the Jewish element in it are allayed, and *Daniel Deronda* is read as a work of literary genius, it will be found not to be the least interesting and important of George Eliot's books. It has the religious interest and inspiration of *Adam Bede*, the historic value of *Romola*, and the critical elements of *Middlemarch;* and these are wrought into a work of lofty insight and imagination, along with a high spiritual ardor and a supreme ethical purpose. In this novel, for the first time, as Professor Dowden says, her poetical genius found adequate expression, and in complete association with the non-poetical elements of her nature.

XVII.

THE SPANISH GYPSY AND OTHER POEMS.

IT was *The Spanish Gypsy*, published in 1868, which brought the name of George Eliot before the public as a poet. This work is a novel written in blank verse, with enough of the heroic and tragic in it to make the story worthy of its poetic form. The story is an excellent one, well conceived and worked out, and had it been given the prose form would have made a powerful and original novel. While it would doubtless have gained in definiteness of detail and clearness of purpose by being presented in the prose form, yet its condensation into a poem is a gain, and the whole setting of the story has been made of greater interest by this method of expression. The poetic form is as original as are the theories of life which the poem is designed to inculcate. In structure it combines, with a method quite its own, the descriptive and dramatic forms of poetry. In this it nearly approaches the method followed in her novels of combining description and dialogue in a unitary structure of great strength and perfection. The descriptive passages in her prose works are strong and impressive, lofty in tone, and yet lovingly faithful in detail. Her conversations are often highly dramatic and add greatly to the whole outcome of these novels. In *The Spanish Gypsy* the surroundings of the story are first described in verse which, if not always perfectly poetic, is yet imaginatively thought out and executed in a manner befitting the subject. Suddenly, however, the narrative and descriptive form ceases and the dramatic begins. By means also of full "stage directions" to the dramatic portions of the poem, the story is wrought out quite as much in detail as it needs to be; and much is gained of advantage over the length of her novels by this concentration of scene and narrative. While the narrative portion of the poem is much less in extent than the dramatic, yet it has in it some of the main elements of the plot, and those without which the action could not be worked out. The dramatic element gives it a real and living power. The characters are strongly conceived, and nearly all of them are individualities of an original type and of an action thoroughly distinct and human.

As a work of art, the most serious defect in *The Spanish Gypsy* is its doctrinal tone. It is speculative in its purpose quite as much as poetical, and the speculation is so large an element as to intrude upon the poetry. Thought overtops imagination, the fervor and enthusiasm of the poet are more than matched by the ethical aims of the teacher. This ethical purpose of unfolding in a dramatic form the author's theories of life has filled the book, as it has her novels, with epigrams which are original, splendid and instructive. Into a few lines she condenses some piece of wisdom, and in words full of meaning and purpose. Into the mouth of Sephardo, a character distinctive and noteworthy, she puts some of her choicest wisdom. He says, —

> Thought
> Has joys apart, even in blackest woe,
> And seizing some fine thread of verity
> Knows momentary godhead.

Again he utters the same idea, but in more expressive words.

> Our growing thought
> Makes growing revelation.

Don Silva is made to use this highly poetic imagery.

> Speech is but broken light upon the depth
> Of the unspoken.

Zarca, that truest and most original character in the poem, says of the great work he purposes to accomplish,

> To my inward vision
> Things are achieved when they are well begun.

Again, he says, —

> New thoughts are urgent as the growth of wings.

Expressive and original as *The Spanish Gypsy* is, yet it gives the impression of lacking in some poetic quality which is necessary to the highest results. Difficult as it may be to define precisely what it is that is wanting, nearly every reader will feel that something which makes poetry has been somehow left out. Is it imagination, or is it a flexible poetic expression, which is absent? While George Eliot has imagination enough to make a charming prose style, and to adorn her prose with great beauty and an impressive manner, yet its finer quality of subtle expression is not to be found in her poetry. Those original and striking shades of meaning which the poet employs by using words in unique relations, she does not often attain to. It is the thought, the ethical meaning, in her poetry as in her prose, which is often of more importance than the manner of expression; and she is too intent on what is said to give full heed always to how it is said. She has, however, employed that form of verse which is best suited to her style, and one which does not demand those lyrical or those imaginative qualities in which she is deficient. The blank verse is well adapted to her realism, though it does not always answer well to the more dramatic and tragical and impassioned portions of the story.

As a study of an historic period, *The Spanish Gypsy* is not so great a success as *Romola;* yet it more perfectly unfolds a unitary moral purpose, and the various types of character are more originally developed. The conflict of motives, the contrasted and opposed national interests, are distinctly brought out, but the aroma of the time and place are wanting. To describe a poetic and heroic era she is never content to do. Her method is totally different from that of Scott, who reflects the spirit and life of the time he depicts with almost absolute faithfulness. No gypsy was ever such a character as Zarca, no gypsy girl ever had the conscience of Fedalma. As in the case of *Romola*, so here, an historic period is used, not so much for artistic as for philosophic purposes, because it is well designed to present her ideas about heredity and tradition. *The Spanish Gypsy* is essentially a romance, and contains much of those more poetic and ideal elements which distinguish *Daniel Deronda* from her other novels. This romantic element, if it does not develop poetry of the highest quality, does bring out in its most perfect form all the finest characteristics of her style.

While *The Spanish Gypsy* affords many points of attack for the critic, yet it cannot be dismissed by saying it is not a great poem. Its strong qualities are too many to permit of its being disposed of in haste. With all its defects it is a noble piece of work, and genuinely adds to the author's expression of genius. It is one of those poems which win, not popularity, but the heartiest admiration of a choice and elect few who find life and highest inspiration in it, because giving strength to their thoughts and purpose to their moral convictions. As a study of some of the deeper problems of the ethical and social life of man, it is unsurpassed, and the teaching imparted by it is singularly well and impressively conveyed by the whole make of the poem. It is also remarkable for its large and impressive style, its rich command of words, and the lofty beauty of its diction. One of its most striking qualities, as Mr. Henry James, Jr., suggests, "is its extraordinary rhetorical energy and eloquence," and "its splendid generosity of diction." The same writer says of the character of Don Silva, that "nowhere has her marvellous power of expression, the mingled dignity and pliancy of her style, obtained a greater triumph." The critics have almost without exception dealt severely with the poem, but they have applied to it the canons of poetic art as interpreted by themselves. Genius creates its own laws, makes its own methods, reverses old decisions and triumphs against the whole brood of critics. The world accepts what is true and excellent, however defective in technical requirements. Imperfect meters, and poetic structures not orthodox, may disturb those who deal in criticism, but such limitations as these are not sufficient to fix the final acceptance of a poem. More than one of the greatest poems could not endure such tests. That *The Spanish Gypsy* has vitality of purpose, enduring interest in treatment, and a lofty eloquence of diction, is doubtless enough to insure it an accepted place among the few greater poems in the language. Its profoundly thoughtful interpretation of some of the greater social problems mankind has to deal with, will necessarily give a permanent interest for the lovers of speculative poetry, while its genuine poetic merits will largely add to that interest, and add to it by its tragic power, its rich ethical wisdom, and its fine portrayal of character.

No other book of George Eliot's is so filled and inspired by the spirit of her teachings as *The Spanish Gypsy*. Its inspiration and its interest lie mainly in the direction of its moral and spiritual inculcations. Verse did not stimulate her, but was a fetter; it clogged her highest powers. The rich eloquence of her prose, with its pathos and sentiment, its broad perspective and vigorous thought, was to her a continual stimulus and incentive. Her poems are more labored than her novels, and for this very reason they show the philosophy which gives them meaning more clearly. Their greater concentration and less varied elements also largely help to make apparent the teachings they contain. Her sympathy with the evolution philosophy of the day is conspicuous in *The Spanish Gypsy*. It is simply a dramatic interpretation of the higher phases of Darwinism. The doctrinal element does not intrude itself, however; it is not on the surface, it is well subordinated to the artistic elements of the poem. Even intelligent readers may not detect it, and the majority of those who read the poem without any preconceptions may not discover its philosophic bearings. Yet to the studious reader the philosophy must be the most conspicuous element which enters into the poem, and it gives character and meaning to the work far more fully than in the case of any of her novels.

The aim of the poem is to show how hereditary race influences act as a tragic element in opposition to individual emotions and inclinations. The teaching of *Romola* is much of it reproduced, at least that portion of it which inculcates renunciation and altruism. Its distinguishing features, however, more nearly resemble those of *Daniel Deronda*. The race element is introduced, and the effect of the past is shown as it forms character and gives direction to duties. One phase of its meaning has been very clearly described by Mr. R. H. Hutton, who says the poem teaches "how the inheritance of the definite streams of impulse and tradition stored up in what we call race, often puts a veto upon any attempt of spontaneous individual emotion or volitions to ignore or defy their control, and to emancipate itself from the tyranny of their disputable and apparently cruel rule." "How the threads," he says again, "of hereditary capacity and hereditary sentiment control as with invisible chords the orbits of even the most powerful characters, — how the fracture of those threads, so far as can be accomplished by mere *will*, may have even a greater effect in wrecking character than moral degeneracy would itself produce, — how the man who trusts and uses the hereditary forces which natural descent has bestowed upon him, becomes a might and a centre in the world, while the man, intrinsically the nobler, who dissipates his strength by trying to swim against the stream of his past, is neutralized and paralyzed by the vain effort, — again, how a divided past, a past not really homogeneous, may weaken this kind of power, instead of strengthening it by the command of a larger experience — all this George Eliot's poem paints with tragical force."

The main thought of *The Spanish Gypsy* is, that the moral and spiritual in man is the result of social conditions which, if neglected, lead to the destruction of all that is best in human nature. In the description of Mine Host, in the opening pages of the poem, this evil result of a severing of life from tradition is described. He was educated in the Jewish faith, but was made a Christian at the age of ten.

> So he had to be converted with his sire,
> To doff the awe he learned as Ephriam,
> And suit his manners to a Christian name.

The poet then delivers one of her doctrinal utterances, and one which is in this case the keynote of the whole poem.

> But infant awe, that unborn moving thing,
> Dies with what nourished it, can never rise
> From the dead womb and walk and seek new pasture.

That awe which grows up in childhood, if destroyed later, brings anarchy into human life. All the characters of the poem exemplify this teaching, and each is but a product of his past, individual or social. Don Silva, Zarca, Fedalma, the Prior, Sephardo, illustrate this idea. The latter gives utterance to the thought of the poem, when Don Silva says to him that he has need of a friend who is not tied to sect or party, but who is capable of following his "naked manhood" into what is just and right, without regard to other considerations.

> My lord, I will be frank; there's no such thing
> As naked manhood. If the stars look down

On any mortal of our shape, whose strength
Is to judge all things without preference,
He is a monster, not a faithful man.
While my heart beats, it shall wear livery —
My people's livery, whose yellow badge
Marks them for Christian scorn. I will not say
Man is first man to me, then Jew or Gentile:
That suits the rich *marranos*;[1] but to me
My father is first father and then man.
So much for frankness' sake. But let that pass.
'Tis true at least, I am no Catholic
But Salomo Sephardo, a born Jew,
Willing to serve Don Silva.

In the conversation between Don Silva and this uncle, the Prior expresses in the strongest language his conviction that Fedalma will in time reveal her gypsy blood, and that any rejection on the part of Don Silva of the life assigned him by his birth will end in sorrow and misery. When Don Silva declares his intention of following his own inclinations the Prior answers, —

Your strength will turn to anguish, like the strength
Of fallen angels. Can you change your blood?
You are a Christian, with the Christian awe
In every vein. A Spanish noble, born
To serve your people and your people's faith.
Strong, are you? Turn your back upon the Cross —
Its shadow is before you. Leave your place:
Quit the great ranks of knighthood: you will walk
Forever with a tortured double self,
A self that will be hungry while you feast,
Will blush with shame while you are glorified,
Will feel the ache and chill of desolation
Even in the very bosom of your love.

This eloquent expostulation against rejection of any of those ties and obligations imposed by birth and race is repeated again in the plea of Zarca to his daughter, when he urges that there is no life and joy for Fedal-

[1] In a note George Eliot gives the following explanation of the word *marranos*: "The name given by the Spanish Jews to the multitudes of their race converted to Christianity at the end of the fourteenth century and beginning of the fifteenth. The lofty derivation from *Maran-atha*, the Lord cometh, seems hardly called for, seeing that *marrano* is Spanish for *pig*. The 'old Christians' learned to use the word as a term of contempt for the 'new Christians,' or converted Jews and their descendants; but not too monotonously, for they often interchanged it with the fine old crusted opprobrium of the name *Jew*. Still, many Marranos held the highest secular and ecclesiastical prizes in Spain, and were respected accordingly."

ma apart from that race to which she belongs and those social conditions which gave her mind its characteristics.

> Will you adopt a soul without its thoughts,
> Or grasp a life apart from flesh and blood?
> Till then you cannot wed a Spanish Duke
> And not wed shame at mention of your race,
> And not wed hardness to their miseries —
> Nay, wed not murder.

Zarca and the Prior are each faithful to race, religion and social tradition. Each knows his duty, is content with the opportunities given him by social inheritance, is thoroughly in harmony with his own past. Both are consequently strong, resolute, successful. Zarca is a grand character, and though a hero in a nation of vagabonds, he wholly identifies himself with his people and accepts their destiny as his own. The Prior is a haughty Spanish Churchman, who has inherited all the traits of a noble family, and is proud of his priestly functions.

In the case of Don Silva and Fedalma there is a conflict between love and race. The one is a Spanish nobleman, the other the daughter of a Zincala chief. Yet they love, and feel that no outward circumstances are sufficient to separate them. This verdict of their hearts is the verdict of mankind in all ages; but it is not the one arrived at by George Eliot in obedience to her philosophy. The reasons why these two should not wed grew entirely out of the social circumstances of the time. An English nobleman of to-day could marry such a woman as Fedalma without social or other loss. The capacities of soul are superior to conditions of race. Virtue and genius do not depend on social circumstances. Yet *The Spanish Gypsy* has for its motive the attempt to prove that the life of tradition and inheritance is the one which provides all our moral and social and religious obligations. In conformity with this theory the conflict of the poem arises, because Don Silva is not in intellectual harmony with his own character. A thoughtful, fastidious, sensitive soul was his, not resolute and concentrated in purpose. He was no bigot, could not be content with any narrow aim, saw good on many sides.

A man of high-wrought strain, fastidious
In his acceptance, dreading all delight
That speedy dies and turns to carrion:
His senses much exacting, deep instilled
With keen imagination's airy needs;—
Like strong-limbed monsters studded o'er with eyes,
Their hunger checked by overwhelming vision,
Or that fierce lion in symbolic dream
Snatched from the ground by wings and new-endowed
With a man's thought-propelled relenting heart.
Silva was both the lion and the man;
First hesitating shrank, then fiercely sprang,
Or having sprung, turned pallid at his deed
And loosed the prize, paying his blood for naught.
A nature half-transformed, with qualities
That oft bewrayed each other, elements
Not blent but struggling, breeding strange effects,
Passing the reckoning of his friends or foes.
Haughty and generous, grave and passionate;
With tidal moments of devoutest awe,
Sinking anon to furthest ebb of doubt;
Deliberating ever, till the sting
Of a recurrent ardor made him rush
Right against reasons that himself had drilled
And marshalled painfully. A spirit framed
Too proudly special for obedience,
Too subtly pondering for mastery:
Born of a goddess with a mortal sire,
Heir of flesh-fettered, weak divinity,
Doom-gifted with long resonant consciousness
And perilous heightening of the sentient soul.

Too noble and generous to accept the narrow views of his uncle, Don Silva insisted on marrying Fedalma, because he loved her and because she was a pure and true woman. He had a poet's nature, was sensitive to all beauty, and his heart vibrated to all ideal excellence. His love became to him a thing apart, a sacred shrine and Fedalma was made one with all joy and beauty.

He thought all loveliness was lovelier,
She crowning it; all goodness credible,
Because of that great trust her goodness bred.

His love gave a delicious content and melody to his day dreams.

O, all comforters,
All soothing things that bring mild ecstasy,
Came with her coming, in her presence lived.
Spring afternoons, when delicate shadows fall
Pencilled upon the grass; high summer morns
When white light rains upon the quiet sea
And cornfields flush with ripeness; odors soft —
Dumb vagrant bliss that seems to seek a home
And find it deep within 'mid stirrings vague
Of far-off moments when our life was fresh;
All sweetly tempered music, gentle change
Of sound, form, color, as on wide lagoons
At sunset when from black far-floating prows
Comes a clear wafted song; all exquisite joy
Of a subdued desire, like some strong stream
Made placid in the fulness of a lake —
All came with her sweet presence, for she brought
The love supreme which gathers to its realm
All powers of loving. Subtle nature's hand
Waked with a touch the far-linked harmonies
In her own manifold work. Fedalma there,
Fastidiousness became the prelude fine
For full contentment; and young melancholy,
Lost for its origin, seemed but the pain
Of waiting for that perfect happiness.

So strong was Don Silva's love, so ardent his passion for Fedalma, that he forsook all duties and social obligations and became a Zincala for her sake. Yet once awakened to the real consequences of his act, he killed Zarca and sought to regain by hard penances his lost knighthood.

With Fedalma also love was an absorbing passion. The passionate devotion of a woman is in her words.

No ills on earth, though you should count them up
With grains to make a mountain, can outweigh
For me his ill who is my supreme love.
All sorrows else are but imagined flames,
Making me shudder at an unfelt smart;
But his imagined sorrow is a fire
That scorches me.

With great earnestness she says she will —

Never forsake that chief half of her soul
Where lies her love.

With what depth of love does she utter these words:

I belong to him who loves me — whom I love —
Who chose me — whom I chose — to whom I pledged
A woman's truth. And that is nature too,
Issuing a fresher law than laws of birth.

Though her love is deep and passionate and full of a woman's devotedness, the mark of race is set deep within her soul. The moment the claim of race is brought clearly before her as the claim of duty, as the claim of father and of kindred, she accepts it. Her love is not thrown hastily aside, for she loves deeply and truly, and it tears her heart in sunder to renounce it; but she is faithful to duty. Her love grows not less, loses none of its hold upon her heart.

No other crown
Is aught but thorns on my poor woman's brow.

Hers is not a divided self, however; to see the way of duty with her, was to follow in it. Her father's invincible will, courage and patient purpose are her own by inheritance. Once realizing the claim of birth and race, she does not falter, love is resolutely put aside, all delight in culture and refinement becomes dross in her eyes.

I will not count
On aught but being faithful. I will take
This yearning self of mine and strangle it.
I will not be half-hearted: never yet
Fedalma did aught with a wavering soul.
Die, my young joy — die, all my hungry hopes!
The milk you cry for from the breast of life
Is thick with curses. O, all fatness here
Snatches its meat from leanness — feeds on graves.
I will seek nothing but to shun base joy.
The saints were cowards who stood by to see
Christ crucified: they should have flung themselves
Upon the Roman spears, and died in vain —
The grandest death, to die in vain — for love
Greater than sways the forces of the world!
That death shall be my bridegroom. I will wed
The curse that blights my people. Father, come!

The poem distinctly teaches that Fedalma was strong, because the ties of blood were strongly marked upon her mind and willingly accepted by her intellect and conscience; while Don Silva was weak, because he did not acknowledge those ties and accept their law. In the end, however, both declare that the inherited life is the only one which gives joy or duty, and that all individual aims and wishes are to be renounced. The closing scene of this great poem is full of sadness, and yet is strong with moral purpose. Don Silva and Fedalma meet for the last time, she on her way to Africa with her tribe to find a home for it there, he on his way to Rome, to seek the privilege of again using his knightly sword. Both are sad, both feel that life has lost all its joy, both believe it is a bitter destiny which divides them from the fulfilment of their love, and yet both are convinced that love must be forsworn for a higher duty. Their last conversation, opened by Don Silva, is full of power, and concentrates into its last words the total meaning of the poem.

I bring no puling prayer, Fedalma — ask
No balm of pardon that may soothe my soul
For others' bleeding wounds: I am not come
To say, "Forgive me:" you must not forgive,
For you must see me ever as I am —
Your father's . . .

FEDALMA.

Speak it not! Calamity
Comes like a deluge and o'erfloods our crimes,
Till sin is hidden in woe. You — I — we two,
Grasping we knew not what, that seemed delight,
Opened the sluices of that deep.

DON SILVA.

We two? —
Fedalma, you were blameless, helpless.

FEDALMA.

No!
It shall not be that you did aught alone.
For when we loved I willed to reign in you,
And I was jealous even of the day
If it could gladden you apart from me.

And so, it must be that I shared each deed
Our love was root of.

DON SILVA.

Dear! you share the woe —
Nay, the worst part of vengeance fell on you.

FEDALMA.

Vengeance! She does but sweep us with her skirts.
She takes large space, and lies a baleful light
Revolving with long years — sees children's children,
Blights them in their prime. Oh, if two lovers leane
To breathe one air and spread a pestilence,
They would but lie two livid victims dead
Amid the city of the dying. We
With our poor petty lives have strangled one
That ages watch for vainly.

DON SILVA.

Deep despair
Fills all your tones as with slow agony.
Speak words that narrow anguish to some shape:
Tell me what dread is close before you?

FEDALMA.

None.
No dread, but clear assurance of the end.
My father held within his mighty frame
A people's life: great futures died with him
Never to rise, until the time shall ripe
Some other hero with the will to save
The outcast Zincali.

DON SILVA.

And yet their shout —
I heard it — sounded as the plenteous rush
Of full-fed sources, shaking their wild souls
With power that promised sway.

FEDALMA.

Ah yes, that shout
Came from full hearts: they meant obedience.
But they are orphaned: their poor childish feet
Are vagabond in spite of love, and stray
Forgetful after little lures. For me —
I am but as the funeral urn that bears
The ashes of a leader.

DON SILVA.

O great God!
What am I but a miserable brand

Lit by mysterious wrath? I lie cast down
A blackened branch upon the desolate ground
Where once I kindled ruin. I shall drink
No cup of purest water but will taste
Bitter with thy lone hopelessness, Fedalma.

FEDALMA.

Nay, Silva, think of me as one who sees
A light serene and strong on one sole path
Which she will tread till death . . .
He trusted me, and I will keep his trust:
My life shall be its temple. I will plant
His sacred hope within the sanctuary
And die its priestess — though I die alone,
A hoary woman on the altar-step,
Cold 'mid cold ashes. That is my chief good.
The deepest hunger of a faithful heart
Is faithfulness. Wish me naught else. And you —
You too will live. . . .

DON SILVA.

I go to Rome, to seek
The right to use my knightly sword again;
The right to fill my place and live or die
So that all Spaniards shall not curse my name.
I sate one hour upon the barren rock
And longed to kill myself; but then I said,
I will not leave my name in infamy,
I will not be perpetual rottenness
Upon the Spaniard's air. If I must sink
At last to hell, I will not take my stand
Among the coward crew who could not bear
The harm themselves had done, which others bore.
My young life yet may fill some fatal breach,
And I will take no pardon, not my own,
Not God's — no pardon idly on my knees;
But it shall come to me upon my feet
And in the thick of action, and each deed
That carried shame and wrong shall be the sting
That drives me higher up the steep of honor
In deeds of duteous service to that Spain
Who nourished me on her expectant breast,
The heir of highest gifts. I will not fling
My earthly being down for carrion
To fill the air with loathing: I will be
The living prey of some fierce noble death
That leaps upon me while I move. Aloud
I said, "I will redeem my name," and then —
I know not if aloud: I felt the words
Drinking up all my senses — "She still lives.

I would not quit the dear familiar earth
Where both of us behold the self-same sun,
Where there can be no strangeness 'twixt our thoughts
So deep as their communion." Resolute
I rose and walked. — Fedalma, think of me
As one who will regain the only life
Where he is other than apostate — one
Who seeks but to renew and keep the vows
Of Spanish knight and noble. But the breach —
Outside those vows — the fatal second breach —
Lies a dark gulf where I have naught to cast,
Not even expiation — poor pretence,
Which changes naught but what survives the past,
And raises not the dead. That deep dark gulf
Divide us.

FEDALMA.

Yes, forever. We must walk
Apart unto the end. Our marriage rite
Is our resolve that we will each be true
To high allegiance, higher than our love.
Our dear young love — its breath was happiness!
But it had grown upon a larger life
Which tore its roots asunder. We rebelled —
The larger life subdued us. Yet we are wed;
For we shall carry each the pressure deep
Of the other's soul. I soon shall leave the shore.
The winds to-night will bear me far away.
My lord, farewell!

What has been said of *The Spanish Gypsy* applies very nearly as well to all her other poems. They are thoughtful, philosophic, realistic; they are sonorous in expression, stately in style, and of a diction eloquent and beautiful. On the whole, the volume containing the shorter poems is a poetical advance on *The Spanish Gypsy*, containing more genuine poetry, more lyrical fire, and a greater proportion of humor, sympathy and passion. They are carefully polished and refined; and yet that indefinable something which marks the truest poetry is wanting. They are saturated with her ideas, the flavor of her thought impregnates them all, with but two or three exceptions.

Her artistic conceptions are more fully developed in some of these poems than in any of her novels, especially in "Armgart" and "The Legend of Jubal." The special thought of "Armgart" is, that no artistic success is of so much worth as a loving sympathy with others. The longing of Armgart was to be —

> a happy spiritual star
> Such as old Dante saw, wrought in a rose
> Of light in Paradise, whose only self
> Was consciousness of glory wide-diffused,
> Music, life, power — I moving in the midst
> With a sublime necessity of good.

Her ambition runs very high.

> May the day be near when men
> Think much to let my horses draw me home,
> And new lands welcome me upon their beach,
> Loving me for my fame. That is the truth
> Of what I wish, nay, yearn for. Shall I lie?
> Pretend to seek obscurity — to sing
> In hope of disregard? A vile pretence!
> And blasphemy besides. For what is fame
> But the benignant strength of One, transformed
> To joy of Many? Tributes, plaudits come
> As necessary breathing of such joy;
> And may they come to me!

Armgart is beloved of the Graf, and he tries to persuade her to abandon her artistic career and become his wife. He says to her, —

> A woman's rank
> Lies in the fulness of her womanhood:
> Therein alone she is loyal.

Again he says to her, —

> Pain had been saved,
> Nay, purer glory reached, had you been throned
> As woman only, holding all your art
> As attribute to that dear sovereignty —
> Concentering your power in home delights
> Which penetrate and purify the world.

Armgart will not listen; her whole heart is enlisted in music. She says to the Graf, —

> I will live alone and pour my pain
> With passion into music, where it turns
> To what is best within my better self.

A year later Armgart's throat has failed, and her career has ended in nothing. Then her servant and friend, Walpurga, who has devoted her life to Armgart, speaks that lesson George Eliot would convey in this little story, that a true life is a life of service. Walpurga chides Armgart's false ambition in these words:

> I but stand
> As a small symbol for the mighty sum
> Of claims unpaid to needy myriads;
> I think you never set your loss beside
> That mighty deficit. Is your work gone —
> The prouder queenly work that paid itself
> And yet was overpaid with men's applause!
> Are you no longer chartered, privileged,
> But sunk to simple woman's penury,
> To ruthless Nature's chary average —
> Where is the rebel's right for you alone?
> *Noble rebellion lifts a common load;*
> But what is he who flings his own load off
> And leaves his fellows toiling? Rebel's right?
> Say, rather, the deserter's.

Armgart learns from her master, the old and noble Leo, that he had also been ambitious, that he had won only small success, and that he now lived for the sake of the good he could do to those about him. He says to her, —

> We must bury our dead joys,
> And live above them with a living world.

Then Armgart is brought to see that there is a noble privilege in living as her friend has lived, in making music a joy to others, and in doing what she can to make .ife better for humanity.

There are two very distinct ideas running through the poem, that a life guided by altruism is better than a merely artistic life, and that woman is to find in home and wedded joys that opportunity for the development of her soul, without which no artistic career can be complete. The words of the Graf speak George Eliot's own thought, that Armgart's life and her art would have been both more perfect and more noble had she held all her art as attribute to the dear sovereignty of affection.

The same artistic conception pervades "The Legend of Jubal." That fame for which Jubal also yearns comes to him, he is taught, in the good which he leaves behind him for humanity to enjoy. He dies, and ceases to be as a personal being. At least this may be inferred from the concluding lines.

> Quitting mortality, a quenched sun-wave,
> The All-creating Presence for his grave.

A *sun-wave* while living, his being is now *quenched*. But he lives on in the life of the race, lives on in man's joy of music, in the deeper life which music awakens in all bosoms through all ages. He is told that he has no need of —

> aught else for share
> Of mortal good, than in his soul to bear
> The growth of song, and feel the sweet unrest
> Of the world's springtide in his conscious breast.

His own loved Past says to him, —

> This was thy lot, to feel, create, bestow,
> And that immeasurable life to know
> From which the fleshly self falls shrivelled, dead,
> A seed primeval that has forests bred.

This poem views death as positivism conceives it, and gives a poetic interpretation of that subjective immortality, or that immortality in the race, in which George Eliot so heartily believed. No other artistic presentation of this theory has ever been made which equals that given in this poem, and in the one beginning, "O may I join the choir invisible." This latter poem is not only beautiful in itself, but it has made altruism attractive and lovely. Its tone of thought is elevated, its spirit lofty and noble, and its ideal pure and gracious. All that can be said to make altruism lovely and winning, to inspire men with its spirit and motive, is here said. The thought presented in these two poems is repeated in "The Death of Moses." Here we have Moses living forever in the human influence he created.

> He dwells not with you dead, but lives as Law.

For her ideas about resignation we must turn to the pages of *The Mill on the Floss* and *Romola*, for those about heredity and the past to *The Spanish Gypsy* and *Daniel Deronda;* but in these shorter poems she has completely unfolded the positivist conception, as she accepted it, of death and immortality. The degree to which she was moved and inspired by this belief in an immortality in humanity is seen in the greater ardor and poetic merit of these poems than any others she wrote.

It is interesting to note that she introduces music into "The Legend of Jubal" and "Armgart." It was the art she most loved. She even said that if she could possess the power most satisfactory to her heart, it would be that of making music the instrument of the homage which the great performers secure. Yet she teaches in "Armgart" that there is a power higher than this, the power of affectionate service. Her books are full of the praise of music. She makes Maggie Tulliver express her own delight in it.

> "I think I should have no other mortal wants, if I could always have plenty of music. It seems to infuse strength into my limbs, and ideas into my brain. Life seems to go on without effort, when I am filled with music."

In *Adam Bede* she becomes most poetic when extolling the power of exquisite music to work on the soul.

> To feel its wondrous harmonies searching the subtlest windings of your soul, the delicate fibres of life wherein memory can penetrate, and binding together your whole being, past and present, in one unspeakable vibration, melting you in one moment with all the tenderness, all the love, that has been scattered through the toilsome years, concentrating in one emotion of heroic courage or resignation all the hard-learnt lessons of self-renouncing sympathy, blending your present joy with past sorrow, and your present sorrow with all your past joy.

In the "Minor Prophet" is to be found George Eliot's theory of progress. That poem also repeats her faith in common humanity, and gives new emphasis to her joy in the common toils and affections of men. In the "College Breakfast Party" and "Self and Life," her thoughts take a more truly philosophic form than in any of her other poems, but the first of these is the poorest piece of poetic work she gave to the public. Nothing new in the way of teaching appears in these or her other poems.

George Eliot is the poet of positivism. What is beautiful, touching and inspiring in that conception of the world she has sung, and in as poetic a manner as that philosophy is ever likely to inspire. Her poetry is full of the thoughts and sentiments of the time. It reflects the mood of her generation. Prof. Sidney Colvin has truly said that "there is nothing in the literature of the day so rousing — to the mind of the day there is scarcely anything so rousing in all literature — as her writing is. What she writes is full of her time. It is full of observation, imagination, pathos, wit and humor, all of a high class in themselves; but what is more, all saturated with modern ideas poured into a language of which every word bites home with peculiar sharpness to the contemporary consciousness." This is true even more of her poetry than of her prose. That poetry lacks where the age lacks, in true poetic quality. The ideal, the breath of eternal spring, is not in it.

XVIII.

LATER ESSAYS.

THE later essays of George Eliot have the same characteristics as the earlier ones, and are mainly of interest because they furnish additional evidences of her philosophical, ethical and political opinions. While they indicate the profound thoughtfulness of her mind, her deep concern about the largest problems of human existence, and her rare ethical tone and purpose, they add little or nothing to her literary reputation. It is very plain that while George Eliot was not a poet in the largest, truest sense, she was still less an essayist in that genial, widely sympathetic sense which has adorned English literature with so many noble books of comment on the foibles and the virtues of man. Her manner is heavy, her thoughts philosophical, her purpose doctrinal; and the result is far from satisfactory to the lover of fine essay-writing.

She needs the glow of her imagination, the depth of her emotions, to relieve and lighten the burden of her thoughts. But in her essays she is less wise, less racy and expressive, than in the didactic passages of her novels. She could best make her comment on the ways of life while describing a character or studying an action. These additions to her narrative and conversation are, to the thoughtful reader, among the best portions of her novels, for they give meaning to all the rest, and throw a flood of light on the hidden facts of life. She is never so great, so wise, so profoundly inspired by her theme, as in many of these passages.

There is need, however, in her case, of the large

surrounding life of her novels in order to draw out this wisdom and inspiration. Her essays lack in the fine sentiment and the fervid eloquence of the chorus-utterances in her novels. They give little evidence that she would have attained to great things had she followed the early purpose of her life. In view of what she has written in the shape of essays, no one can regret that she confined her chief efforts to her imaginative prose creations. Yet her essays have a special value on account of their subjects, and they will be read by many with a hearty appreciation, simply because they were George Eliot's. No one thoroughly interested in the work done by the great realistic novelist can afford to overlook her essays, even if they do not nearly touch the highest mark in their kind.

After she began her career as a novelist George Eliot wrote about twenty essays, nearly all of which are included in her last book, *Impressions of Theophrastus Such*. Previous to this, however, she had published in the first number of the *Fortnightly Review*, issued May 15, 1865, and edited by Lewes, an article on "The Influence of Rationalism," in review of Mr. W. H. Lecky's book on that subject. A year after the appearance of *Felix Holt* she wrote out her views on the subject of political reform, in the shape of an "Address to Workingmen by Felix Holt," which appeared in *Blackwood's Magazine* for January, 1868. These essays are significant, because of the light they afford concerning the author's views on religious and political subjects. The first is a piece of thorough reviewing, and shows what George Eliot might have done in that direction. She is a merciless critic, and yet one inclined to appreciate all that is best in an author. Her sympathies with positivism and with the "scientific method" in philosophy find expression in the pages of this essay. In it she gives a most expressive utterance to her ideas about the universality of law and the influence of tradition. Her point of view is so antagonistic to Mr Lecky's that she does not do full justice to his work. His idealism is repugnant to her, and he does not give prominence enough to please her to those positivist influences in which she so strongly believed. Her dissatisfaction with his idealism appears in her very first words.

There is a valuable class of books on great subjects which have something of the character and functions of good popular lecturing. They are not original, not subtle, not of close logical texture, not exquisite either in thought or style; but by virtue of these negatives they are all the more fit to act on the average intelligence. They have enough of organizing purpose in them to make their facts illustrative, and to leave a distinct result in the mind even when most of the facts are forgotten; and they have enough of vagueness and vacillation in their theory to win them ready acceptance from a mixed audience. The vagueness and vacillation are not devices of timidity; they are the honest result of the writer's own mental character, which adapts him to be the instructor and the favorite of "the general reader." For the most part, the general reader of the present day does not exactly know what distance he goes; he only knows that he does not go "too far." Of any remarkable thinker, whose writings have excited controversy, he likes to have it said "that his errors are to be deplored," leaving it not too certain what those errors are; he is fond of what may be called disembodied opinions, that float in vapory phrases above all systems of thought or action; he likes an undefined Christianity which opposes itself to nothing in particular, an undefined education of the people, an undefined amelioration of all things in fact, he likes sound views—nothing extreme, but something between the excesses of the past and the excesses of the present. This modern type of the general reader may be known in conversation by the cordiality with which he assents to indistinct, blurred statements. Say that black is black, he will shake his head and hardly think it; say that black is not so very black, he will reply, "Exactly." He has no hesitation, if you wish it, even to get up at a public meeting and express his conviction that at times, and within certain limits, the radii of a circle have a tendency to be equal; but, on the other hand, he would urge that the spirit of geometry may be carried a little too far. His only bigotry is a bigotry against any clearly defined opinion; not in the least based on a scientific scepticism, but belonging to a lack of coherent thought—a spongy texture of mind, that gravitates strongly to nothing. The one thing he is staunch for is the utmost liberty of private haziness.

But precisely these characteristics of the general reader, rendering him incapable of assimilating ideas unless they are administered in a highly diluted form, make it a matter of rejoicing that there are clever, fair-minded men who will write books for him—men very much above him in knowledge and ability, but not too remote from him in their habits of thinking, and who can thus prepare for him infusions of history and science that will leave some solidifying deposit, and save him from a fatal softening of the intellectual skeleton. Among such serviceable writers, Mr. Lecky's *History of the Rise and Influence of the Spirit of Rationalism in Europe* entitles him to a high place. He has prepared himself for its production by an unusual amount of well-directed reading; he has chosen his facts and quotations with much judgment; and he gives proof of those important moral qualifications, impartiality, seriousness and modesty. This praise is chiefly applicable to the long chapter on the history of Magic and Witchcraft, and to the two chapters on the antecedents and history of Persecution.

A further evidence of her wide culture and reading, and of her large critical ability, may also be found in the first number of the *Fortnightly Review*, for which she wrote the first of the "notices of new books" which it published. This was a review of Mr. Owen Jones's *Grammar of Ornament*. The author was one of her friends, and the decorator of the rooms in which her Sunday receptions were held. She praised the book very highly. The first paragraph of this notice betrays her appreciation of the æsthetic movement in England, and her sympathy with its objects and spirit. The moral value of æsthetic influences is characteristically expressed. The influence of the environment, as she understood it, is here seen. The largeness of her faith in the moral efficiency of material causes is nowhere so strongly expressed by her as in the words which follow.

The inventor of movable types, says the venerable Teufelsdröckh, was disbanding hired armies, cashiering most kings and senates, and creating a whole new democratic world. Has any one yet said what great things are being done by the men who are trying to banish ugliness from our streets and our homes, and to make both the outside and the inside of our dwellings worthy of a world where there are forests, and flower-tressed meadows, and the plumage of birds; where the insects carry lessons of color on their wings, and even the surface of a stagnant pool will show us the wonders of iridescence and the most delicate forms of leafage? They, too, are modifying opinions, for they are modifying men's moods and habits, which are the mothers of opinions, having quite as much to do with their formation as the responsible father — Reason. Think of certain hideous manufacturing towns where the piety is chiefly a belief in copious perdition, and the pleasure is chiefly gin. The dingy surface of wall pierced by the ugliest windows, the staring shop-fronts, paper-hangings, carpets, brass and gilt mouldings, and advertising placards, have an effect akin to that of malaria; it is easy to understand that with such surroundings there is more belief in cruelty than in beneficence, and that the best earthly bliss attainable is the dulling of the external senses. For it is a fatal mistake to suppose that ugliness which is taken for beauty will answer all the purposes of beauty; the subtle relation between all kinds of truth and fitness in our life forbids that bad taste should ever be harmless to our moral sensibility or our intellectual discernment; and — more than that — as it is probable that fine musical harmonies have a sanative influence over our bodily organization, it is also probable that just coloring and lovely combinations of lines may be necessary to the complete well-being of our systems, apart from any conscious delight in them. A savage may indulge in discordant chuckles and shrieks and gutturals, and think that they please the gods, but it does not follow that his frame would not be favorably wrought upon by the vibrations of a grand church organ. One sees a person capable of choosing the worst style of wall-paper become suddenly afflicted by its ugliness under an attack of illness. And if an evil state of blood and lymph usually goes along with an evil state of mind, who shall say that the ugliness of our streets, the falsity of our ornamentation, the vulgarity of our upholstery, have not something to do with those bad tempers which breed false conclusions?

The address to workingmen which George Eliot put into the mouth of Felix Holt is a suggestive and valuable piece of political writing. Tradition is therein presented as a moral and political influence. The spiritual treasures mankind possesses she says are the products of tradition, and these must be preserved. This can be done only by keeping the old institutions and forms until they can be organically supplanted by others. All the various portions of society are mutually dependent, and the destruction of any one of them will be to the injury of all. This she says to workingmen as a reason why they should not antagonize the social orders above them, whose work is as important as their own. The organs of society are the various social classes of which it is composed, and society is to be improved by turning class interests into the functions by which Humanity is to be developed. The spiritual treasures of the past are only to be preserved by order and good government; hence all revolutionary methods are suicidal. Life is to be advanced by giving social influence into the hands of the wisest. True principles must regulate society, and these George Eliot would have rest on science and altruism.

Such are some of the ideas of this remarkable essay, one of the most suggestive and instructive of all she wrote. The emphasis she laid on retribution, tradition, heredity and duties appears here in all its force. Perhaps nothing else she wrote so clearly brings out some of the characteristics of her mind. Her intense distrust of individualism does not permit her to say a single word of the *rights* of the laboring classes. The right of rebellion and revolution is totally disregarded, rather it is not recognized that any rights whatever exist. The workingman is not to think of himself or his class, but of society and humanity ; he is to become an altruistic worker for the common good. While this is fine in theory, yet history indicates that the aristocratic classes have yielded to the broader social spirit only when they have been compelled to do so. The concessions must come from above, not from beneath. George Eliot's political philosophy, if carried into actual life, would keep the proletariate where they are, and strengthen the social power of the aristocratic classes. These words may indicate the drift of the essay :

But I come back to this: that, in our old society there are old institutions, and among them the various distinctions and inherited advantages of classes, which have shaped themselves along with all the wonderful slow-growing system of things made up of our laws, our commerce and our stores of all sorts, whether in material objects, such as buildings and machinery, or in knowledge, such as scientific thought and professional skill. Just as in that case I spoke of before, the irrigation of a country, which must absolutely have its water distributed or it will bear no crop; these are the old channels, the old banks and the old pumps, which must be used as they are until new and better have been prepared, or the structure of the old has been gradually altered. But it would be fool's work to batter down a pump only because a better might be made, when you have no machinery ready for a new one : it would be wicked work, if villages lost their crops by it. Now the only safe way by which society can be steadily improved and our worst evils reduced, is not by any attempt to do away directly with the actually existing class distinctions and advantages, as if everybody could have the same sort of work or lead the same sort of life (which none of my hearers are stupid enough to suppose), but by turning of Class Interests into Class Functions or duties. What I mean is, that each class should be urged by the surrounding conditions to perform its particular work under the strong pressure of responsibility to the nation at large; that our public affairs should be got into a state in which there should be no impunity for foolish or faithless conduct. In this way, the public judgment would sift out incapability and dishonesty from posts of high charge, and even personal ambition would necessarily become of a worthier sort, since the desires of the most selfish men must be a good deal shaped by the opinions of those around them; and for one person to put on a cap and bells, or to go about dishonest or paltry ways of getting rich that he may spend a vast sum of money in having more finery than his neighbors, he must be pretty sure of a crowd who will applaud him. Now changes can only be good in proportion as they help to bring about this sort of result: in proportion as they put knowledge in the place of ignorance, and fellow-feeling in the place of selfishness. In the course of substitution class distinctions must inevitably change their character, and represent the varying Duties of men, not their varying Interests. But this end will not come by impatience. "Day will not break the sooner because we get up before the twilight." Still less will it come by mere undoing, or change merely as change. And moreover, if we believed that it would be unconditionally hastened by our getting the franchise, we should be what I call superstitious men, believing in magic, or the production of a result by hocus-pocus. Our getting the franchise will greatly hasten that good end in proportion only as every one of us has the knowledge, the foresight, the conscience, that will make him well-judging and scrupulous in the use of it. The nature of things in this world has been determined for us beforehand, and in such a way that no ship can be expected to sail well on a difficult voyage, and reach the right port, unless it is well-manned: the nature of the winds and the waves, of the timbers, the sails and the cordage, will not accommodate itself to drunken, mutinous sailors.

You will not suspect me of wanting to preach any cant to you, or of joining in the pretence that everything is in a fine way and need not be made better. What I am striving to keep in our minds is the care, the precaution, with which we should go about making things better, so that the public order may not be destroyed, so that no fatal shock may be given to this society of ours, this living body in which our lives are bound up. After the Reform Bill of 1832, I was in an election riot, which showed me clearly, on a small scale, what public disorder must always be; and I have never forgotten that the riot was brought about chiefly by the agency of dishonest men who professed to be on the people's side. Now the danger hanging over change is great, just in proportion as it tends to produce such disorder by giving any large number of ignorant men, whose notions of what is good are of a low and brutal sort, the belief that they have got power into their hands and may do pretty much as they like. If any one can look round us and say that he sees no signs of any such danger now, and that our national condition is running along like a clear broadening stream, safe not to get choked with mud, I call him a cheerful man; perhaps he does his own gardening, and seldom takes exercise far away from home. To us who have no gardens, and often walk abroad, it is plain that we can never get into a bit of a crowd but we must rub clothes with a set of roughs, who have the worst vices of the worst rich — who are gamblers, sots, libertines, knaves, or else mere sensual simpletons and victims. They are the ugly crop that has sprung up while the stewards have been sleeping; they are the multiplying brood begotten by parents who have been left without all teaching save that of a too-craving body, without all well-being save the fading delusions of drugged beer and gin. They are the hideous margin of society, at one edge drawing towards it the undesigning ignorant poor, at the other darkening imperceptibly into the lowest criminal class. Here is one of the evils which cannot be got rid of quickly, and against which any of us who have got sense, decency and instruction have need to watch. That these degraded fellow-men could really get the mastery in a persistent disobedience to the laws and in a struggle to subvert order, I do not believe; but wretched calamities would come from the very beginning of such a struggle, and the continuance of it would be a civil war, in which the inspiration on both sides might soon cease to be even a false notion of good, and might become the direct savage impulse of ferocity. We have all to see to it that we do not help to rouse what I may call the savage beast in the breasts of our generation — that we do not help to poison the nation's blood, and make richer provision for bestiality to come. We know well enough that oppressors have sinned in this way — that oppression has notoriously made men mad; and we are determined to resist oppression. But let us, if possible, show that we can keep sane in our resistance, and shape our means more and more reasonably towards the least harmful, and therefore the speediest, attainment of our end. Let us, I say, show that our spirits are too strong to be driven mad, but can keep that sober determination which alone gives mastery over the adaptation of means. And a first guarantee of this sanity will be to act as if we understood that the fundamental duty of a government is to preserve order, to enforce obedience of the laws. It has been held hitherto that a man can be depended on as a guardian of order only when he has much money and comfort to lose. But a better state of things would be, that men who had little money and not much comfort should still be guardians of order, because they had sense to see that disorder would do no good, and had a heart of justice, pity and fortitude to keep them from making more misery only because they felt some misery themselves. There are thousands of artisans who have already shown this fine spirit, and have endured much with patient heroism. If such a spirit spread and penetrated us all, we should soon become the masters of the country in the best sense and to the best ends. For, the public order being preserved, there can be no government in future that will not be determined by our insistence on our fair and practicable demands. It is only by disorder that our demands will be choked, that we shall find ourselves lost amongst a brutal rabble, with all the intelligence of the country opposed to us, and see government in the shape of guns that will sweep us down in the ignoble martyrdom of fools.

The eighteen essays published as the *Impressions of Theophrastus Such* purport to have been the work of a bachelor of singular habits and tastes, who had written a book which proved a failure, and who left this volume to appear posthumously. He had been in the habit of giving an account to himself of the characters he met with, and he begins his book by describing his own weaknesses. He classes himself as one of the blunderers he would portray, as having the faults and foibles he finds in others. Expressively the author says, "If the human race has a bad reputation, I perceive that I cannot escape being compromised." This may be taken as the sentiment of George Eliot herself; and it is she who really speaks in these words concerning the satirical criticisms of those she describes:

If I laugh at you, O fellow-men! if I trace with curious interest your labyrinthine self-delusions, note the inconsistencies in your zealous adhesions, and smile at your helpless endeavors in a rashly chosen part, it is not that I feel myself aloof from you: the more intimately I seem to discern your weaknesses, the stronger to me is the proof that I share them. How otherwise could I get the discernment?—for even what we are averse to, what we vow not to entertain, must have shaped or shadowed itself within us as a possibility before we can think of exorcising it. No man can know his brother simply as a spectator.

After the second essay Theophrastus disappears, and no further hint is given that it is he who is the reputed author. This slight fictitious machinery is too weak to carry the load put upon it. The reader soon feels that it is George Eliot who is talking, and the opinions put forth, the sentiments expressed, are recognized as her own. Indeed, it would have been better, so the reader may probably come to say to himself, if this attempted disguise had been entirely dispensed with. By the time he has reached the sixth essay, "Only Temper," the discerning reader, familiar with George Eliot's books, will be ready to affirm that this is no other than the author herself speaking very frankly and finely her own sentiments. In this essay the moral temper of her mind appears, and her strong inclination to subordinate the individual to the social requirements of life.

These papers are modelled on those of the great essay-making period in English literature. Old-fashioned names are adopted, which have a greater or less significance in connection with the purpose of the essay. The man with the excitable temper is called Touchwood, while the man who slides into a deferential acceptance of opinions made for him is Mixtus. This method of the old essayists seems antiquated, cumbersome and unsuitable to the subjects discussed. The persons described lose their individuality by its use, and the reader forgets that they were meant to be creatures of flesh and blood. For the most part, they are mere abstractions, mere figures of straw, to be knocked over by the ingenious pen of the author. Some special fault or sin is given the name of a personality, but it is too much isolated from actual existence to produce the impression of a living thing.

These essays much resemble occasional chapters in her novels, and might have been studies for a new work. They are studies simply, done with a fine skill and polish, but fragmentary. The large setting of her novels is needed to give them relief and proportion. They disappoint as they are, for the satire is too apparent, and we do not see these characters in action, where their follies would obtain for them a more living interest. They are studies of individual character, portraying types of social and literary weakness, such as may have come under George Eliot's observation. They are careful dissections of motives and conduct, and full of a minute analysis of the moral and intellectual nature of her characters. There is abundance of candid criticism, shrewd observation and compressed wisdom of statement. Occasionally she is at her very best; but she uses many long, cumbersome sentences, the satire is too harsh and the wisdom too unwieldy. Her sympathy, love, pathos and pity are not so apparent as in her novels; she takes less delight in these creations, and evidently created them for purposes of dissection. She is never so weak in her other writings as in these essays, so wanting in genius and large-heartedness. She scourges many of the intellectual follies of the time, the conceit of culture, the pride of literature, and the narrowness of politics; but in most of the essays this is all.

The artistic conception of the book is too slight and fragmentary, and it gives the impression of being unfinished in execution and desultory in purpose. Yet there is in it much of fine feeling, pure sentiment, lively satire and apt wisdom. Sometimes the thought is labored; but there is a wealth of clear-cut conviction, strong thoughts and rich experience. There is force in the arguments, richness of ideas throughout, and a wonderful aptness of allusion and illustration. Her culture and learning are everywhere apparent in the fine perception of the most exact analogies and in the ease with which she brings science to the support of morals. Those of her admirers who come closest to her spirit, thoroughly appreciate her ideas, and delight in them, will read this book with satisfaction, and feel thankful that she wrote it. No one who would know the mind of George Eliot can afford to overlook it.

When George Eliot writes on subjects involving a moral purpose or ideal, she is always wise and interesting. When, however, she attempts to satirize some weakness or laugh at some folly, she is not always successful. Rich as may be the satire and the wit of her novels, both are often heavy and dull in her essays.

The greater number of essays in this volume are devoted to the analysis of special types of character, but a few are given to moral problems. These latter are of the more interest and value, and they present some new discussions of those problems with which George Eliot was so much fascinated. Her earnest faith in altruism, realism, tradition, natural retribution and the social value of morality, is as distinct here as in her novels or poems. In the essay on "False Testimonials" she gives a good realistic definition of imagination, which she says is "always based on a keen vision, a keen consciousness of what *is*, and carries the store of definite knowledge as material for the construction of its inward visions." She is no realist, however, in the sense of confining poetry merely to a photographic picture of outward nature. She accepts Dante as a genuine realist, for "he is at once the most precise and homely in his reproduction of actual objects, and the most soaringly at large in his imaginative combinations." She would have faithfulness to facts, but no limitation of vision; she would have the imagings exact and legitimate, but she would give our moral and intellectual insights no narrow bounds. Her realism is well defined when she criticises one of those persons who take mere fancy for imagination, to whom all facts are unworthy of recognition.

In at least two of these essays, those on "Debasing the Moral Currency" and "The Modern Hep, Hep, Hep!" she has newly expressed herself concerning tradition. In the first she protests against the too-common custom of satirizing what is noble and venerable. Our need of faith in the higher things of life is very great, and that faith is to be established only through our regard for what has been given us by those who have gone before us. Whatever lowers our trust in the results of human efforts is corrupting, for it breaks down our faith in the true sources of human authority. "This is what I call debasing the moral currency," she says; "lowering the value of every inspiring fact and tradition so that it will command less and less of the spiritual products, the generous motives which sustain the charm and elevation of our social existence — the something besides bread by which man saves his soul alive." With her conception of tradition, as the legitimate source of the moral and spiritual life in man, and as the influence which builds up all which is truest and purest in our civilization, she can endure to see no contempt put upon its products. This essay, more perhaps than anything else she wrote, gives an insight into her conception of the higher life and her total lack of faith in any idealistic sources of human motive or inspiration. Contempt for the traditional, with her, implies contempt for the spiritual and moral. To destroy the traditional is revolutionary, dangerous and immoral. She cannot reject tradition in the name of higher wisdom, in the name of higher truth and authority. It gone, and all is gone; hence her fear of all iconoclastic and revolutionary methods. So she would keep whole and pure the national memories of every people. In the last essay of the book she says, "The preservation of national memories is an element and a means of national greatness, and their revival a sign of reviving nationality." It is "the divine gift of memory" as it expresses itself in the life and purposes of a people, "which inspires the moments with a past, a present and a future, and gives the sense of corporate existence that raises man above the brutes." All which lowers the influence or the sacredness of this memory is debasing. The corrupting of this memory "is the impoverishment that threatens our posterity;" and this "new famine, a meagre fiend, with lewd grin and clumsy hoof, is breathing a moral mildew over the harvest of our human sentiments." That eager yearning of the nineteenth century for truth and reality, for something more than traditions and national memories, which displays itself in reforms and revolutions of every kind, had little of George Eliot's sympathy. Yet this spirit is stronger even than tradition, and creates for us a new world and a higher life.

Throughout these essays it is the social side of morality which is praised and commended. What will increase the altruistic spirit, what will widen sympathy and helpfulness, is regarded as truly ethical in its import. Ideal aims are brought to the level of present needs and the possibilities of human nature as it now exists.

Wide-reaching motives, blessed and glorious as they are, and of the highest sacramental virtue, have their dangers, like all else that touches the mixed life of the earth. They are archangels with awful brow and flaming sword, summoning and encouraging us to do the right and the divinely heroic, and we feel a beneficent tremor in their presence; but to learn what it is they summon us to do, we have to consider the mortals we are elbowing, who are of our own stature and our own appetites. . . . On the whole, and in the vast majority of instances, the action by which we can do the best for future ages is of the sort which has a certain beneficence and grace for contemporaries. A sour father may reform prisons, but considered in his sourness he does harm.

In another essay, that entitled "Only Temper," the social side of morality is again presented. Especially does it appear in that on "Moral Swindlers." "Let us refuse to accept as moral," says George Eliot, "any political leader who should allow his conduct in relation to great issues to be determined by egoistic passion, and boldly say that he would be less immoral even though he were as lax in his personal habits as Sir Robert Walpole, if at the same time his sense of the public welfare were supreme in his mind, quelling all pettier impulses beneath a magnanimous impartiality." George Eliot is almost without exception sound and just in her moral judgments, but here her theories have made her overlook the true conditions of a moral life.

Seeing that Morality and Morals under their *alias* of Ethics are the subject of voluminous discussion, and their true basis a pressing matter of dispute — seeing that the most famous book ever written on Ethics, and forming a chief study in our colleges, allies ethical with political science, or that which treats of the constitution and prosperity of States, one might expect that educated men would find reason to avoid a perversion of language which lends itself to no wider view of life than that of village gossips. Yet I find even respectable historians of our own and of foreign countries, after showing that a king was treacherous, rapacious, and ready to sanction gross breaches in the administration of justice, end by praising him for his pure moral character, by which one must suppose them to mean that he was not lewd nor debauched, not the European twin of the typical Indian potentate whom Macaulay describes as passing his life in chewing bang and fondling dancing-girls. And since we are sometimes told of such maleficent kings that they were religious, we arrive at the curious result that the most serious wide-reaching duties of man lie quite outside both Morality and Religion — the one of these consisting in not keeping mistresses (and perhaps not drinking too much), and the other in certain ritual and spiritual transactions with God which can be carried on equally well side by side with the basest conduct toward men. With such a classification as this, it is no wonder, considering the strong re-action of language on thought, that many minds, dizzy with indigestion of recent science and philosophy, are fain to seek for the grounds of social duty; and without entertaining any private intention of committing a perjury which would ruin an innocent man, or seeking gain by supplying bad preserved meats to our navy, feel themselves speculatively obliged to inquire why they should not do so, and are inclined to measure their intellectual subtlety by their dissatisfaction with all answers to this "Why?"

It would be quite impossible for George Eliot to write an essay without some fresh thought or some new suggestion. To those who admire her genius and are in sympathy with her teachings this volume will have a special interest. Its few essays which touch upon moral or speculative subjects are of the utmost value as interpretations of her life and thought.

All her essays, the later as the earlier, are mainly of interest as aids to an understanding of her philosophy. Nothing is worthless which helps us clearly to comprehend an original mind.

XIX.

THE ANALYTIC METHOD.

GEORGE ELIOT'S literary method was that of Fielding and Thackeray, both of whom evidently influenced her manner. Their realism, and especially their method of comment and moral observation, she made her own. She had little sympathy with the romanticism of Scott or the idealism of Dickens. Her moral aims, her intense faith in *altruism*, kept her from making her art a mere process of photographing nature. Nature always had a moral meaning to her, a meaning in reference to man's happiness and health of soul; and that moral bearing of all human experiences gave dignity and purpose to her art.

It was the method of Scott to present the romantic, picturesque and poetic side of life. He was not untrue to nature, but he cared more for beauty and sentiment than for fact. He sometimes perverted the historic incidents he made use of, but he caught the spirit of the time with which he was dealing with absolute fidelity. In this capacity for historic interpretation he surpassed George Eliot, who had not his instinctive insight into the past. Scott had no theory about the past, no philosophy of history was known to him; but above all novelists he had the power to see by the light of other days, and to make the dead times live again. Not George Eliot and not Thackeray was his rival in this historic insight and poetic power of interpretation; and his superior success was due not only to his peculiar genius but also to his romanticism. Scott failed where

George Eliot succeeded, in giving an intellectual interpretation of life. With certain social and moral tendencies he was clearly at home. On its side of adventure and social impulse and craving for a wider life, as a single instance of his power, he was a true interpreter of the age of Elizabeth. Its deeper spirit, its intellectual movements, he did not, and could not, bring within the range of his story. It was here George Eliot was superior, as is abundantly shown in *Romola*. The thoughtful aspects of Florentine life she truthfully presented; but its more romantic elements it needed a Scott to make living and real. In *The Spanish Gypsy* there is very little of genuine interpretation. Certain local features may be accurate, but the spirit of the time is not there; the characters are not such as that age and country developed. Scott, with all his romanticism, would have introduced *reality* into such an historic picture.

Within her own lines of power George Eliot is much greater than Scott, who could not have written *Adam Bede* or *Middlemarch*, or brought out what is best in those works. Adventure was necessary to Scott; he could not have transfigured the plain and homely with beauty as George Eliot has done. Where she is at her best, as in the simple scenes of *Silas Marner*, there is a charm, pathos and sympathy in her work which must endear it to all hearts. That peculiar power Scott did not have; yet it would be most difficult to decide which is the truer to nature. Genuine art, it is true, has its foundation in the realities of human experience; but those realities are not always best interpreted by the methods of realism. In his own province Scott was truer to nature than George Eliot was in the same field, as may be seen at once by comparing *The Spanish Gypsy* with *Ivanhoe*, or any of Scott's novels dealing with the mediæval and feudal ages. He took the past into himself, caught its spirit, reflected it in its wholeness. In this he was a genuine realist, and all the more faithful to reality because he did not accept realism as a theory.

In comparing George Eliot with Dickens, it must first of all be noted that each is the superior of the other in his own special province. Dickens has more imagination; he appeals to more universal sentiments, touches a wider circle of experiences, captivates his readers with a resistless interest and tenderness of spirit. His characters are unreal, mere caricatures often, mere puppets. Yet he had an imagination of marvellous power, so that his characters appeared to his own mind as if real, and he describes them as if they actually stood before him, making them intensely real to his readers. Many of his persons never lived, never could have lived; yet they are types or certain traits of character made living and brought out into a distinctive existence. What those traits of character are he makes all the more apparent by this method.

Dickens had not a fine literary taste, he had no clear insight into some of the purer human sentiments, he was grossly untrue and false in many of his pictures. Yet all in all, with his many faults, it is to be said that his idealism, which was not of a high type, made him a true interpreter of life. If his characters are less faithfully drawn than George Eliot's, his insight into some of the sentiments and emotions was truer. His pictures may be false in some particulars, but he has given them the true spirit with which they should be animated.

In thoughtful fidelity to the facts of life, George Eliot surpasses Scott or Dickens. Scott by his insight, Dickens by his imagination, were able to do what she could not; but they put little thought into their work. They did not think about what life meant; she did. They worked instinctively, she thoughtfully. Her characters are more often to be met with than theirs; and there is a freshness, a wholesomeness, about them theirs do not have. She is more simple and refined than Fielding, more elevated in tone of thought, there is a deeper and a richer purpose in her work. None of the cynicism and hardness of Thackeray appear in her pages. She is fresher, more genuine, more poetic than he, with more of humanity.

In her essay on "The Natural History of German Life" she said of Dickens that he was "gifted with the utmost power of rendering the external traits of our town population." City life Dickens and Thackeray most truly photographed in all its features of snobbishness and selfishness. Its better side, its nobler sentiments, its humanity, they did not succeed in so well; not so well as George Eliot did, and simply because they did not so much sympathize with it. Country life they did not understand, and could not have sketched. Where George Eliot best succeeded they would have failed. Her real advance upon Dickens and Thackeray, however, lay in another direction. She says in the essay just quoted, speaking of Dickens's portraitures of town populations, that "if he could give us their psychological character — their conception of life and their emotions — with the same truth as their idiom and manners, his books would be the greatest contribution art has ever made to the awakening of social sympathies." In the two directions here indicated lay her superiority over other novelists, — her humanitarian sympathies and her psychologic insight. In reality, she did not contribute anything new to the realism of literary art. All which can be said for faithfulness to nature in art and poetry has been said by Ruskin, and George Eliot was early a reader of his books. Her predecessors, especially Thackeray, opened the way in the application of the realistic principles in its newer spirit. The enlargement of realism, however, was carried on to a much greater extent by the pre-Raphaelites in painting and poetry, and George Eliot was influenced by them as well. Their principle of loyal fidelity to the time and circumstances depicted was her own, at least in theory.

It was in another direction her chief characteristic lay, that of describing "psychologic character." Here she was no imitator, but she made a way of her own, and developed a new method. The method of science she applied to literature. Science has adopted the method of analysis, of inductive inquiry, of search in all the facts of nature for the laws which underlie them. So magnificent have been the results obtained by this process in the study of the material world, that it has been applied with the hope of securing the same thorough investigation of the phenomena presented by history, ethics and religion. Even here the method has justified itself, and has in recent years opened up new and valuable results, giving to the world an enriched conception of the life of man. The speculative mind has been stimulated to fresh activity, and new philosophies, of vast and imposing proportions, have been the result. The studies of Charles Darwin, and the elaboration of the theory of evolution, have given a marvellous incentive to the new method, resulting in its wide-spread application to all the questions of nature and life.

A method so productive in all directions must have its effect on literature. What claims the attention of all thinking men cannot long be kept out of poetry and art. In painting and in music it has been largely developed in the direction of a more intimate and sympathetic interpretation of nature and man. In literature the new method has been mainly brought into application hitherto in the form of photographic studies of human life. To describe what is, to make a true word-picture, has been the chief aim. With George Eliot began a wider use of the new method and its application in a more sympathetic spirit to the deeper problems of the mind and heart. She was not content to paint the surface of nature, to give photographic sketches of the outside of human life, but she wished to realize every subtle fact and every most secret impulse. An admirer of the Dutch school in painting, and of Jane Austen as a novelist, she was not content with their results and methods, wishing to interpret the spirit as well as the letter of nature and life.

In literature, the new method as developed in recent years consists in an application of psychology to all the problems of man's nature. George Eliot's intimate association with the leaders of the scientific movement in England, naturally turned her mind into sympathy with their work, and made her desirous of doing in literature what they were doing in science. In the special department of physiological psychology, no one did more than George Henry Lewes, and her whole heart went out in genuine appreciation of his work. He studied the mind as a function of the brain, as being developed with the body, as the result of inherited conditions, as intimately dependent on its environment. Here was a new conception of man, which regarded him as the last product of nature, considered as an organic whole. This conception George Eliot everywhere applied in her studies of life and character. She studied man as the product of his environment, not as a being who exists above circumstances and material conditions. "In the eyes of the psychologist," says Mr. James Sully, "the works of George Eliot must always possess a high value by reason of their large scientific insight into character and life." This value consists, as he indicates, in the fact that she interprets the inner personality as it is understood by the scientific student of human nature. She describes those obscure moral tendencies, nascent forces, and undertones of feeling and thought, which enter so much into life. She lays much stress on the subconscious mental life, the domain of vague emotion and rapidly fugitive thought.

The aim of the psychologic method is to interpret man from within, in his motives and impulses. It endeavors to show why he acts, and it unfolds the subtler elements of his character. This method George Eliot uses in connection with her evolutionary philosophy, and uses it for the purpose of showing that man is a product of hereditary conditions, that he has been shaped into his life of the emotions and sentiments by the influence of tradition. The psychologic method may be applied, however, without connection with the positive or evolutionary philosophy. The mind may be regarded as a distinct force and power, exercised within social and material limits, and capable of being studied in all its inner motives and impulses. Yet in her mental inquiries George Eliot did not regard man as an eternal soul in the process of development by divine methods, but as the inheritor of the past, moulded by every surrounding circumstance, and as the creature of the present. Instead of regarding man as *sub specie eternitatis*, she regarded him as an animal who has through feeling and social development come to know that he cannot exist beyond the present. This limitation of his nature affected her work throughout.

The psychologic method in literature has also been that of Robert Browning, and he has been as faithful to it as any other. He, too, analyzes his characters, penetrates all the hidden causes of motive and deed, lays bare the soul. No other poet has surpassed him in power to unveil the inner workings of the mind, to discover all the influences affecting it or in revealing how motives are created and how motives lead up to deeds. In two important particulars Robert Browning differs from George Eliot. His characters speak for themselves, reveal the secrets of their own minds. He does not talk about them, does not criticise their words and conduct, does not stand off from them as a spectator. He differs from her also in his conception of man as a being who is here developing an eternal existence under the laws of an Infinite Spirit. He, too, believes in the natural, and believes that the highest law of the soul is, to be true to every pure impulse arising within us. To calculate, to philosophize, he holds to be always to man's injury, that nature when perfectly obeyed is the only guide. He studies man as affected by all the circumstances of his existence, and as wrought upon by the great social forces which have made him what he is. His analysis is as keen as George Eliot's; he makes the soul appear before us in all its reality. His is a more creative, a more dramatic method than hers; yet he is fully as subjective, as much an interpreter of the soul. Neither is content to record the deeds of men; both wish to know why men act.

Browning has fittingly been called the poet of psychology. He is a dissecter, a prober, an analyzer in the full spirit of scientific research. He spares no pains to get at and to completely unfold the truth about man's nature, to show all the hidden causes of his action, all the secret motives of his life, using this method as thoroughly as George Eliot. It is interesting to note his attitude towards the great religious problems. His faith in God is intensely passionate and sublime in its conception. In words the most expressive in their meaning, and indicating a conviction the deepest, he reveals his faith.

"He glows above
With scarce an intervention, presses close
And palpitatingly, His soul o'er ours."

The lifting and inspiring power of faith in an Infinite Being he has sung with a poet's purity of vision. Along with this faith goes his belief that man is being slowly perfected for a higher and nobler existence.

'To whom turn I but to Thee, the ineffable Name?
Builder and maker. Thou, of houses not made with hands!
What, have fear of change from Thee, who art ever the same?
Doubt that Thy power can fill the heart that Thy power expands?

There shall never be one lost good! What was, shall live as before;
The evil is null, is naught, is silence implying sound;
What was good, shall be good, with, for evil, so much good more;
On the earth the broken arcs; in the heaven the perfect round.

" All we have willed or hoped or dreamed of good, shall exist;
Not its likeness, but itself; no beauty, nor good, nor power
Whose voice has gone forth, but each survives for the melodist
When eternity confirms the conceptions of an hour.
The high that proved too high, the heroic for earth too hard,
The passion that left the ground to lose itself in the sky,
Are music sent up to God by the lover and the bard;
Enough that He heard it once: we shall hear it by and by."

He teaches that progress is the true mark and aim of man's being, a progress sure and glorious.

"Progress, man's distinctive mark alone,
Not God's and not the beast's; God is, they are,
Man partly is, and wholly hopes to be."

Man yearns after more than he can gain here; that yearning is the mark of his higher nature and the means of progress. If he follows the better impulses of his nature, all experience will help to unfold his soul into higher attainments, and impulse will at last become, in clearer moments, revelation.

"Oh, we're sunk enough here, God knows!
But not quite so much that moments,
Sure tho' seldom, are denied us,
When the spirit's true endowments
Stand out plainly from its false ones,
And appraise it if pursuing
Or the right way or the wrong way
To its triumph or undoing.
There are flashes struck from midnights,
There are fireflames noondays kindle,
Whereby piled-up honors perish,
Whereby swol'n ambitions dwindle,
While just this or that poor impulse
Which for once had play unstifled
Seems the sole work of a lifetime,
That away the rest have trifled."

More impersonal and dramatic than George Eliot, Browning introduces his doctrines less often. It is not easy to discover what are his theories as distinguished from those of his characters, for he makes no comments, and is faithful in developing the unity and integrity of his *dramatis personæ*, whether in his monologues or dramas. Great as his other faults may be, he surpasses George Eliot in his power to reveal character, but not in his power to make his characters stand out distinctly and unprejudiced from his own mind. His obscurity of expression and his involved style are serious defects in much of his work; and to most readers his thoroughly dramatic manner is puzzling. He gives but faint clue to the situation in his monologues, little explanation of the person, time or place. All is to be discovered from the obscurest allusions and hints. Defective as this method is in Browning's treatment, it is the true psychologic method, wherein motive and character are developed dramatically and without labored discussion. It is a more vital and constructive process than that followed by George Eliot, because nothing of the meaning and fulness of life is lost in the process of analysis. That Browning can never be read by more than a few, indicates how great are his faults; but in lyric passion, dramatic power and psychologic analysis he is one of the greatest poets of the century. The value and range of the new method are well illustrated in its use by two such thinkers and poets.

The analytic method as applied by George Eliot regards man as a social being, studies him as a member of society. All that he is, and all the influences working upon him, are understood only as affected by his connection with the life of the race. This fact gives the most distinguishing characteristic to her literary methods. Her imitators may not, and nearly all of them do not, follow her into positivism; but they all study man as a social being. They deal with him as affected by heredity, education, and social characteristics. Even here it is not her theories, but her artistic methods, which are imitated. The novel is no longer regarded as a story to be told dramatically and with moving effect, but as a study of character, as an analysis of situations and motives. The advocates of the new method say that "in one manner or another the stories were all told long ago; and now we want merely to know what the novelist thinks about persons and situations."[1] This interpretation of the mission of the novelist well describes George Eliot's work, for she never hesitated to tell her reader what she thought about the situations and the persons of whom she wrote.

The new method, as developed in sympathy with agnosticism, fails in literature just as science fails to be a complete interpretation of the universe. The process which answers in the material world does not answer in the spiritual. The instruments which tell the secrets of matter, close the avenues to the revelations of mind. The methods of experiment and demonstration which have brought the universe to man's knowledge, have not been sufficient to make the soul known to itself. Any literary methods imitating physical science must share in its limitations without its power over the materials with which it has to deal. Literature has hitherto been made helpful and delightful and acceptable because of its ideal elements. Belief in a spiritual world, belief in the imperative law of righteousness as a divine command, runs through all effective literature. However realistic the poets have been when they have reached their highest and best, they have believed that the soul, and what belongs to it, is the only *reality*. Divorced of this element, literature is at once lowered in tone, a dry-rot seizes upon it and eats away its finest portions. If Goethe and Shakspere are realists in literary method, as some of their interpreters would claim, yet to them the spiritual is supreme, the soul is monarch. So it is with Homer, with Dante, with Scott, with Cervantes, with Victor Hugo, with every supremely artistic and creative mind. Great minds instinctively believe in the creative power of the mind, in its capacity

[1] W. D. Howells in the Century for November, 1882.

for self-direction. An unbiassed mind gifted with genius sees over and through all obstacles, leaps to magnificent results, will not be restrained by the momentary conditions of the present. Education or social environment, however adverse, will not long hinder the poet from his work. He writes for the future, if the present will not accept him, confident that what his soul has to utter can be truly uttered only as his own individuality impels, and that if he is faithful to his genius the world will listen in due time. This power of personality lies at the basis of all genuine literature, teaching faith in the soul, faith in a providential ordering of the world, and overturning all agnostic theories about realism and environment.

This instinctive faith in mind is the basis of all genuine idealism. The idealist is not the creator of an imaginary world, peopling it with shapes that never existed; but he is one who believes in ideas, and in mind as their creator and the vehicle of their expression. Contemporary with George Eliot was a group of men who believed in the mind as something other than the temporary product of an evolutionary process. With them she may be contrasted, her work may be measured by theirs. Carlyle, Tennyson, Browning and Ruskin shared with her the radical ideas of the time. Not one of them has been fettered by narrow theories or cramped by old social doctrines. The broad, inquiring, scientific spirit of the time has been shared by them all. Ruskin is a realist, Carlyle believed in the enduring realm of facts, and they have all accepted the spirit of naturalism which has ruled the century. The scientific, philosophic and social theories of the time have been their inspiration. Certain ideas about law, progress and social regeneration have affected them through and through. Yet as regards the one great characteristic of idealism, all have widely departed from George Eliot, for all regard mind as supreme, all believe in a spiritual realm environing man. This fact appears throughout their work. To them the spiritual is objective; they are the true realists. To George Eliot the spiritual is subjective, the result of our own feelings, to which it is limited. When the feelings are gone, all is gone. In the pages of these men there is consequently to be found a power and an inspiration not to be found in hers. Wonderful as is her skill as an artist, and in the analysis of character, yet we feel that we are walking over mocking graves whenever we reach her spiritual conception of the world. She deceives us with a shadow, offers us a name in place of what we crave for with every nobler instinct of the soul. Our own feelings are given us, mirrored in the feelings of others, in place of the reality we desire to possess.

These men have linked their work with those spiritual convictions which have been the moral sustenance of the ages. They have gained in strength and effectiveness thereby. Tennyson has his many doubts, his teachings have been questioned; and yet he sings, —

"That each, who seems a separate whole,
Should move his rounds, and passing all
The skirts of self again, should fall,
Remerging in the general soul, —

Is faith as vague as all unsweet:
Eternal form shall still divide
The eternal soul from all beside;
And I shall know him when we meet."

His flight of song is more sustained for this faith. He is a truer poet, of stronger wing and loftier flight, because life has for him an infinite meaning, because he opens his mind to the impressions which come of man's spiritual existence. In the same way, Carlyle has a grander meaning running through his books, more of sublimity, a finer eloquence, because the spiritual is to him real. Doubter and scorner as he was, he could not but see that man's being reaches beyond the material world and interprets some higher realm. Vague as that faith was with him, it was a source of the most effective literary power and stimulus. He bursts forth, under its impulse, into impassioned passages of the noblest poetic beauty.

"Perhaps my father, all that essentially was my father, is even now near me, with me. Both he and I are with God. Perhaps, if it so please God, we shall in some higher state of being meet one another, recognize one another. As it is written, we shall be forever with God. The possibility, nay (in some way) the certainty, of perennial existence daily grows plainer to me."

Ruskin has made it plain how necessary is that tone of mind which is religious to the best work in art. His own faith has been earnest and strong in the reality of the spiritual. Realist as he is in art, he believes in the original and creative power of the mind, and his work has all taken on a higher spirit and a finer expression because of his religious convictions. Writing in *Modern Painters* of man as made in the image of God, he answers the objection which is raised to the idea that all the revelation man has is contained in a being so imperfect.

"No other book, nor fragment of book, than that, will you ever find, — nothing in the clouds above, nor in the earth beneath. The flesh-bound volume is the only revelation that is, that was, or that can be. In that is the image of God painted; in that is the law of God written; in that is the promise of God revealed. Know thyself; for through thyself only thou canst know God. Through the glass, darkly; but except through the glass, in no wise. A tremulous crystal, waved as water, poured out upon the ground; — you may defile it, despise it, pollute it at your pleasure and at your peril; for on the peace of those weak waves must all the heaven you shall ever gain be first seen; and through such purity as you can win for those dark waves must all the light of the risen Sun of Righteousness be bent down by faint refraction. Cleanse them, and calm them, as you love your life. Therefore it is that all the power of nature depends on subjection to the human soul. Man is the Sun of the world; more than the real sun. The fire of his wonderful heart is the only light and heat worth gauge or measure. Where he is, are the tropics; where he is not, the ice-world."

Such words may not be scientific, but they convey real meaning. Their assertion that the world is to be tested and understood by man, not man by the world, is one worthy of attention. The conviction of this truth has a literary power and incentive not to be found in "the scientific method" or any of its corollaries.

To this group of writers may be added Mrs. Browning, who, as a poet, did great and lasting work. Its value, in large measure, rests on its depth of spiritual conviction, and on its idealism in purpose and spirit. Her conception of love is finer and truer than George Eliot's, because she gave it an ideal as well as an altruistic meaning; because she thought it has an eternal as well as a social significance. As a poet she lost nothing of charm or of power or of inspiration because she could herself believe, with simple trust, what she has embodied in "A Child's Thought of God."

> "God is so good, He wears a fold
>   Of heaven and earth across his face—
> Like secrets kept, for love, untold.
>   But still I feel that his embrace
> Slides down by thrills, through all things made,
>   Through sight and sound of every place."

That art is to be nothing more than a copying and interpretation of nature Mrs. Browning did not believe. In *Aurora Leigh* she says,—

> "Art's the witness of what is
> Beyond this show. If this world's show were all,
> Mere imitation would be all in art."

The glow of genius burns up out of all her pages, and there is an aroma and a subtle power in them which comes alone of this conception of art. She could not rest content with the little round of man's experience, but found that all the universe is bound together and all its parts filled with a God-spirit.

"No lily-muffled hum of a summer bee
But finds some coupling with the spinning stars;
No pebble at your foot but proves a sphere;
No chaffinch but implies the cherubim:
. . . Earth's crammed with heaven,
And every common bush afire with God."

That is a larger faith and a truer faith than appears anywhere in the pages of George Eliot, and it is one which impregnates most of the best literature the world posseses with light and life. It is a faith which gives hope and impulse where the other saddens and unnerves.

There is wanting in George Eliot's books that freshness of spirit, that faith in the future, and that peaceful poise of soul which is to be found in the writings of Tennyson, Ruskin and Mrs. Browning. Even with all his constitutional cynicism and despair, the teachings of Carlyle are much more hopeful than hers. An air of fatigue and world-weariness is about all her work, even when it is most stimulating with its altruism. Though in theory not a pessimist, yet a sense of pain and sorrow grows out of the touch of each of her books. In this she missed one of the highest uses of literature, to quicken new hopes and to awaken nobler purposes. There is a tone of joy and exultation in the power life confers, an instinctive sense of might to conquer the world, in the best writing. To make men think, to move men to action, to confer finer feelings and motives, is the power of the true poet. When he does not accomplish this he has written to a lesser purpose. Literature aims either to please or to quicken the mind. It cannot please when it leaves the heart depressed and burdened with the failures and sadness of the world. If it is to please, it must make use of that goodness and joy which are in excess of evil and misery. It cannot quicken when it unnerves the mind and brings despair of moral purpose. If it is to inspire it must show that something great is to be done, and awaken the courage to do it.

That life has its sad and painful elements is a terrible fact, and the novelist who would paint life as it is must recognize them. It is quite as true that the good and the hopeful are more than the sad and painful, that right is more powerful in human life than wrong. The novelist who would paint life with an exact and even-handed justice, must not make all his endings sorrowful, for very many in real life are not so. *The Mill on the Floss* would have been a more powerful and effective book could Maggie have been made to conquer. It would have been quite as true to nature to have represented her as overcoming her defects, and as being purified through suffering. Is all suffering to conquer us, instead of our being able to conquer it, and gaining a more peaceful and a purer life through its aid? If Maggie is George Eliot in her youthful experiences, then the novel is untrue to fact in that Marian Evans conquered and Maggie failed. The same fault is to be found in *Middlemarch*, that Dorothea, great as she is, deserved a much better fate than that accorded to her. The elements of womanly greatness were in her character, and with all the barriers created by society she would have done better things had her creator been true to her capacities in unfolding her life-history. The effect of both these great novels is one of depression and disappointment. The reader always expects more as he goes on his way through these scenes, depicted with such genius, than is realized at the end. Disappointment is almost inevitable, for the promise is greater than the fulfilment. The like result is produced by those books which have the brightest closing scenes, as in *Adam Bede* and *Daniel Deronda*, where the author's aim was evidently hopeful and constructive. *Silas Marner* and *Felix Holt* are the only exceptions to this pessimistic tone, and in which justice is done to the better side of life. In all her later books the ending is painful. In *The Mill on the Floss*, Maggie and Tom are drowned after Maggie had been led to a most bitter end of her love-affairs. In *Romola* the heroine is left a widow, after her husband's treachery had brought him to a terrible death, and after Savonarola had suffered martyrdom. Dorothea marries into a life of ordinary drudgery, and Lydgate fails. Daniel Deronda and Gwendolen are separated from each other, and Deronda goes to the east in furtherance of a wild scheme of Jewish colonization. Fedalma loses her father by the treachery of her lover, and without hope conducts her tribe to Africa. Jubal dies dishonored, and Armgart loses her voice. Yet it is not merely that the conclusion does not lead to the expected result, but throughout there is a tone of doubt and failure. That George Eliot purposed to give life this tinge of sadness is not to be accepted as the true explanation of it. It is known that she did not have such a purpose, that she was surprised and disappointed that her books should produce such a result on her readers. The explanation is to be found in another direction.

She was an agnostic; life had no wide horizon for her. The light of a genuinely ideal and spiritual conception of life was not hers. The world was bounded to her vision, rounded into the little capacity possessed by man. Where others would have cast a glow of hope and sunset brilliance, promise of a brighter day yet to dawn over the closing scenes of her novels, she could see nothing beyond but the feeble effect of an earthly transmitted good. In this regard her books afford a most interesting contrast to those of the two other great women who have adorned English literature with their genius. The lot of Mrs. Browning and Charlotte Brontë was much sadder and more depressing than that of George Eliot; more of darkness and pain affected their lives. A subtle tone of sadness runs through their books, but it is not burdensome and depressing as is the case of George Eliot. There is hope with it, and a buoyant faith in the good, which lies above and beyond all pain and sorrow. With neither of them was this faith conventional, a mere reflection of the religion taught them in childhood. It was a thoughtful result of a large experience, and of hard contact with many of the severest facts of human experience. That wide horizon of spiritual reality which shone for them on every hand, lights all their work with a brilliance which almost puts out of sight the pain and sorrow of the world. The reader of their books is made to believe that life is an endless good; he is cheered and made stronger for what life offers him.

Agnosticism may have its great and heroic incentives, it may impel men to a nobler activity, but its literary effect, as a motive towards a more inspiring life, has not been satisfactory in the hands of George Eliot. Shakspere is not a teacher of philosophy or ethics, he has no doctrines to preach, no theories to advocate. What he believed, it would be difficult to ascertain from his writings; yet he is an effective teacher of morals, he stimulates into activity all that is best in man, life widens and deepens under the touch of his genius. So is it with Milton, Schiller, Molière, Calderon, Montaigne and Wordsworth. So is it with George Eliot in all that concerns our duties, and even with our human sympathies. In the one direction of trust she is wanting, and her books are devoid of it. Shakspere makes us realize that God rules over the world; George Eliot leaves us with the feeling that we know nothing, and can hope for but little. That her theories really cast a shadow over the world, may be seen in all her dealings with love. Love is with her a human passion, deep, pure, blessed. It crowns some of her characters with joy and peace and strength; it is never impure and base in her pages. Yet it is human, it is a social force, it is to be made altruistic. It never gains that high poetic influence and charm which glorifies it in the writings of Mrs. Browning, Browning and Tennyson. Browning conceives of it as an eternal passion, as one with all that is divinest in man, as a medium of his spiritual development. In his pages it glows with moral promise, it inspires and regenerates. The poet should deal with love, not as a thing base and susceptible of abuse, but as an influence capable of the most beneficent results in the uplifting of man's nature. If it degrades, it also sweetens; and only that is love which makes life richer and more worthy. The true artist can afford to deal with that which pleases, not with that which saddens and disgusts. The real love is the pure love, not the depraved. The natural is the noble, not the debased life.

George Eliot's originality of method has given rise to a new school in fiction. Her imitators, even when at their best, are not her equals, and they have degraded her methods oftentimes to paltry uses. They have tried to take photographs of life, supposing that art has for its aim to copy nature. They have failed to see, what she did see, though not so clearly as could have been desired, that art must do much more than imitate some scene or fact out of nature. It must give beauty, meaning and expression to what it copies. And it must do more than imitate: it must go beyond mere description, and introduce unity, purpose and thought into its work. True art has a soul as well as a body, says something to the mind as well as to the eye, appeals to the soul as well as to sense. Had George Eliot done nothing more than to describe common English life there would have been small excuse for her work. She did more, touched that life with genius, made it blossom into beauty, and gave to it deep moral meanings. The defects of her method are to be seen in the fact that her imitators cannot get above life's surface, and deal mainly with shallow or degraded natures. Her methods do not inspire great work, while her own genius redeemed the false ways into which she was led by her philosophic theories.

Science can dissect the human body, but it can do little towards an explanation of the subtler meanings of life and mind. Its methods are analytical; it has reached no truly synthetic results in the regions where knowledge is most to be desired. Its effects on literature are destructive. Science destroys poetry, dries up the poetic sense, closes the doors of imagination. The attempt to make science co-operate with poetry is in itself the promise of failure. The limitations of George Eliot's work are the limitations of poetry subdued by science. Could she have rid herself of that burden, been impelled by a faith and an ideal purpose commensurate with her genius, the result would have been much greater. This limitation suggests the fact that literature is synthetic and constructive in its purpose and spirit. It is this fact which has made the classic literatures so powerful in their effect on modern Europe. They have given unity, spiritual purpose and ideal aims to the whole modern world. The freshness as of an eternal spring was in the literature of Greece, the naturalness of a healthy manhood. That literature is organic, it is one with life, it is refreshing as nature itself. That literature lives and flames with power because it is synthetic, buoyant, touched with an eternal spiritual beauty, great with promise of a growing earth. Its poets do not dissect, but build; they do not analyze, but create. And this is the literary need of the present time. There is need of more poetry, a more poetic interpretation of life, a richer imagination and a finer sense of beauty. The common is everywhere, but it is not necessarily great or beautiful or noble. It may have its elements of pathos and tragedy, its touches of beauty and its motives of heroism. It has in it also the promise of better things to be. That is the true poetry, the true fiction, which brings out this promise so that we know it, so that it moves us to better deeds and enchants us with music of purer living. The world is bad enough without dragging to the light all its evils and discords; let us rather know what promise it contains of the better. In one word, the real oppresses and enthralls; the ideal liberates, and brings us to ourselves.

Genius redeems every fault. It must be taken for what it is, must not be criticised, is to be used to the highest ends. Only when genius unites itself to false methods and checks itself by false theories, has the critic a right to complain. Genius, obedient to its own laws, accepts every fact life presents, and lifts each one to be an instrument for the enlargement of man's life. When it deliberately strikes out all that is not human, however, from man's experience, denies the realty of that impression and that conviction which comes from other than material sources, it cripples and denies itself.

XX.

THE LIMITATIONS OF HER THOUGHT.

IT must be remembered that George Eliot does not use the novel merely for the purpose of inculcating certain doctrines, and that her genius for artistic creation is of a very high order. In dealing with her as a thinker and as a moral and religious teacher, she is to be regarded, first of all, as a poet and an artist. Her ethics are subordinate to her art; her religion is subsidiary to her genius. That she always deliberately set about the task of introducing her positivism into the substance of her novels is not to be supposed. This would be to imply a forgetfulness on her part of her own methods, and a prostration of art to purposes she would have scorned to adopt. This is evidently true, however, that certain features of the positive and the evolution philosophy had so thoroughly approved themselves to her mind as to cause them to be accepted as a completely satisfactory explanation of the world, so far as any explanation is possible. So heartily were they received, so fully did they become incorporated with the substance of her thinking, that she viewed all human experiences in their light. They had ceased to be theory and speculation with her. When she thought about the world, when she observed the acts of men, the positivist explanation was at once applied, and instinctively.

That she did teach positivism is unfortunately true, so far as her literary touch and expression is concerned. That philosophy affects all her books with its subtly insinuating flavor, and it gives meaning and bias to most of them. They thus gain in definiteness of purpose, in moral vigor, in minutely faithful study of some phases of human experience, and in a massive impression of thoughtfulness which her work creates. At the same time, they undoubtedly lose in value as studies of life; in free range of expression for her genius, her poetry and her art; and in that spiritual vision which looks forward with keen gazing eyes of hope and confident inquiry.

Her teaching, like most teaching, is a mingled good and evil. In more than one direction her ethical and religious influence was most wholesome and effective. She brought into clear light a few great facts, and made them the more conspicuous by the strong emphasis she gave them. This is, in the main, the method of all teaching and of all progress. Development seldom proceeds in a direct line, but rather, so far as man is concerned, by forcible emphasis laid on some great fact which has been previously neglected. The idealism of a previous age had shown the value of certain facts and tendencies in human nature, but it had exaggerated some faculties and capacities of man, as well as neglected others. In consequence, our own time swings to the other extreme, and cannot have too much of evolution and positivism.

Idealism is in human nature, and will give itself expression. Positivism is also a result of our experience and of our study of the universe, both material and mental; it is a result of the desire for definite knowledge. As a re-action against the excesses of idealism it is a powerful leaven, and it brings into necessary prominence those facts which are neglected by the opposite philosophy. It takes account of facts, and scorns mysticism; and it thus appeals to a deep-seated bias of the time.

George Eliot's books have an interest as an attempt at an interpretation of life from its more practical and realistic side, and not less as a re-action against the influences of very nearly all the great literary minds of the earlier half of the century in England. Under the lead of Coleridge and Wordsworth, and influenced by German thought and literature, a remarkable movement was then developed in English literature. The outcome of that movement has been surpassed only by that of the age of Shakspere. Freshness of thought, love of nature, profound humanitarian convictions, and spontaneity wedded to great largeness of ideas, characterize this period and its noble work. Such an age is almost invariably followed by an age of re-action, criticism, realism and analysis. An instinctive demand for a portrayal of the more positive side of life, and the influence of science, have developed a new literary school. For doctrine it teaches agnosticism, and in method it cares mainly for art and beauty of form. Towards the development of the new school George Eliot has been a leading influence, though her sympathies have not gone with all its tendencies and results.

If Wordsworth exaggerated the importance of the intuitive and personal, George Eliot equally exaggerated the value of the historic and hereditary. It was desirable, however, that the relations of life to the past should be brought out more distinctly by a literary development of their relations to the present, and that the influence of social heredity should be seen as affecting life on all sides. Tradition is a large and persistent element in the better life of the race, while the past certainly has a powerful influence over the present. This fact was neglected by Wordsworth, and especially is it neglected by the intuitive philosophies. They ignore the lessons of the past, and assume that a new and perfect world is to be evolved from the depths of consciousness. That to think a better world is to create a better world, they seem to take for granted, while the fact is that the truer life is the result of a painful and long-continued struggle against adverse conditions. What has been, persists in remaining, and the past, with all its narrowness and prejudices, continues to influence men more powerfully than does clear thought or regard for the truth. Emotion and sentiment cling about what has become sacred with age. Channels for thought and activity having once been made, it is very difficult to abandon them for untried paths approved even by reason.

The historic view is one of much importance, and is likely to be overlooked by the poets and novelists. It is also ignored by the radicals in morals and religion. Much which George Eliot says on this subject is of great value, and may be heeded with the utmost profit. Her words of wisdom, however, lose much of their value because they utterly ignore those spontaneous and supernatural elements of man's higher life which lift it quite out of the region of dependence on history.

There is something to be said in behalf of George Eliot's attitude towards religion, which caused her to hold it in reverence, even when rejecting the objective validity of its dogmas. Yet much more is to be said for that other attitude, which is faithful to the law of reason, and believes that reason is competent to say some truer and larger word on a subject of such vital importance and such constant interest to man. That both reason and tradition are to be listened to reverently is true, but George Eliot so zealously espoused the cause of tradition as to give it an undue prominence. Her lesson was needed, however, and we may be all the better able to profit by it because she was so much an enthusiast in proclaiming its value. The even poise of perfect truth is no more to be had from her pages than from those of others.

The emphasis she laid on feeling and sentiment was a needed one, as a counterpoise to the exaggerations of rationalism. Man does live in his feelings more than in his reason. He is a being of sentiment, a creature of impulse, his social life is one of the affections. In all the ranges of his moral, religious and social life he is guided mainly by his emotions and sentiments. It cannot be said, however, as George Eliot would have us say, that these are human born and have no higher meaning. They are the outgrowth of spiritual reality, as well as of human experience; they repeat the foregleams and foresights of a

> "far-off divine event,
> To which the whole creation moves."

Life is enriched and flooded with light by the emotions, and feeling, true and tender and pure, is as much the symbol of humanity as reason itself. It was therefore well that some one should attempt to justify the emotional life against the aspersions of those who have done it grave injustice. It is true that man is not a being who wholly arrives at his method of life through reason, but feeling lends quite as important aid. He does not only think, but he has emotions as well; he not only weighs evidence, but he acts by impulse. He is continually led by the emotions, sentiments and impulses created for him by the life of ages past. Without emotion there could be no art, no poetry and no music. Without emotion there would be no religion and no spiritual life. Sentiment sweetens, beautifies and endears all that is human and natural.

Emotion and the affections, however, seem to be shorn of their highest beauty and glory when they are restricted to a merely earthly origin and compass of power. It is altogether impossible to believe that their own impulse to look beyond the human is a delusion, and that they really have nothing to report that is valid from beyond the little round which man treads. To believe in the human beauty and glory of the feelings, and to rejoice in their power to unite us to our kind, need imply no forgetfulness of their demand for a wider expression and a higher communion.

Her theory of the origin of feeling is not to be accepted. It means something more than an inheritance of ancestral experience. It is the result rather than the cause of reason, for reason has an influence she did not acknowledge, and an original capacity which she never saw. Her view of feeling was mainly theoretical, for she was led in her attitude towards the facts of life, not by sentiment, but by reason. Hers was a thoughtful rather than an impulsive mind, and given to logic more than to emotion.

Her enthusiasm for altruism, her zeal for humanity, lends a delightful feature to her books. It gives a glow and a consecration to her work, and makes her as great a prophet as positivism is capable of creating. And it is no idle power she awakens in her positivist faith in man. She shames those who claim a broader and better faith. Zeal for man is no mean gospel, as she gives life and meaning to it in her books. To live for others, too many are not likely to do. She made altruism beautiful, she made it a consecration and a religion. Those who cannot accept her agnosticism and her positivism may learn much from her faith in man and from her enthusiasm for humanity. No faith is worth much which does not lead to a truer and a more helpful love of man. Any faith is good in so far as it makes us more humane and sympathetic. In this regard, the radicalism of George Eliot was a great advance on much of the free-thinking of our century. She desired to build, not to destroy. She was no iconoclast, no hater of what other men love and venerate. Her tendencies were all on the side of progress, good order and social growth.

Her conception of the organic social life of the race is one of great value. It led her to believe in the possibility of a social organization in the future based on science, and better capable of meeting all the wants of mankind than the more personal and competitive methods have done. This belief in the organic unity of the race is not necessarily positivist in its character, for Hegel entertained it as fully as does Herbert Spencer. The larger social life will come, however, as individuals are moved to lead the way, and not alone as the result of a general evolutionary process. On its mental side, her social theory is to be regarded with grave suspicions, for it brings all minds to the same level. No mind of commanding influence is to be found in her books. No powerful intellect gives greatness to any of her plots. Her Felix Holt is not a man of original and positive thought. We accept, but do not enthusiastically admire him. Deronda is a noble character, but he in no sense represents the largest things of which a social leader is capable. He disappoints and is weak, and he has no power to create the highest kind of leadership. In other words, he is not a great man. The world's reformers have been of another temper and mettle. He is no Mazzini, no Luther. George Eliot's social theories left no room for such men. They were superfluous in her social system. The man not to be explained by heredity and tradition had no place in her books; and no genius, no great man, can ever be explained by heredity and tradition alone.

George Eliot evidently desired to destroy individualism as a social force. The individual, according to her teaching, is to renounce himself for the sake of the race. He is to live, not as a personal being, but as a member of the social organization; to develop his altruistic nature, not to perfect his personal character. The finer flavor of personality is brushed mercilessly away by this method.

Reason needs to be justified in opposition to her excessive praise of feeling. Meanwhile, the capacity of man to live a life higher than that of his social state is to be asserted. He is indeed a member of humanity, but humanity does not absorb him to the cost of his personality. Life is strong in those ages in which the individual is able to assert his own personality, in opposition to what is imperfect and untrue in the life of his time. This failure to recognize the worth and capacity of the individual is a most serious defect in George Eliot's work, and mars it in many directions.

A very competent critic has shown how serious is the limitation arising in this manner, and permeating her books with a false conception of life.

"So far as George Eliot's life is concerned," says Mr. Stopford Brooke, "she was eager in her self-development, and as eager in her sympathies. But it was a different matter in the main drift of her work. She lowered the power of individualism. Nay, she did not believe in its having any self-caused or God-caused existence. Few have individualized their characters more than she did, and of these characters we have many distinct types. But she individualized them with, I may say, almost the set purpose of showing that their individualism was to be sacrificed to the general welfare of the race. The more her characters cling to their individuality the more they fail in reaching happiness or peace. If they are noble characters, they are finally obliged, through their very nobility, to surrender all their ideals, all their personal hopes, all the individual ends they hoped to develop; and they reach peace finally only through utter surrender of personality in humanity. The characters in her books who do not do this, who cling to their individuality and maintain it, succeed in life, for the most part, if they are strong; are broken to pieces if they are weak; but in all cases, save one, are not the noble but the ignoble characters. The whole of her books is a suppressed attack on individualism, and an exaltation of self-renunciation as the only force of progress, as the only ground of morality. I leave aside here, as apart from the moral side of the subject, the view that individual power or weakness of any kind is the consequence of the past, of race, of physical causes. What a man is found to do is not affected by that, in her view. . . . No one can deny that the morality is a lofty one, and, as far as it asserts self-renunciation, entirely useful; we have with all our hearts to thank George Eliot for that part of her work. But when sacrifice of self is made, in its last effort, equivalent to the sacrifice of individuality, the doctrine of self-renunciation is driven to a vicious extreme. It is not self-sacrifice which is then demanded, it is suicide . . . Fully accepted, it would reduce the whole of the human race to hopelessness. That, indeed, is the last result. A sad and fatal hopelessness of life broods over all the nobler characters. All their early ideals are sacrificed, all their early joys depart, all the pictures they formed are blotted out. They gain peace through renunciation, after long failure; some happiness in yielding to the inevitable, and harmonizing life with it; and some blessedness in doing all they can for the progress of those who follow them, for the good of those that are with them. Their self is conquered, not through ennoblement of personality, but through annihilation of personality. And having surrendered their separate personality, they then attain the fitting end, silence forevermore. It is no wonder that no characters are so sad, that none steep the reader in such hopelessness of joy, as the noble characters of the later works of George Eliot. They want the mighty power, the enkindling hopes, the resurrection of life, the joy and rapture which deepens towards death and enables man to take up the ideals of youth again."

If too severe in some directions, this criticism is substantially sound. It does not matter what theory of personality we adopt, in a philosophical sense, if that theory upholds personal confidence and force of will. If it does not do this, the whole result is evil. This lack of faith in personality saddened all the work done by George Eliot. In theory a believer in an ever-brightening future, and no pessimist, yet the outcome of her work is dark with despondency and grief.

Life is sad, hard and ascetic in her treatment of it. An ascetic tone runs through all her work, the result of her theories of renunciation. The same sternness and cheerlessness is to be seen in the poetry and painting of the pre-Raphaelites. The joy, freshness and sunniness of Raphael is not to be found in their work. Life is painful, puritanic and depressing to them. Old age seems to be upon them, or the decadence of a people that has once been great. Human nature does not need that this strain be put upon it. Life is stronger when more assertive of itself. It has a right to assert itself in defiance of mere rules, and only when it does so is it true and great. The ascetic tone is one of the worst results of a scientific view of the world as applied to literature; for it is thoroughly false both in fact and in sentiment. The strong, hopeful, youthful look at life is the one which literature demands, and because it is the nearest the heart and spirit of life itself. The dead nation produces a dead literature. The age made doubtful by an excess of science produces a literature burdened with sadness and pain. Great and truthful as it may be, it lacks in power to conquer the world. It shows, not the power of Homer, but the power of Lucretius.

Her altruism has its side of truth, but not all of the truth is in it. Any system of thought which sees nothing beyond man is not likely to find that which is most characteristic in man himself. He is to be fathomed, if fathomed at all, by some other line than that of his own experience. If he explains the universe, the universe is also necessary to explain him. Man apart from the supersensuous is as little to be understood as man apart from humanity. He belongs to a Universal Order quite as much as he belongs to the human order. Man may be explained by evolution, but evolution is not to be explained by anything in the nature of man. It requires some larger field of vision to take note of that elemental law. Not less true is it that mind does not come obediently under this method of explanation, that it demands account of how matter is transformed into thought. The law of thought needs to be solved after mind is evolved.

There is occasion for surprise that a mind so acute

and logical as George Eliot's did not perceive that the evolution philosophy has failed to settle any of the greater problems suggested by Kant. The studies of Darwin and Spencer have certainly made it impossible longer to accept Locke's theory of the origin of all knowledge in individual experience, but they have not in any degree explained the process of thought or the origin of ideas. The gulf between the physiological processes in the brain and thought has not been bridged even by a rope walk. The total disparity of mind and matter resists all efforts to reduce them to one. The utmost which the evolution philosophy has so far done, is to attempt to prove that mind is a function of matter or of the physiological process. This conclusion is as far as possible from being that of the unity of mind and matter.

That man is very ignorant, and that this world ought to demand the greater share of his attention and energies, are propositions every reasonable person is ready to accept. Granted their truth, all that is necessarily true in agnosticism has been arrived at. It is a persistent refusal to see what lies behind outward facts which gives agnosticism all its practical justification. Art itself is a sufficient refutation of the assertion that we know nothing of what lies behind the apparent. That we know something of causes, every person who uses his own mind may be aware. At the same time, the rejection of the doctrine of rights argues obedience to a theory, rather than humble acceptance of the facts of history. That doctrine of rights, so scorned by George Eliot, has wrought most of the great and wholesome social changes of modern times. Her theory of duties can show no historic results whatever.

To separate George Eliot's theories from her genius it seems impossible to do, but this it is necessary to do in order to give both their proper place. All praise, her work demands on its side where genius is active. It is as a thinker, as a theorizer, she is to be criticised and to be declared wanting. Her work was crippled by her philosophy, or if not crippled, then it was made less strong of limb and vigorous of body by that same philosophy. It is true of her as of Wordsworth, that she grew prosy because she tried to be philosophical. It is true of her as it is not true of him, that her work lacks in the breadth which a large view of the world gives. His was no provincial conception of nature or of man. Hers was so in a most emphatic sense. The philosophy she adopted is not and cannot become the philosophy of more than a small number of persons. In the nature of the case it is doomed to be the faith of a few students and cultured people. It can stir no common life, develop no historic movements, inaugurate no reforms, nor give to life a diviner meaning. Whether it be true or not, — and this need not here be asked, — this social and moral limitation of its power is enough to condemn it for the purposes of literature. In so far as George Eliot's work is artistic, poetic, moral and human, it is very great, and no word too strong can be said in its praise. It is not too excessive enthusiasm to call her, on the whole, the equal of any novelist. Her genius is commanding and elemental. She has originality, strength of purpose, and a profound insight into character. Yet her work is weakened by its attachment to a narrow theory of life. Her philosophy is transitory in its nature. It cannot hold its own, as developed by her, for any great length of time. It has the elements of its own destruction in itself. The curious may read her for her speculations; the many will read her for her realism, her humanity and her genius. In truth, then, it would have been better if her work had been inspired by great spiritual aims and convictions.

XXI.

BIBLIOGRAPHY.

AS an aid to those who may wish to carry further the preceding study of George Eliot, the following bibliography and lists of references have been compiled. In their preparation constant use has been made of Poole's *Index of Periodical Literature*, the bibliography contained in *The Manchester Literary Club Papers* for 1881, and a list of references published in *The Literary World* (Boston) for February 24, 1883. Numerous additions have been made to these bibliographies, while the references have been verified as far as possible. An occasional reference given in these lists has not been discoverable, as that of the Manchester Club to the *London Quarterly Review* for January, 1874, for an article on "George Eliot and Comtism," and Poole's reference to the same article in the *London Quarterly*, 47 : 446. This will be found in the number for January 1877, volume ninety-four.

1. Writings.

1846. *The Life of Jesus*, by Strauss. Translated from the fourth German edition, 3 vols. Chapman Brothers, London.

1852–3. Assistant editor of the Westminster Review.

1852. The Westminster Review for January contained her notice of Carlyle's Life of John Sterling.

In the July number appeared her article on *The Lady Novelists.*

1854. *The Essence of Christianity*, by Feuerbach. Translated from the second German edition. John Chapman, London.

The Westminster Review for October published her *Woman in France: Madame de Sablé.*

She wrote, it is supposed, occasionally for The Leader

newspaper, of which journal Lewes was the literary editor None of her contributions have been identified.[1]

1855. Westminster Review, October, *Evangelical Teaching: Dr. Cumming.*

1856. Westminster Review, January, *German Wit: Heinrich Heine.* July, *The Natural History of German Life.* October, *Silly Novels by Lady Novelists.*

1857. Westminster Review, January, *Worldliness and other-Worldliness: the Poet Young.*

In Blackwood's Magazine for January and February appeared *The Sad Fortunes of the Reverend Amos Barton;* in March, April, May and June, *Mr. Gilfil's Love Story;* from July to December, *Janet's Repentance.* In December these stories were published in two volumes under the title of *Scenes of Clerical Life*, by George Eliot. Edinburgh, Blackwood & Sons. Reprinted in Living Age from April to December, 1857.

1859. In February, *Adam Bede* appeared in three volumes, Blackwoods.

Blackwood's Magazine for July contained *The Lifted Veil.*

1860. In April, *The Mill on the Floss* was published in three volumes, Blackwoods.

1861. *Silas Marner* in March, one volume, Blackwoods.

1863. *Romola* appeared in the Cornhill Magazine from July, 1862, to July, 1863, and was illustrated. It was published in three volumes in July; Smith, Elder & Co., London.

1864. The Cornhill Magazine for July contained *Brother Jacob*, with illustrations.

1865. The Fortnightly Review for May 15 contained *The Influence of Rationalism*, and a review of Owen Jones's Grammar of Ornament.

1866. In June, *Felix Holt* was issued in three volumes, Blackwoods.

1868. Blackwood's Magazine, January, contained an *Address to Workingmen, by Felix Holt.*

In June, *The Spanish Gypsy* was published by Blackwoods.

1869. Blackwood's Magazine for May printed *How Lisa Loved the King.*

The Atlantic Monthly for August contained *Agatha.*

1870. In Macmillan's Magazine for May, *The Legend of Jubal.*

1871. Macmillan's Magazine for July, *Armgart.*

Middlemarch was issued in twelve monthly numbers, beginning with December, by Blackwoods.

1874. *The Legend of Jubal and other Poems* was published by Blackwoods. It contained: *The Legend of Jubal, Agatha,*

[1] There is a nearly complete set of The Leader in the Boston Athenæum Library.

Armgart, *How Lisa Loved the King*, *A Minor Prophet*, *Brother and Sister*, *Stradivarius*, *Two Lovers*, *Arion*, *O May I Join the Choir Invisible*.

1876. *Daniel Deronda* was issued in eight monthly parts, beginning in February, by Blackwoods.

1878. Macmillan's Magazine for July, *A College Breakfast Party*.

1879. *The Impressions of Theophrastus Such* was published in June by Blackwoods.

The Legend of Jubal and Other Poems, Old and New, was issued by Blackwoods, containing, in addition to those in the first edition, *A College Breakfast Party*, *Self and Life*, *Sweet Evenings Come and Go*, *Love*, *The Death of Moses*.

In Blackwood's cabinet edition of George Eliot's complete works, *The Lifted Veil* and *Brother Jacob* are reprinted with *Silas Marner*.

After the death of Lewes she edited his *Study of Psychology* and his *Mind as a Function of the Organism*.

1881. The Pall Mall Gazette of January 6 contained her letter to Sara Hennell concerning the origin of *Adam Bede*.

Three letters to Professor David Kaufmann appeared in the Athenæum of November 26, 1881.

The following articles also contain sayings of George Eliot's, or extracts from her letters: In the Contemporary Review, by "One who knew her," on the Moral Influence of George Eliot; C. Kegan Paul in Harper's Magazine; F. W. H. Myers in The Century; W. M. W. Call in the Westminster Review, and a nephew of William Blackwood in Blackwood's Magazine.

1882. In Harper's Magazine for March, Elizabeth Stuart Phelps published numerous extracts from George Eliot's letters under the title of *Last Words from George Eliot*.

1883. George Eliot, by Mathilde Blind, — London, W. H. Allen, and Boston, Roberts Brothers, — contains extracts from several letters.

The Essays of George Eliot, collected by Nathan Sheppard, — New York, Funk & Wagnalls, — contains *Carlyle's Life of Sterling*, *Woman in France*, *Evangelical Teaching*, *German Wit*, *Natural History of German Life*, *Silly Novels by Lady Novelists*, *Worldliness and other-Worldliness*, *The Influence of Rationalism*, *The Grammar of Ornament*, *Felix Holt's Address to Workingmen*.

The Complete Essays of George Eliot, Boston, Estes & Lauriat, 1883, in addition to the above, contains *The Lady Novelists*, *George Foster, the German Naturalist*, *Weimar and its Celebrities*.

2. Selections, Translations and Portraits.

Wise, Witty and Tender Sayings in Prose and Verse, Selected by Alexander Main. Blackwoods, 1872.

Wit and Wisdom of George Eliot. Boston, Roberts Brothers, 1878; enlarged and with a biographical memoir prefixed, 1881.

George Eliot Birthday Book. Blackwoods, 1878.

George Eliot: Fragments et Pensées, extraits et traduits des ses Œuvres, par Ch. Ritter. Genève, Georges, 1879.

Character Readings from George Eliot, selected and arranged by Nathan Sheppard. New York, Harpers, 1882.

The following translations have been published: —

French. — Adam Bede, by A. Durade; Mill on the Floss, by A. Durade; Silas Marner, by Durade; Romola, by Durade; Mr. Gilfil's Love Story, by E. Pasquet; Dorlcote Mill, by E. D. Forques in Revue des Deux Mondes, June 15, 1860; The Lifted Veil, in Revue des Deux Mondes, September, 1880.

Dutch. — Felix Holt, by Merv. Van Westrheeve, 1867, and by P. Bruyn, 1873; Middlemarch, by Merv. Van Westrheeve, 1873; Adam Bede, by P. Bruyn, 1870; Mill on the Floss, by P. Bruyn, 1870; Romola, by P. Bruyn, 1870, and by J. C. Van Deventer, 1864; Novelettes, by P. Bruyn, 1870.

German. — Adam Bede, by J. Frese; Silas Marner, by J. Frese, 1861; Mill on the Floss, by J. Frese, 1861; Romola, by A. v. Metzsch, 1864; Middlemarch, by E. Lehmann, 1872–3; Daniel Deronda, by Strodtmann, 1876; Felix Holt (no translator's name given), 1867. Der Gelüftche Schleier, Bruder Jakob, by Lehmann.

The portrait of George Eliot appearing as the frontispiece to this volume is from that published in The Century for November, 1881. Accompanying it was the following account of it and of other portraits: —

"We have the pleasure of presenting to our readers an authentic portrait of George Eliot, the only one by which it is likely that she will be known to posterity. We are indebted for this privilege, as we shall presently explain, to the kindness and courtesy of her husband, Mr. J. W. Cross, who has allowed us to be the first to usher this beautiful work of art to the world. In doing so, we believe it will interest readers of The Century Magazine to learn, for the first time, the exact truth regarding the portraits of George Eliot, and we have therefore obtained from the three artists to whom, at different times in her life, she sat, some particulars of those occasions.

"Miss Evans passed the winter of 1849–50 at Geneva, in the house of M. F. d'Aldert Durade, the well-known Swiss water-color painter, who is also the translator of the authorized French version of her works. At that time she had, however, written nothing original, and had attracted no general interest. While she stayed with M. Durade and his wife, the Swiss painter amused himself by making a small portrait of her in oils — a head and shoulders. This painting remains in the possession of M. Durade, who has not merely refused to sell it, but will not allow it to be photographed or reproduced in any form. He has, however, we understand, consented to make a replica of it for Mr. Cross. We have not seen this interesting work, but we hear that it is considered, by those who still remember the great writer as she looked in her thirtieth year, to be remarkably faithful. M. Durade recently exhibited this little picture for a few days at the Athénée in Geneva, but has refused to allow it to be brought to London.

"Ten years after this, in 1859, as the distinguished portrait-painter, Mr. Samuel Laurence, was returning from America, he happened to meet with 'Adam Bede,' then just published. He was so delighted with the book that he was determined to know the author, and it was revealed to him that to do so he had but to renew his old acquaintance with Mr. George Henry Lewes, whom he had met years before at Leigh Hunt's. He made George Eliot's acquaintance, and was charmed with her, and before long he asked leave to make a study of her head. She assented without any affectation, and, in the early months of 1861, Mr. Lewes commissioned the painter to make a drawing of her. She gave him repeated sittings in his studio at 6 Wells Street, London, and Mr. Laurence looks back with great pleasure on the long conversations that those occasions gave him with his vivacious sitter. The drawing was taken front face, with the hair uncovered, worn in the fashion then prevalent, and it was made in chalks. While it was proceeding, Mr. Laurence asked her if he might exhibit it, when finished, at the Royal Academy, and she at once consented. But when the time for sending in drew near, the artist received a letter from Mr. Lewes absolutely withholding this consent, and a certain strain, of which this was the first symptom, began to embarrass the relations of the two gentlemen, until Mr. Lewes finally refused to take the drawing at all. But before the summer was out, Mr. Langford, the reader of Messrs. Blackwood of Edinburgh, who published George Eliot's works, called on Mr. Laurence, and asked if he would consent to make a copy of the drawing for the firm. The artist replied that he should be happy to sell them the original, and accordingly it passed from his studio, in June, 1861, into the back parlor of Mr. Blackwood's shop, where it now hangs. Like that of M. Durade, Mr. Laurence's portrait of George Eliot is not to be in any way reproduced.

"The remaining portrait is that which we reproduce with this number. It is an elaborate chalk drawing, in black and white, with a slight touch of color in the eyes, and was executed in the latter part of 1866 and the early part of 1867, by Mr. Frederick W. Burton, at that time member of the Society of Painters in Water-colors, and now director of the National Gallery in London. George Eliot gave Mr. Burton many sittings in his studio at Kensington, and the picture was eventually exhibited in the Royal Academy, in 1867, as No. 735, 'The Author of "Adam Bede."' It passed into Mr. Lewes's possession, was retained at his death by George Eliot, and is now the property of Mr. J. W. Cross. In the spring of this year, Mr. Cross came to the conclusion that —as the shop windows were likely to become filled with spurious and hideous 'portraits' of George Eliot—it was necessary to overcome the dislike felt by the family of the great novelist to any publication of her features, to which in life she had been averse, and he thereupon determined to record in a monumental way what he felt to be the best existing likeness. Mr. Cross took the drawing over to M. Paul Rajon, who is acknowledged to be the prince of modern etchers, and in his retirement at Auvers-sur-Oise, the great French artist has produced the beautiful etching which we have been permitted to reproduce in engraving. For this permission, and for great courtesy and kindness under circumstances the peculiar nature of which it is not necessary here to specify, we have to tender our most sincere thanks to Mr. J. W. Cross and to Mr. Burton.

"These are regarded by her friends to be the only important portraits of George Eliot which exist, but Mr. Cross possesses a very interesting black silhouette, cut with scissors, when she was sixteen. In this profile, the characteristics of the mature face are seen in the course of development. There is also a photograph, the only one ever taken, dating from about 1850, the eyes of which are said to be exceedingly fine. As an impression of later life, there should be mentioned a profile drawn in pencil by Mrs. Alma Tadema, in March, 1877. Of all the portraits here alluded to, the one we engrave is the only one at present destined for publication. It may be added that there exist one or two other profile sketches, which, however, are not approved by the friends of George Eliot."

3. Biographical.

Atlantic Monthly, 14:66, December, 1864, Kate Field on "English Authors in Florence." Louise M. Alcott in the Independent for Nov. 1, 1866. The Galaxy, 7:801, June, 1869, Justin McCarthy on "George Eliot and George Lewes;" reprinted in "Modern Leaders," 1872. "Home Sketches in France and other Papers," by the late Mrs. Henry M. Field, G. P. Putnam's Sons, 1875, p. 208, "The Author of Adam Bede in Her own Home." International Review, 10:447, 497, May and June, 1881, W. Fraser Rae. The Century, 23:55, with portrait, F. W. H. Myers, reprinted in Essays: Modern, London, 1883; 23:47, "The Portrait of George Eliot." The Nineteenth Century, 9:778, Edith Simcox. Blackwood's Magazine February, 1881. Harper's Magazine, May, 1881, C. Kegan Paul; reprinted in Biographical Sketches, London, 1883; March, 1882, E. S. Phelps. Westminster Review, 116:154, July, 1881, W. M. W. Call, "George Eliot: her Life and Writings." Le Livre, April 10, 1881, "Life in Geneva." London Daily Graphic, 23:27, January 8, 1851, "Reminiscences of George Eliot." Lippincott's Magazine, 31:510, May, 1883, J. A. Dickson, "An Afternoon at Ashbourne." Inquirer, January, 1881, Dr. Sadler's address. Pall Mall Gazette, December 30, 1880, "Early Life." London Daily News, December, 30, 1880, account of her funeral. Eclectic Magazine, March, 1881, account of her early life and of her funeral; April, A personal sketch. "George Eliot," Mathilde Blind, 1883, W. H. Allen, London. "Pen pictures of Modern Authors," Wm. Sheppard, 1882, G. P. Putnam's Sons, New York. The Congregationalist, May 28, 1879, Mrs. Annie Downs, "A Visit to George Eliot." The Christian Leader, October 27, 1881, Mrs. M. E. Bruce.

4. General Criticisms.

Quarterly Review, 108:469. Macmillan's Magazine, 14:272, J. Morley; same, Eclectic Magazine, 67:488; reprinted in "Critical Miscellanies," first series. Atlantic Monthly, 18:479, H. James. Christian Examiner, 70:227, I. M. Luyster. North British Review, 45:141, 197, H. H. Lancaster; reprinted in "Essays and Reviews," Edinburgh, 1876. National Review, 11:191. Home and Foreign Review, 3:522, Richard Simpson. Fraser's Magazine, 103: 263, February, 1881, T. E. Kebbel, "Village Life according to George Eliot;" same, Living Age, 148:608. National Quarterly, 1:455, E. L. Wentworth. Potter's American Monthly, 9:260, 334. British Quarterly Review, 45:141. Catholic World, 17:775, J. McCarthy, "Comparison between George Eliot and Fleurange." Canadian Monthly, 11:261, "Later Manner of George Eliot." Dublin Review, 88:371. Southern Review (new style), 13:205, Mrs. S. B. Herrick. R. H. Hutton, "Essays, Theological and Literary," 2d vol. 1871. Contemporary Review, 20:403; same, Living Age, 115:109, Eclectic Magazine, 79 : 562, Professor E. Dowden; reprinted in "Studies of Literature." Atlantic Monthly, 33:684, June, 1874, George P. Lathrop, "The Growth of the Novel." A. C. Swinburne, "A Note on Charlotte Brontë," 1877. International Review, 7 : 17, July, 1879, Francis Maguire, Jr. Cornhill Magazine, 43 : 152, Leslie Stephen, "Critical Study of George Eliot;" same, Living Age, 148 : 731, Eclectic Magazine, 96 : 443. Month, 42 : 272. Every Saturday, 10 : 186. North British Review, 33:165, "George Eliot and Hawthorne." Eclectic Magazine, 88:111, "George Eliot and George Sand." The Nation, 32:201, J. Bryce, "George Eliot and Carlyle;" 31:456, W. C. Brownell. London Quarterly, 57:154. Blackwood's Magazine, 129 : 255; same, Living Age, 148 : 664; Eclectic Magazine, 96:433. St. Paul's, 12:592, G. B. Smith. Living Age, 58:274: 148:318. Eclectic Magazine, 96:353. Southern Monthly, 14:65. Tinsley's Monthly, 3:565. Victoria, 31:56. The Century, 23:619, February, 1882, "George Eliot and Emerson." Library Magazine, 7 : 84, Nathan Sheppard, "George Eliot's Analysis of Motives;" reprinted as an introduction to George Eliot's Essays, Funk & Wagnalls, 1883. Macmillan's Magazine, 46:488, October, 1882, Annie Matheson, "George Eliot's Children;" same, Living Age, 155 : 211. The Critic, January, 1881, Edward Eggleston; reprinted in Essays from the Critic, 1881. Christian Union, February, 1881, Noah Porter. The Independent, February 17, 1881, Mrs. Lippincott, "Three Great Women." A History of English Prose Fiction from Sir Thomas Malory to George Eliot, Bayard Tuckerman, New York, 1882. The English Novel and the Principle of its Development, Sidney Lanier, New York, 1883. Modern Review, 2:399, April, 1881, George Sarson, "George Eliot and Thomas Carlyle." Literary World (London), January, 1881, Peter Bayne. Athenæum, January 1. 1881 : 20. The Academy, 19 : 27, January 8, 1881. Temps, December 26, 1880, Edmond Scherer. Le Roman Naturaliste, Ferdinand Brunetère, 1883, has a chapter on

"English Naturalism: a Study of George Eliot." Études sur la Littérature Contemporaine, E. Scherer, Paris, 1878. The Pen, 1880, Robert E. Francillon. East and West: 1:203, June, 1881. Papers of the Manchester Literary Club, 1881; Bibliography, Charles W. Sutton; "George Eliot as a Poet," George Milner; "George Eliot as a Novelist," John Mortimer; "George Eliot's Use of Dialect," William E. A. Axon. National Review, April, 1883, "New School of Fiction." Merry England, May, 1883, C. Kegan Paul, "The Rustic of George Eliot and Thomas Hardy." Blackwood's Magazine, April, 1883. Nineteenth Century, October, 1881, John Ruskin on "Fiction: Fair and Foul."

5. Discussions of her Teachings.

Penn Monthly, 10:579, "The Art of George Eliot." Dublin Review, 89:433, "Religion of George Eliot." Unitarian Review, 3:357, J. E. Carpenter, "Religious Influence of George Eliot." "The Ethics of George Eliot's Works," J. C. Brown, Wm. Blackwood & Sons. Edinburgh, 1879. Mind, 6:378, July, 1881, "George Eliot's Art," James Sully. The Spectator, 52:751, "George Eliot's Ideal Ethics;" same, Littell's Living Age, 142:123, July 12, 1879. Scribner's Magazine, 8:685, Wm. C. Wilkinson; reprinted in "A Free Lance in the Field of Life and Letters," 1874. Westminster Review, 117:65, January, 1882, "George Eliot as a Moral Teacher." Contemporary Review, 39:173, February, 1881, "Moral Influence of George Eliot;" same, Living Age, 148:561. Unitarian Review, 16:125, 216, August and September, 1881, John A. Bellows, "Religious Tendency of George Eliot's Writings." Atlantic Monthly, 51:243, February, 1883, M. L. Henry, "The Morality of Thackeray and George Eliot." The Independent, March 24, 1883, Stopford A. Brooke, "George Eliot and Thomas Carlyle." "The Religion of Our Literature," George MacCrie, London, 1875. "George Eliot and Judaism," David Kaufmann, Blackwoods, 1878.

6. Scenes of Clerical Life.

Atlantic Monthly, 1:890.

7. Adam Bede.

Blackwood's Magazine, 85:490, April, 1859. Dublin Review, 47:33, November, 1859. Edinburgh Review, 110:223, July, 1859. Westminster Review, 71:486, April, 1859. Athenæum, February 26, 1859. Saturday Review, February 26, 1859:194. Atlantic Monthly, 4:521. Christian Examiner, 70:227, I. M. Luyster. "Seth Bede, the Methody: his Life and Labors," chiefly by Himself. London: Tallant & Co., 1859. "George Eliot in Derbyshire," London Society, 27:311, 439; 28:20, by Guy Roslyn (Joshua Hatton); reprinted in book form, London, 1876.

8. The Mill on the Floss.

Blackwood's Magazine, 87:611. May, 1860. Dublin University Review, 57:192. Macmillan's Magazine, 3:441. Westminster

Review, 74 : 24, July, 1860. Christian Examiner, 69:145, L. G. Ware.

9. Silas Marner.

Christian Examiner, 70:227, I. M. Luyster. Macmillan's Magazine, 4:305. Revue des Deux Mondes, September, 1861, C. Clarigny.

10. Romola.

Blackwood's Magazine, 116:72. Land we Love, 1:134. Westminster Review, 80:344, October, 1863. Christian Remembrancer, 52:445. Revue des Deux Mondes, December, 1863, E. D. Forques.

11. Felix Holt, the Radical.

Blackwood's Magazine, 100 : 94, July, 1866. Edinburgh Review, 124:435, October, 1866; same, Living Age, 91:432. North American Review, 103 : 557, July, 1866, A. G. Sedgwick. The Nation, 3:127, Henry James. Contemporary Review, 3:51. Eclectic Review, 124 : 34. Chambers's Journal, 43 : 508. Westminster Review, 86:200, July, 1866.

12. The Spanish Gypsy.

Atlantic Monthly, 22:380, W. D. Howells. North American Review, 107:620, October, 1868, Henry James. The Nation, 7:13, July 2, 1868, Henry James. Edinburgh Review, 128:525. Westminster Review, 90:183. Macmillan's Magazine, 18 : 281, J. Morley; same, Eclectic Magazine, 71:1276. Blackwood's Magazine, 103 : 760. British Quarterly Review, 48:503. Fraser's Magazine, 78:468, J. Skelton. St. James's, 22:478. St. Paul's, 2:583. London Quarterly, 31:160. Southern Review (new style), 4:383, W. H. Browne. Every Saturday, 6:1.

13. Poems.

Contemporary Review, 8:387, July 1868, Matthew Browne (W. B. Rands); same, Every Saturday, 6:79. Every Saturday, 16:667, G. A. Simcox. The Argosy, 2:437, November, 1866, Matthew Browne. Saturday Review, 37:75. Macmillan's Magazine, 22:1. North American Review, 119:484, Henry James. Atlantic Monthly, 34:102, July, 1874, W. D. Howells. Harper's Magazine, 49:887. Academy, 5:33, May 10, 1874, G. A. Simcox. Edinburgh Review, 128:523, October, 1868. Papers of the Manchester Literary Club, 1881, p. 108, George Milner. The Nation, 19:124. "Our Living Poets: an Essay in Criticism," H. Buxton Forman, London, 1871.

14. Middlemarch.

Quarterly Review, 134:336, April, 1873. Edinburgh Review, 137:246, January, 1873. Fortnightly Review, 19:142, Sidney Colvin. Blackwood's Magazine, 112:727; same, Living Age, 116 : 131; Eclectic Magazine, 80 : 215. The Nation, 16:60, 76, January, 1873, A. V. Dicey. North American Review, 116:432,

April, 1873, T. S. Perry. British Quarterly Review, 57:407, April 1883. London Quarterly Review, 40:99, April, 1873. Canadian Monthly, 3:549. Old and New, 7:352, H. G. Spaulding. Southern Monthly, 12:373, W. H. Browne. Atlantic Monthly, 31:490, A. G. Sedgwick. Catholic World, 17:775, September, 1873. Die Gegenwart, 1874, Freidrich Speilhagen.

15. DANIEL DERONDA.

Atlantic Monthly, 38:684, Henry James, December, 1876. North American Review, 124:31, E. P. Whipple, January, 1877. Edinburgh Review, 144:442, October, 1876. Fortnightly Review, 26:601, November, 1876, Sidney Colvin. The Nation, 23:230, 245, October, 12, 19, 1876, A. V. Dicey. British Quarterly Review, 64:472. Eclectic Magazine, 87:657. International Review, 4:68, R. R. Bowker. The Western, 3:603, O. G. Garrison. Potter's American Monthly, 8:75. Gentleman's Magazine (new style), 17:593, November, 1876, J. Picciotto; 17 : 411, R. E. Francillon. Canadian Monthly, 9:250, 343; 10:362. Victoria, 28:227, A. S. Richardson. Temple Bar, 49:542, "Deronda's Mother;" same, Living Age, 133:248; same, Eclectic Magazine, 88:751. Macmillan's Magazine, 36:101, J. Jacobs, "Mordecai: a Protest against the Critics, by a Jew;" same, Living Age, 134:112. Athenæum, 1876:160, 327, 461, 593, 762. Westminster Review, 106:280, 574. Appleton's Journal (new style), 3:274, September, 1877, Wirt Sikes. Deutsche Rundschau, February 7, 1877. Contemporary Review, 29:348, February, 1877, Edward Dowden, reprinted in "Studies of Literature."

16. IMPRESSIONS OF THEOPHRASTUS SUCH.

Edinburgh Review, 150:557. Fortnightly Review, 32:144, G. Allen. Westminster Review, 112:185, July, 1879. The Nation, 28:422, June 19, 1879, G. E. Woodberry. Fraser's Magazine, 100:103. Canadian Monthly, 16:333. Unitarian Review, 12:292, R. W. Boodle.

INDEX.

A.

B.

C.

D.

M.

N.

P.

R.

S.

T.

W.

Y.

www.ingramcontent.com/pod-product-compliance
Lightning Source LLC
Chambersburg PA
CBHW031828270326
41932CB00008B/589

* 9 7 8 3 3 3 7 2 3 6 7 6 2 *